DECADENCE AND LITERATURE

Decadence and Literature explains how the concept of decadence developed since Roman times into a major cultural trope with broad explanatory power. No longer just a term of opprobrium for mannered art or immoral behaviour, decadence today describes complex cultural and social responses to modernity in all its forms. From the Roman emperor's indulgence in luxurious excess as both personal vice and political control, to the Enlightenment libertine's rational pursuit of hedonism, to the nineteenth-century dandy's simultaneous delight and distaste with modern urban life, decadence has emerged as a way of taking cultural stock of major social changes. These changes include the role of women in forms of artistic expression and social participation formerly reserved for men, as well as the increasing acceptance of LGBTQ+ relationships, a development with a direct relationship to decadence. Today, decadence seems more important than ever to an informed understanding of contemporary anxieties and uncertainties.

JANE DESMARAIS is Professor of English and Director of the Decadence Research Unit in the Department of English and Comparative Literature at Goldsmiths, University of London. She has written numerous essays on the theme of decadence and has co-edited several works, including *Decadence: An Annotated Anthology* (with Chris Baldick, 2012), *Arthur Symons: Selected Early Poems* (with Chris Baldick, 2017), and *Decadence and the Senses* (with Alice Condé, 2017). Her monograph, *Monsters under Glass: A Cultural History of Hothouse Flowers, 1850, to the Present* was published in 2018.

DAVID WEIR is Professor Emeritus of Comparative Literature at The Cooper Union in New York City, where he taught literature, linguistics, and cinema. He has published books on Jean Vigo, James Joyce, William Blake, orientalism, and anarchism, as well as three books on decadence. Those books have had a major role in the development of decadence as an academic field of study, beginning with *Decadence and the Making of Modernism* (1995), *Decadent Culture in the United States* (2009), and, most recently, *Decadence: A Very Short Introduction* (2018). He now lives in a Hudson Valley village in upstate New York.

CAMBRIDGE CRITICAL CONCEPTS

Cambridge Critical Concepts focuses on the important ideas animating twentieth- and twenty-first-century literary studies. Each concept addressed in the series has had a profound impact on literary studies, as well as on other disciplines, and already has a substantial critical bibliography surrounding it. This series captures the dynamic critical energies transmitted across twentieth- and twenty-first-century literary landscapes: the concepts critics bring to reading, interpretation and criticism. By addressing the origins, development and application of these ideas, the books collate and clarify how these particular concepts have developed, while also featuring fresh insights and establishing new lines of enquiry.

Cambridge Critical Concepts shifts the focus from period- or genre-based literary studies of key terms to the history and development of the terms themselves. Broad and detailed contributions cumulatively identify and investigate the various historical and cultural catalysts that made these critical concepts emerge as established twenty-first-century landmarks in the discipline. The level will be suitable for advanced undergraduates, graduates and specialists, as well as to those teaching outside their own research areas, and will have cross-disciplinary relevance for subjects such as history and philosophy.

Published Titles

Law and Literature
Edited by KIERAN DOLIN University of Western Australia

Time and Literature
Edited by THOMAS M. ALLEN University of Ottawa

The Global South and Literature
Edited by RUSSELL WEST-PAVLOV University of Tübingen

Trauma and Literature
Edited by ROGER KURTZ The College at Brockport, State University of New York

Food and Literature
Edited by GITANJALI SHAHANI San Francisco State University

Animals, Animality, and Literature
Edited by BRUCE BOEHRER, MOLLY HAND AND BRIAN MASSUMI Florida State University, University of Montreal

Terrorism and Literature
Edited by PETER HERMAN San Diego State University

Climate and Literature
Edited by ADELINE JOHNS University of Surrey

Orientalism and Literature
Edited by GEOFFREY NASH SOAS, University of London

DECADENCE AND LITERATURE

EDITED BY

JANE DESMARAIS
Goldsmiths, University of London

DAVID WEIR
The Cooper Union for the Advancement of Science and Art

CAMBRIDGE
UNIVERSITY PRESS

CAMBRIDGE
UNIVERSITY PRESS

University Printing House, Cambridge CB2 8BS, United Kingdom

One Liberty Plaza, 20th Floor, New York, NY 10006, USA

477 Williamstown Road, Port Melbourne, VIC 3207, Australia

314–321, 3rd Floor, Plot 3, Splendor Forum, Jasola District Centre, New Delhi – 110025, India

79 Anson Road, #06–04/06, Singapore 079906

Cambridge University Press is part of the University of Cambridge.

It furthers the University's mission by disseminating knowledge in the pursuit of education, learning, and research at the highest international levels of excellence.

www.cambridge.org
Information on this title: www.cambridge.org/9781108426244
DOI: 10.1017/9781108550826

First published 2019

Printed in the United Kingdom by TJ International Ltd. Padstow Cornwall

A catalogue record for this publication is available from the British Library.

Library of Congress Cataloging-in-Publication Data
NAMES: Desmarais, Jane, editor. | Weir, David, 1947 April 20– editor.
TITLE: Decadence and literature / edited by Jane Desmarais, Goldsmiths, University of London ; David Weir, The Cooper Union for the Advancement of Science and Art.
DESCRIPTION: New York : Cambridge University Press, 2019. | Series: Cambridge critical concepts
IDENTIFIERS: LCCN 2019008391 | ISBN 9781108426244 (hardback)
SUBJECTS: LCSH: Decadence in literature. | Modernism (Aesthetics) – History. | Intellectual life – History. | Degeneration – Social aspects – History. | Social change – History. | BISAC: LITERARY CRITICISM / Semiotics & Theory.
CLASSIFICATION: LCC PN56.D45 D424 2019 | DDC 809/.93353–dc23
LC record available at https://lccn.loc.gov/2019008391

ISBN 978-1-108-42624-4 Hardback

For Alcide Bava and Vic le Fesq

Contents

Figures

Contributors

CHRIS BALDICK is Professor of English in the Department of English and Comparative Literature at Goldsmiths, University of London. His research interests are chiefly in British and European writing of the twentieth century, especially English poetry and fiction 1900–1950; the history of English literary criticism; literary terminology; and the work of W. H. Auden. Among his several books are *Literature of the 1920s: Writers Among the Ruins* (2012).

MATTHEW BRADLEY is Senior Lecturer in English at the University of Liverpool, specializing in the intersections between late-Victorian literature, religion and culture. He is the editor of the Oxford World Classics edition of William James' *The Varieties of Religious Experience* (2012) and, with Juliet John, of *Reading and the Victorians* (Ashgate, 2015), and is currently writing a book on the Victorian end of the world.

ALICE CONDÉ is Associate Tutor in the Department of English and Comparative Literature at Goldsmiths, University of London. She is co-editor of *Decadence and the Senses* (with Jane Desmarais, 2017) and is currently co-editing *In Cynara's Shadow: Collected Essays on Ernest Dowson (1867–1900)* (with Jessica Gossling, 2019). She is Deputy Editor of *Volupté: Interdisciplinary Journal of Decadence Studies.*

CHAD DENTON is a writer and historian who grew up in Amherst County, Virginia. Fascinated by underdogs and outcasts, he has written about prostitutes, mad monarchs, culture wars, and dying empires. He holds an MA in History from George Mason University and a PhD, also in History with a minor in Gender Studies, from the University of Missouri. His publications include *Decadence, Radicalism, and the Early Modern French Nobility: The Enlightened and Depraved* (2016).

JANE DESMARAIS is Professor of English and Director of the Decadence Research Unit in the Department of English and Comparative Literature at Goldsmiths, University of London. She has written numerous essays on the theme of decadence and has co-edited several works, including *Decadence: An Annotated Anthology* (with Chris Baldick, 2012), *Arthur Symons: Selected Early Poems* (with Chris Baldick, 2017), and *Decadence and the Senses* (with Alice Condé, 2017). Her monograph, *Monsters under Glass: A Cultural History of Hothouse Flowers, 1850 to the Present* was published in 2018.

STEFANO EVANGELISTA is Fellow and Tutor in English at Trinity College, Oxford. His research brings English literature together with a number of other disciplines: classics, art history, modern European literatures, and the history of sexuality. He is the editor of *The Reception of Oscar Wilde in Europe* (2010) and the author of *British Aestheticism and Ancient Greece: Hellenism, Reception, Gods in Exile* (2009).

GERALD GILLESPIE is Emeritus Professor of German Studies and Comparative Literature at Stanford University. He is the author of some twenty books, including *Proust, Mann, Joyce in the Modernist Condition* (2nd rev. edn, 2010); Ludwig Tieck's *Puss-in-Boots and Theater of the Absurd* (2013); *The Nightwatches of Bonaventura* (2014).

SACHA GOLOB is Senior Lecturer in Philosophy and Director of the Centre for Philosophy and the Visual Arts at King's College London. He has published extensively on modern French and German Philosophy and the Philosophy of Art. His current research looks at contemporary conceptions of ethical degeneration, transformation, and virtue. His publications include *Heidegger on Concepts, Freedom, and Normativity* (2014) and the *Cambridge History of Moral Philosophy* (Cambridge University Press, 2018).

MELANIE HAWTHORNE is Professor of French in the Department of International Studies at Texas A&M University in College Station, Texas. Her specialty is nineteenth- and twentieth-century French literature, with special emphasis on prose fiction of the decadent period and on women writers. Well-known as a translator of the novels of Rachilde (Marguerite Eymery Vallette, 1860–1953), she is currently engaged in a series of projects related to the work of the Anglo-French writer known as Renée Vivien (Pauline Tarn, 1877–1909).

KATHARINA HEROLD is Stipendiary Lecturer in English at Brasenose College, Oxford. Her research focuses on the ways in which Orientalism shaped English and German Decadent writing between 1880 and 1920. She is a member of the international research network 'Writing 1900' led by Gesa Stedman and Stefano Evangelista. Her book chapter 'Dancing the Image – Sensoriality and kinaesthetics in the poetry of Stéphane Mallarmé and Arthur Symons' appeared in *Decadence and the Senses* (2017). More recently, she contributed a chapter on Arthur Symons and Gypsy lore to *Arthur Symons: Poet, Critic, Vagabond* (ed. Elisa Bizzotto and Stefano Evangelista, 2018).

ISOBEL HURST is Lecturer in English in the Department of English and Comparative Literature at Goldsmiths, University of London. Her research interests are in nineteenth- and twentieth-century poetry and fiction, women's writing, and the reception of classical epic and tragedy. She is the author of *Victorian Women Writers and the Classics: The Feminine of Homer* (2006).

JORDAN KISTLER is Lecturer in Nineteenth-Century Literature at the University of Keele, Staffordshire. Her interests include Victorian poetry, literature, and science, the New Woman and women's writings of the fin de siècle, and gothic fiction. She is the author of *Arthur O'Shaughnessy, a Pre-Raphaelite Poet in the British Museum* (2016).

KATE KRUEGER is the Director of Honors for the College of Liberal Arts and Sciences at the University of Illinois. She is the author of *British Women Writers and the Short Story, 1850–1930: Reclaiming Social Space* (2014).

DEBORAH LONGWORTH is Senior Lecturer and Head of English Literature at the University of Birmingham. Her research focuses on English literature from 1880 to 1940, with a specific focus on gender and modernism and the modernist novel. Her publications include *Djuna Barnes* (2003) and *Streetwalking the Metropolis* (2000).

SHUSHMA MALIK is Lecturer in Classics at the University of Roehampton, London. Her research interests include the role of Roman emperors in the classical tradition, Roman religions, and imperial historiography. In particular, she has worked extensively on the Emperor Nero's portrayal in Christian history as the Antichrist and has published on portrayals of Roman emperors in the works and letters of Oscar Wilde.

NICHOLAS D. MORE is Professor of Philosophy at Westminster College in Salt Lake City. He studies Nietzsche and the relation of philosophy to the humanities. His publications include *Nietzsche's Last Laugh: Ecce Homo as Satire* (2014).

LAURA MOURE CECCHINI is Assistant Professor of Art and Art History at Colgate University in Hamilton, New York. Her research investigates how transnational networks and the internationalization of artistic forms have shaped the modernist canon, focusing on Italy and Mexico as case studies. She is currently at work on a book titled *Baroquemania: the Allure of the Baroque in Italian Modern Visual Culture, 1898–1945*.

JEFFREY K. SACHS is a PhD student in the Department of Sociology at Yale University. His research focuses on social theory and organizational studies.

MICHAEL SHAW is Lecturer in Scottish Literature at the University of Stirling. His research focuses on fin-de-siècle literature and art, with a particular emphasis on the performance of aestheticism, decadence, and celticism in Scotland and Ireland. He is currently at work on a monograph, *The Fin-de-Siècle Scottish Revival: Romance, Decadence and Celtic Identity*.

EMMA SUTTON is Senior Lecturer in the School of English at the University of St Andrews. Her principal research interest is the relationship between literature and music in the late-nineteenth and early-twentieth centuries, particularly the contentious relationship between music and politics. Her publications include *Aubrey Beardsley and British Wagnerism* (2002) and *Virginia Woolf and Classical Music: Politics, Aesthetics, Form* (2013).

JERRY TONER is Fellow and Director of Studies at Churchill College and Director of Studies at Hughes Hall, Cambridge University. His research looks at Roman social and cultural history, with a focus on trying to look at history 'from below'. Key publications include *Homer's Turk: How Classics Shaped Ideas of the East* (2013), *Roman Disasters* (2013), *Popular Culture in Ancient Rome* (2009), and *Leisure and Ancient Rome* (1995).

DAVID WEIR is Professor Emeritus of Comparative Literature at The Cooper Union in New York City, where he taught literature, linguistics, and cinema for thirty years. He has published books on Jean Vigo, James

Joyce, William Blake, orientalism, anarchism, and decadence. His most recent publication is *Decadence: A Very Short Introduction* (2018).

THERESA ZEITZ-LINDAMOOD is an artist living and working in New York City. A graduate of The Cooper Union for the Advancement of Science and Art, she received a Fulbright Scholarship in 2014 to study painting in Bologna and Rome. In addition to painting, her interests include architecture and urban design.

Acknowledgements

How can we acknowledge the debt of decadence we owe to so many who would doubtless feel a mixture of shame and outrage to be so acknowledged, or, possibly, deny the tribute altogether? Hélas, to those we say that we both understand and sympathize. Hence, we are left to express our gratitude only to those hapless few who for reasons still unknown to us have refused to shun our company and – mirabile dictu! – have even gone so far as to participate amicably and help this project along. And so, it is with no small sense of wonder that we withhold moral judgement (a judgement that is always best withheld anyway) and offer our still incredulous gratitude to these inexplicably amicable and generous enablers of decadence. Among this group no one has done more than our research assistant Jessica Gossling of Goldsmiths, University of London (who is recovering quite well, thank you). We must also acknowledge our degenerate contributors and advisers, who should have known better but, happily, did worse. Special thanks to Geoffrey Nash for sharing his wisdom, and to our anonymous reader, thank you so much for being both anonymous and constructive, and for taming the CCC beast in its early stages. And what can we say of Edgar Mendez of Cambridge University Press in New York? Not enough, surely, or too much. By far our most incredulous debt of thanks for bringing this questionable project to its unquestioned conclusion goes to Ray Ryan, the series editor at Cambridge University Press, whose own most fulsome failure of moral judgement made this book possible. To him we offer our sincere gratitude, not only without qualification but also (doubt it not) without irony.

We are grateful to the following for permission to publish the images that appear in this book:

To Getty Images / Heritage Images for Thomas Couture, *The Romans of the Decadence* (1847).

To Getty Images / DEA Picture Library for Sir Lawrence Alma-Tadema, *The Favourite Poet* (1888).

To Getty Images / DEA Picture Library for Édouard Manet, *Music in the Tuileries Gardens* (1862).

To Getty Images / David Soanes Photography for Palazzo Zuccari (1590–1603).

To Getty Images / ullstein bild Dtl. for Erich von Stroheim (c. 1929).

To Musée Rops, Namur, Belgium, for *La Dame au Pantin* (1883–1885), gouache, coloured pencil, lead pencil, black stone and pastel on paper, 39.4 × 27.4 cm. Collection Fondation Roi Baudouin.

To Museo Nacional de Arte, INBA Acervo constitutive, 1982, Mexico City, Mexico, for Julio Ruelas, *La crítica* (1906–1907), etching.

To Hammer Museum, Los Angeles, for Gustave Moreau, *Salome Dancing before Herod* (1874–1876), oil on canvas, 143.5 × 104.3 cm. Collection: The Armand Hammer Collection; Gift of the Armand Hammer Foundation; photo: Robert Wedemeyer.

To Artists Rights Society / Art Resource, New York for Otto Dix, *Großstadt* (1927–1928), tryptich, wood, distemper, 181 × 401 cm. Collection: Kunstmuseum Stuttgart, Stuttgart, Germany.

To Estate Brassaï, ©RMN-Grand Palais / Art Resource, New York for *Lulu de Montparnasse dressed in a tuxedo with a woman at The Monocle*, c. 1933. Gelatin-silver print. Photo: Michèle Bellot.

Quotations from the published works of W. H. Auden appear by kind permission of the Estate of W. H. Auden.

Introduction

Jane Desmarais and David Weir

> To master the concept of decadence and to free it from inconsistency has been for students of nineteenth-century European cultural history, if not exactly the quest of the Grail, at least an important part of their intellectual agenda.
>
> (Richard Drake, 1982: 69)

The observation that Richard Drake made in 1982 seems more pertinent than ever, now that decadence has gained a secure place as the object of scholarly investigation. But the concept is no longer solely confined to the domain of 'nineteenth-century European cultural history'. Since 1982, the study of decadence has been extended well into the twentieth century, and some would argue, as several of our contributors do here, that the concept has contemporary relevance as well. Moreover, nineteenth-century concerns about decadence did not occur in a cultural or historical vacuum, which means that earlier investigations of decadence need to be taken into account. At the same time, decadence has assumed a multidisciplinary dimension, broadening the concept beyond the field of cultural history alone into such areas as philosophy, sociology, psychology, and more. In some instances, decadence seems to have served as a kind of shadow concept haunting the thought of those writers engaged in more traditional disciplines, while in others the concept appears to have played a role in the very foundation of new fields of inquiry. A well-known example of the former is the philosophy of Friedrich Nietzsche, for whom the concept was at once troubling and inescapable: 'Nothing has occupied me more profoundly than the problem of decadence' (1967: p. 155). A lesser-known example of the latter is the sociology of Émile Durkheim, for whom disharmony between individual interests and the good of society at large emerged as a signal concern. Durkheim may not have always used the word *décadence* in the analysis of such disharmony (he preferred the word *anomie*), but the concept is clear, in part because earlier writers, such as the critic Paul Bourget, had used that very word to identify precisely the condition Durkheim described: 'The word "decadence" is often used to designate the state of a society that produces too few individuals suited to the labors of communal life' (2009: 98).

Bourget's analysis of social disharmony dates from 1883 and owes its origins to the critic's interest in the poetry of Charles Baudelaire, whose 1857 collection *Les fleurs du mal* [*The Flowers of Evil*] remains a touchstone text of literary decadence. Bourget understood Baudelaire's poetry as 'decadent' because of an earlier analysis by Théophile Gautier that emphasized the relationship between literary style and the state of society at large. In particular, Gautier understood certain stylistic features of Baudelaire's poetry as reflective of imperial decline, finding in *The Flowers of Evil* a number of elements also evident in the literature of the Latin decadence. For Gautier, Baudelaire's style

> recalled the speech of the Lower Empire that was already veined with the greenish streaking of decomposition and the complex refinement of the Byzantine school, the ultimate form of decadent Greek art. Such, however, is the necessary, the inevitable speech of nations and civilizations when fictitious life has taken the place of natural life and developed in man wants till then unknown. (1903: p. 40)

Gautier's analysis of 'le style de décadence' has been influential for a number of reasons. First, the analysis shifts the meaning of the term *decadent* as a literary descriptor: whereas in the past a work might have been understood as decadent because of a lack of originality or an excess of conventionality, now a work of decadence could be regarded as something innovative and necessary, a means of expressing the new and hitherto unknown feelings produced by the experience of historical decline. Second, the analysis conveys the sense that decadence is more than a style because of the sense of social malaise the style conveys. The style, in short, shows that society itself has changed: no longer healthy, it is now decadent. Third, and most important, the analysis argues for an alignment of artistic values and social values under the shared rubric of decadence as a concept common to both. This is the point at which complications inevitably ensue, because the concept has become so dynamic as to belie coherence. This semantic instability results from the double interference of artistic and social meanings alongside the negative and positive valorization of those meanings. No single artistic context allows for positive aesthetic judgement in every case, just as no single social context permits negative moral judgement in every case. The poetry of the fourth-century Roman poet Ausonius and that of the nineteenth-century English poet Ernest Dowson are both decadent, but in different senses. Paedophilia in ancient Greece was noble, but in Victorian England it was so decadent as to be criminal.

Conceptually, decadence accommodates such contradictory meanings; it has been used to describe racial degeneration, historical decline, philosophical pessimism, personal immorality, physical entropy, artistic imperfection, and more. The fact that decadence has been studied using the analytical procedures of such disparate disciplines as eugenics, history, philosophy, psychology, physics, and aesthetics illustrates just how complex the concept is. Decadence appears to be what linguists call a semantic field, the understanding of which depends on an aggregation of related associations. The temporal and spatial dimensions of decadence are captured by 'decline' and 'decay', decline necessarily occurring over time and decay (or degeneration) being a property of objects. These two dimensions may merge through a metaphorical process, as when we speak of 'the decay of society', as if a society were an object – like a human body – subject to dissolution. Of course, decay occurs over time, so decadence is mostly an organic metaphor (rooted in the Latin verb *decadēre*, formed by the root verb *cadēre* 'to fall' plus the prefix *de-* 'down') with a wide range of associations.

To explain what we mean when we say that decadence is 'conceptually complex', and to speak in less metaphorical terms, we need to start from the basic idea that decadence is the resultant of both etymology and history, that the root sense of decadence as 'falling away' or decline gained currency because of certain historical instantiations of that meaning, with the fall of Rome as the paradigm case subsequently applied to other periods and cultures. Aesthetic meanings of decadence follow from this etymologically grounded historical assessment of certain cultures as 'decadent', that is, artistic inferiority is seen as an effect of imperial decline and social decay. Interest in decadence as historical decline begins in the eighteenth century just as the modern nation-state emerges in something like its full maturity, at least in Great Britain and France, for understandable reasons: as modern nations began to extend their political and commercial powers territorially into new colonial domains, it made sense for Montesquieu, Edward Gibbon, and others to examine the history of empires, the reasons for their successes and failures. Such concerns were part of the enlightenment project and the ideology of progress. Decadence originates as a cautionary component in the progressive paradigm of enlightenment thought, the obverse 'other' of reason and progress. The dynamism and complexity of decadence inheres in the way this otherness is valorized. For some, decadence is simply negation: it is *not* moral, *not* tasteful, and so on. For others, such negation is necessary as a critique of social norms or as a creative alternative to artistic conventions. Most artistic expressions of decadence combine the two and offer creative alternatives that include social critique. The way decadence functions, conceptually, allows for some remarkably dynamic reversals of meaning, such that the idea of decay or decline becomes – or can become – generative, inventive, creative, even progressive. The cross-over is evident in a number of areas, whether historical, social, or aesthetic, as in the aforementioned example of Gautier's assessment of Baudelaire as a poet whose powers of artistic invention proved adequate to the decadent era in which he lived. The critic had nothing but praise for the poet because of his capacity to create new forms of expression to capture sensations and ideas hitherto unknown.

In 1898, the critic Remy de Gourmont took stock of the conceptual transmutations of decadence in late nineteenth-century France, beginning with this essential observation:

> Just as the political history of the Romans has furnished us with the conception of historical decadence, so the history of their literature has furnished us with the conception of *literary* decadence – the double face of the same conception, for it is easy to point out the coincidence of the two movements, and easy to establish the belief that their developments were necessarily connected. (de Gourmont, 1966: p. 68)

De Gourmont takes issue with this formulation by questioning the connection between literary and political history. He casts doubt on the idea by noting that 'it is precisely now, when their political power has become nil, that the Scandinavian kingdoms find themselves adorned with original talents'. The comment about the originality of Henrik Ibsen and other Scandinavian authors reflects the critic's signal concern with 'the idea of decadence' as 'identical to the idea of imitation' in an effort to understand how the most original of his literary contemporaries, Stéphane Mallarmé, has come to be construed – and valued – as *décadent.* The effort is all the more interesting in the light of de Gourmont's rejection of political decline as a means of explaining literary decadence: 'no reasonable relationship can be established between the strength of a people and the genius of a man'; on the contrary, it might well be that 'political decadence is the condition most favourable for intellectual flowering' (p. 69). In making that last point, de Gourmont follows Gautier in his earlier analysis of Baudelaire's innovations as a necessary response to historical decline, but de Gourmont perhaps goes further than Gautier by allying the decadence of Mallarmé to an artistic rebellion against certain aesthetic conventions that appear to have been more persistent in the literary culture of France than elsewhere. Those conventions include imitation itself, understood in the positive sense as a respect for tradition; and clarity, another positive value that, like imitation, descends from the *classicisme* of Racine and other seventeenth-century writers. Mallarmé's cultivation of a contrasting aesthetic of innovation and obscurity, then, is a noteworthy departure from classical conventions that traditionalist critics inevitably decry as 'decadent'. While this juxtaposition of 'decadence' and 'classicism' is nothing new, de Gourmont's explanation of their relationship is: if Mallarmé's originality and obscurity are decadent, so much the better – such decadence is far preferable to obligatory imitation and vacuous clarity. In other words, classicism itself has become decadent, which opens the way for the innovative *décadence* of Mallarmé.

But it is not solely in literature that the concept of decadence serves as an impetus to renewal. Various inflections of decadence play a foundational role in a number of liberal arts fields, an obvious example being art history. Johann Winckelmann's *Geschichte der Kunst des Alterthums* [*History of Ancient Art*] (1774) established the modern field of art history by proposing that culture is subject to organic development – periods of growth, maturity, and decline. His theory that Greek art provided a pattern of perfection and that subsequent periods of art were therefore decadent in relation to classical perfection was to be far reaching. Other examples of the foundational role of decadence in the development of entire intellectual fields are less well known but no less important. Again, the modern social science of sociology might not exist if the founders of that field had not engaged with the concept of decadence. In addition to the conceptual echoes of Bourget's decadent discourse in Durkheim's descriptions of the breakdown in the social bonds between the community and the individual, other social theories during the early years of sociology reveal a certain conceptual kinship with decadence. Thorstein Veblen, another foundational figure in sociology, described the theory of conspicuous consumption in his *Theory of the Leisure Class* (1899), a theory with a clear debt to decadence. That debt is clear because the American decadent novelist Henry Blake Fuller had earlier described the same Chicago social scene – and the same consumerist dynamic – in his fiction that Veblen analysed in his social theory some years later. It is a harder argument to make, but one could also argue that anthropology is another field that emerged in its modern form as the result of an intellectual dialogue with decadence.

A classic formulation understands decadence and primitivism as the dialectical terms in a social process of decay and renewal, and this positive conception of primitivism as socio-cultural renewal may lie behind the foundational thinking of certain anthropologists, notably Franz Boas and Edward Sapir, both of whom rejected the racist paradigm that construed Native American and other indigenous cultures as somehow 'primitive'. The larger point here is that decadence, conceptually considered, has a range and a relevance that is not limited to literature alone.

For this reason, the essays in this book often investigate decadence as something more than a cultural moment or movement in an effort to establish its value as a critical concept whose origins may lie in history and literature but whose relevance and application extend to areas outside those two seminal fields. At the same time, the discussion of the concept of decadence in the context of such non-literary disciplines as philosophy, science, geography, sociology, and so on, should prove invaluable to students of literature because all those disciplines are variously represented in literature itself. Our multidisciplinary approach comes at a crucial time in the brief history of decadence as an academic field. Prior to the recent academic burgeoning of decadence as a discipline (which began sometime in the late-1970s to the mid-1990s), 'decadent' existed as little more than a term of opprobrium for literature that was construed as mannered, derivative, or unoriginal. The assessment of inferiority also made the term useful for certain periods of literary history, notably the Roman fourth century or the last decade of the nineteenth century in Great Britain, where 'The Decadence' once functioned as a period label to describe the work – and the lives – of such figures as Oscar Wilde and Aubrey Beardsley. The label was given life by the idea that this fin-de-siècle literature formed a kind of aesthetic parallel to the precious, excessively artificial poetry of Ausonius and other authors of the late Roman Empire – the original Decadence.[1] With the publication in 1987 of Linda Dowling's *Language and Decadence in the Victorian Fin de Siècle* and the expanded edition of Matei Calinescu's *Five Faces of Modernity: Modernism, Avant-Garde, Decadence, Kitsch, Postmodernism*, decadence was well on its way to becoming a complex topic in its own right that merited serious research. Dowling's book was notable for depth of investigation, Calinescu's for breadth of coverage. Two years later Barbara Spackman's *Decadent*

[1] Usage varies with respect to capitalization, but the convention seems to be that 'decadence' is capitalized when it refers to the late Roman Empire but not when it refers to more recent cultural and social developments.

Genealogies: The Rhetoric of Sickness from Baudelaire to D'Annunzio combined depth and breadth by taking a comparative approach to decadence. The approach was comparative in two senses, in that Spackman sought to engage with more than one national literature while also interpreting literature itself in the light of the nineteenth-century science of eugenics. The comparative approach continued in 1995 with David Weir's *Decadence and the Making of Modernism*, which argued for the transitional role of decadence in the cultural modulation of romanticism into modernism by examining works by Gustave Flaubert, Walter Pater, Joris-Karl Huysmans, Gabriele D'Annunzio, James Joyce, André Gide, and others. The study of decadence seemed poised to develop along the broad, comparative, interdisciplinary lines that marked its emergence thirty years ago.

Generally speaking, the ensuing development of decadence as an academic field has been less comparative and interdisciplinary than scholarship at the end of the last century seemed to portend. In our view, some of the recent scholarship on decadence has become specialized to the point that the concept risks losing the status it once had as a major cultural trope with broad explanatory power, as it was in the eighteenth century, for example, in the historiography of Gibbon; in the nineteenth century, in the philosophy of Nietzsche; or, in the twentieth century, in the critical theory of Theodor Adorno. Taught within the confines of late-Victorian literature and culture, or its more cosmopolitan variant, fin-de-siècle studies, decadence is understandably perceived as a niche area. Hence our purpose here is to restore a sense of depth and complexity to the concept by including essays that examine the role of decadence in fields other than the literary, a manoeuvre that does not, by any means, gainsay the considerable value of the numerous specialized, monographic studies that have appeared over the last twenty years or so.

The approach to the concept of decadence represented here is both multidisciplinary and chronological, or, rather, developmental, as reflected in the three main sections of the volume: 'Origins', 'Developments', and 'Applications'. The 'Origins' section of the volume sees decadence originating in ancient Rome, in Enlightenment France, and in nineteenth-century modernity, with decadence being a particularly complex response to the dual industrial and political revolutions that produced the urban, bourgeois values of liberal society. This section includes two chapters on the decline of Rome, the first describing Roman decadence from the perspective of the Romans themselves (although, strictly speaking, the Romans did not have a word for what was later termed 'decadence', but their *luxuria* [extravagance, luxury] comes close to the modern concept), the second from that of Roman historiographers. These two chapters are followed by an essay on the literary and artistic extensions of Roman historiography, in which the decline of Rome and Roman history in general are treated as a kind of cultural template for creative explorations of contemporary anxieties over both the failures (e.g., the 1848 revolutions) and the successes (e.g., urban renovation programs) of modernity. The second point of origin for decadence is the libertine enlightenment, a culture closely associated with the reign of Louis XV (Chapter 4). Not only the libertine hedonism of that period but also the aesthetic contrast of rococo art with the earlier classicism associated with Louis XIV's reign acquired resonance for later decadents. These two points of origin – the Roman decadence and French libertinage – combined in the nineteenth century to provide a means of reacting against both the politics and the morality of bourgeois modernity, as Thomas Couture's 1847 painting, *The Romans of the Decadence* (fig. 3.1), an allegory of contemporary France, reveals. The third point of origin for decadence is a less allegorical and more direct challenge to the progressive paradigm of modernity, wherein progress itself is regarded as a form of decadence. This foundational phase of decadence is the subject of the two chapters on nineteenth-century bourgeois modernity – one on urban experience and the decadent sensibility (Chapter 5), the second on decadence as a critique of the modernity that urban experience entails (Chapter 6). Both show the foundational importance of the modern metropolis to cultural manifestations of decadence. The 'Origins' section also includes a transitional chapter on aesthetics, a discipline that originates with enlightenment thought but is critical to the development of decadence as a retreat from both the old morality that modernity negates and the new ideology of progress that modernity entails (e.g., art for art's sake, *l'art pour l'art*).

The chapter on aesthetics forms the link to a chapter on the art-historical meanings of decadence, the first of several chapters in the 'Developments' section that show how the concept has evolved in different ways, depending on the discipline or field under examination. We understand aesthetics as originary and art history as developmental because aesthetic philosophy provided the critical rationale that made the assessment of decadence possible with respect to particular works of art. The fact that 'decadent' began to serve as a positive designation for the work of certain artists (Gustave Moreau, Aubrey Beardsley, Gustav Klimt) only in the late nineteenth century is a further justification for the inclusion of the chapter on art history in the 'Developments' section. The relationship between aesthetics and art history illustrates a critical dynamic because art history is not the only field where the concept of decadence 'crossed over', ameliorated, or otherwise underwent some kind of transvaluation in meaning. We understand such transvaluation as developmental, not least because Nietzsche described the process as occurring in the field of philosophy in the late nineteenth century. Surely it makes sense to take note of occurrences of the same process in other cultural fields as one way of justifying and unifying the chapters designated as 'Developments'. Additional unifying strategies include the complementary positioning of certain chapters (religion and science, for example) and the continuity of topics and issues from the 'Origins' section to the 'Developments' section (both the philosophy and the psychology chapters echo, in different ways, the enlightenment chapter in the 'Origins' section). The chapter on parody, pastiche, satire, and New Women's writing might seem out of place at first, but our thinking is that this particular literary and cultural dimension of decadence is one form of the aesthetic development of the concept, hence its positioning along with the chapters on visual arts and music, which also echo the transitional chapter on aesthetics.

The 'Developments' section focuses mostly on traditional disciplines and fields that emerged in the nineteenth century or prior. This point needs stressing because it is what distinguishes development from application. The focus of the 'Developments' section is on those fields that were either well established in the nineteenth century or were in the process of becoming so. Various branches of the physical and biological sciences were sufficiently established in the nineteenth century to allow physicists, for example, to elaborate a theory of entropy that could be transposed as a social theory of decadence, as happened in 1895 with Brooks Adams's *Law of Civilization and Decay*. Most of the social sciences, psychology especially, were in the process of becoming established in the nineteenth century, and here again the concept of decadence plays a role in that establishment. After all, it is hard to imagine Sigmund Freud's invention of psychoanalysis without such 'sexological' precursors as Richard von Krafft-Ebing, whose *Psychopathia Sexualis* (1886) remains a foundational text for anyone seeking to investigate the development of decadence in terms of sexual perversion. The chapters in the 'Developments' section move from such aesthetic fields and topics as visual arts, music, and literature to other types of nineteenth-century disciplines, either established or emerging. Just as Chapter 7, 'Decadence and Aesthetics', serves as a transition to the discussion of decadence and aesthetic topics in the 'Developments' section, so Chapter 15, 'The Sociology of Decadence', serves as a bridge to the 'Applications' section, which includes several chapters that take stock of the social meanings and implications of the concept of decadence.

The 'Applications' section employs a different logic from the 'Developments' section (where, again, the principle of selection is grounded in fields of human knowledge that were familiar or becoming familiar in the nineteenth century) by seeking to elucidate the ways in which the concept of decadence has been or might be applied to fields that have emerged most forcefully in the twentieth century (cinema studies and popular culture being good examples). Here also the chapters echo earlier ones, with the chapter on urban geography combining with the transitional chapter on sociology, for instance, to carry forward the emphasis on decadence and the urban condition from the 'Origins' section. The 'Applications' section includes theoretical and historical examinations of literary applications that are becoming somewhat familiar (such as the use of decadence to investigate modernism), plus some applications that are quite new and unusual (cinema, again, as well as interwar avant-garde culture). The opening chapter on urban geography functions almost as an introduction to the section, given the emphasis on the urbanist importance of Vienna 1900 and Weimar Berlin, as well as interwar Paris, to the broader application, or set of applications, of the concept of decadence. The chronological progression of the closing chapters merits emphasis, beginning with transnational applications that originate in the fin de siècle but extend well into the twentieth century. These chapters are followed by the modernist application of decadence to both fiction and poetry, and then by a further application during the interwar period that includes not only fiction and poetry, but also photography (e.g., Brassaï). The final chapter brings decadence into the twenty-first century, revealing the continuing relevance and application of decadence to our own times. To that assessment we might add that not only is the concept of decadence still a part of contemporary life, but also that it may be, in some sense, necessary to an informed understanding of the anxieties and uncertainties that beset us today.

References

Bourget, Paul (2009). The Example of Baudelaire. Nancy O'Connor, trans., *New England Review*, 30(2), 90–104.

Drake, Richard (1982). Decadence, Decadentism and Decadent Romanticism in Italy: Toward a Theory of Decadence. *Journal of Contemporary History*, 17, 69–92.

Gautier, Théophile (1903). Charles Baudelaire. In vol. XXIII of *The Complete Works of Théophile Gautier*, S. C. de Sumichrast, ed. and trans., New York: George D. Sproul, pp. 17–126.

Gourmont, Remy de (1966). Stéphane Mallarmé and the Idea of Decadence. In Glenn S. Burne, ed. and trans., *Selected Writings*, Ann Arbor: University of Michigan Press, pp. 67–76.

Nietzsche, Friedrich (1967). '*The Birth of Tragedy' and 'The Case of Wagner*,' Walter Kaufmann, trans., New York: Random House.

PART I

Origins

CHAPTER 1

Decadence in Ancient Rome

Jerry Toner

'La décadence, c'est Rome', as the French historian, Pierre Chaunu, put it (1981: p. 165). As a result of well-known stories, such as the emperor Nero's extravagance or the aristocracy's supposed nightly round of orgies, ancient Rome has become almost synonymous with luxury and excess: the place where people first set out to enjoy themselves without restraint (Dalby, 2000). This chapter will examine how far the evidence supports this somewhat melodramatic view of Rome by looking at the ways in which luxury spread in the Roman world. It will also look at the ways this growth in luxury compelled the Romans to create new concepts to understand the phenomenon. Luxury was almost never seen as a simple index of increased wealth. Rather, it raised all manner of moral issues among Rome's ruling classes, many of which long outlived the end of the Roman Empire itself.

The Growth of Luxury

The Romans might have invented decadence, but they did not possess an exact term for it. The word 'decadence' derives from medieval Latin, whereas the Romans' own discussions focus more on the concept of *luxuria* [luxury]. Roman writers agree that Rome experienced a significant increase in the availability and the display of luxury goods, and there is no doubt that their depictions are true. Rome's conquest of the Mediterranean world opened up a whole new network of trade routes. Notably, when the future emperor Augustus cemented his control over the empire by defeating Mark Antony and Cleopatra at Actium in 31 BCE, new routes to the east were established. Now that Rome controlled Egypt, direct shipping lanes from the Red Sea to Arabia, East Africa, and India were opened. These gave access to goods which were, by Roman standards, exotic in the extreme, including silks from China, incenses from Arabia, and spices from India (Wallace-Hadrill, 2014). Previously the perilous journeys through intervening states, such as the Persian Empire, meant that these high-value goods had reached Rome only in small quantities. The first-century CE writer, Pliny the Elder, gives us a sense of the range of goods that made it into Rome's markets when he analyses Roman luxury by listing the available items and their prices. Pepper from India, for example, could fetch as much as fifteen denarii per pound, enough to feed a family of four at subsistence level for a month. The volume of the trade, however, also meant that far cheaper black pepper was also available, allowing it to become widely popular as a way to spice up dishes and wines and even medicines (Pliny the Elder, *Natural History* 12.29).[1] Imported in bulk, black pepper was stored in a specially constructed warehouse, the *Horrea Piperataria*, which still partly survives under the Basilica of Constantine. The quantities were so large that when Alaric the Goth held Rome to ransom in 408 CE, part of the deal to buy him off was 3,000 pounds of pepper.

Rome was a steeply hierarchical society, with legal gradations from the highest senator down to the lowest slave. The Romans were, as a result, acutely alert to distinctions of personal status and rank, so luxury items offered an easy way for individuals and families to display their status. The wealthy decorated their villas with coloured paints, white being cheapest, then red and yellow, with blue and black being reserved for grand rooms to create an aura of high value, luxury, and prestige (Zarmakoupi, 2014). In the same way, perfumed water might be sprinkled on bathroom walls (Pliny, *Natural History* 13.5; on the sensory expansion of the empire, see Betts, 2017). Lower down the social scale, individuals might own decorated oil lamps, good quality tableware or wear amulets and jewellery made from imported stones.

There was another, more cultural necessity behind the importation of luxury. Rome needed to create a new form of its culture that was fitting for its vast empire. Faced with the cultural superiority of the conquered Hellenistic world, the Romans responded by culturally appropriating all manner of Greek practices, ranging from statuary to new kinds of food and forms of literature. This new type of mannered artifice did not, therefore, simply represent indulgence in new-found luxuries. It was part of a cultural revolution in the Roman world, one that saw Rome change from a relatively uncultured backwater to the centre of a huge empire's artistic and aesthetic life (Wallace-Hadrill, 2008).

[1] For classical references, numbers refer to sections in the standard original texts; translations are my own unless otherwise stated.

Luxury as Moral Decline

What becomes clear is that luxury was thought to possess meaning beyond simple display. Social display served as a way to mark off both the elite from those beneath them and Rome as a whole from its empire. Taste itself became a means of social distinction, which was then itself used as evidence of the cultural superiority of both the elite and Rome. But the importation of a foreign high culture was not unproblematic. It explicitly recognized aspects of traditional Roman simplicity as being inferior. The adoption of Greek artifice, or *cultus* as the Romans called it, also explicitly accepted that Roman culture was changing. The poet Horace, writing under the first emperor Augustus, famously complained that the rough Romans had themselves been conquered by the attractions of Greek culture: 'Graecia capta ferum victorem cepit et artes intulit agresti Latio' [Captive Greece has captured her savage conqueror, and brought the arts into rustic Latium] (Horace, *Epistles* 2.1.156). Discussions about luxury, therefore, came to be central to how Romans perceived that they had changed from their ancestors and to how they understood the implications of that change.

Precisely what luxury consisted of, however, was never such a clear-cut issue. The first problem was one of degree. How much luxury could a society indulge in without affecting standards of behaviour? In many ways the Romans revelled in luxury. Readily accepting the financial rewards of empire, they spent huge sums on their own pleasure. Whether in the colossal public games in the amphitheatre and the circus, in the opulent imperial bath complexes, or in extravagant private villas, Romans of all social levels delighted in the very best that life was thought to offer. In the late Republic, one of the main driving forces behind this huge public expenditure had been the vigorous competition between aristocrats for political office and the great riches it could bring. Needing to be elected by the Roman people, they sought to win their votes by providing food and luxuries on a vast scale. This practice led to a wider dissemination of luxury than would otherwise have been the case (Toner, 1995).

But the Romans also felt a profound sense of unease about the effect that all this new luxury seemed to be having upon them. Assessing luxury always involved a degree of comparison with the simplicity of old Rome, itself something of a mythological creation. Roman writers frequently harked back to a golden age when the values of Rome were uncorrupted and simple (see, for example, Livy, *Ab Urbe Condita* 39.6 and Pliny the Elder, *Natural History* 9.58.117–18). In part, this disquiet reflected a very practical concern that the Roman citizen body, having won the empire through its legendary military toughness, was likely to soften under the influence of the many luxuries Rome now offered. The kind of man who bathed daily, dined on delicacies, and composed fine verses was hardly likely to make much of a soldier. War exacerbated these concerns. During the conflicts with Carthage in the second century BCE, Scipio the Younger arrived at one camp only to find all manner of licentiousness and luxury. He issued orders for all the soothsayers and prostitutes to be driven out of the camp. He even commanded that the only utensils a soldier should be allowed to possess were a pot, a fork, and an earthenware drinking-cup. The troops were forbidden from reclining at dinner, which he ordered should consist only of bread, porridge, or boiled meat. The only luxury he allowed was that each man if he so wished could keep a silver tankard of not more than two pounds in weight. Scipio himself went about wearing a plain black cloak, saying that he was in mourning for the army's lost honour.

Many Roman writers, therefore, condemned individual actions which broke what they saw as the proper limits of luxury. Pliny, for example, complains that painting was by the first century CE thought worthless if it was not executed in a multitude of costly and exotic pigments (Pliny the Elder, *Natural History* 35.39). The popularity of bathing was of particular concern. Petronius describes the fictional nouveau riche character Trimalchio as luxuriating in the baths, his skin glistening all over with perfumed oil. He was rubbed down, not with ordinary linen, but with towels of the purest and softest wool, then wrapped in a blazing scarlet robe (*Satyricon* 28). Romans now seemed to have so much money that moralists fulminated that, 'Everyone thinks himself impoverished and distressed unless the walls of his bathing area sparkle with marble, paintings and glass; or unless Thasian marble, once a rare sight even in a temple, lines the swimming pools and the water pours out of silver taps' (Seneca, *Epistulae Morales* 78.23). Expensive spices and perfumes were associated with the supposedly decadent Greek and Persian East, which added to their connotations of immorality. Even slaves allegedly had silver mirrors (Pliny, *Natural History* 34.160). The emperors themselves provided the most extreme examples of such sensuous excess. Nero supposedly used to fish with a golden net, drawn by silken cords of purple and scarlet (Suetonius, *Nero* 30). The description of immoral luxury became a core part of the Roman literary tradition.

There was an element of financial concern about the growth in luxury. Pliny was outraged at the 100 million sesterces which he claims was being spent on luxury imports from the east, 50 million of which went to India alone. These numbers need to be treated with great caution since they are based more on the literary effect they were designed to generate rather than on hard data (in reality 100 million sesterces would have represented a very modest figure and the reality must have been far higher). Pliny also does not seem to take into account the value of goods that were exported from the Roman Empire in partial exchange for such luxury goods. And then there was an additional fiscal upside to this trade since the Roman authorities imposed a 25 per cent tax on imported luxury goods, which must have generated substantial revenues for the state (Wallace-Hadrill, 2014: pp. 74–5).

But the financial scale of the trade in luxury items only seemed to exaggerate the moral fears. We can see this effect in relation to seemingly unproblematic practices, such as personal grooming. Traditionally, Roman men did not shave, but the practice became widespread as Rome expanded and skilled barbers arrived from Greece. There is an interesting story that the fourth-century emperor Julian summoned a barber to trim his hair. The barber duly arrived, wearing a splendid outfit. The emperor was amazed and asked him how much he earned. The barber revealed that he made the equivalent of twenty daily allowances of bread and the same amount of fodder for pack animals, as well as having an annual salary, not to mention many generous tips. Incensed, Julian discharged all attendants of that kind as unnecessary (Ammianus Marcellinus, *Res Gestae* 22.4.9). This dismissal covered barbers, eunuchs, and cooks, the kinds of worthless people who pandered to individual luxury and vice and, in Julian's eyes, had corrupted the palace with dissolute life and the lavish use of silk and fancy food. Military discipline had weakened as a result, with soldiers practising effeminate tunes in place of war-songs and sleeping on feather beds. Stories of barbers making impossibly large fortunes reflected a combination of financial and moral anxieties: a fear that so much money was being wasted on pointless indulgence and a concern that such personal grooming only helped to soften the tough Roman male (Toner, 2015). Seneca contrasts the unshorn Romans of old with the full-length gold mirrors of his own time, when 'luxury, encouraged by sheer opulence, has gradually developed for the worst, and vices have taken on enormous growth', even 'amongst soldiers' (*Naturales Quaestiones* 1:17.7–10). It was a concern that made the first satirist, Juvenal, take a moral stand. When he saw that the man 'who made my stiff beard rasp while he shaved me in my youth can single-handedly challenge all the aristocrats with his wealth', then it was 'hard not to write satire' (*Satires* 1.24–5). A new literary form, satire, had to be created to cope with a world which was literally satiated with luxury.

The city sat at the heart of many of these moral concerns. The sprawling mass of Rome horrified many elite writers. It was the city where the masses wasted their days in idleness or in imperially sponsored leisure. It was in the city that luxury, extravagance, and devotion to pleasure seemed to make the bodies of young men 'so fat and weak that death seems likely to bring no change in them' (Columella, *On Agriculture* 1 preface 17). It was the city that had challenged the traditional relationship between the wealthy classes and the people, dividing the non-elite into the 'dirty plebs and worst slaves who are used to the Circus and the theatre' and the 'respectable part of the people attached to the great households' (Tacitus, *Histories* 1.4). Anxieties about the manliness of Roman men were reflected in attempts to adopt a more macho style of posturing in urban public spaces, with, for example, elite orators during the second century using their physical appearance to construct a suitably aggressive form of masculinity (Gleason, 1995: pp. 55–81, 131–58). A societal debate was clearly taking place about how men should best present themselves in public.

This attitude partly reflected a cyclical view of power, whereby the victorious would be brought low by the fruits of their own success. The texts of Roman historians were peppered with tales carefully selected to deliver an appropriate moral message. Luxury was thought to corrupt the individual and lead to a decline in standards. Faced with the multiple temptations that empire brought, many Romans worried that their society was slipping into a hubristic quagmire of disgraceful behaviour, which could only result in one thing – the loss of the support of the gods. Put simply, the Romans believed the gods were on their side. They referred to this rather cosy arrangement as the *pax Deorum* [the peace of the gods]. It seemed perfectly reasonable to ascribe positive outcomes in human affairs to divine will; divine favour, the Romans believed, had allowed them to establish their control over the whole Mediterranean world: the *pax Romana*. Similarly, misfortune was understood as a scourge sent by the gods to punish Rome for any acts which had upset them. Luxury, therefore, was believed to pose a very potent threat to Roman security.

Resisting Luxury

One response to the grave threat posed by luxury was legislation. The law reflected the authorities' concern about the impact of what was seen as immoral behaviour upon the wider community. Losing the support of the gods because of the immoral behaviour of certain individuals meant that what might look to us like victimless crime, from the Roman point of view risked bringing disaster down on everyone's heads (see Zanda, 2013).

The Roman state had a long tradition of enacting what are called sumptuary laws – laws made for the purpose of limiting or preventing expenditure on certain items of personal consumption, especially luxury items. The second-century CE writer Aulus Gellius discusses these laws, noting how they were introduced to maintain the frugality of the early Romans (*Attic Nights* 2.24). One of the earliest of these was a decree of the senate concerning the Megalensian games ordering all leading citizens to swear an oath before the consuls that they would not spend on dinner more than one hundred and twenty asses in addition to vegetables, bread, and wine, nor would they serve any foreign wine, nor use more than one hundred pounds' weight of silverware at the table. Clearly, such measures were originally targeted at those at the top of Roman society. The fear was that society would rot from the top down if these leaders were corrupted, hence the high level of concern with the weakening effect of anything perceived to be luxurious over-consumption. The emphasis on the foreignness of the wine might also contain a hint of economic protectionism to ensure that the Romans bought Roman goods, but such aims coincided with larger moral aims so closely that they did not need to be articulated separately.

The law tried to act as a check on the steady rise in expenditure on luxury items which accompanied the increase in Rome's power and wealth. The Licinian law, probably passed in 103 BCE, limited the financial outlay on designated holiday feasts while permitting larger sums for weddings. It allowed for a fixed weight of dried meat and other preserved products to be served but permitted unlimited use of anything grown in the earth, on a vine, or in an orchard. Morally acceptable food was that produced naturally from the ground and eaten fresh rather than anything salted, including meat. Meat was a valuable commodity, best reserved as an offering to the gods. But, as Gellius sadly notes, these laws were soon forgotten: many wealthy men were gourmandizing and 'recklessly pouring their family fortune into an abyss of [. . .] banquets' (*Attic Nights* 2.24). Finally, he lists the Julian law of the emperor Augustus, which limited expenditure on dining to two hundred sesterces on a working day, three hundred on holidays, and a thousand at weddings and banquets, and another edict which increased the holiday limit from three hundred to two thousand, which itself says something of the high level of dinner-party inflation. The thinking behind this increase, he says, was that it was better to put some kind of limit on luxury than to allow it to increase uncontrollably. Such laws had no effect because they were widely disregarded and simply lagged behind the increased outlay of the rich on their parties.

Sumptuary laws attempted to regulate more than just the consumption of food and wine. In the aftermath of the crushing defeat at Cannae in 216 BCE, when the Romans lost fifty thousand men in a single day and found themselves facing defeat at the hands of Carthage and its brilliant general, Hannibal, one of the Roman responses was an attempt to place legal limits on the amount of jewellery a woman could wear, what colour clothing she could wear, and how far she could travel in a horse-drawn carriage. The Oppian law, as it was known, stood for twenty years. Then, in 195 BCE, with Rome having defeated Carthage and becoming even richer with the added inflows of tribute from the many provinces formerly in the possession of its opponent, authorities proposed a repeal of the law. It probably seemed irrelevant to many now that the fighting was over and, with the Roman aristocracy never having had it so good, the limits seemed positively draconian. Livy gives a long account of the great public debate the proposed abolition of the law generated (*Ab Urbe Condita* 34.1–8). The very length of the description underlines how important these laws concerning luxury were in the Roman mind. But the two sides of the debate also give us an insight into the wider Roman psychology. At heart, the Romans found themselves in a completely contradictory position: hooked on frugality, addicted to wealth.

What is also clear is that whenever the Roman men failed to win on the battlefield, a natural response was to blame the women back home. It was as if the women of the household were somehow at fault for having softened their male offspring by wearing too much finery. Again, we see a direct relationship in the Roman mind between personal consumption and military prowess. And while the law was aimed primarily at the elite, given it limited the wearing of gold jewellery, the use of that most expensive colour, purple, and travel by means of expensive horse-drawn transport, the entire Roman people seemed to have held strong views about the issue and crowded into the Capitol to hear the debate. The women of Rome came out in numbers to voice their strong support for the law's repeal. They filled the streets, imploring men on their way to the forum to overturn the regulation now that Rome was doing so well. Every day more and more women came into the city from the surrounding towns and villages until they even summoned up the courage to press the consuls and other officers of the state with their demands.

Livy recounts how one of the consuls, the famously hawkish Cato the Elder, had little truck with this band of female protesters. If only Roman husbands had better control of their wives, he argued, there would not now be this trouble with the whole sex. Now women were even entering the forum and interfering in the world of male politics. This was a breach of traditional roles, and Cato was outraged: 'What sort of behaviour is this, running out in public, filling the streets, and speaking to other women's husbands?' In Cato's view, we also find a clear link expressed between luxury and religion. He complains how many people admire the decorations of Greek culture and ridicule the earthenware images of the Roman gods that stand at the entrances of their temples. 'For my part,' he says, 'I prefer these gods', since these were the gods who had won Rome its empire. There was another problem with luxury: it was like a disease which could never be sated. The more individuals indulged in personal pleasure the more they would want it. It was, Cato claimed, like a wild beast.

Cato was a traditionalist and a reactionary. He could see no benefit in Rome changing its all too successful ways. But his voice sat at the extremes of the debate. More moderate speakers argued that now Rome was victorious there was no need for a law passed in the depths of despair following a massive defeat. Austerity had been understandable then, when everyone was trying to save money to help the war effort. It had been right for Rome's women to shoulder their share of the burden and not to waste money on decorative items and pleasure. But now it was only right for Roman women to benefit from the rewards of victory. The crowd of women continued to protest and hammered on the doors of the homes of those who had spoken against the proposed repeal. And their pressure won. The Oppian law was annulled.

Roman laws on luxury reflected a range of moral concerns: fear of a loss of military prowess, fear that luxury was an addiction which would lead to ever more consumption, and fear that lavish expenditure would erode the family fortunes of Rome's aristocratic class. The laws represented an attempt at self-regulation by Rome's elite to prevent luxury from corrupting the ruling class and so undermining the social order. But as the Oppian law shows, all Romans had a strong interest in these matters. Such interest was perhaps partly the result of rising real wealth in Roman society, with more people finding themselves brought into the scope of the expenditure limits of the laws. But we also find increasing concern from the Roman state about the behaviour of the lower classes in certain areas. Bars in particular became a focus of elite concern at what ordinary Romans were now getting up to in their free time.

Popular Luxury

For two centuries the senate had produced ever more complex legislation to try to control the consumption of luxury items. By the time of the empire, it had become patently futile to try and limit such consumption. But that did not mean an end to attempts to legislate against what was regarded as excessive consumption. Rather, the laws were targeted at certain sections of society thought to be most at risk. Taverns, above all, became the focus of a range of laws aimed at limiting the spread of luxury downwards to the ordinary people. It might have been too late to stop the excesses of the aristocracy, but there was still time to save the Roman people.

Taverns featured prominently in the daily life of the people of Rome. These places served as mini-leisure centres and, since most people did not have access to cooking facilities, as places to get hot food. Cold food and wine (usually mixed with hot water) were also served. This centrality to daily life is seen in Pompeii, where something like one hundred forty bars have been found (although it is often impossible to tell for sure when a bar is actually a bar and not a shop). Often these places offered other entertainments, including music, prostitution, and gambling, even though the latter was illegal.

But where ordinary people found food and entertainment, the Roman elite saw gross immorality. Taverns appeared as dens of all kinds of vice. In Apuleius' novel, *Metamorphoses*, one character, Thrasyllus, a young man of wealth and high birth, is given to the pleasures of the tavern. He spends his time in whoring and daytime drinking, falls into the evil company of a band of thieves, and even commits murder (*Metamorphoses* 8.1). A simple drink in a bar was, from an elite perspective, the first step on a slippery slope leading to potential ruin.

Various emperors, therefore, issued sumptuary laws concerning what could be sold in taverns. Tiberius banned the sale of pastries, and Claudius banned cooked meats and hot water (which would have been mixed with wine). Even though Nero is alleged to have spent practically his whole life in bars, he forbade the sale of anything boiled except vegetables and pea-soup (no meat, that is). Vespasian allowed nothing cooked to be sold in bars except chickpeas and other legumes. It might be possible to see some level of economic justification for these bans but the main driver was the fear that in the big, imperial city of Rome, luxury was not limited to the upper classes – it was even filtering down to the plebs. And just as the Oppian law had sought to restrain what women consumed, so laws against taverns and gambling attempted to set limits on what was considered appropriate for an average Roman to consume.

For all this legislation, there seems to have been little real effort to enforce it. The vocal and legal attacks on taverns, the foods they served, and the entertainments they offered were largely a way of letting off moral steam. Fulminating about these new kinds of urban institutions reflected some level of anxiety about the limited control of the elites over the mass population of the huge city Rome had become because the authorities lacked the resources to enforce their legislative regime in any other than an exemplary way. The sheer number of bars certainly suggests that what little they did had no significant effect. Instead, we can see the hostility in elite texts, both legal and literary, towards taverns as reflecting unease at the alternative culture operating so commonly around them. We can also see anti-tavern sumptuary laws as representing a symbolic attempt to limit and confine the problem, making a public statement about the unacceptability of this kind of behaviour, rather than a serious attempt to eradicate it.

The Emperors and Morality

The transition from republic to empire at the turn of the first century BCE saw a profound shift in the nature of Roman political and public life. The sole ruler, Augustus as he came to be known, was faced with unifying a society that had been fractured by decades of civil war. Augustus sought to recreate Roman identity, based on traditional themes of piety, virtue, and loyalty. The emperor himself represented the epitome of these values and served as the cultural centre-point for Roman society as a whole. Luxury, in the form of lavish games, now became the means by which he sought to clearly exhibit this new identity. Pleasure and politics were fused into a powerful alloy which overcame traditional objections to the non-elite having access to leisure and luxury. The games were not thought to corrupt the people because they established imperial legitimacy, maintained social hierarchy, and created social consensus.

The new political ideology sought to contrast itself with the chaos of the previous republic (Toner, 2009). Luxury was shorn of some of its decadent connotations as a way of emphasizing the revitalization of Roman society. It was as if the previous chaos of the late Republic had itself reflected the lack of control over excessive consumption. The emperors could not argue that they were reducing luxury (nor would they want to risk such an unpopular act), but they could show that luxury was now being directed towards a moral political purpose. The previous disorder was presented, almost, as a necessary stage for Roman society to have passed through before it could undergo a profound moral rebirth (see Morley, 2004).

Augustus did not want to be seen as an innovator. He wanted to be seen to have restored the republic. He portrayed his rule as re-establishing traditional morality, not as introducing any unsettling novelty. We might well see this strategy as political spin designed to camouflage the reality of the autocracy of his rule, but establishing controls of supposedly excessive personal behaviour was a cornerstone of his claim to legitimacy. Sumptuary laws, therefore, received a new articulation under Augustus. His moral laws made adultery a public, criminal offence. The law now required a husband to prosecute his wife if he discovered her having an affair, otherwise he risked being charged as a pimp. If convicted, the wife must be immediately divorced. Under the terms of the law, a father could kill his daughter and her lover, provided that he caught them in the act, that they were having sex either in his own house or that of his son-in-law, and that he killed them both immediately. Adultery did not apply to all, since it depended upon the woman's status. Married men could only commit adultery with respectable married women. A wife committed adultery if she slept with any other man, even a slave. By contrast, it was impossible for a female slave or prostitute to commit adultery. As an indication of how seriously Augustus took these laws, if an accusation went to court, slaves were permitted to give evidence against their masters and mistresses.

In introducing these laws against what was regarded as immoral sexual behaviour, Augustus was making a determined effort to reinforce the sanctity of marriage as an institution and the integrity of the family home. After two generations of civil strife during the collapse of the Republic, his moral laws acted as a core part of the first emperor's attempt to reinstate order to all aspects of the Roman world. In this view, political chaos had itself been a reflection of moral chaos and the family sat at the heart of his attempt to restore order. What is less clear is whether the legislation had any real impact. Some openly flouted the legislation, including Augustus' own daughter, Julia, who was banished to an island without access to wine (Suetonius, *Augustus* 65). The poet Ovid shows that elite authors could also delight in subverting the official position. During the reign of Augustus Ovid wrote *Ars amatoria* [*The Art of Love*], a poetic textbook on how to conduct a love affair. This blatant subversion of Augustus' attempts at moral reform probably contributed to his being later exiled to the miserable Black Sea town of Tomis.

Overall, it seems likely that the adultery laws were aimed at the upper classes but, in the process, gave out a strong message about the moral purpose of the new regime to Romans of all levels. The laws were largely symbolic, designed to state an aim and establish an atmosphere rather than to be meticulously prosecuted. In this regard, the adultery laws were no different from other Roman sumptuary laws, where the ability to enforce them was severely limited by the modest resources allocated by the state to do so. What the ineffectiveness of the sumptuary laws also reveals is how the Romans maintained a general belief in the beneficial power of tradition while simultaneously recognizing that things had to change. By reasserting old-fashioned values, Augustus reinvented the past to suit a very different set of political circumstances. People generally accepted this manoeuvre because tradition promised to deliver stability and the continued success of Rome.

Decadent Emperors

How do we square Roman attempts at moral rebirth with the behaviour of the notorious emperors, such as Caligula and Nero, who showed little sign of restraint in any of their personal behaviour? First, we should bear in mind that many of the stories regarding these 'bad' emperors are exaggerated (Elsner and Masters, 1994). We can never know what element of truth, if any, lies behind these tales. But the stories do highlight the paradox that emperors could stand above the very laws they created if they so wished. We might think that such behaviour would undermine the law. But this kind of imperial misbehaviour was not the norm. If anything, these acts were the exceptions that reinforced the norms of society. Immoral emperors generated a moral backlash, which we find expressed in the negative accounts these rulers received from later Roman historians, such as Tacitus and Suetonius. These immoral emperors also suffered directly: they were all assassinated and their memories obliterated.

Emperors as a whole reflected the kind of double standard that seems to have operated in Roman society, making repeated attempts to maintain public standards of behaviour in the same manner as Augustus had done. After sexual permissiveness and luxury had allegedly flourished without restraint, for example, the emperor Vespasian pressured the senate to vote that any woman who had an affair with another person's slave should herself be treated as a slave (Suetonius, *Vespasian* 11). Likewise, Domitian also attempted a moral rebirth by introducing a slew of measures, ranging from expelling senators who had appeared on the stage, preventing women from using sedan chairs, and executing Vestals who had been involved in affairs (Suetonius, *Domitian* 8). The fourth-century CE emperor Julian banned taverns from opening early, prohibited the sale of cooked meat, and forbade ordinary people from heating water (in case they mixed it with wine). He even forbade eating in public (Ammianus Marcellinus, *Res Gestae* 28.4.4). These measures were undoubtedly only very occasionally enforced. But at the same time, almost all emperors continued to indulge in all manner of luxury and extravagance, even though the degree seems to have varied dramatically from one emperor to the next.

It would be easy to see such behaviour as simple hypocrisy. Another way of looking at it is that the Romans were concerned to enjoy the fruits of their conquests while safeguarding their favourable relationship with the gods – always a delicate balancing act. In addition, what counted as luxury changed significantly over the centuries, with an upward inflationary trend seemingly existing throughout Roman history. Perceptions of what constituted acceptable consumption were always, therefore, variable. And while most of the extravagant expenditure was carried out by those at the top of society, the ordinary people of the city of Rome also benefited from an ever-increasing supply of entertainments and foodstuffs. Subsequent Roman emperors kept up Augustus' interest in maintaining public morals and in doing so targeted a range of supposedly immoral behaviours. It was felt to be a fundamental duty of an emperor, as father to his people, to regulate what his people consumed and, by limiting their indulgence in luxuries, to protect their moral health and prevent any wider social decay.

References

Ammianus Marcellinus (1963–1964). *Res Gestae*, J. C. Rolfe, trans., Cambridge, MA: Harvard University Press.

Apuleius (1989). *Metamorphoses*, J. A. Hanson, trans., Cambridge, MA: Harvard University Press.

Aulus Gellius (1961). *Attic Nights*, J. C. Rolfe, trans., Cambridge, MA: Harvard University Press.

Betts, Eleanor, ed. (2017). *Senses of the Empire: Multisensory Approaches to Roman Culture*, London: Routledge.

Chaunu, Pierre (1981). *Histoire et décadence*, Paris: Perrin.

Columella (1954–1955). *On Agriculture*, H. B. Ash, E. S. Forster, and E. H. Heffner, trans., Cambridge, MA: Harvard University Press.

Dalby, Andrew (2000). *Empire of Pleasures: Luxury and Indulgence in the Roman World*, London: Routledge.

Elsner, Jaś, and Jamie Masters (1994). *Reflections of Nero: Culture, History, and Representation*, London: Duckworth.
Gleason, Maud W. (1995). *Making Men: Sophists and Self-presentation in Ancient Rome*, Princeton: Princeton University Press.
Horace (1929). *Satires, Epistles and Ars Poetica*, H. R. Fairclough, trans., Cambridge, MA: Harvard University Press.
Juvenal (2014). *Satires*, S. M. Braund, trans., Cambridge, MA: Harvard University Press.
Livy (1976). *Ab Urbe Condita*, B. O. Foster, trans., Cambridge, MA: Harvard University Press.
Morley, Neville (2004). Decadence as a Theory of History. *New Literary History*, 35, 573–85.
Petronius (2014). *Satyricon*, M. Heseltine, trans., Cambridge, MA: Harvard University Press.
Pliny (1968). *Natural History*, H. Rackham, trans., Cambridge, MA: Harvard University Press.
Seneca (1962–1967). *Epistulae Morales*, R. M. Gummere, trans., Cambridge, MA: Harvard University Press.
Seneca (1971–1972). *Naturales Quaestiones*, T. H. Corcoran, trans., Cambridge, MA: Harvard University Press.
Suetonius (1970). *The Lives of the Caesars*, J. C. Rolfe, trans., Cambridge, MA: Harvard University Press.
Tacitus (1962). *The Histories*, C. F. Moore, trans., Cambridge, MA: Harvard University Press.
Toner, Jerry (1995). *Leisure and Ancient Rome*, Cambridge: Polity.
Toner, Jerry (2009). *Popular Culture in Ancient Rome*, Cambridge: Polity.
Toner, Jerry (2015). Barbers, Barbershops, and Searching for Roman Popular Culture. *Papers of the British School at Rome*, 83, 91–109.
Wallace-Hadrill, Andrew (2008). *Rome's Cultural Revolution*, Cambridge: Cambridge University Press.
Wallace-Hadrill, Andrew (2014). The Senses in the Marketplace: The Luxury Market and Eastern Trade in Imperial Rome. In Jerry Toner, ed., *A Cultural History of the Senses in Antiquity*, London: Bloomsbury, pp. 69–89.
Zanda, Emanuela (2013). *Fighting Hydra-Like Luxury: Sumptuary Regulation in the Roman Republic*, London: Bloomsbury.
Zarmakoupi, Mantha (2014). *Designing for Luxury on the Bay of Naples: Villas and Landscapes (c.100 BCE–79 CE)*, Oxford: Oxford University Press.

CHAPTER 2

Decadence and Roman Historiography

Shushma Malik

Decadence and historiography have an uneasy relationship. The word itself does not readily feel at home in historical accounts, but its definition, 'the process of falling away or declining (from a prior state of excellence, vitality, prosperity, etc.); decay; impaired or deteriorated condition' (*OED*), can be situated far more comfortably as an idea connected to historical change. As Neville Morley explains, the idea of decadence 'rests on a sense of difference between the past and the present, and a sense of meaning in that difference' (2005: 574–5). Decay supplies the difference and immorality the meaning. However, the word still poses problems. It is too metaphorical, too subjective, and too caught up with artistic and aesthetic movements. Instead, historians have preferred the term 'decline' as it can apparently be quantified in a way metaphorical decadence cannot. Graphs, for example, can show population change to support an argument for 'decline'; 'decadence' does not easily sit as its synonym (2005: 574–5). Yet, while retaining seemingly objective language, the reasons for the change can still be explained using the semantic field that defines decadence. In other words, historians can have it both ways; a discussion of decline can employ the rhetoric of immorality without having to use the offending word 'decadence' outright.

Of course, not all decline is related to decadence. Decline can be caused by a wide range of factors that have nothing whatsoever to do with morality or its lack. What's more, the reverse is also true. Decadence can exist in a society without causing its deterioration on a grand scale. The question of whether or not to link decadence and historical decline in the story of Rome has, over many centuries, produced conflicting answers. Setting the tone in the late first-century BCE by following such predecessors as Sempronius Asellio and Sallust, Livy described an idealized past in order to draw a contrast with an immoral, inferior present. The culprit was *libido dominandi*, the lust for domination that led the Romans down the path of imperial expansion to wealth and luxury (Sallust, 2013: p. 33). Like Livy,

Tacitus saw decline all around him. The imperial period, in contrast to the republic, 'was thus an altered world, and of the old, unspoilt Roman character not a trace lingered' (Tacitus, 1931: p. 249). There were pockets of respite, but the overall picture was one of an empire subject to the whims of a sovereign monarch, instead of one administered by a wise council of elders (i.e., the elected magistrates and the Roman senate).

Sallust, Livy, and Tacitus firmly fixed the relationship between decadence and historical decline for the transition of the Roman republic to the principate, but the problem for later historiographers was that Rome continued to stand under the emperors for another four centuries. As a result, the 'fall' of the Roman empire in the west – a series of attacks by barbarian tribes that took place during the fifth century CE – appeared to be a better candidate for the paradigm case of decline's climax. Despite the range of explanations presented in late-antique accounts, by the end of the eighteenth century it seemed indisputable that Rome declined and collapsed because of weakness caused by internal decadence. Not everyone could agree on where and when in Roman history to find that decadence, but it was definitely there somewhere. That was the case, at least, until the development of new methodologies changed the way in which historiography was practised. The rise of a scientific history in the nineteenth century complicated responses to Rome's fall; on the one side, Bartold Georg Niebuhr and his followers promoted a providentialist view, and on the other Theodor Mommsen advocated a positivist approach, inspiring John Bagnell Bury to reject the relationship between decadence and decline altogether. Thus, decadence fell out of favour with Roman historiographers – a situation that remains, broadly speaking, the case today.

Progress vs. Decline

The 'fall' of Rome has not always been straightforwardly connected with either decadence or decline.[1] In the immediate responses to the sack of Rome by Alaric and the Goths in August 410, two dominant approaches emerged: that barbarians entering Rome for the first time since 390 BCE marked a catastrophe caused by decline (Zosimus), or that the sack was a relatively minor event and should not be over-dramatized (Augustine and Orosius). The choice of approach was not dictated by religion, *per se.*

[1] The year 476 CE, the exile of Romulus Augustulus, is traditionally used to date the 'fall' of Rome in the west. However, Croke has shown that 476 was proposed as a turning point by Byzantines in the sixth century (Croke, 1983: 103–19). For the period's contemporaries, particularly those in the west, 410 is the more significant date.

Jerome's reaction from Bethlehem fits better with the pagan Zosimus' than the Christian Augustine and Orosius' (e.g., Jerome, 1893: p. 252). However, Orosius and Augustine engaged far more with the historical ideas of progress and decline in their extended works than Jerome in his short epistolary and prefatory statements. These historical ideas were shaped by their religion.

For the Byzantine historian Zosimus (writing in the early sixth century but using Eunapius' and Olympiodorus' contemporary histories as his sources), Rome was in a deep state of decline.[2] Zosimus starts his *Historia Nova* with a quick summary of the fifth century BCE to the third century CE (dealt with in a mere eight paragraphs) before proceeding with a more detailed account of events up to 410 CE. Two key ideas come from Zosimus' history: that Rome's decline began with the fall of the republic, and that the immorality of Christianity accelerated the process.

In his first idea, Zosimus was not alone. We have already seen Tacitus lamenting the end of an idealized republic as it slid into a degenerate monarchy. But, Zosimus' history placed this slide firmly in the context of the sack of Rome.[3] He begins, 'the civil wars between Sulla and Marius and then between Julius Caesar and Pompey Magnus destroyed the government, and abolishing the aristocracy, they chose Octavianus [Augustus] as sole ruler' (Zosimus, 1982: p. 2). For Zosimus, the principate was autocratic even when a good emperor reigned. When an immoderate man came to power, the growth of decline was rapid: '[If he] became a tyrant, throwing the government into confusion, overlooking crimes, selling justice and regarding subjects as slaves, then everything would prove that a ruler's power without restraint is a universal calamity' (pp. 2–3). Unsurprisingly, when decline tips over into fall, Zosimus blames an emperor (and not just for his Christianity): 'In plain terms, Constantine was the origin and beginning of the present destruction of empire' (p. 39). Zosimus' second idea saw Christianity and its abuse act as indicators of decadence and deterioration. Here, he targets the monks:

> They renounce lawful marriage and fill populous colleges of bachelors in cities and villages: they are useless for war or any other service to the state. Moreover, from that time to this, they have taken over most of the land and, under the pretext of giving everything to the poor, have reduced almost everyone else to beggary. (p. 111)

[2] Eunapius' history ends in 404 CE, and Olympiodorus' picks up in 407 CE (Liebeschuetz, 2003: pp. 206–18). Both these texts are now lost.

[3] Fragments suggest that Olympiodorus did not condemn individuals on religious grounds alone (Liebeschuetz, 2003: p. 205).

The monks, by following their religious rules properly, flouted Roman convention regarding service to the state. Even worse, when they yielded to corruption, the land and power they commanded meant they caused all of Roman society to suffer. Again, the point is not that Zosimus came up with this idea (he did not; e.g., Ammianus Marcellinus, 1939: pp. 19–21), but that he introduced it into a context of decline and fall. This passage appears in the midst of the events of 403–404 CE as Zosimus recounts the build-up to a failed attempt to take Rome by the Goths and the Germans. In later centuries, Gibbon in particular found these arguments persuasive.

Orosius and Augustine saw things differently.[4] Christians were already developing their own version of Roman history as seen through a religious lens. One noticeable difference was to pinpoint Augustus' reign, which saw the birth of Christ, as marking the beginning of an era of progress, not of decline. Christian historians such as Eusebius understood the imperial period as one of peace and prosperity, one that allowed the fledgling religion to flourish (Van Nuffelen, 2012: pp. 192–4). Progress culminated in Christianity's triumph under the emperor Constantine. The story is one of ascent into morality, not of descent into decadence (2012: pp. 6–8, 191).

After Rome was sacked, Augustine and Orosius encountered a disturbing response from the people they met: Rome had incurred the wrath of its traditional gods by turning to Christianity (e.g., Augustine, 1972: pp. 44–5). In the months and years following August 410, Augustine developed his own theological response to the accusation in his sermons and philosophical tour de force, *City of God*. But he also wanted to refute the claim on historical grounds; this task he entrusted to his pupil Orosius who in 416–17 CE wrote *Seven Books of History against the Pagans*. Both agreed that corruption in Rome could be found long before the fall of the republic and the rise of Augustus. However, their opinions on what happened after the birth of Christ diverge – Orosius saw a form of Eusebian-like progression, whereas Augustine refuted the need to take into account historical progress or decline on earth at all. What mattered was the individual's personal relationship to God.

Unlike Sallust or Livy, Augustine and Orosius saw decadence right from the foundation of Rome. Romulus was a prime example; he committed fratricide to become Rome's first king, and then instigated the abduction of Sabine women to provide wives for Roman men. Neither of these acts were 'moral' or 'just' (Orosius, 2010: p. 78; Augustine, 1972: p. 66). More importantly, Romulus' corruption infected the rest of the city:

[4] While Augustine did not write history, his views informed both Orosius and later historiography.

'[the crime] certainly should have been avenged, and therefore the whole community was guilty, because the whole community took no heed of it. And that was worse than fratricide; it was patricide' (Augustine, 1972: p. 94). Corruption continued to colour Rome's history as the kingdom gave way to the republic. Augustine uses Cicero's *De Republica* to show that the Romans (or, at least, Cicero) knew what the ideal republic was but could not achieve it (pp. 72–5). Condemning the Roman republic was not problematic for Augustine and Orosius because their framework for history was vastly different from, say, that of Zosimus. The point to which they built was the birth of Christ, not the sack of Rome. In other words, the traditional model of morality giving way to immorality (Livy, Tacitus, Zosimus, etc.) was discarded. Before Christianity, corruption was constant; regal and republican Rome had no high point from which to decline and, until the incarnation, no way to improve.

At this point, the two authors separate. Orosius took the view that Christianity brought overall progress. For him, the empire since the reign of Augustus and the arrival of Christ had certainly improved, and while war and strife continued to occur, they lasted for a shorter time than before (Orosius, 2010: pp. 322, 327). Emperors could still be tyrants and Christians might face periods of persecution, but there was an attitude of moral advancement brought about by the church that the sack of Rome could not halt. In fact, the city had never been in any real danger as Alaric, the Gothic king who led the siege, was a Christian himself. Instead of causing death and destruction in toto, the barbarians helped believers to escape, punishing only heathens (Van Nuffelen, 2012: pp. 182–4). Indeed, the barbarians even made better masters, offering 'freedom in poverty' rather than 'trouble and taxation under Rome' (Orosius, 2010: p. 407). In Orosius' account, progress could continue so long as the empire remained Christian. If Christianity were abandoned, Rome would fall (p. 54). But that was not what had happened in 410 CE.

Where Orosius advocates historical progress, Augustine explains the futility of focusing on the earthly city at all. Since the incarnation, Christ had acted as a mediator for Christians to gain access to the heavenly city (Augustine, 1972: pp. 443–4). Everything other than the individual's relationship with God was secondary: 'in the one history of the world there is [for Augustine] so little that counts: creation, fall, redemption, judgement, that is all' (Bittner, 1998: p. 356). In the story of the earthly city, there can be nothing but sin, and redemption is an existential, not a historical process (Pocock, 2003: p. 104). This perspective accounts for Augustine's somewhat abrupt message to his congregation in Carthage following the sack: 'But the retort is made to me: "It is manifest that God did not spare the city." My answer is: "No, it is not at all manifest to me"' (Augustine, 1955: p. 57). He reminds them of God's destruction of Sodom, from which no one escaped alive. From Rome, on the other hand, many escaped and later returned (p. 57). Any Christian who did die was better off at peace in heaven (Augustine 1994: pp. 207–8). Since Rome still stood, sweeping notions of progress, decadence, and decline did not resonate with Augustine – only whether or not the individual person knew the wisdom of God (Clark, 2014: pp. 35–52).

Orosius' and Augustine's arguments commanded great authority in the Middle Ages, when their works were at their most popular point (Formisano, 2013: p. 153). Instead of an empire that fell, medieval writers understood the events of the fifth century in retrospect as a transfer of power (*translatio imperii*) by way of the papacy from the western Romans to the eastern Romans (the Greeks) to the Franks (Pocock, 2003: p. 99). Otto von Freising's *Chronicle or History of the Two Cities* (1143–1147, revised 1157) provides an example of such a view. To reinforce continuity, von Freising contends that the Romans and the Franks shared a common ancestor, the Trojans (1928: p. 309, n. 5). Also, like Augustine, von Freising is not concerned with the concept of historical decline. At the end of book four (which takes the reader up to roughly 476), a turning point has certainly been reached – a diminished Rome hands over power to a rising Francia – but this is a mere distraction that draws attention away from contemplating the heavenly city (pp. 320–1). Rome did not succumb to decadence, as sin was always a feature of the earthly city, but rather the empire came to the end of its natural lifespan, as Babylon, Medo-Persia, and Macedonia had done before (pp. 318, 151).

Embedding Decadence and Decline

Orosius' and Augustine's impact was not to last. Humanists and Enlightenment thinkers saw little value in a version of history focused through a Christian lens. For historians like Leonardo Bruni and Flavio Biondo, *translatio imperii* did not work because the continuation of the church was not sufficient to show progression from one state to the next. Moreover, Renaissance Italy saw a renewed interest in the nature of Rome's government as many of its historiographers came from the small, republican states that were formed following the collapse of the medieval empire. Thus, in works such as Biondo's *Decades of History from the Decline of the Roman Empire* (1438–1452), decline and fall resurfaced. Biondo retells the familiar story: 'it is no wonder that Rome, [...] pride increasing with power and vices overcoming wealth, should have been torn by civil wars, and at last in about its seven hundredth year bowed to the lordship of a single Caesar' (Pocock, 2003: p. 189).

Decadence was not truly embedded, however, until Enlightenment historians and philosophers began to explore in detail the species of decline that caused Rome's fall. Chief among these were Voltaire, Montesquieu, and Gibbon. The Frenchmen were the pioneers of philosophic history; a history not caught up in facts and footnotes, but one that considered larger questions of civilization and humanity through, for example, religion, law, and trade (Momigliano, 1954: 452–3). Voltaire pursued these themes in his *Essay on the Manners and Spirit of Nations* (1756) and Montesquieu in his *Considerations on the Causes of the Greatness of the Romans and of their Decline* (1734, rev. 1748) and *Spirit of the Laws* (1748). Gibbon used their works extensively.

Fighting against the apologetic Christian history and the triumphalism of his predecessors (Volpilhac-Auger, 2009: p. 143), Voltaire locates Roman decadence not in the reigns of emperors, even the worst emperors, but in the corruption of Christianity. Taking Nero's punishment of innocent Christians falsely accused of setting fire to Rome as an example, he mutates Tacitus' criticism of the emperor's extreme cruelty into a reason to vindicate Nero (Tacitus, 1937: p. 285; Voltaire, 2009: pp. 166, 504). The Jews and the people of Rome threw the blame onto the Christians, and Nero, who did not set the fire either, acted only as required in order to keep the peace. Instead, for Voltaire decadence lies in a church allowed to grow in relative peace that has lapsed into complacency and corruption. He refutes the seriousness of the pagan persecutions (pointing out that the Christian persecutions of each other were far more ferocious), and accuses Christians of descending into *le luxe, la mollesse, l'avarice* [luxury, effeminacy, avarice] (Voltaire, 2009: p. 175). Voltaire singles out Rome's first Christian emperor as directly responsible for the fall (unlike Zosimus, because of his Christianity): 'De savoir s'il [Constantin] fut cause de la ruine de l'empire, c'est une recherche digne de votre esprit. Il paraît évident qu'il fit la décadence de Rome' [To know if [Constantine] was to blame for the fall of the empire is a worthwhile pursuit. It seems clear that he caused the decline of Rome] (p. 204; editors' translation). As Rome falls, Voltaire continues to emphasize the religion's decadence: 'C'est qu'il y a de déplorable, c'est qu'à peine la religion chrétienne fut sur le trône, que la sainteté en fut profanée par des chrétiens qui se livrèrent à la soif de la vengeance, lors même que leur triomphe devait leur inspirer l'esprit de paix' [What is so deplorable is that, no sooner had the Christian religion taken up the throne than its sanctity was profaned by Christians who set about quenching their thirst for vengeance, even though their triumph should have imbued them with a spirit of peace.] (p. 205; editors' translation).

Montesquieu's views did not follow Voltaire's; the former mentions Christianity rarely (Montesquieu, 1965: pp. 175–6). Montesquieu's main concerns were to warn those in power against despotism (1965: p. 94; 1989: pp. 28–9) and to warn his own country against the sort of imperial expansion that caused Rome to decline and fall (Rahe, 2011: 134; 2005: 75). In *Considerations*, he contemplates the various indicators of Rome's decay: citizenship rights following the social war, inadequate provision of laws, moral corruption, and overuse of auxiliary troops. But all these indicators hinge on one overarching problem: 'an empire founded by arms needs to be sustained by arms' (Montesquieu, 1965: p. 170). While the cruel antics of despotic emperors facilitated Rome's laxity – Caligula, Nero, Commodus, and Caracalla were all mad populists with a love of luxury and bloodshed – their real contribution to decline was to beat down civil power to such an extent that no emperor was in the position to control the military that controlled the empire (pp. 137, 139). Here Montesquieu echoes Tacitus: following the death of Nero, the 'secret of empire' – that real power lay with the military outside of Rome – was revealed (Tacitus, 1925: p. 9).[5]

Empire is the key theme for Montesquieu. For a while, Rome maintained greatness through prudence and audacity in war, and through impeccable statecraft (Montesquieu, 1965: pp. 33–41). However, as time passed and men's ambitions grew, rapid expansion began to yield unforeseen consequences. Rome started to lose *l'esprit de citoyens* [the citizen spirit], 'a single love of liberty, a single hatred of tyranny' (p. 92). Among the soldiers, long years spent on military campaigns resulted in loyalty to their general, the man who allowed them to plunder, above their city (pp. 74, 91). In Rome itself, the populace had become disparate and distracted through the extension of citizenship to subjugated people. The people 'no longer saw Rome with the same eyes, [. . .] the same love of country' (p. 93; De Senarclens, 2003: pp. 161–5). Rome's decline was caused not by its wealth or a love of luxury (Montesquieu, 1965: p. 98), but by a crisis of identity caused by diversity.[6] Here Montesquieu departs from the ancient

[5] Montesquieu used a range of classical writers (Livy, Sallust, Appian, Vegetius, etc.), but Tacitus seems to be the most influential for both his ideas and his form (Volpilhac-Auger, 1985).

[6] Montesquieu's 'problem' of diversity is a consistent theme across his works (Courtney, 1988: pp. 61–81).

evidence; usually, imperial expansion caused decay through the extreme spending of vast riches and individuals' unhealthy desire for empire (Lintott, 1972: 626–38). In fact, Tacitus suggests the opposite to Montesquieu's thesis: luxury had long been the ruin of Rome's traditional families, whereas men coming to Rome from Italian towns and the provinces had not yet been corrupted by Rome's luxurious ways and actively rejected such immoral practices (Tacitus, 1931: p. 611). Montesquieu, on the other hand, used Rome to deliver a lesson in the shortcomings of universal monarchy to such monarchs as Louis XIV, who dreamt of conquest (Rahe, 2005: 89). The world did not share universal values; even if luxury could be tamed, the same regional and cultural differences that brought down Rome would bring down any aspiring successor. Montesquieu's decadence via diversity coloured decline and fall in a very different hue.

All this gave Edward Gibbon much food for thought. Like Voltaire and Montesquieu, he saw value in the philosophic method, but was not willing to sacrifice facts and footnotes in the way of (particularly) Voltaire. Gibbon knew through and through the ancient sources available to him, and he had sympathy for the approach of the older generation of antiquarians (Momigliano, 1954: 452). Thus, his multi-volume *History of the Decline and Fall of the Roman Empire* (1776–1789), covering the period from the reign of Commodus (180–192 CE) to the siege of Constantinople (1453), contained elements of both philosophic and traditional history. As Gibbon's methodology was broad, so his results were wide-ranging. Like Voltaire, he contemplated Christianity's effects, and like Montesquieu, he lamented the expansion of empire at all costs.

Gibbon's most famous epigram seemingly sums up his thoughts about Rome's decline and fall; his project describes 'the triumph of Barbarism and religion' (1909–1914: vol. VII, p. 321).[7] However, enemy invasion by barbarians is the result, not the cause, of decline. Rome was already deteriorating when the barbarians turned their attention to the borders (vol. I, p. 210). Regarding religion, Gibbon expands on Zosimus' views, but with a sympathetic twist that would not be found in the works of Voltaire. Christianity practised properly had an indirect role in decline because it flouted Roman values. Bishops with the best of intentions 'preached doctrines of patience and pusillanimity', but this meant 'the last remains of the military spirit were buried in the cloister' (vol. IV, p. 175). Just as serious were the theological squabbles of religious factions

[7] Gibbon takes this phrase from Voltaire (2009: p. 212).

that distracted emperors who should have been focusing on the army.[8] But here is the twist: Christianity's role in decline is tempered by its ability to improve society. For example, as a 'pure and humble religion', primitive Christianity helped to curb otherwise rampant Roman luxury (vol. II, p. 1; vol. IV, p. 81). However, this tempering effect was not to last as centuries of abuse stripped the religion of its primitivism: 'Prosperity had relaxed the nerves of discipline. Fraud, envy, and malice prevailed in every congregation' (vol. II, pp. 125–6). When Christians gain power, the effects of abuse are acutely felt. Describing Theodosius' demolition of pagan temples (c. 381 CE), Gibbon compares zealous Christians to barbarians:

> But, in almost every province of the Roman world, an army of [Christian] fanatics, without authority and without discipline, invaded peaceful inhabitants; and the ruin of the fairest structures of antiquity still displays the ravages of *those* Barbarians, who alone had time and inclination to execute such laborious destruction. (vol. III, p. 209)

Yet, while Gibbon's notion of decadence certainly includes Christianity, in the grand scheme of his work it plays a relatively small part when compared to other indicators of immorality.[9]

The far larger part of the story of decadence in Gibbon's *History* is familiar from Montesquieu's: the expansion of empire. To Gibbon it was 'simple and obvious' that 'prosperity ripened the principle of decay; the causes of destruction multiplied with the extent of conquest; and [. . .] the stupendous fabric yielded to the pressure of its own weight' (vol. IV, pp. 173–4). The Romans simply were not strong enough to stand up to the onslaught of riches and luxury that empire afforded them. Individual emperors did not help (e.g., Commodus, Septimius Severus, Constantine), but as Gibbon set the scene for Alaric's invasion of Rome, he returned to the laxity of Roman society as a whole. This is where Gibbon and Montesquieu part ways. *La diversité* in the peoples who made up society was not to blame for the weakening of the military and citizen spirit, but outright luxury was. Far more than his French predecessors, Gibbon returned to the Roman sources, in particular to Sallust's claim that the end of Rome's wars with Carthage paved the way for luxury and idleness even among the city's greatest men (Sallust, 2013: pp. 259–61). Gibbon compares the 'heroes who had repulsed the arms of Hannibal' to

[8] However, Gibbon does concede that the barbarians' adoption of Christianity also served to mollify them (vol. IV, p. 175).

[9] Gibbon's depiction of Christianity is both the most famous and the most misunderstood part of his work (Womersley, 1997: pp. 190–216; Pocock, 2000: pp. 48–68).

the late-republican 'opulent nobles of an immense capital, who were never excited by the pursuit of military glory, and seldom engaged in the occupations of civil government, naturally resigned their leisure to the business and amusements of private life' (1909–1914: vol. III, pp. 306, 310). The Romans corrupted themselves with an a priori desire for luxury that could be realized as Rome's size and wealth multiplied. For Gibbon, the Romans themselves bore the brunt of the blame for the decadence that caused decline and fall, not the Christian or provincial 'other'. His meaning was clear: using Rome as an example, Gibbon advocated a cautious approach to imperialism (one at odds with his contemporaries) as his own (British) empire continued to form colonies and strive towards expansion (Black, 1995: 457).

Detaching Decadence

Gibbon's work was not lacking in impact. Upon publication of the first volume, he faced substantial criticism for his views on Christianity and earned himself the label 'the infidel writer' (Anon., 1863: 504). However, his work was also the standard against which all other histories of Rome for at least the following century were judged. Charles Merivale was so conscious of Gibbon's achievement that he finished his *History of the Romans* (1850–1862) at the point at which Gibbon started, the end of Marcus Aurelius' reign. That said, one of the most substantial criticisms levelled against Gibbon remains his weakness in source criticism; he generally took the accounts of ancient writers at face value (Momigliano, 1954: 450–1). Further, through no fault of his own, Gibbon did not have access to the numerous catalogues of archaeological inscriptions that would be edited and published in the centuries after his death. New sources and a new era produced a modern type of professional historian who made extensive use of material evidence and rejected plot-driven narrative. Thus, Gibbon's history became the primary target for the next 'scientific' generation.

As Linda Dowling has shown, scientific historians eventually came to reject the idea of decline via decadence (1985: 599–600). But it took some time to arrive at this conclusion. At the beginning of the nineteenth century, the German historian Niebuhr's *Römische Geschichte* (1811–1812, rev. 1827–1832) explored the history of Rome from its earliest period to the republic. Niebuhr was highly and widely praised for his sophisticated source criticism (in particular, of Livy's history), but he still composed the sort of providentialist story reminiscent of Gibbon. By showing that Rome's earliest period could be understood historically (instead of as a series of myths), the city could enjoy a 'youth' before its maturity and old age (Dowling, 1985: 586). Niebuhr readily adopted the language of decline: 'At the close of the time which I purpose to embrace [the Augustan period], the nation resolves itself into a fermenting mass, in which the form, now that the soul has abandoned it, daily becomes more indistinct and decays' (1828: p. 1). Niebuhr had some influential followers, including Thomas Arnold, Charles Merivale, Charles Kingsley, and Thomas Hodgkin. As the century progressed, their teleological accounts clashed against the (supposedly) 'colourless' and systematic history of the young Mommsen (Dowling, 1985: 594).[10]

Mommsen held himself to extremely high standards and refused to write a 'story' of Rome that produced an uncomplicated plot. However, the clash with Niebuhr and his followers ends there; Mommsen shows us that the scientific method did not necessarily demand the exclusion of decadence and decline. As Demandt summarizes, 'he saw nothing in [late antiquity] beyond overthrow, failure, decadence (*Zerfall*) and protracted death-throes' (1996: p. 10). Mommsen's willingness to take the long view of Rome's decline is evident from his review of the state of affairs after the death of the dictator Sulla (78 BCE):

> The sun of freedom with all its endless store of blessings was constantly drawing nearer to its setting, and the twilight was settling over the very world that was still so brilliant. It was no accidental catastrophe which patriotism and genius might have warded off; it was ancient social evils – at the bottom of all, the ruin of the middle class by the slave proletariate – that brought destruction on the Roman commonwealth. (Mommsen, 1867: vol. III, p. 394)

'Social evils' capture the language of decadence but, as the republic falls, Mommsen suggests there might still be hope for recovery:

> [S]uch calm considerations do not mould history; it is not reason, it is passion alone, that builds for the future. The Romans had just to wait and to see how long their commonwealth would continue unable to live and unable to die, and whether it would ultimately find its master and, so far as might be possible, its regenerator, in a man of mighty gifts, or would collapse in misery and weakness. (vol. III, p. 394)

His speculation is rhetorical; collapse in misery and weakness was, of course, the true destiny of Rome.

[10] There is, however, much to recommend Mommsen's prose (Mattenklott, 2005: pp. 163–80, esp. pp. 176–7).

While Mommsen's long-awaited volume of Roman imperial history remained unfinished upon his death in 1903, the discovery and publication of his students' lecture notes by Alexander and Barbara Demandt now give us a reconstructed version of his views. As Mommsen turns his attention to Alaric, the Goths, and the early fifth century, he says:

> We can similarly observe how the Goths – for example, in the administration of justice, or the levying of taxes – simply worked according to Roman models. They fell victim to the same fate as all uncivilized peoples who conquer civilized Empires, and which to a certain extent the Romans themselves succumbed to in relation to the Greeks. The warm baths, the villas, the good food, luxury in general, as well as the poetry and rhetoric, the science and art, all affected them – they became Romanized. (1996: p. 494)

Despite his advocacy of the scientific method, Mommsen could not bring himself to revise the history of Roman decadence and decline (Demandt, 1995: 24–39). Influencing his decision was his view that history had a pedagogical purpose: 'History [. . .] is not a toy, but a serious matter, and the history of that period [Diocletian and the tetrarchy], in particular, is of the greatest importance for the immediate present' (Mommsen, 1996: p. 368). As a member of the Prussian parliament (1873–1879) and of the Reichstag (1881–1884) during the reign of Kaiser Wilhelm I (the man who had founded the German empire) Mommsen, like Gibbon, urged his contemporaries to take heed of Rome's example.

Bury was more willing to change the script. In direct contrast to Mommsen, he refused to write a history that would allow British imperialists to continue to find lessons in the Roman past: 'Historical parallels are almost always superficial, and, like classical quotations, useful to embellish an oration, not to determine a policy' (1896: p. 645). Bury sums up neatly the historiographical advances and pitfalls of his age, '[I]t was not till the scientific period began that laxity in representing facts came to be branded as criminal. [. . .] But a stricter standard of truth and new methods for the purpose of ascertaining truth were not enough to detach history from her old moorings' (1930: p. 7). In his *Later Roman Empire* (1889, rev. 1923), he identified '*a series of contingent events*', and not inevitable 'general causes', as the explanation for the empire's 'gradual collapse' (1923: vol. I, p. 311). The contingent events were: the movement of the Huns into the empire, which occurred independently of Roman strength of weakness; the death of Valens at Hadrianople (378 CE); the death of Theodosius I (395 CE); and finally that Theodosius' son and heir was a 'feeble-minded boy'. None of these events, says Bury, had anything to do with the condition of empire, moral or otherwise (p. 311). That is not to say that Bury did not see immorality in ancient Rome, he just did not consider such practices as Nero's orgies and Domitian's dinners as symptoms of decay. In other words, Romans did indulge in bouts of excess, but this had absolutely nothing to do with why the western Roman empire fell (1896: p. 645). As far as decadence was concerned, Bury's was a triumph of the scientific method.

Conclusion

All that remains is to consider where things stand in the present day. Decline, fall, and the 410 CE sack of Rome are still the subjects of considerable debate (Van Nuffelen, 2015: 322–9). However, the argument is no longer about where to find decay, but whether we should see the events of the fifth century as 'fall' at all. Historians led by Peter Brown's *World of Late Antiquity* have seen the Later Roman Empire as a period of transition rather than collapse. Walter Goffart (2006), for example, maintained that the so-called invasion of Rome should be understood in terms of migration and that most Germanic tribes simply integrated themselves into an already changing Roman world. Not all agree with this school of thought, but even those who do not still keep decadence at a distance from decline. In 2005, Peter Heather and Bryan Ward-Perkins both dedicated books to the case for decline and fall, but neither were tempted to identify any sort of moral decay as the cause (Heather, 2005: pp. xii–xiii; Ward-Perkins, 2005: pp. 179–83). Decadence, once so firmly entrenched as a species of decline, no longer occupies a place in the history of its paradigm case. Perhaps the relationship of decadence with history is approaching a decisive fall of its own.

References

Ammianus Marcellinus (1939). *History*, vol. III, J. C. Rolfe, trans., Cambridge, MA: Harvard University Press.

Anon. (1863). A History of the Romans Under the Empire by Charles Merivale. *North American Review*, 96(199), 503–58.

Augustine (1955). *De Excidio Urbis Romae Sermo*, M. V. O'Reilly, trans., Washington, DC: Catholic University of America Press.

Augustine (1972). *Concerning the City of God against the Pagans*, H. Bettenson, trans., London: Penguin.

Augustine (1994). *Sermons. Vol. VIII of The Works of Saint Augustine, Part III*, E. Hill, trans., Brooklyn, NY: New City Press.

Bittner, Rüdiger (1998). Augustine's Philosophy of History. In Gareth B. Matthews, ed., *The Augustinian Tradition*, Berkeley: University of California Press, pp. 345–60.
Black, Jeremy (1995). Empire and Enlightenment in Edward Gibbon's Treatment of International Relations. *International History Review*, 17(3), 441–58.
Bury, J. B. (1896). The British and the Roman Empire. *Saturday Review of Politics, Literature, Science and Art*, 27 June, 645.
Bury, J. B. (1923). *A History of the Later Roman Empire from the Death of Theodosius I to the Death of Justinian*, 2 vols., London: Macmillan.
Bury, J. B. (1930). The Science of History. In H. Temperley, ed., *Selected Essays of J. B. Bury*, Cambridge: Cambridge University Press, pp. 3–22.
Clark, Gillian (2014). Fragile Brilliance – Augustine, Decadence, and 'Other Antiquity'. In Marco Formisano and Thérèse Fuhrer, eds., *Décadence: 'Decline and Fall' or 'Other Antiquity'?*, Heidelberg: Universitätsverlag, pp. 35–52.
Courtney, Cecil P. (1988). Montesquieu and the Problem of 'la diversité'. In Giles Barber and Cecil P. Courtney, eds., *Enlightenment Essays in Memory of Robert Shackleton*, Oxford: Voltaire Foundation, pp. 61–81.
Croke, Brian (1983). AD. 476: The Manufacture of a Turning Point. *Chiron*, 13, 81–119.
De Senarclens, Vanessa (2003). *Montesquieu, historien de Rome*, Geneva: Droz.
Demandt, Alexander (1995). Mommsen zum Niedergang Roms. *Historische Zeitschrift*, 261(1), 23–49.
Demandt, Alexander (1996). Introduction to Theodor Mommsen, *A History of Rome under the Emperors*, Thomas Wiedemann, ed., Clare Krojzl, trans., London: Routledge, pp. 1–35.
Dowling, Linda (1985). Roman Decadence and Victorian Historiography. *Victorian Studies*, 28(4), 579–607.
Formisano, Marco (2013). Grand Finale. *Orosius' Historiae adversus paganos* Or the Subversion of History. In Henriette Harich-Schwarzbauer and Karla Pollmann, eds., *Der Fall Roms und seine Wiederauferstehungen in Antike und Mittelalter*, Berlin: De Gruyter, pp. 153–76.
Gibbon, Edward (1909–1914). *The History of the Decline and Fall of the Roman Empire*, J. B. Bury, ed., 7 vols., London: Methuen.
Goffart, Walter (2006). *Barbarian Tides: The Migration Age and the Later Roman Empire*, Philadelphia: University of Pennsylvania Press.
Heather, Peter (2005). *The Fall of the Roman Empire*, London: Macmillan.
Jerome (1893). *The Principal Works of St. Jerome*, W. H. Fremantle, trans., Grand Rapids, MI: Eerdmans.
Liebeschuetz, Wolf (2003). Pagan Historiography and the Decline of the Roman Empire. In Gabriele Marasco, ed., *Greek and Roman Historiography in Late Antiquity: Fourth to Sixth Century A.D.*, Leiden: Brill, pp. 177–218.
Lintott, A. W. (1972). Imperial Expansion and Moral Decline in the Roman Republic. *Historia: Zeitschrift für Alte Geschichte*, 21(4), 626–38.

Mattenklott, Gert (2005). Mommsens Prosa – Historiographie als Literatur. In Alexander Demandt, Andreas Goltz, and Heinrich Schlange-Schöningen, eds., *Theodor Mommsen: Wissenschaft und Politik im 19. Jahrhundert*, Berlin: Walter de Gruyter, pp. 163–180.

Momigliano, A. (1954). Gibbon's Contribution to Historical Method. *Historia: Zeitschrift für Alte Geschichte*, 2(4), 450–63.

Mommsen, Theodor (1867). *History of Rome*, 5 vols., William Purdie Dickson, trans., London: Richard Bentley.

Mommsen, Theodor (1996). *A History of Rome under the Emperors*, Clare Krojzl, *trans.*, Thomas Wiedemann, ed., London: Routledge.

Montesquieu (1965). *Considerations on the Causes of the Greatness of the Romans and their Decline*, David Lowenthal, trans., New York: The Free Press.

Montesquieu (1989). *The Spirit of the Laws*, Anne M. Cohler, Basia Carolyn Miller, and Harold Samuel Stone, ed. and trans., Cambridge: Cambridge University Press.

Morley, Neville (2005). Decadence as a Theory of History. *New Literary History* (35), 573–85.

Niebuhr, Barthold Georg (1828). *The History of Rome*, vol. I, J. C. Hare and C. Thirlwall, trans., Cambridge: Cambridge University Press.

Orosius (2010). *Seven Books of History against the Pagans*, A. T. Fear, trans., Liverpool: Liverpool University Press.

Pocock, J. G. A. (2000). Gibbon and the Primitive Church. In Stefan Collini, Richard Whatmore, and Brian Young, eds., *History, Religion, and Culture: British Intellectual History 1750–1950*, Cambridge: Cambridge University Press, pp. 48–68.

Pocock, J. G. A. (2003). *The First Decline and Fall.* Vol. III of *Barbarism and Religion*. Cambridge: Cambridge University Press.

Rahe, Paul A. (2005). The Book That Never Was: Montesquieu's Considerations on the Romans in Historical Context. *History of Political Thought*, 26(1), 43–89.

Rahe, Paul A. (2011). Montesquieu's anti-Machiavellian Machiavellianism. *History of European Ideas*, 37(2), 128–36.

Sallust (2013). *The War with Catiline and the War with Jugurtha*, John T. Ramsey, ed., J. C. Rolfe, trans., Cambridge, MA: Harvard University Press.

Tacitus (1925). *The Histories*, vol. II, J. Jackson, trans., Cambridge, MA: Harvard University Press.

Tacitus (1931). *The Annals*, vol. III, J. Jackson, trans., Cambridge, MA: Harvard University Press.

Tacitus (1937). *The Annals*, vol. V, J. Jackson, trans., Cambridge, MA: Harvard University Press.

Van Nuffelen, Peter (2012). *Orosius and the Rhetoric of History*, Oxford: Oxford University Press.

Van Nuffelen, Peter (2015). Not Much Happened: 410 and All That. *Journal of Roman Studies*, 105, 322–9.

Volpilhac-Auger, Catherine (1985). *Tacite et Montesquieu*, Oxford: Voltaire Foundation.

Volpilhac-Auger, Catherine (2009). Voltaire and History. In Nicholas Cronk, ed., *The Cambridge Companion to Voltaire*, Cambridge: Cambridge University Press, pp. 139–52.

Voltaire (2009). *Essai sur les mœurs et l'esprit des nations: avant-propos et chapitres 1–37*. Vol. XXII *of Œuvres complètes de Voltaire*, Bruno Bernard, John Renwick, Nicholas Cronk, and Janet Godden, eds., Oxford: Voltaire Foundation.

Von Freising, Otto (1928). *The Two Cities: A Chronicle of Universal History to the Year 1146 AD*, C. C. Mierow, ed. and trans., New York: Columbia University Press.

Ward-Perkins, Bryan (2005). *The Fall of Rome and the End of Civilization*, Oxford: Oxford University Press.

Womersley, David (1997). Gibbon and the 'Watchmen of the Holy City': Revision and Religion in the *Decline and Fall*. In Rosamond McKitterick and Roland Quinault, eds., *Edward Gibbon and Empire*, Cambridge: Cambridge University Press, pp. 190–216.

Zosimus (1982). *New History*, R. T. Ridley, trans., Canberra: Australian Association for Byzantine Studies.

CHAPTER 3

Nineteenth-Century Literary and Artistic Responses to Roman Decadence

Isobel Hurst

Désiré Nisard's 1834 *Études de mœurs et de critique sur les poètes latins de la décadence* [*Cultural-Critical Studies of Latin Poets of the Decadence*] pioneered the application of the term 'decadence' to literature, suggesting an analogy between the Silver Age of Latin and French Romanticism (Vance, 1997: pp. 251–2). Nisard's readings of poets such as Persius, Juvenal, Seneca, Statius, Martial, and Lucan identify characteristics which remain central to our understanding of literary decadence, 'from the imagery of Roman decline to sensual indulgence, extreme erudition, and linguistic complexity' (Potolsky, 2013: p. 3). Yet for Nisard's British contemporaries the literature of the Silver Age was derivative, over-decorated, and not representative of Rome's greatness. G. H. Lewes, in his 1842 essay 'The Roman Empire and Its Poets', considers these 'puny poets' from a corrupt and crumbling empire to be 'tawdry, florid, and wearisome', distinctly inferior to predecessors such as Virgil, Ovid, Lucretius, Horace, and Catullus, and worthy of attention only because they are Roman (36). Even that Roman identity is disputed when Lewes emphasizes the foreign ancestry of these poets from the far reaches of an empire too unwieldy to give its heterogeneous peoples any sense of unity – 'Macedonians, Carthaginians, Spaniards, Etrurians, &c.' (37). The qualities that are here seen as characteristic of foreign influences weakening Rome, such as 'abundant artifice' and 'corrupt language', become strengths when celebrated by decadent writers such as Lewes' French contemporaries Théophile Gautier and Charles Baudelaire (36). Half a century after Nisard's study of decadence in Latin literature, in Joris-Karl Huysmans's *À rebours* [*Against Nature*] (1884), Des Esseintes deliberately builds up a library of neglected Latin writers, disdaining the Augustan authors who remained prominent in the nineteenth-century reception of ancient Rome: he considers the language of Horace, Cicero, Virgil, and Caesar tedious and unoriginal, restricted in idiom, inflexible in syntax, colourless and flat.

He suggests that hackneyed university lectures on 'decadence' discourage students from reading the Latin writers he values most, Lucan and Petronius (Huysmans, 2003: p. 27).

i

Des Esseintes does not share the tastes of 'dilettante scholars' who relish numerous authors of the Silver Age, including Seneca, Suetonius, Tacitus, Juvenal, Persius, Statius, Martial, and others. He reserves his admiration for Petronius' *Satyricon*, a fragmentary collection of prose fiction, and the 'fine craftsmanship of Lucan's enamelled and jewelled verse' in the *Pharsalia* (p. 29). These two Neronian authors are significant for the decadent reception of antiquity, prefiguring the celebration of artificiality and the grotesque, the morbid fascination with dismemberment and death. He is charmed by the eclectic use of language in Petronius' *Satyricon*, the 'style that makes free of every dialect, that borrows expressions from all the languages imported into Rome, that extends the frontiers and breaks the fetters of the so-called Golden Age' (p. 30). His preference for linguistic freedom extends to the Christian Latinists of the tenth century CE, well into a mediaeval period conventionally identified as the Dark Ages. Matthew Potolsky describes Des Esseintes' taste for the Latin of late antiquity as a decadent canon, 'an alternative version of existing traditions' which privileges the stylistic hybridity of authors from Africa, Greece, and other countries colonized by Rome (2013: pp. 86–8). The poet and critic Remy de Gourmont dedicated his *Le Latin mystique: les poètes de l'Antiphonaire et la Symbolique au Moyen Âge* [Mystic Latin: Poets of the Antiphonary and Symbolism in the Middle Ages] (1892) to Huysmans. In the introduction to the volume, Huysmans characterizes mediaeval Latin as fertile and reinvigorated by vulgar and barbaric diction, the introduction of gamey idioms, the foreign words and concepts of Christianity, and the language of the streets, after the exhaustion of the pagan language.

Huysmans also finds parallels between the *Satyricon* and the naturalist fascination with representing the sordid contemporary world. Rodolphe Gasché notes Huysmans's preoccupation with the similarities between modern French literature and the transitional nature of Silver Latin, emerging in 'times of appalling storm and stress, profoundly marked by contrast and antithesis' (1988: 185). Des Esseintes describes the *Satyricon* in terms of its realism, its detailed and dispassionate analysis of the scandalous antics of the common people in Rome:

> unnatural old men with their gowns tucked up and their cheeks plastered with white lead and acacia rouge; catamites of sixteen, plump and curly-headed; women having hysterics; legacy-hunters offering their boys and girls to gratify the lusts of rich testators, all these and more scurry across the pages of the *Satyricon*, squabbling in the streets, fingering one another in the baths, beating one another up like characters in a pantomime. (Huysmans, 2003: p. 30)

In contrast to Des Esseintes' critical engagement with the *Satyricon,* the hero of Oscar Wilde's *The Picture of Dorian Gray* (1891) has a superficial idea of Petronius, based on the commonplace but unverified identification of the author with the arbiter of elegance in Nero's court (described by Tacitus, Pliny the Elder, and Plutarch). Dorian finds 'a subtle pleasure in the thought that he might really become to the London of his own day what to imperial Neronian Rome the author of the *Satyricon* once had been, yet in his inmost heart he desired to be something more than a mere *arbiter elegantiarum* [judge of taste or excellence], to be consulted on the wearing of a jewel, or the knotting of a necktie' (Wilde, 1985: p. 161). Laura Eastlake examines the 'distinctly Neronian figure of the Decadent' as a notable image of masculinity at the fin de siècle, an expression of anxiety about modern urban life set against 'the health and vigour of the New Imperialist', which represents a divergent reception of Roman history (2016: 474). Wilde affected a Neronian haircut and bestowed on Dorian Gray his own 'aesthetic fascination with elegant and luxurious evil' embodied in emperors such as Tiberius, Nero, Caligula, and Elagabalus (Vance, 1997: p. 258). Despite his reputation for tyranny and personal cruelty, Nero could be regarded more favourably as an artist and patron of the arts, presiding over and participating in a flourishing literary and artistic culture. He 'demonstrated an aptitude and enthusiasm for such activities as sculpture, painting, poetic composition, song, the playing of the lyre, and horsemanship', and has been described as 'a full-time performance artist' (Leigh, 2017: p. 21).

ii

The imperial taste for performance and spectacle extends into the world of less exalted citizens in the *cena* [banquet] or *convivium* (the Roman equivalent of the Greek symposium), a frequent motif in representations of decadence. The most substantial surviving fragment of the *Satyricon* depicts a *cena* given by the vulgar and dissolute freedman Trimalchio, who is obsessed with displaying his extraordinary wealth. He surrounds himself and his guests with reminders of the brevity of life as a justification for their greed and drunken indulgence. Among the dishes served to the guests is a wild boar with suckling pigs made from pastry arranged around its teats. When the boar is carved, live thrushes fly out to be caught by fowlers and distributed to the guests. The lavishness of the food and entertainment and the elaborate artistry of the delicacies served at the feast stimulate the reader's senses: Victoria Rimell notes that the repeated metaphor of literature as food suggests that the reader is participating in the 'tasting of a layered dish of the kind that graces Trimalchio's table' (2002: p. 40). The banquet is an occasion of sexual freedom as well as gluttony. While women are present, Trimalchio's attention is focused on the long-haired slave boys (*capillati*); his wife becomes angry when he kisses a pretty boy, but is silenced by Trimalchio's reminder that he himself had once been a slave who won his master's favour and eventually inherited his estate (Richlin, 2009: pp. 82–101). Nikolai Endres describes Trimalchio's *cena* as a 'fully physicalized version of the Platonic *symposion*' within a text which extends the representation of homosexuality beyond the pederastic dynamic (2018: pp. 259–61).

The extravagance and conviviality of the *cena* also finds a place in the genre of historical painting, which offered artists the opportunity to depict scenes of debauchery in lavish detail by accompanying them with a moral meaning. Thomas Couture's huge painting *Les romains de la décadence* [*The Romans of the Decadence*] (1847) displays exhausted pleasure-seekers sprawling on dining couches, drinking wine, and entwined with naked courtesans; two disapproving foreigners and a melancholy youth remain apart from the revels (fig. 3.1). They are surrounded by statues representing Rome's heroic past, and the dignified architecture of past generations recedes into a shadowy background. A. E. Carter describes the scene as a typical representation of 'the metropolis, at the zenith of its glory, seeking relief from boredom and satiety in all manner of excess' (1958: p. 26). Couture's painting was understood to be a 'pictorial commentary, indirect but unmistakable' on France (Weir, 1995: p. 28). Norman Vance explains that the reinvention of an idealized version of the Roman Republic was used to enhance the dignity of the French Revolution of 1789 (1997: pp. 24–6). Analogies between ancient Rome and modern France became less flattering with the rise of a new Caesar in Napoléon Bonaparte and could be used to suggest the likelihood of a decline yet to come. Couture's painting was exhibited a year before the 1848 revolution, a time of bitter disappointment with the failings of the July Monarchy, a period of bourgeois influence and colonial expansion (1830–1848). While the

Fig. 3.1 In *The Romans of the Decadence* (1847), Thomas Couture transforms the classical *cena* into a pictorial allegory of excess [Getty Images / Heritage Images].

representation of corrupt and decadent Romans failing to live up to the ideals of their ancestors was understood to reflect on contemporary Paris, the habit of appropriating images of antiquity for contemporary purposes allowed viewers to discover a variety of political or social interpretations of the painting according to existing ideological biases (Boime, 1980: p. 137). In the catalogue, the painting's title was accompanied by a quotation from Juvenal's sixth Satire (lines 292–3): 'saeuior armis | luxuria incubuit uictumque ulciscitur orbem' [luxury, more brutal than war, weighs heavy on us and avenges the world we have conquered] (Musée Royal, 1847: p. 46). Juvenal casts wealth and luxury as weaknesses, suggesting that Rome's long period of peace and prosperity (the *pax Romana*, which began in the reign of the emperor Augustus and was to end two centuries later with the death of Marcus Aurelius) had deleterious effects. Juvenal claims that Roman *virtus* [manliness] has been further weakened by the increasing influence of women, foreigners, and homosexuals, 'by nature slaves to the senses, helpless to control their lust and given to drunkenness, materialism and all manner of irrational impulses' (Shumate, 2006: pp. 21–3).

The Roman Empire could be used as both model and warning by countries with ambitions to extend their imperial power, like Britain and France. Patrick Brantlinger, in describing the decadent approach to the ancient world as 'negative classicism' – a reaction against industry, mass culture, and bourgeois notions of progress – argues that Imperial Rome and Byzantium function as 'the ironic mirror' of nineteenth-century societies, 'a model of decadent behavior to be admired and imitated but also an exemplar of imperial hubris and futility' (1983: pp. 114–15). As France attempted to establish a colonial empire, the example of Rome seemed pertinent, and French commentators not only identified France with Rome but also disparaged Britain as a modern Carthage (Davies, 2018: pp. 281–2). Gustave Flaubert questions this comforting analogy in his novel *Salammbô* (1862), which aligns post-Napoleonic France with Rome's bitter enemy. The question of genre – whether Flaubert's text was to be regarded as a form of history, historical fiction, or an 'epic poem', as Gautier described it – was confused by Flaubert's contradictory attitude towards acknowledging sources such as the Greek historians Polybius, Herodotus, and Diodorus Siculus, the philosopher Theophrastus, and the Roman naturalist and historian Pliny the Elder. Charles Bernheimer notes that Flaubert told Jules and Edmond de Goncourt that his book was not historical but defended it to others on the basis of his painstaking research (2002: pp. 38–9). Flaubert not only chooses a relatively unknown period but also critiques the idea of progressive history by subordinating events to the pictorial and stylistic aspects of the text. The critic Charles-Augustin Sainte-Beuve censured Flaubert's focus on the otherwise forgotten Mercenary War, remote from modern times and petty by comparison with Rome's long conflict with Carthage. *Salammbô* is set in the aftermath of the First Punic War (264–241 BCE), a protracted conflict between the Romans and the combined forces of Carthage and Syracuse, with the occupation of Sicily acting as a proxy for control of the western Mediterranean. At the end of the war, Carthage was forced to accept humiliating terms and pay an indemnity which rendered Carthage unable to pay the foreign mercenaries who had fought in the war; these soldiers became Carthage's enemies in the Mercenary War of 240–238 BCE.

Flaubert's fantastical depictions of opulent banquets; outlandish clothing and jewellery; extraordinary architecture; and religious and magical rituals draw on historical sources that are embellished with an Orientalist exoticism. Elaborate and painstaking passages of description of bizarre settings and characters frequently impede the progress of the plot, which is subordinated to stylistic embellishment and the ostentatious demonstration of obscure erudition. Political corruption and physical degradation are embodied in the Carthaginian leader, Hanno, a leper whose monstrously obese body is covered with running sores inadequately concealed by cosmetics. In describing Carthaginian banquets, Flaubert draws on the representation of food in Roman satire, which 'tends towards the putrid, disgusting, or taboo, exposing the tenuous and often arbitrary divide between what is considered edible or inedible' (Gowers, 1993: p. 109). The descriptions of the meat dishes recall Roman extravagance, but also evoke disgust at barbarian tastes:

> antelopes with their horns, peacocks with their feathers, whole sheep cooked in sweet wine, haunches of she-camels and buffaloes, hedgehogs in garum, fried grasshoppers and preserved dormice. [. . .] Pyramids of fruit tumbled over honey-cakes, and they had not forgotten a few little dogs with big bellies and pink bristles, fattened on olive-pulp, that Carthaginian delicacy which other people found revolting. (Flaubert, 1977: pp. 18–19)

Even after Rome's decisive victory in 146 BCE after more than a century of conflict, Carthage retained a hold on the Roman cultural imagination as a significant threat: in Virgil's *Aeneid*, the threat is projected into the past, so that the anger of Carthage's patron goddess Juno imperils the foundation of Rome by repeatedly endangering the hero Aeneas. The most powerful threat to Rome's destiny is the love between Aeneas and Dido, Queen of Carthage, whose tragic death prefigures Rome's destruction of Carthage. The pathos with which Virgil portrays her undermines the imperial mission with a reminder of the human cost of Rome's triumph, yet Dido is also reminiscent of a recent threat to Rome, the Eastern femme fatale Cleopatra. Flaubert's Salammbô, who performs a dance with a black python (Swinburne praised the 'mystic marriage [. . .] between the maiden body and the scaly coils of the serpent' [quoted in Bernheimer, 2002: p. 34]) is akin to the Egyptian queen. There are echoes of Virgilian epic in *Salammbô*: Mâthô, the chief of the barbarian soldiers, who falls in love with the daughter of his Carthaginian enemy, dares to steal a lavishly bejewelled veil belonging to a statue of the moon goddess Tanit (the Phoenician deity identified with the Roman Juno Caelestis). This violation of a sacred artefact identified with the welfare of the state recalls the theft of the Palladium by the Greeks in Book 2 of the *Aeneid*.

Flaubert's delight in the portrayal of carnage connects the text with Silver Latin literature, such as Seneca's lurid tragedies and Lucan's *Pharsalia* or *Bellum Civile* [*The Civil War*], a poem 'strewn with mangled limbs and severed heads' (Most, 1992: p. 397). In one of Flaubert's set pieces of sadism, Mâthô's body is torn apart until it is no longer recognizably human: 'just a long shape, completely red from top to bottom; his broken bonds hung along his thighs, but could not be distinguished from the tendons of his wrists which had been completely stripped of flesh' (Flaubert, 1977: p. 281). Lucan depicts similar scenes with a bloodthirsty relish which sets the decadent poet apart from epic predecessors such as Homer and Virgil, extending scenes of wounding or killing to three or four times the length of those in other epics (Most, 1992: p. 400). The literary fascination with mutilation connects with Roman audiences' taste for spectacles of cruelty and human suffering, such as gladiatorial combat and staged animal hunts (*venationes*) in which the human hunters might be savaged by lions, bears, or crocodiles, followed by the display of 'extreme cases of human injuries' (p. 402). In Neronian literature, the fragmentation and mutilation of the human body stand for larger failures of moral and political order. Although he praised Nero in the early years of his reign, Lucan was later involved in a conspiracy to assassinate the emperor; his glorification of the Roman Republic and resistance to the Virgilian narrative of Rome's imperial destiny are expressed in the *Pharsalia*, an epic celebrating the losers of Rome's civil war and representing the establishment of the Julio-Claudian dynasty as a catastrophe for Rome. Lucan's poem depicts 'a world out of joint, a history that cannot be organized by imperial apologists into the plot of destiny' (Quint, 1993: p. 147). *Salammbô* similarly reflects unfavourably on colonial power, evoking the 'military occupation and brutal French tactics in Algeria in the 1830s and 1840s', including 'conditions similar to the slavery, barbarity, and planned massacres of the indigenous populations' (Goellner, 2018: p. 72). The decadent culture of Carthage in *Salammbô* is sadistically cruel, grotesquely violent, rapacious, and immoral.

Images of Roman decadence are often drawn from the Julio-Claudian era, highlighting the depravity of emperors such as Caligula and Nero. For some Roman observers, decline could be traced further into the past, to the beginning of the empire or even the late republic. Juvenal attributes the weakening of the Roman character to the influence of foreigners from the empire: he claims that filthy money and shameful indulgences have softened and corrupted Rome. Virgil had acknowledged the supremacy of the Greeks in music and literature while praising the practical and military skills of the Romans; Horace claimed that colonizing Greece had enriched the cultural heritage of Rome when the captive Greeks taught the conquering Romans their arts; by Juvenal's time there was a concern that the weak and effeminate Greeks would contaminate Roman civilization. Such fears are echoed (in the *Juvenal* volume of the Blackwood's series *Ancient Classics for English Readers*) in concerns about the expanding British Empire, and the conquered peoples who might infect the colonizers with 'mean, low, sneaking vices':

> they have a strong, not to say irresistible, tendency to lead their captors captive, and stupefy their minds with the insinuating enervating poison which is their essential character. This process may be traced recurring again and again [. . .] the same cycle of deterioration, decay and subjugation, being ensnared by the luxurious and effeminate customs of those whom they had vanquished. (Walford, 1872: p. 70)

Walford writes of the Romans living in 'luxury and sluggish peace' and 'feeling the emptiness in their own times, the total absence of any field in which a spirit cast in the old heroic mould could find a worthy sphere of action' (p. 48), evoking similar anxieties about British heroism and readiness for action in the century after the Battle of Waterloo (1815). Such enervating foreign influences recalled the seductive influences luring hardened warriors towards indolence and despair about the cruelty of the gods in Alfred Lord Tennyson's poem 'The Lotos-Eaters'.

iii

Responses to Latin literature illuminate close connections between the romanticism of Tennyson and the decadence of his fin-de-siècle counterparts. When George C. Schoolfield observes that the decadent 'regards himself as being set apart, more fragile, more learned, more perverse, and certainly more sensitive than his contemporaries' (2003: p. xiii), the sense of being set apart from the crowd evokes Horace's *Odes* 3.1 on the role of the *vates* [poet-priest]: 'odi profanum vulgus et arceo' [I hate the uninitiated masses and keep my distance from them] (2004: p. 140). Arthur Henry Hallam's review of Tennyson's *Poems, Chiefly Lyrical* (1830) represents poets as men who are set apart because they feel more acutely than others: 'whose senses told them a richer and ampler tale than most men could understand, and who constantly expressed, because they constantly felt, sentiments of exquisite pleasure or pain, which most men were not permitted to experience' (1972: p. 88). Tennyson could also be interpreted as a precursor of decadence as a *doctus poeta* [scholar poet], whose 'linguistic and philological self-consciousness' assimilates his poetry to the 'Alexandrian' influences on Roman poets such as Catullus and Horace (Dowling, 1986: p. 142). Allusions to classical poetry enable Tennyson to explore an obsession with mortality that anticipates the work of fin-de-siècle poets such as Oscar Wilde, Ernest Dowson, and Lionel Johnson in their intertextual dialogues with Sappho, Propertius, Horace, and Ovid. Joseph Bristow notes that these poets use classical models to 'articulate dissident desires that proved hard to express elsewhere', as the poet and Latin scholar A. E. Housman also does in the 'quietly rebellious volume *A Shropshire Lad* (1896), whose hardly outspoken homosexual and atheist sentiments have become critically more audible in recent years' (Bristow, 2013: pp. 28–9). Tennyson's *In Memoriam* frequently invokes the love poems of Catullus, Ovid, Propertius, and Tibullus (Markley, 2004: pp. 75–9), as well as an elegiac sensibility connected with mourning, as in Catullus 101, the poem addressed to the poet's dead brother. In turn, Swinburne appropriates Catullus' phrase 'ave atque vale' [hail and farewell] in the title of his elegy for Baudelaire (1868). In lamenting the death of a brother author, Swinburne links private and public mourning by mingling the motifs of the praise of the dead in the pastoral elegy tradition with the tropes of the funeral oration expressing an ideal of brotherhood as a revolutionary political ideal (Potolsky, 2013: pp. 49–69).

The *Odes* of Horace presented Victorian poets with a world of masculine camaraderie in which the presence of women (usually slaves, prostitutes, or entertainers) is incidental and fleeting. Stephen Harrison (2017) examines the reworking of themes from the *Odes* in poems by Tennyson, Matthew Arnold, and Arthur Hugh Clough, and in Edward FitzGerald's *The Rubiáyat of Omar Khayyám*. Horatian conventions could be adapted to express a socially acceptable system of *amicitia* [male friendship] (as in Tennyson's invitation poem 'To the Rev. F. D. Maurice') or to imply a countercultural discourse of love between men. Indulgence in wine and other pleasures is tempered by an Epicurean awareness of the brevity of life and the uncertainty of the future. In *Odes* 1.11 Horace memorably urges the celebration of the present with the phrase 'carpe diem' [seize the day] (2004: p. 44). There is much that a decadent poet might exploit in the conventions of the Latin love elegy, such as the cruelty of the *domina* [mistress] and the subversion of Roman notions of masculinity in the prevalent conceit of *militia amoris* [soldiery of love], in which the poet is unfit for conventional warfare but skilled in a metaphorical battle of love. Dowson's 'Non Sum Qualis Eram Bonae sub Regnum Cynarae' ['I am not what I was in the reign of good Cynara'] notoriously borrows its title from Horace *Odes* 4.1 (p. 218), a poem marking Horace's return to lyric a decade after the publication of his first three books of *Odes*. Yet Dowson does not engage with the rest of the poem from which the line is taken (or the other three odes in which Horace refers to Cynara). The allusion serves to intensify the distance between Horace's expression of nostalgia for a long-lost girl, even as he pleads with Venus not to reawaken his desires after so many years, and Dowson's complaint that the shadow of his 'old passion' for Cynara interrupted what should have been an easy sexual encounter with a prostitute. Linda Dowling argues that Dowson alludes to classical texts to establish his remoteness from a 'nobler, more active poetic tradition'; the reference to Cynara (whose name recalls both Horace's Cynara and Propertius' Cynthia) marks a cultural distance between the 'guiltless pleasures' of the Roman poets and the 'oppressed consciousness' of the disaffected speaker (1986: pp. 203–4). Dowson's brief reference to Horace's former mistress not only underlines the unfamiliar sexual morality underpinning a standard school text, Horace's *Odes*, but also highlights his indebtedness to notably dissident poets such as Sappho and Catullus.

iv

In the Victorian period, threats to religion are often associated with developments in science. Concerns about how to live in a universe not governed by a benevolent deity connect with the Epicurean materialism of Lucretius: Arnold planned to write a play about Lucretius but reworked some of the material into *Empedocles on Etna* (1852), a drama which could more closely express Arnold's awareness of 'living in an age of intellectual transition', poised between faith and doubt (Shrimpton, 2015: pp. 476–82). Tennyson makes use of a legend that Lucretius' jealous wife gave him a love potion to restore his passion, subjecting him to such vivid and terrible dreams that he killed himself. In his nightmares, the juxtaposition of images of blood and disintegration with erotic torment anticipates decadent preoccupations (Markley, 2004: pp. 141–8). Linda K. Hughes suggests that 'Lucretius' belongs to a time in which Tennyson is emboldened to 'approach sensual content more frankly' after the publication of Swinburne's controversial *Poems and Ballads* (1866), prompting an intertextual dialogue: 'the Roman pagan becomes a site where Tennyson and Swinburne can meet' (2009: pp. 306–10). Depicting the era of transition from paganism to Christianity offered writers the opportunity to suggest that the dominance of Christianity might be coming to an end. In 'Hymn to Proserpine' (1866), Swinburne highlights a time of doubt after the emperor Constantine had established Christianity as the official religion in Rome: his nephew and successor Julian converted to paganism and unsuccessfully attempted to re-establish the old religion. Swinburne's poem takes the emperor's last words – 'vicisti, Galilæe' [you have conquered, Galilean] – as a recurrent motif in the last hymn of a dying pagan. The poem casts Christianity as a pale, barren and macabre creed by comparison with the cruel and beautiful sensuality of the chthonic cult of Proserpina [Persephone]. The speaker suggests that Christianity will become obsolete in its turn and the pagan deities will return.

Norman Vance identifies a shift from an era of creative appropriation of Republican Rome in the Romantic era to a late-Victorian focus on imperial Rome, 'initially pagan and a persecutor of Christians but progressively Christianized' (1997: p. 197). In historical fiction, colourful, sensationalized accounts of the persecution of early Christians often take place against the backdrop of the Roman Empire; sympathetic pagan characters are ripe for conversion, as in Edward Bulwer-Lytton's *The Last Days of Pompeii* (1834). Such narratives were used to intervene in contemporary sectarian debates: Charles Kingsley's anti-Catholic *Hypatia* (1853) provoked ripostes by Cardinal Wiseman in *Fabiola or, The Church of the Catacombs* (1854) and by J. H. Newman in *Callista, A Tale of the Third Century* (1855). Walter Pater's *Marius the Epicurean* (1885) takes a more tentative approach to the conversion plot – the hero spends much of the novel attempting to find an acceptable version of Epicureanism before he befriends Christian converts, witnesses the celebration of the Eucharist, receives the last rites and is treated as a martyr without having ever committed himself to Christianity.

Uncertainties about the morality of traditional religion and the lack of a satisfying philosophy to replace monotheistic or polytheistic worship link the worlds of the hero and the nineteenth-century reader. The narrator explicitly points out an analogy between the reign of Marcus Aurelius in second-century Rome and that of Queen Victoria in Britain, a similarity suggested by Arnold in an essay on Marcus Aurelius published in 1863 (Weir, 1995: pp. 76–7). This kind of comparative approach, applying ancient philosophy and history to the problems of the contemporary world, was encouraged by the programme of classical studies in which authors such as Pater were engaged, Oxford's *Literae Humaniores* [literally, 'the more humane letters'] or 'Greats'. Like Huysmans, Pater finds the transitional nature of imperial decline and the rise of Christianity germane to the present. He is also impressed by the linguistic fertility of the period and in particular by the elaborate literary Latin of Apuleius' *Metamorphoses*.

v

Decadence is associated not just with the imperial city of Rome but also with southern Italy (a region once colonized by the Greeks and known as Magna Graecia), and in particular the Bay of Naples. The eruption of Vesuvius in 79 CE (chronicled in an eyewitness account by Pliny the Younger) both obliterated and preserved the cities of Pompeii and Herculaneum. Excavations began in the mid-eighteenth century, and archaeological evidence proved a rich source of erotic and pornographic images, statues, and inscriptions. One response to such discoveries is found in texts such as *The Last Days of Pompeii*: the idea that the eruption of the volcano was a divine punishment. Versions of Pompeii presented for widespread consumption were selective and sanitized, such as those at the Great Exhibition at the Crystal Palace in the 1850s, where the Pompeian Court offered a 'domestic and anglicized vision of the ancient world' (Nichols, 2015: p. 240). Those who visited the ruins or the Naples museum could see much more: Kate Fisher and Rebecca Langlands argue that the 'myth of censorship' – that the excavators were so shocked by the licentious material discovered in Pompeii and Herculaneum that they concealed it from the public – was greatly embellished by later generations to suit stereotypical notions of Victorian prudery (2011: pp. 302–3). In the late-nineteenth century, Naples and Capri were associated with sexual tourism, partly because of the legendary decadence of certain Roman emperors. The cruel and paranoid Tiberius spent the latter half of his reign on the island of Capri; the distance from Rome fed the rumours of his depravity. Suetonius dwells on Tiberius surrounding himself with erotic paintings, sculptures, and books which were instruction manuals for the prostitutes of both sexes who engaged in orgies watched by the emperor. Jon L. Seydl comments that ancient sites in the Bay of Naples were seen as a 'subversive sexual environment', represented by painters as a 'homoerotic Arcadia, populated by young men and boys', and associated with sexualized encounters between men (2012: p. 22). The city that saw the reunion of Oscar Wilde and Lord Alfred Douglas following Wilde's release from prison had become 'an established destination for northern European homosexual tourists' (Murray, 2016: pp. 27–8).

Imagery based on archaeological discoveries from Pompeii and Herculaneum is prominent in the popular Roman paintings of artists such as Edward Poynter and Lawrence Alma-Tadema. Pictures of 'the minutiae of everyday life' in the ancient world replaced the grand tradition of moralizing history painting about the deeds of heroes, as archaeology encouraged an interest in the domestic (Prettejohn, 1996b: p. 56). The sumptuous interiors Alma-Tadema depicts are full of details inspired by his study of recent archaeological discoveries, but they do not represent specific Roman buildings. Some of his fictional spaces evoke the homes of the wealthy in ancient Rome and Victorian London, in which young women in a diaphanous but respectable version of Roman dress may be observed reading, talking, and lounging against a background of elaborately decorated marble. In *The Favourite Poet* (1888) (fig. 3.2), the scroll one woman is reading from could be replaced with a volume of Homer to create a contemporary version of the scene. In other pictures, historical accuracy provides an excuse for the representation of hedonistic and erotic scenes in a Roman context that would have been controversial in a contemporary setting. Female nudes could be depicted in the setting of the Roman baths in Alma-Tadema's *Tepidarium* (1881), *The Baths of Caracalla* (1899), and *A Favourite Custom* (1909), or in Poynter's *Diadumenè* (1884) and *Water Babies* (1900) (Prettejohn, 1996a: pp. 147–70). While the scale of Alma-Tadema's *The Roses of Heliogabalus* (1888) evokes the tradition of history painting, the artist 'parodies the conventions' of such images of exemplary virtue (Prettejohn, 1996b: p. 60). Alma-Tadema uses the familiar setting of the *cena*, with the teenage emperor Elagabalus and his favoured guests surrounded by imagery associated with the wine-god Dionysus (Bacchus to the Romans), watching as diners on a lower level (described as 'parasites' in the *Historia Augusta*) are gradually smothered by the accumulation of pink rose petals which fall from a false ceiling.

Fig. 3.2 Sir Lawrence Alma-Tadema's *The Favourite Poet* (1889) uses a Roman scene to evoke the domestic pleasures of the contemporary Victorian leisure class [Getty Images / DEA Picture Library].

Rosemary Barrow suggests that Alma-Tadema's frequent use of roses in his paintings combines a 'distinctive Roman aura of excess' (associated with the extravagant banquets of Cleopatra, Nero, and Vitellius) with the familiarity of the Victorian language of flowers (1997–1998: 183–5). The image of the rose could evoke corruption and death: Swinburne alludes in the poem 'Dolores' (1866) to 'the raptures and roses of vice' (2000: p. 124). Elizabeth Prettejohn notes the erotic implications underlying the superficial prettiness of the scene: the 'abandoned poses' of the guests suggest that they experience a brief ecstasy as they suffocate and die (1996b: p. 60). Elagabalus' extravagant tastes included the use of immensely heavy silver vessels, decorated with lewd designs, at banquets which were themed by colour and different for every day of the summer, and he required his banqueting rooms to be strewn with flowers such as lilies, violets, narcissi, and hyacinths. Such indulgences could be portrayed without overt allusions to Elagabalus' notorious sexual escapades with his wives, courtesans, numerous male lovers, and the charioteer 'husband' to whom Elagabalus played the 'empress'. Richard Jenkyns criticizes Alma-Tadema's approach to painting classical scenes as mere 'fancy dress' – 'dressing up and playing at having an orgy; and remaining careful not to go too far' so as not to offend contemporary taste (1992: pp. 234–9). However, an outraged response by Archdeacon F. W. Farrar suggests that the more subversive interpretations perceptible below the superficial prettiness of the rose petals did not escape the contemporary gaze: for Farrar this is a 'picture of unquestionable power' which 'can hardly fail to awaken very painful reflections'. He finds the perversion of the symbol of the rose particularly disconcerting: an 'avalanche of these sickening, crumpled, decaying blossoms for vile purposes vilely abused' (Farrar, 1891: 543). For Farrar such a painting debases not only the tradition of historic painting but the history of Rome itself:

> In all the stately and noble scenes of Roman rule, its lofty figures, its heroic ideals, its magnificent magnanimities, the all but Christian grandeur of its endurance and its patriotism, was there nothing worth the infinite toil of this skilled hand but this carnival of bejewelled sensualism, this portent of abysmal depravity [. . .]? (543)

With so many historical figures who could be used to uphold Roman virtues – dutifulness to family and the gods, self-sacrificing patriotism, heroic manliness – to focus instead on the extravagance, weakness, and sexual deviance of the emperors was to exhibit the perversity for which decadent culture is renowned. A sense of belatedness, a feeling that the greatness of the past is gone forever, connects the Silver Age and the late-nineteenth century, inspiring a pessimistic world view but also a freedom from the artistic and linguistic restrictiveness of a self-consciously great era. Yet the transition from virtuous to dissolute impressions of Rome is not simply a phenomenon of the fin de siècle: the subversive insinuations of melancholy, self-indulgence, effeminacy, extravagance, embellishment, and foreign influences in the literature of the Golden Age resonate with romantic sensibilities and react against imperial ambitions to destabilize exemplary images of Rome throughout the nineteenth century.

References

Barrow, Rosemary J. (1997–1998). The Scent of Roses: Alma-Tadema and the Other Side of Rome. *Bulletin of the Institute of Classical Studies*, 42, 183–202.

Bernheimer, Charles (2002). *Decadent Subjects: The Idea of Decadence in Art, Literature, Philosophy and Culture of the Fin de Siècle in Europe*, Baltimore, MD: Johns Hopkins University Press.

Boime, Albert (1980). *Thomas Couture and the Eclectic Vision*, New Haven, CT: Yale University Press.

Brantlinger, Patrick (1983). *Bread and Circuses: Theories of Mass Culture as Social Decay*, Ithaca, NY: Cornell University Press.

Bristow, Joseph (2013). How Decadent Poems Die. In Jason David Hall and Alex Murray, eds., *Decadent Poetics: Literature and Form at the British Fin de Siècle*, Basingstoke: Palgrave Macmillan, pp. 26–45.

Carter, A. E. (1958). *The Idea of Decadence in French Literature 1830–1900*, Toronto: University of Toronto Press.

Davies, Rachel Bryant (2018). *Troy, Carthage and the Victorians: The Drama of Classical Ruins in the Nineteenth-Century Imagination*, Cambridge: Cambridge University Press.

Dowling, Linda C. (1986). *Language and Decadence in the Victorian Fin de Siècle*, Princeton, NJ: Princeton University Press.

Eastlake, Laura (2016). Metropolitan Manliness: Ancient Rome, Victorian London, and the Rhetoric of the New, 1880–1914. *English Literature in Transition, 1880–1920*, 59, 473–92.

Endres, Nikolai (2018). From *Eros* to Romosexuality: Love and Sex in *Dorian Gray*. In Kathleen Riley, Alastair J. L. Blanshard, and Iarla Manny, eds., *Oscar Wilde and Classical Antiquity*, Oxford: Oxford University Press, pp. 251–66.

Farrar, F. W. (1891). Historic and Genre Pictures. *Good Words*, 32, 542–7.

Fisher, Kate, and Rebecca Langlands (2011). The Censorship Myth and the Secret Museum. In Shelley Hales and Joanna Paul, eds., *Pompeii in the Public Imagination from Its Rediscovery to Today*, Oxford: Oxford University Press, pp. 301–15.

Flaubert, Gustave (1977). *Salammbô*, A. J. Krailsheimer, trans., Harmondsworth: Penguin.

Gasché, Rodolphe (1988). The Falls of History: Huysmans's *À Rebours*. *Yale French Studies*, 74, 183–204.

Goellner, Sage (2018). *French Orientalist Literature in Algeria, 1845–1882: Colonial Hauntings*, Lanham, MD: Lexington Books.

Gowers, Emily (1993). *The Loaded Table: Representations of Food in Roman Literature*, Oxford: Clarendon Press.

Hallam, Arthur Henry (1972). On Some of the Characteristics of Modern Poetry. In Isobel Armstrong, ed., *Victorian Scrutinies: Reviews of Poetry, 1830–1870*, London: Athlone Press.

Harrison, Stephen (2017). *Victorian Horace: Classics and Class*, London: Bloomsbury.

Horace (2004). *Odes and Epodes*, Niall Rudd, trans., Cambridge, MA: Harvard University Press.

Hughes, Linda K. (2009). 'Frater, Ave'? Tennyson and Swinburne. In Robert Douglas-Fairhurst and Seamus Perry, eds., *Tennyson among the Poets: Bicentenary Essays*, Oxford: Oxford University Press, pp. 296–314.

Huysmans, Joris-Karl. (2003). *Against Nature*, Robert Baldick, trans., London: Penguin.

Jenkyns, Richard (1992). *Dignity and Decadence*, London: Fontana.

Leigh, Matthew (2017). Nero the Performer. In Shadi Bartsch, Kirk Freudenburg, and Cedric Littlewood, eds., *The Cambridge Companion to the Age of Nero*, Cambridge: Cambridge University Press, pp. 21–33.

Lewes, G. H. (1842). The Roman Empire and Its Poets. *Westminster Review*, 38, 33–58.

Markley, Arnold A. (2004). *Stateliest Measures: Tennyson and the Literature of Greece and Rome*, Toronto: University of Toronto Press.

Most, Glenn W. (1992). *Disiecti Membra Poetae*: The Rhetoric of Dismemberment in Neronian Poetry. In Ralph Hexter and Daniel Selden, eds., *Innovations of Antiquity*, London: Routledge, pp. 391–419.

Murray, Alex (2016). *Landscapes of Decadence: Literature and Place at the Fin de Siècle*, Cambridge: Cambridge University Press.

Musée Royal (1847). *Explication des ouvrages de peinture, sculpture, architecture gravure et lithographie des artistes vivants*, Paris: Vinchon.

Nichols, Kate (2015). *Greece and Rome at the Crystal Palace: Classical Sculpture and Modern Britain, 1854–1936*, Oxford: Oxford University Press.

Potolsky, Matthew (2013). *The Decadent Republic of Letters: Taste, Politics, and Cosmopolitan Community from Baudelaire to Beardsley*, Philadelphia: University of Pennsylvania Press.

Prettejohn, Elizabeth (1996a). Catalogue II: Recreating Rome. In Michael Liversidge and Catharine Edwards, eds., *Imagining Rome: British Artists and Rome in the Nineteenth Century*, London: Merrell Holberton, pp. 125–70.

Prettejohn, Elizabeth (1996b). Recreating Rome in Victorian Painting: From History to Genre. In Michael Liversidge and Catharine Edwards, eds., *Imagining Rome: British Artists and Rome in the Nineteenth Century*, London: Merrell Holberton, pp. 54–69.

Quint, David (1993). *Epic and Empire: Politics and Generic Form from Virgil to Milton*, Princeton, NJ: Princeton University Press.

Richlin, Amy (2009). Sex in the Satyrica: Outlaws in Literatureland. In Jonathan Prag and Ian Repath, eds., *Petronius: A Handbook*, Oxford: Wiley-Blackwell, pp. 82–101.

Rimell, Victoria (2002). *Petronius and the Anatomy of Fiction*, Cambridge: Cambridge University Press.

Schoolfield, George C. (2003). *A Baedeker of Decadence: Charting a Literary Fashion, 1884–1927*, London: Yale University Press.

Seydl, Jon L. (2012). Decadence, Apocalypse, Resurrection. In Victoria C. Gardner Coates, Kenneth Lapatin, and Jon L. Seydl, eds., *The Last Days of Pompeii: Decadence, Apocalypse, Resurrection*, Los Angeles: J. Paul Getty Museum, pp. 15–31.

Shrimpton, Nicholas (2015). Matthew Arnold. In Norman Vance and Jennifer Wallace, eds., *The Oxford History of Classical Reception in English Literature: 1790–1880*, vol. IV, Oxford: Oxford University Press, pp. 471–94.

Shumate, Nancy (2006). *Nation, Empire, Decline: Studies in Rhetorical Continuity from the Romans to the Modern Era*, London: Duckworth.
Swinburne, A. C. (2000). *Poems and Ballads* and *Atalanta in Calydon*, Kenneth Haynes, ed., London: Penguin.
Vance, Norman (1997). *The Victorians and Ancient Rome*, Oxford: Blackwell.
Walford, Edward (1872). *Juvenal*, Edinburgh: W. Blackwood.
Weir, David (1995). *Decadence and the Making of Modernism*, Amherst, MA: University of Massachusetts Press.
Wilde, Oscar (1985). *The Picture of Dorian Gray*, Harmondsworth: Penguin.

CHAPTER 4

Decadence and the Enlightenment

Chad Denton

In one of many saturnalias depicted in the Marquis de Sade's *Juliette* (1797), the libertine protagonist is treated to a magnificent banquet hosted by the impossibly wealthy Russian cannibal Minski. Pastries, exotic fruits, blood sausages, and 'eighteen magnums of Greek wine' are served by 'a swarm of half-naked boys' performing unspecified lewd acts. Entertainment comes in the form of Minksi whipping and stabbing the boys and breaking their arms, followed by the vicious libertines being brought to a room where mostly naked young women are already neatly arranged, with typical Sadean meticulousness, in preparation for torture (Sade, 1968: p. 603). Such a violent orgy was not, by this point in the narrative, unknown to Juliette, who was already firmly established in a career of accumulating wealth and absolute self-gratification, a frantic and insatiable lifestyle that invokes one of Richard Gilman's definitions of decadence as 'an irritated ennui stealing over those of the rich or powerful who don't feel themselves bound by prevailing tastes or standards' (1979: p. 11). Whether fictional or actual, libertines like Juliette represented a concept of decadence born out of the Enlightenment era. It was a notion of decadence shaped by new and developing ideas about luxury and morality, and it is perhaps this vision of decadence that still seduces the modern imagination.

Sadean heroes like Justine and Minski were grotesquely extravagant representations of a particular early modern figure, the *libertine*. Although the term had its origins in John Calvin's condemnations of heretics who allegedly sought to justify their own sins theologically, libertinage came to signify a man or (more rarely) a woman who was educated, privileged, and irreligious, a sophisticated consumer of luxuries unbound from traditional moral and social restrictions. This one persona encapsulated the Enlightenment concept of decadence, which itself resulted from the interconnected social and economic upheavals of Europe's early modern era. Unprecedented prosperity, urbanization, and the emergence of a modern consumer culture produced a cosmopolitan intellectual and global outlook that galvanized the intellectual currents of the seventeenth and eighteenth centuries, but also informed a particular model of decadence revealed in two distinctive cultural forms of the era, the libertine and political pornography, as well as the efforts of individuals and groups to combat such influences.

i

The presentation of decadence in the early modern period was predominantly informed by the expansion of European wealth and consumer culture and the resulting shifting attitudes towards luxury, a subject which Maxine Berg and Elizabeth Eger in *Luxury in the Eighteenth Century* understandably deem the most important debate in early modern Europe. For the economic theorists of the era, luxury did not just entail consumption and questions of economic utility, but also the social and moral improvement of the middle and upper classes (Berg and Eger, 2003). The growing consumer market driven by globalization and colonization made possible a connection between wealth and self-improvement. These consumption habits were also tied inexorably to the expansion of knowledge in the seventeenth and eighteenth centuries. Publications about the experiences and observations of pioneering adventurers, colonists, naturalists, missionaries, and merchants in the Americas, Polynesia, and East Asia stoked popular curiosity and the desire for knowledge about cultures outside Europe. This market for new information nearly matched the market for exotic objects (Peck, 2005: pp. 112–13, 121–2).

These market forces inaugurated a dramatic shift away from what had been the philosophical and theological consensus about luxury. Ancient Greek and Roman philosophy as well as Christian tradition cast luxury as a constant driver of weak and effeminate behaviour, an idea that persisted well into the eighteenth century and beyond (Wahnbaeck, 2004: pp. 13–15). However, the notion that luxury was instead value-neutral began to dominate by the late seventeenth century. As Christopher J. Berry says of these claims, 'luxury can be looked upon as socially useful and not as a source of social and individual corruption' (1994: p. 124). The 'demoralization' of luxury was contested by those who insisted that luxury encouraged not only immoral but also selfish and unpatriotic behaviour (Hont, 2006: p. 379). Nonetheless, a utilitarian understanding of luxury did penetrate official thinking. Widely read celebrities of the Enlightenment like Daniel Defoe, Montesquieu, and Adam Smith persuasively extolled the practical virtues of industry and trade that luxury encouraged, but it was not just a debate relegated to pamphlets and books. In the Grand Duchy of Tuscany, for example, the economist Pompeo Neri (1706–1776) influenced the course of the government's policies, shaping them through the argument that luxury must be treated as a purely economic issue that had nothing to do with individual or societal morality (Wahnbaeck, 2004: pp. 106–7, 131–4). Even the effeminacy and softness traditionally associated with luxury was sometimes recast as refinement and sensibility. These attributes were, according to Mary Peace, 're-spun as the mildness, softness, and humanity necessary to the success of the modern state' (2017: p. 95).

Still, in the same era the idea of luxury as decadence was revitalized by Jean-Jacques Rousseau. He formulated a moral but nonetheless secularized argument against luxury, associating it with upper-class idleness, corruption, and the decline of societal order. 'Almighty God [. . .] give us back ignorance, innocence, and poverty, which alone can make us happy and precious in Thy sight', Rousseau wrote in *The Social Contract*, desiring what was essentially a complete inversion of the decadent values held by enlightened libertines (1920: p. 152). Even a philosophical supporter of the new, 'demoralized' conception of luxury like David Hume described the desire for luxury as innate and universal, but still 'destructive of society' and requiring constant 'regulating and restraining' of the human impulse towards avarice (1888: p. 492).

It was not just a relic of older attitudes that inspired commentators to link the new luxuries with societal decadence. Supporters and pessimists alike recognized that the expansion of consumerism and luxury economies in Europe had broad consequences for day-to-day life, especially for those living in the highly commercialized societies of the Dutch Republic and England. For example, Linda Levy Peck has argued that a more cosmopolitan and global outlook inspired by new patterns of consumption had already formed in early Stuart England (2005: pp. 112–13, 121–2). Rather than leading to decadence, luxury – or at least the moderate enjoyment of it – could lead to more refined and virtuous individuals as well as a less rigidly hierarchical society (Shovlin, 2006). For a Europe where memories of devastating wars driven largely by sectarian fissures were still fresh, commerce and consumption even seemed to promise an enduring unity. At least this was the opinion of the English diplomat William Temple, who was impressed by how in the Dutch Republic the profusion of commerce and the resulting social ties meant that religious differences no longer did the harm they still caused elsewhere (Gregory, 2012: p. 277).

ii

For all the good contemporaries attributed to this diffusion of wealth, the effeminate, luxury-addicted man-about-town became a commonplace figure by the eighteenth century. At the same time as Enlightenment writers idealized the sensible bourgeois consumer, native terms roughly equivalent to 'dandy' or 'fop' surfaced across western and central Europe. Britain had the *macaroni*, Germany the *Stutzer*, Spain the *afeminado* and the *petimetra*, Italy the *cicesbo*, and Poland the *fircyk*. The images and concepts conveyed in this language varied widely, but they were universally seen as young, well-to-do men who tended to have in common traits of effeminacy and superficiality, as well as an association with sexual deviance (whether homosexuality or adultery with married women), an urban sophistication, and an appetite for trendy, flamboyant consumption. Also, they were usually seen as influenced – or rather tainted – by foreign cultures, namely France, always seen as the cancerous source of corruption in both fashion and thought.

The spread of wealth and cosmopolitanism was blamed not only for the enfeeblement of young, upper-class men but also for the number of women who appeared to be disrupting the gendered order and encroaching on men's social and political spaces. Upper-class and bourgeois women alike hosted European and American salons held in homes with luxurious displays of cultural taste and operated commercial coffee houses, inviting and offering financial support to writers, artists, and philosophers. By the second half of the seventeenth century, these female-guided locations became important centres for intellectual and cultural sociability. Of course, intellectual and social spaces on the whole remained more restricted to women (although women were present in coffee houses as both proprietors and customers), but the idea that women were not only valuable participants in respectable sociability but also civilizing agents became a core truism in Enlightenment discourse (Melton, 2001: pp. 200–4).

Even though the journalist Joseph Addison disliked French influences over English society and culture, so much so that he mused on the idea of the English Parliament outlawing 'French fopperies', he admitted in an article for *The Spectator* that the French had a distinct advantage in allowing women to more freely converse with men than the English, since 'Man would not only be an unhappy, but a rude unfinished Creature, were he conversant with none but those of his own make' (1712: 168). Likewise, Voltaire even wrote that, because of the benefits arising from the 'commerce between the sexes', society 'depends on women' (quoted by Gordon, 1992: 902). In practice, the women who hosted salons did value decorum and tangible signs of intellectual polish. For example, joining the salon of Rahel Varnhagen in late-eighteenth century and early nineteenth-century Berlin was, according to a Swedish ambassador, not a matter of class or wealth, but of having a 'cultivated personality' (Arendt, 1974: p. 56). French women, in particular, were seen as proof of such trends. In Spain, the widely published friar and scholar Benito Feijóo (1676–1764) openly hailed French women as models of erudition and examples of the benefits of an equal education for women (Peruga, 2005: pp. 395–6).

By the later eighteenth century, some French commentators came to see these same highly educated and somewhat independent women as sources of political and social corruption. This was one of the pivotal claims of Rousseau, who (in)famously complained that, 'Unable to make themselves into men, the women make us into women' (1968: pp. 100–1). Rousseau's misogynistic declaration is oft-quoted, but he was not alone in fearing a feminine corruption of the male upper class. Even the Cardinal de Bernis, who agreed with the Cartesian idea that inequality between the sexes was merely the result of unequal education and social conditioning, blamed women for spreading softness and frivolity among France's elite young men (1903).

Certainly, handwringing over the moral failings of the rising generation can be found in any historical era. However, was there perhaps something more particular and tangible behind such anxieties over both the women and the men who comprised the elite? At a glance, Enlightenment Europe seemed to have a bumper crop of royals and aristocrats who openly exhibited libertine characteristics, from Catherine II 'the Great' of Russia openly taking a series of male lovers to the last Medici Grand Duke of Tuscany, Gian Gastone de' Medici, having a male lover-*cum*-procurer, Giuliano Dami, to King Louis XV of France 'secretly' maintaining the *parc-aux-cerfs* [stag-park], a house where he kept women for casual trysts. For all the fierce competition, none perhaps better represented the *zeitgeist* than King George IV of Britain, a notorious dilettante throughout his life who put himself into heavy debt by indulging in luxuries like colognes and clothing while having a long series of mistresses, some married women.

The nobilities of early modern Europe were no less prolific than royalty. In France, even though until the Revolution French law allowed for the punishment of female adultery with indefinite imprisonment in a convent, upper-class wives and husbands living separately and taking their own lovers had become de rigueur since the second half of the seventeenth century (Gibson, 1989: pp. 65–6). Montesquieu has his fictional Persian observers of French high society remark with astonishment that husbands did not care if their wives took lovers (2008: pp. 72–3). A popular comedy from 1735, *Le préjugé à la monde* [The tyranny of fashion], describes a young nobleman who actually loves his wife dearly, but bows to pressure from high culture until, of course, the happy ending in the final act when he breaks with fashion and openly declares his marital bliss. No doubt there is some exaggeration, but there is ample evidence of real-life arrangements made between couples. For instance, the influential economist, the Marquis de Mirabeau (1715–1789), agreed that his wife should be allowed to have lovers as long as she met them on her own estates. One aristocratic couple, the Choiseul-Stainvilles, maintained a similar arrangement. However, when it became publicly known that Madame de Stainville (1746–1789) had become the lover of a famous actor, and not a member of the aristocracy as was conventional, her husband Jacques Philippe (1727–1789) had her imprisoned for the rest of her life in a convent (Carré, 1920: pp. 189–90). Such practices did not seem to make much headway outside France, although according to one observer the eccentric and francophile King Christian VII of Denmark apparently thought it was déclassé to show any affection towards his queen, Caroline Matilda of Hanover (Wraxall, 1864: vol. I, pp. 29).

It is perhaps obvious that this period in history did not invent the effete, elite, and immoral personage. Such figures can be traced back to Alcibiades in classical Athens, if not further. Still, as nobles across Europe left their country estates for the growing cities, a particular image of a noble who was urban, debauched, and detached from the rhythms of traditional life emerged. After all, as Craig Koslofsky argues, royal and princely courts were becoming increasingly nocturnal. As late as the end of the sixteenth century, King Henri III of France did not retire until eight o'clock whereas a century later Louis XIV and his court remained awake until at least midnight (2011: pp. 211–14). Who knew what deceptions and deviant activity courtiers could enact in the safety of the dark?

However, some expressions of elite decadence were performed within the gaze of the public. Prime examples include the libertine clubs of Britain and Ireland, like the Society of Dilettanti in London, the Monks of the Order of St. Francis (better known as the Hellfire Clubs of London and Dublin), and the Beggar's Benison of Edinburgh, groups that combined aristocratic masculinity, avant-garde intellectual knowledge, alcoholic excess, and sexual promiscuity (Kelly, 2006: 759–95). Such groups were upper class and male, savouring spectacles such as being served excessive alcohol by topless women or sharing pornography, but they were also known for inviting artists, writers, and politicians and, in the case of the Society of Dilettanti, sponsoring archaeological expeditions and funding scholarships. These were inherently exclusive spaces, but the lifestyles and gossip such organizations represented were conveyed to a much wider public through the popular press and internationally bestselling autobiographical books like the famous Venetian libertine Casanova's *Histoire de ma vie* (c. 1789–1794) and the memoirs of the Irish courtesan and brothel-keeper, Peg Plunkett (1727–1797). Such works invited the reader to be a voyeur to illicit activities and a sophisticated milieu where pleasures were freely enjoyed and traditional prohibitions were sometimes observed, but also sometimes flaunted or even deconstructed.

Gossip about the elites and published works about the lives of those who avoided traditional lives of monogamous domesticity (at least before their retirement or their 'reform'), communicated a possibility of sexual freedom, at least for those privileged or bold enough to find their own way. At the same time, in both philosophical works and novels circulated by the ever-growing popular press, traditional religious and social assumptions about sexuality and morality were subjected to open mockery and aggressive questioning. Still, unlike today when shifts in moral and social norms often culminate in political campaigns and legislative reforms, changes in prevailing sexual regulations were glacial if they occurred at all. It is true that Enlightenment writers satirized or outright dismissed traditional Christian morals, such as Hume deeming celibacy and mortification to be values 'everywhere rejected by men of sense [. . .] because they serve to no manner of purpose' (Hume, 1875: p. 246). Likewise, Diderot's *Supplément au voyage de Bougainville* [*Addendum to the Journey of Bougainville*] (1772) compared the strict, ascetic morals of the Catholic missionaries on the island unfavourably to the more free and unrestrained lives of the native Tahitians. 'The notion of sin and the fear of disease came among us only from you. Our enjoyments, once so sweet, are accompanied by guilt and dread', Diderot has one elderly Tahitian declare. 'That man in black standing near you, listening to me, has spoken to our boys; I don't know what he said to our girls, but our boys hesitate, our girls blush' (Diderot, 1955: p. 53; my translation).

State-imposed and private punishments and even strong censorious attitudes among the upper class against adultery as well as executions for sodomy did on the whole decline, save for waves of persecution for sodomy in the Dutch Republic and Britain (Sibalis, 1996: pp. 80–96). It was a development urged on by Enlightenment literati, who generally condemned torturous and public punishments. However, it was also part of a widespread decline of violence in judicial punishments and executions that had already been unfolding since the sixteenth century (Ruff, 2001: pp. 109–14). Even as Enlightenment writers mocked and rationally deconstructed traditionalist attitudes about celibacy, indissoluble marriage, asceticism, female promiscuity, illegitimacy, and natural law, divorce remained very difficult to obtain even under Protestant governments, especially for women, no matter how exploited and abused they were (Hufton, 1995: pp. 262–3). There were no widespread campaigns challenging marital laws and customs or questioning the existence of sodomy laws until the revolutionary era.

Prominent public figures like the highly influential Milanese jurist Cesare Beccaria (1738–1794) openly questioned the utility and humaneness of sodomy laws (Tobin, 2015: p. 7), while in private, elite figures such as Anne-Marie-Louise d'Orléans envisioned the liberation of women from the onerous institution of marriage altogether (d'Orléans, 2002). Her correspondence laid the groundwork for a pastoral utopia where marriage would be banned, and women would be free to study and write in their own private libraries. Despite such images of radical change, however fanciful, circulating among the upper classes, even at the peak of the Enlightenment actual tangible reforms of legislation on sexual and marital matters were, at best, usually incremental. Even a well-known enlightened despot like Emperor Joseph II in 1787 reduced the penalty for sodomy in Austria and Hungary from burning to imprisonment as part of a general legal reform (Wachenfeld, 1901: pp. 24–5). It was a far cry from those very few voices like Beccaria and the British philosopher Jeremy Bentham who advised outright decriminalization.

This backdrop informs the prevailing feeling that members of the educated elite could liberate themselves from the hypocritical and irrational demands of traditionalist morality, since they had the knowledge to understand the flaws in age-old concepts like natural and universal moral laws and to understand the value in pleasure and personal freedom. The 'extreme refinement' (1979: p. 11) that Gilman noted in the word 'decadence' is telling in this regard; decadence, especially if we trace modern notions of decadence to the Enlightenment era, was very much an elite preserve. Knowledge, especially that gained through a superior education and resources, was required to access decadence and libertinage. Such elitism was not unlike how the foundational atheist author Baron d'Holbach imagined that atheism was 'not made for the masses, nor for the majority of humanity' (1966: vol. II, p. 337). The idea that certain forms of enlightened knowledge should be limited to the privileged few also echoes in Benjamin Franklin's concern, expressed in a letter to an atheist friend (probably Thomas Paine), that 'how great a portion of mankind consists of weak and ignorant Men and Women [. . .] who have need of the motives of religion' (1853: p. 488); and in Voltaire's quip that, despite his personal Deism, he would want his wife, his tailor, his servants, and his lawyer to all be traditional Christians so that he would not be cheated or cuckolded (Gay, 1988: p. 262). More than expressing anxieties about the social ramifications of the open and blunt scepticism that was apparently spreading in the eighteenth century, the assumption was that only those who had a sophisticated intellectual understanding, likely provided through an elite education, could be trusted to challenge traditional standards and restraints.

iii

For some, knowledge itself, either of the wider world or of the past, was a threat to morals. To defend the sensitivities of readers, for example, the first Renaissance scholars to discover Plato and Socrates and their deep connection to pederasty were careful to replace language that could be read as sexually suggestive with more innocent or ambiguous phrasing. This went as far as editing out from the *Symposium* Alcibiades' entire seductive monologue addressed to Socrates (Reeser, 2016: pp. 30–3). Even travel and exposure to foreign cultures could lead to the corruption of morals, at least according to the philosopher Jean de La Bruyère, speaking of libertines in his *Caractères* (1951: p. 450). The threat of knowledge coalesced even further by the eighteenth century. Once the secular study of philosophical history had fully developed out of seventeenth-century Christian apologetics, its practice legitimized and made broadly accessible earlier heretical and forbidden authors (Mulsow, 2015: p. 83). With this menace of new and redeemed knowledge approaching on multiple fronts, it is perhaps no surprise that, after 1755, the clergy of France regularly condemned the *philosophes* for ruining religion and morals (Anonymous, 1759), or that in Sweden one year earlier a university professor who advocated Enlightenment ideas was heavily fined for the vague crime of 'seducing the young' (Frängsmyr, 1981: p. 169).

Such intellectual liberations were bluntly articulated in that most distinctive of genres in the early modern era, what Robert Darnton categorizes as 'philosophical pornography' (1996: p. 85–114). The use of the ribald and the bawdy to make subversive observations about people's behaviour was a common trope in ancient Greek and Latin literature and was known in medieval vernacular literature, from authors embraced by the elites of their time such as Boccaccio and Chaucer to folk tales, songs, and poems. However, the rediscovery of Plato's and Xenophon's Socratic dialogues in the late fifteenth and sixteenth centuries provided the basic structure for the nascent genre of philosophical pornography. In these works, often an older and worldlier figure initiates a younger, sexually inexperienced person into the erotic realm and beyond the limits of Christian decency through the use of Socratic arguments that challenged moral assumptions. A prime example of such work was *La cazzaria* (c. 1525) by Antonio Vignali (1501–1559). In the text, which takes place in an ancient, pagan Athens that nevertheless observes Catholic prohibitions against sodomy, Arsiccio uses reasoning to disprove to his pupil Sodo the idea that anal sex is unnatural. The dialogue ends with the implication that Arsiccio and a convinced Sodo are about to become lovers.

The influence of such works increased over the course of the seventeenth century. As James Turner observes, the growing popularity in central and western Europe of theories like those of John Locke that posited sensory experience as the basis for the development of complex ideas, gave a further nudge to the genre of philosophical pornography (2003: p. 20). If sensation is the origin of knowledge, then erotic experience too can be a source of intellectual enlightenment, especially in learning the arbitrariness and historicity of moral regulations. As the Socratic erotica that began in humanist Italy spread to France and beyond with the rapid development of print media across Europe, these works promoted what Lisa Z. Sigel terms a 'cosmopolitan sexuality' (2005: p. 9). It was an attitude towards sex that was not only grounded in an intellectual liberation but also defined by its opposition to traditional restraints.

This literature spread deeply through the complex web of the underground book trade that had developed by the seventeenth century. Throughout the era, France was the undisputed major producer of erotica, while Russia, Finland, Germany, the Dutch Republic, and Spain had few indigenous pornographers of their own. Nonetheless, translations and imitations, especially of French texts, still abounded and developed large readerships in those countries (Sigel, 2005: pp. 8–9; Mijnhardt, 1993: pp. 287–8).

Jean-Marie Goulemont deems the 'first libertine *Bildungsroman*' (1994: p. 11) to be the anonymously written *L'école des filles* [The school for girls] which was published in 1655 and appeared in English as *The School of Venus*. Using the form of Socratic discourse, an older woman teaches a younger one methods for achieving sexual pleasure and avoiding pregnancy. It was *L'école des filles* that the famous English diarist Samuel Pepys called the 'most bawdy, lewd book that ever I saw' but still admitted that, after reading it, he masturbated before burning it (2000: pp. 21–2, 59). Beyond the rebellious implications of a book that provided tips on how to pursue non-procreative sex, some texts were explicit in their pronouncement on social matters. The anonymously written *Whores Rhetorick* (1683), which took its title from and was based on an earlier Italian text by Ferrante Pallavicino (1615–1644), has its aged courtesan Madame Creswell explain to her young pupil Dorothea (and to readers) that '[t]he World, and so all men in it are governed by fancy and opinion: good and evil are therefore little understood as they are in themselves, but rather as they come represented to Mens various and vitiated places' (Anonymous, 1683: p. 113). Later works, including the anonymous *Histoire de Dom Bougre, portier de Chartreux* (1741), John Cleland's *Fanny Hill: Memoirs of a Woman of Pleasure* (1749), and Honoré-Gabriel Riqueti de Mirabeau's *Le rideau levé ou l'éducation de Laure* [*The Curtain Drawn Up, or The Education of Laura*] (1786), tended to depict upper-class milieus where conventional morality was flaunted and promoted the idea that happiness and even material success can follow from a libertine attitude towards sexuality.

New threads of thought spearheaded by the likes of Locke, Descartes, and Spinoza aided the development of this Socratic erotica because it was actively responsive to the revolutionary philosophical trends that seemed to accelerate by the middle of the seventeenth century and beyond. The pivotal example is *Thérèse philosophe* [*Theresa the Philosopher*], anonymously published in 1748 but likely written by the Marquis d'Argens (1704–1771) (Darnton, 1996: p. 86), who was intimate with such Enlightenment celebrities as Voltaire and Frederick the Great. The narrative follows the life of a young bourgeoise, the eponymous Thérèse, who is suddenly stricken by a mysterious, debilitating illness. The 'enlightened' Abbé T. and Madame C. diagnose Thérèse as suffering from an unnatural lack of pleasure, which is affecting her body. The abbé teaches Thérèse how to masturbate without compromising the signs of her virginity, and how to have sexual intercourse without risking pregnancy. Not only does he teach her that some moderate amount of bodily pleasure is essential for healthy living, a principle that had already long been axiomatic in mainstream Enlightenment thought (Porter, 1996: p. 9), but that God and Nature are one and the same, a central theme in Spinoza's philosophy. After being empowered by her pleasurable experiences and her exposure to philosophy,

Thérèse falls in love with the Count, who in the book's finale challenges Thérèse to peruse the erotic tomes in his library while resisting the urge to masturbate. When she loses the bet, the Count rushes in to take her into his arms, and they embark on a truly 'philosophical' relationship. As Darnton summarizes, it is a story of 'philosophical hedonism' in which Thérèse herself confronts a readership whom she describes as 'know-nothings' and 'ill-humored critics' (p. 100, pp. 298–9). The work still carried a decadent and transgressive flavour, especially through the sensibilities of the audience. Philosophical erotica had a dialectical relationship with the prevailing social norms that condemned non-procreative and non-marital expressions of sexuality, but it also claimed legitimacy from lived experience as well as validation as philosophical and rational truth.

Of course, Enlightenment decadence was moulded not only by the champions of libertinism, but also by its enemies. The rapidly growing cities of the early modern era sharpened anxieties about large urban populations freed from the age-old moral constraints of community and family and enticed by the new cultures of consumption and luxury goods. Driven by these fears, middle-class Londoners founded the Society for the Reformation of Manners in 1691 and similar societies soon spread across the urban centres of England and Scotland. These societies focused on exposing moral corruption and bringing persecutions for prostitution and sodomy, the two crimes that seemed to thrive particularly well amid the anonymity of the early modern city (Hunt, 1999: pp. 28–54).

Such grassroots crusades against urban vice were rare outside Britain, but on the Continent governments were more willing to intervene in moral domains that in the past had been within the purview of ecclesiastical institutions. In Vienna, Empress Maria Theresa founded in 1751 the short-lived *Keuscheitskommission* [Chastity Commission], an organization consisting of hundreds of vice agents and police who were empowered to arrest those suspected of promiscuity and adultery (Brechka, 1970: pp. 107–8). More lasting and effective was Louis XIV's establishment in 1667 of police forces in Paris tasked with arresting those whose sexual improprieties could not be curbed by traditional family authority (Riley, 2001: p. 18). Nor was it likely a coincidence that the two governments in Europe that were the most violent when it came to persecuting sodomites during the eighteenth century, the Dutch Republic and Great Britain, were also responsible for vast urban centres that had become notorious for their homosexual subcultures (Crompton, 2003: pp. 451–5, 462–71).

One can speak of Enlightenment decadence as the product of a society that had become wealthy and more openly sceptical of the doctrines of the past, but where ancient conceptions of morality and religion still broadly prevailed in the leading social and political institutions. The French Revolution brought this age of enlightened, libertine decadence to an end. In the wake of the age of revolutions, as Lynn Hunt points out, pornography was both democratized and depoliticized (1993: p. 306); open and liberated sexuality became a means by which anyone, regardless of their class, could achieve personal happiness rather than an offensive tactic for exposing the hypocrisies and irrationalities of social and religious orthodoxies. In effect, by the end of the eighteenth century, to some extent decadence, along with pornography, had become democratized.

The influence of the libertine still lingers centuries later, particularly in the iconography associated with the Hellfire Club, the name that Francis Dashwood (1708–1781) used for his secret libertine society, which made the stereotypical trappings of eighteenth-century European high society – powdered wigs, frock coats, elaborate dresses – symbols of high-class decadence. Take, for example, an episode from the 1961 BBC television series, *The Avengers*, titled 'A Touch of Brimstone', where the eponymous heroes cross paths with a modern-day Hellfire Club that mixes contemporary S&M culture, occult imagery, and eighteenth-century and Regency-era costumes. Here and elsewhere libertinism is not unknown even to modern pop culture, as such well-known films as *The Draughtsman's Contract* (1983), *Dangerous Liaisons* (1988), *Ridicule* (1996), and *Marie Antoinette* (2006) show, all of which explore the contrasts between the refined manners and the decadence of the upper class. Yet despite its comprehensibility and even its power and attractiveness today, Enlightenment decadence thrived within a unique nexus of material wealth, transgressive intellectualism, and politicized eroticism that was very much of its time.

References

Addison, Joseph (1712). No. 433. *The Spectator*, July 17, 167–8.

Anonymous (1759). *Censure de la faculté de théologie de Paris, contre le livre qui a pour titre, de l'Esprit*, Paris: Garnier.

Anonymous (1683). *Whores Rhetorick*, London.

Arendt, Hannah (1974). *Rahel Varnhagen: The Life of a Jewish Woman*, New York: Harcourt.

Berg, Maxine, and Elizabeth Eger (2003). The Rise and Fall of the Luxury Debates. In Maxine Berg and Elizabeth Eger, eds., *Luxury in the Eighteenth Century: Debates, Desires and Delectable Goods*, New York: Palgrave Macmillan, pp. 7–27.

Bernis, François-Joachim de Pierre, Cardinal (1903). *Mémoires et lettres*, 3 vols., Paris: Société d'éditions littéraires et artistiques, Librairie Paul Ollendorf.

Berry, Christopher J. (1994). *The Idea of Luxury: A Conceptual and Historical Investigation*, Cambridge: Cambridge University Press.

Brechka, Frank T. (1970). *Gerard van Swieten and His World*, The Hague: Martinus Nijhoff.

Carré, Henri (1920). *La noblesse de France et l'opinion publique au XVIII ^{e} siècle*, Paris: Libraire Ancienne Honoré Champion.

Crompton, Louis (2003). *Homosexuality & Civilization*, Cambridge, MA: Harvard University Press.

Darnton, Robert (1996). *The Forbidden Best-Sellers of Pre-Revolutionary France*, New York: Norton.

Diderot, Denis (1955). *Supplément au voyage de Bougainville*, Herbert Dieckmann, ed., Geneva: Droz.

d'Orléans, Anne-Marie-Louise (2002). *Against Marriage: The Correspondence of La Grande Mademoiselle*, Joan DeJean, ed. and trans., Chicago: University of Chicago Press.

Frängsmyr, Tore (1981). The Enlightenment in Sweden. In Roy Porter and Mikuláš Teich, eds., *The Enlightenment in National Context*, Cambridge: Cambridge University Press, pp. 164–75.

Franklin, Benjamin (1853). *The Select Works*, Epes Sargent, ed., Boston: Phillips, Sampson.

Gay, Peter (1988). *Voltaire's Politics: The Poet as Realist*, New Haven, CT: Yale University Press.

Gibson, Wendy (1989). *Women in Seventeenth Century France*, Houndmills: Macmillan.

Gilman, Richard (1979). *Decadence: The Strange Life of an Epithet*, New York: Farrar, Straus, and Giroux.

Gordon, Daniel (1992). Philosophy, Sociology, and Gender in the Enlightenment Conception of Public Opinion. *French Historical Studies*, 17, 882–911.

Goulemont, Jean Marie (1994). *Forbidden Texts: Erotic Literature and Its Readers in Eighteenth-Century France*, James Simpson, trans., Philadelphia: University of Pennsylvania Press.

Gregory, Brad S. (2012). *The Unintended Reformation: How a Religious Revolution Secularized Society*, Cambridge, MA: Belknap Press.

Holbach, Paul-Henri Thiry, Baron d' (1966). *Système de la Nature*, Hildesheim: George Olms Verlagsbuchhandlung.

Hont, Istvan (2006). The Early Enlightenment Debate on Commerce and Luxury. In Mark Goldie and Robert Wokler, eds., *The Cambridge History of Eighteenth-Century Political Thought*, Cambridge: Cambridge University Press, pp. 379–418

Hufton, Olwen (1995). *The Prospect before Her: A History of Women in Western Europe*, vol. I, New York: Alfred A. Knopf.

Hume, David (1875). An Inquiry Concerning the Principles of Morals. In *The Philosophical Works of David Hume*, vol. IV, London: Longmans, Green and Co., pp. 169–287.

Hume, David (1888). *A Treatise of Human Nature*, Oxford: Clarendon Press.

Hunt, Alan (1999). *Governing Morals: A Social History of Moral Obligation*, Cambridge: Cambridge University Press.

Hunt, Lynn (1993). Pornography and the French Revolution. In Lynn Hunt, ed., *The Invention of Pornography: Obscenity and the Origins of Modernity, 1500–1800*, New York: Zone Books, pp. 301–39.

Kelly, Jason M. (2006). Riots, Revelries, and Rumor: Libertinism and Masculine Association in Enlightenment London. *Journal of British Studies*, 45(4), 759–95.

Koslofsky, Craig (2011). *Evening's Empire: A History of the Night in Early Modern Europe*, Cambridge: Cambridge University Press.

La Bruyère, Jean de (1951). *Les Caractères*. In *Œuvres complètes*, Julien Benda, ed., Paris: Gallimard.

Melton, James Van Horn (2001). *The Rise of the Public in Enlightenment Europe*, Cambridge: Cambridge University Press.

Mijnhardt, Wijnand W. (1993). Politics and Pornography in the Seventeenth- and Eighteenth-Century Dutch Republic. In Lynn Hunt, ed., *The Invention of Pornography: Obscenity and the Origins of Modernity, 1500–1800*, New York: Zone Books, pp. 283–300.

Montesquieu (2008). *Persian Letters*, Margaret Mauldon, trans., Oxford: Oxford University Press.

Mulsow, Martin (2015). *Enlightenment Underground: Radical Germany, 1680–1720*, H. C. Erik Midelfort, trans., Charlottesville: University of Virginia Press.

Peace, Mary (2017). *Changing Sentiments and the Magdalen Hospital: Luxury, Virtue, and the Senses in Eighteenth-Century Culture*, London: Routledge.

Peck, Linda Levy (2005). *Consuming Splendor: Society and Culture in Seventeenth Century England*, New York: Cambridge University Press.

Pepys, Samuel (2000). *The Diary of Samuel Pepys, 1668–1669*, Robert Latham and William Matthews, eds., Berkeley and Los Angeles: University of California Press.

Peruga, Mónica Bolufer (2005). 'Neither Male Nor Female': Rational Equality in the Early Spanish Enlightenment. In Sarah Knott and Barbara Taylor, eds., *Women, Gender, and the Enlightenment*, New York: Palgrave Macmillan.

Porter, Roy (1996). Enlightenment and Pleasure. In Roy Porter and Marie Mulvey Roberts, eds., *Pleasure in the Eighteenth Century*, New York: New York University Press, pp. 1–18.

Reeser, Todd W. (2016). *Setting Plato Straight: Translating Ancient Sexuality in the Renaissance*, Chicago and London: University of Chicago Press.

Riley, Philip F. (2001). *A Lust for Virtue: Louis XIV's Attack on Sin in Seventeenth-Century France*, Westport, CT: Greenwood Press.

Rousseau, Jean-Jacques (1920). *The Social Contract & Discourses*, G. D. H. Cole, trans., London: J. M. Dent.

Rousseau, Jean-Jacques (1968). *Politics and the Arts: Letter to M. d'Alembert on the Theatre*, Allan Bloom, trans., Ithaca, NY: Cornell University Press.

Ruff, Julius R. (2001). *Violence in Early Modern Europe*, Cambridge: Cambridge University Press.

Sade, Donatien-Alphonse-François, Marquis de (1968). *Juliette*, Austryn Wainhouse, trans., New York: Grove Press.

Shovlin, John (2006). *The Political Economy of Virtue: Luxury, Patriotism, and the Origins of the French Revolution*, Ithaca, NY, and London: Cornell University Press.

Sibalis, Michael David (1996). The Regulation of Male Homosexuality in Revolutionary and Napoleonic France, 1789–1815. In Jeffrey Merrick and Bryan T. Ragan, Jr., eds., *Homosexuality in Modern France*, New York and Oxford: Oxford University Press, pp. 80–96.

Sigel, Lisa Z. (2005). Introduction: Issues and Problems in the History of Pornography. In Lisa Z. Sigel, ed., *International Exposure: Perspectives on Modern European Pornography, 1800–2000*, New Brunswick, NJ: Rutgers State University Press, pp. 1–26.

Tobin, Robert Deam (2015). *Peripheral Desires: The German Discovery of Sex*, Philadelphia: University of Pennsylvania Press.

Turner, James (2003). *Schooling Sex: Libertine Literature and Erotic Education in Italy, France, and England, 1534–1685*, Oxford: Oxford University Press.

Vignali, Antonio (2003). *La cazzaria: The Book of the Prick*, Ian Frederick Moulton, trans., New York: Routledge.

Wachenfeld, Friedrich (1901). *Homosexualität und Strafgesetz*, Leipzig: Dieterich.

Wahnbaeck, Till (2004). *Luxury and Public Happiness: Political Economy in the Italian Enlightenment*, Oxford: Clarendon Press.

Wraxall, C. F. Lachelles (1864). *The Life and Times of Her Majesty, Caroline Matilda*, 3 vols., London: William H. Allen.

CHAPTER 5

Decadence and the Urban Sensibility

Michael Shaw

In his 1895 essay, 'The Sociology of Autumn', published in the Scottish 'little magazine' *The Evergreen*, the town planner and sociologist Patrick Geddes comments on the relationship between decadent writers and the urban realm. Geddes, who was deeply committed to urban renewal projects, including the revival of Edinburgh's Old Town, was often critical of the indolence and individualism that he associated with decadence. But, in this essay, Geddes highlights aspects of aestheticism and decadence (he uses the terms interchangeably) that he finds commendable:

> Sheltered amid the wealth and comfort of our city life our aesthete develops as never before, his impressionist mirror growing more and more perfect in its polished calm. So develop new subtleties of sense; and given this wealth of impressions, this perfection of sensibility, new combinations must weave themselves in the fantasias of reverie. Our new Merlins thus brighten our winter with their gardens of dream. (1895: 36)

Geddes here advocates the aesthetes and decadents' freshness of thinking: in their detachment from modern life, they are able to imagine the world 'as it might be' (p. 38), which Geddes regards as a crucial catalyst for civic and cultural revival. In making these comments on aestheticism and decadence, Geddes depicts a curious relationship between decadents and the urban environment. The experience of the city for decadents is one of simultaneous immersion and detachment, centrality, and dislocation: they may exist within cities, but they are also 'sheltered' from them through the 'calm' enclaves they inhabit amidst urban commotion. Geddes is primarily discussing urban renewal in this passage, but beneath his comments on that topic he acknowledges the complex relationship between decadents and urban life, one ultimately characterized by ambivalence.

This ambivalence is a defining feature of decadent engagements with modernity in general, but it also defines the decadent relationship to the increasing dominance of urban cultures in particular. As a consequence of rapid industrialization and urbanization throughout the nineteenth century, urban cores became dominant in a way they had never been before. By the turn of the century, one in seven people in England and Wales lived in London alone, which housed six million inhabitants; by 1905, Berlin was five times larger than it had been in 1848 (Fritzsche, 2015: pp. 29–30). The decadent response to this increasingly industrialized, utilitarian, democratized, and urbanized society was one of resistance, a sense of defiance reflected throughout decadent writing. But the urban environments of the fin de siècle also captivated decadent writers. Even the proto-decadent James Thomson, who distilled the atomization, alienation, and despair of city life in *The City of Dreadful Night* (1874), characterizing city dwellers as 'inconceivably remote, as stars and star systems in infinite space' (1892: p. 261), was entranced by the city and relied on it as his poetic muse. Holbrook Jackson expanded on this idea in 1913, arguing that the writers of fin-de-siècle London 'reasserted the romance of London as an incident in their new-found love of the artificial' (1950: p. 105). For Jackson, the city did not simply inspire the decadents' critiques of modernity – it also helped to further their ideals. Decadents may have abhorred urban modernity and positioned themselves in opposition to it, but their indulgence in artifice was befitting to urban life too.

To negotiate these varied, even conflicting, responses to the dominance of urban life at the fin de siècle, decadent writers adopted a range of sensibilities that facilitated their simultaneous participation in, and resistance to, urban modernity. This chapter examines three of these sensibilities, as represented by the flâneur, the flâneuse, and the dandy. Both nineteenth-century and more recent figures define these sensibilities as supportive of the decadent ambivalence towards the city, but in differing ways. The variety of decadent negotiations with the city emerges through an examination of the works of Oscar Wilde, Amy Levy, and Arthur Symons, wherein we observe how each of these three sensibilities supported ambivalent decadent interactions with urban life.

Flâneur

Flânerie and dandyism are both assessed, at times in opposition to each other, in Charles Baudelaire's 'Le peintre de la vie moderne' ['The Painter of Modern Life'] (1863). In his essay on Edgar Allan Poe, author of 'The Man of the Crowd' (1840), Baudelaire asserts his own credentials as a proto-decadent thinker. In step with decadence, he positions himself in opposition to industrial modernity, mourning the culture of 'bourgeois mediocrity' that took hold in the nineteenth century, and he welcomes Poe's work as a remedy to this culture of 'democracy, progress and *civilisation*' (Baudelaire, 1995: p. 95). These sentiments, which would be echoed at the fin de siècle, marked Baudelaire as a critic of utility, commerce, and uniformity, one who questioned whether progressiveness was truly 'civilized'. To successfully resist this culture (while still permitting participation in it), Baudelaire advocates the adoption of two differing sensibilities in 'The Painter of Modern Life', the flâneur and the dandy. With the flâneur especially, Baudelaire defined a sensibility that allowed individuals to immerse themselves in the urban sphere, and even receive pleasure from it, while concurrently subverting it. Baudelaire's flâneur was enthusiastically adopted at the fin de siècle, its influence extending across decadent literature, as in Oscar Wilde's short story *Lord Arthur Savile's Crime* and Arthur Symons's essay 'At the Alhambra'.

The flâneur sensibility responded to a key aspect of the increasing urbanization that came with industrialization: the crowd. In contrast to Geddes' portrayal of decadents as sheltered from the masses, Baudelaire's flâneur did not hide from the crowds of the urban realm: he entered them as a willing spectator. In 'The Painter of Modern Life', Baudelaire stresses the flâneur's absorption in the crowd as he reflects on the artwork of Constantin Guys ('Monsieur G.'):

> The crowd is his element, as the air is that of birds and water of fishes. His passion and his profession are to become one flesh with the crowd. For the perfect flâneur, for the passionate spectator, it is an immense joy to set up house in the heart of the multitude, amid the ebb and flow of movement, in the midst of the fugitive and the infinite. [. . .] The spectator is a prince who everywhere rejoices in his incognito. (p. 9)

Here, Baudelaire stresses the flâneur's joy in receiving a panorama of impressions from modern life and experiencing a sense of anonymity. The vivacity that the flâneur finds in urban modernity raises the question of why this sensibility appealed to Baudelaire and the decadents who were, at the very least, sceptical towards it. One answer lies in Guys' sensibility: the flâneur may experience joy within urban crowds, but his demeanour is at odds with the industry and utility that underpins the modern city. Baudelaire's depiction of Guys' sensibility reveals what he finds commendable in the flâneur. The flâneur is not a figure who celebrates function and commerce in his engagement with the city, but one who subverts these values by advocating purposelessness, beauty, curiosity, 'barbarity', and sensation.

Curiosity is a key feature of the flâneur in Baudelaire's estimation: 'The mainspring of his genius is *curiosity* [. . .] a fatal, irresistible passion' (p. 5). This inquisitiveness, the desire to experience the new, is likened by Baudelaire to that of a child, who 'sees everything in a state of newness; he is always drunk' (p. 8). In associating the flâneur with the child's 'fixed and animally ecstatic gaze' (p. 8) that captures the vividness of life freshly, Baudelaire evokes the vitalism of the flâneur, which distances him from rationality and commerce. Indeed, the flâneur is explicitly set in opposition to the 'stale' sensibility of the bourgeoisie: 'for most of us, and particularly for men of affairs, the fantastic reality of life has become singularly diluted. Monsieur G. never ceases to drink it in; his eyes and his memory are full of it' (pp. 9, 15). The perceptiveness and sensitivity of Guys' 'childlike barbarousness' (p. 15) is what Baudelaire celebrates: Guys may want to interact with the urban scene, but his style is markedly distinct from the masses and their culture of 'progress and *civilisation*'.

This 'childlike barbarousness' is not the only way that Baudelaire styles the flâneur in opposition to 'men of affairs'. Walter Benjamin observes of Baudelaire's flâneur that the figure 'protests against the production process with his ostentatious nonchalance' (2006: p. 57). The casualness of the flâneur – his 'slow[ness]' (p. 84), his 'indolence' (p. 72), and his drifting through society – detaches him from an industrious sensibility. Benjamin's stress on lethargy and lack of clear purpose reveals the flâneur's 'unwilling[ness] to forego the life of a gentleman of leisure' (p. 84), a trait that is highly reminiscent of languid characters such as Des Esseintes that feature in decadent literature. Guys' stress on aesthetic form defines another tie between decadence and the flâneur. The flâneur intensely appreciates beauty and style, arrested by 'gilding, colours, shimmering stuffs, or the magic of physical beauty assisted by the cosmetic art' (Baudelaire, 1995: p. 8). He is 'obsessed and possessed by form' (p. 8). In 'The Painter of Modern Life', as in Wilde's preface to *The Picture of Dorian Gray,* beauty and form are privileged over utility. By elevating beauty, lethargy, and perception over the productiveness and industriousness of the urban realm, Baudelaire juxtaposes the flâneur with the crowds of urban modernity. In doing so, the flâneur is presented as a sensibility that permits engagements with, and even enthusiasm for, the modern city, while remaining detached and subversive. The flâneur, in Baudelaire's presentation, is decidedly 'on the threshold' of urban life (Benjamin, 2006: p. 40).

The ambivalence that underpins the flâneur's relationship to the urban environment was deeply appealing to writers of decadence. One of the clearest decadent embodiments of the flâneur sensibility that Baudelaire articulates lies in Wilde's *Lord Arthur Savile's Crime*. In that short story, the protagonist learns from a cheiromantist that his future will be defined by murder. After learning his fate, Lord Arthur wanders through the streets of London and encounters a key locale that Benjamin associates with the flâneur, the marketplace:

> Where he went he hardly knew. He had a dim memory of wandering through a labyrinth of sordid houses, of being lost in a giant web of sombre streets, and it was bright dawn when he found himself at last in Piccadilly Circus. As he strolled home towards Belgrave Square, he met the great waggons on their way to Covent Garden. The white-smocked carters, with their pleasant sunburnt faces and coarse curly hair, strode sturdily on, cracking their whips, and calling out now and then to each other; on the back of a huge grey horse, the leader of a jangling team, sat a chubby boy, with a bunch of primroses in his battered hat, keeping tight hold of the mane with his little hands, and laughing; and the great piles of vegetables looked like masses of jade against the morning sky, like masses of green jade against the pink petals of some marvellous rose. Lord Arthur felt curiously affected, he could not tell why. [. . .] It gave him pleasure to watch them as they went by. (Wilde, 1891: pp. 26–8)

Like Baudelaire's understanding of the city as a 'death-fraught idyll' (quoted in Benjamin, 2006: p. 41), ambivalence towards the urban sphere is clearly articulated here. London, the largest metropolis in the world at this point, however 'sordid' and 'sombre', nonetheless becomes in Wilde's hands an urban Arcady, with carters possessing 'pleasant sunburnt faces'. The deeply aestheticized representation of the urban scene, achieved by comparing vegetables and the sky to 'green jade against [. . .] pink petals', not only extends the idyllic metaphor but also reflects the flâneur's ability to see 'everything in a state of newness'. The stress on Savile's aimless 'wandering' and 'stroll[ing]' through the city, as well as the 'curious' pleasure he receives by focusing on the varied 'masses', further align him with the flâneur. Wilde here asserts 'the romance of London', to use Jackson's phrase; like the flâneur, Savile encounters mercantile industriousness but transforms it into an aestheticized experience.

Another decadent figure attracted to the flâneur sensibility was Arthur Symons, whose work highlights a particular dimension of Baudelaire's flâneur – gender. For Baudelaire, flânerie was a male activity. In 'The Painter of Modern Life', he not only genders the flâneur as male but also frames women as visual stimuli for the flâneur Guys: women are figures to 'astonish' and charm the artist (1995: p. 33); they are 'idol[s]' to be worshipped (p. 30). This portrayal of women as the subjects of creativity and observation – rather than being observational, creative agents themselves – is also reflected in Symons's work. In many of his poems and essays, Symons traverses the London cityscape, hoping to capture 'transitory, fugitive' modernity (p. 12). In 'At the Alhambra: Impressions and Sensations', Symons acknowledges his 'perverse and decadent way of thinking' (1896: 75) when he styles himself a flâneur who surveys a ballet dance at the Alhambra Theatre in Leicester Square. While Elizabeth Wilson has noted that the flâneur is not necessarily the 'embodiment of the male gaze' (1992: 98), Symons's spectatorship of the 'jostling crowd' on stage clearly blurs the distinction between flâneur and voyeur, as his comments on a ballet dancer's make-up show:

> [T]he exact line of red paint along the lips, every shading of black under the eyes, the pink of the ears and cheeks, and just where it ends under the chin and along the rim of throat. In a plain girl make-up only seems to intensify her plainness: for make-up does but give colour and piquancy to what is already in a face, it adds nothing new. But in a pretty girl how exquisitely becoming all this is, what a new kind of exciting savour it gives to her real charm! It has [. . .] a certain sense of dangerous wickedness, the delight of forbidden fruit. The very phrase, painted woman, has come to have an association of sin; and to have put paint on her cheeks, though for the innocent necessities of her profession, gives to a woman a sort of symbolic corruption. (1896: 77)

Like Baudelaire's flâneur, the narrator here is arrested by the 'magic of physical beauty assisted by the cosmetic art' (1995: p. 8). In observing the 'painted woman', Symons participates in several misogynist discourses – endorsing the image of the femme fatale and the 'idol of perversity' (see Dijkstra, 1986) through his comments on women's sinfulness, corruption, and capacity to mesmerize. While attempting to style the woman as powerful and enticing here, Symons instead reveals his own credentials as a predatory flâneur, manifesting the imbalance in power between the flâneur and the object of the flâneur's gaze. 'At the Alhambra' discloses the ways that the male flâneur could exploit his privileged observational agency to subject those he surveys.

Flâneuse

While nineteenth-century flânerie has typically been defined as a masculine sensibility, there were fin-de-siècle attempts to both arrest the male gaze and to assert the observational agency of women in the urban space, attempts that further complicate the relationship between decadence and the urban environment. Countering the common notion that flânerie is exclusively reserved for men, Lauren Elkin's *Flâneuse* traces various literary instances of women wandering and observing urban spaces in the nineteenth and twentieth centuries. She demonstrates the ways that women were (and are) excluded from full participation in public realms, arguing that 'space is not neutral. Space is a feminist issue' (2016: p. 286). Among the writers she examines are Virginia Woolf, Jean Rhys, and George Sand, the nineteenth-century French novelist who dressed as a man to participate in the urban crowd. These women, Elkin argues, attempted to claim women's 'place in the city' as 'observing entities' in order to challenge the limitations placed upon them (p. 288).

A key fin-de-siècle figure with decadent connections and an interest in the flâneuse sensibility was Amy Levy, whom Elkin briefly mentions. Levy was a poet, novelist, and essayist who became a protégée of Wilde, the editor of *Woman's World* while Levy was a contributor. Wilde described Levy as a genius and, following her suicide in 1889, mourned the fact that 'the world must forgo the full fruition of her power' (1890: 51). In addition to her connections to Wilde, Levy's Sapphic poetry and the influence of Walter Pater and Thomson on her work have led critics to define her 'Decadent poetic[s]' (Boyiopoulos and Sandy, 2016: p. 14). But although Levy was clearly influenced by male decadent figures, we find far less scepticism or ambivalence towards the urban scene in her work than in Wilde's and Thomson's. On the contrary, her writing exhibits Levy's concerted efforts to claim a stake for women within modern urban and commercial space, both as 'observing entities' and as participants. As such, several distinctions can be drawn between the observational sensibility she develops in her work and that of Baudelaire's flâneur.

Levy was also one of the early articulators of the flâneuse sensibility, and even used the term in her essay 'Women and Club Life', published in *Woman's World*, which posits that marriage should not prohibit women from joining social clubs. Levy notes that 'the female club-lounger, the flâneuse of St. James Street, latch-key in pocket and eye-glasses on the nose, remains a creature of the imagination' (quoted in Nord, 1995: p. 184). For Levy, the female observer of urban life, with privileges equivalent to those the flâneur enjoyed, was yet to be fully realized. Levy, however, endeavoured to resist the limitations placed on women in the urban sphere, in both her writing and in her life. She was known for traversing the city independently, controversially seating herself on the top deck of omnibuses, which were usually reserved for men; her sister, Katie Solomon, stated that she was 'among the first women in London to show herself on the tops of omnibuses' (quoted in Vadillo, 2005: p. 39) – a vantage point that permitted a fuller view of the city. In 'The Ballade of an Omnibus', Levy expresses joy in female spectatorship, beholding the full 'city pageant' that unfolds as she moves. As Deborah Parsons notes, for Levy (as for Baudelaire) the city was her 'muse' (2010: p. 93), and the omnibus was one way for a woman to experience it as fully as she could.

Of Levy's several novels, the one that best embodies her concern with advancing the flâneuse sensibility, as well as arresting the male gaze, is her first, *The Romance of a Shop* (1888). This novel concerns four sisters who, following their father's death, decide to move to Bloomsbury to set up a photography business. By establishing a supposedly unwomanly business and becoming professional photographers with their own observational agency, the sisters' shop counters patriarchal expectations. The women increasingly engage with both London society and the city environment itself, which provides opportunities for the sisters to immerse themselves into the same crowds they observe. As such, the novel negotiates the transition from the established domestic roles middle-class women were expected to fulfil to more public roles in the city.

Wilde described *The Romance of a Shop* as a 'clever' novel (1890: 52), and *The Woman's World* noted that it was full of 'quick observation' (quoted in Bernstein, 2006: p. 37). The choice of words in the latter appraisal could hardly have been accidental: observation is a central feature of the novel. In addition to the sisters being placed in crowds and given the ability to look at life through the camera lens, the language of surveillance suffuses the novel, the words 'glance' and 'glimpse' appearing frequently throughout. For instance, Gertrude, the protagonist who is most keen to observe the urban environment, glimpses other figures with 'wistful interest' (Levy, 2006: p. 113). When her future husband, Lord Watergate, offers to find her a seat at the 'Show Sunday' exhibition, she says, 'No; thank you; I prefer to stand. One sees the world so much better' (p. 115). At this event, Gertrude meets her antagonist, Sidney Darrell, an artist whose observational capacities rival hers: she seeks to observe the full panorama of society and he possesses an 'all-seeing languid glance' (p. 150). Darrell's 'languid glance' and 'all-seeing' capabilities associate him with the flâneur here, making him an embodiment of the male gaze. He predatorily stares at other women in the novel and manipulates them through his artistic gaze; for instance, he seeks to paint Gertrude's sister Phyllis, with whom he later has an affair, as Cressida, thus casting Phyllis as a fallen woman. As in 'At the Alhambra', the male gaze is used to align women with corruption. Here, however, Levy equips Gertrude with an 'intense gaze' to counter the male stare (p. 115). What Susan Bernstein calls a 'battle of the gendered gazes' (2006: p. 38) reveals this rivalry towards the conclusion of the novel:

> His face was livid with passion; his prominent eyes, for once wide open, glared at her in rage and hatred.
>
> Gertrude met his glance with eyes that glowed with a passion yet fiercer than his own.
>
> Elements, long smouldering, had blazed forth at last. Face to face they stood; face to face, while the silent battle raged between them.
>
> Then with a curious elation, a mighty throb of what was almost joy, Gertrude knew that she, not he, the man of whom she had once been afraid, was the stronger of the two. For one brief moment some fierce instinct in her heart rejoiced. (Levy, 2006: p. 172)

Overcoming the desire to 'snatch her heavy camera and flee from his presence', Gertrude confronts the 'man's gaze' here (p. 107). Darrell's stare is portrayed as especially predatory – an enraged, incensed gaze, keen to overcome its rival – but Gertrude returns it with equal ferocity. Here, Levy is not only concerned with confronting the male gaze of the predatory flâneur but also with challenging the 'vacant gaze' that Baudelaire ascribes to women (1995: p. 35); instead, Levy presents her readers with women who can claim their own observational agency in the urban realm.

But Levy does not stop at resisting the male gaze; she also presents brief moments where women can perform flânerie in urban crowds. At the risk of being associated with prostitutes, or 'street walkers', Levy's female protagonists traverse the urban labyrinth without a chaperon and observe it. Gertrude's deep pleasure in observing the urban realm is expressed in Chapter 4, when she travels to the British Museum to undertake a photography course:

> Gertrude mount[ed] boldly to the top of an Atlas omnibus.
>
> 'Because one cannot afford a carriage or even a hansom cab', she argued to herself, 'is one to be shut up away from the sunlight and the streets?'
>
> Indeed, for Gertrude, the humours of the town had always possessed a curious fascination. She contemplated the familiar London pageant with an interest that had something of passion in it; and, for her part, was never inclined to quarrel with the fate which had transported her from the comparative tameness of Campden Hill to regions where the pulses of the great city could be felt distinctly as they beat and throbbed. (2006: p. 80)

Unlike the private, enclosed carriages portrayed by Constantin Guys that Baudelaire describes, Levy focuses on a public, open form of transport, the omnibus. The passage echoes Levy's other writings, and her own life: as in

'The Ballade of an Omnibus', the city is represented as a 'pageant' – a spectacle to be viewed by the passing flâneuse – and Gertrude positions herself where she can achieve a panoramic perspective, on top of the omnibus, as Levy herself did. The emphasis on Gertrude's 'curious' fascination and 'passion' for the urban realm is akin to Baudelaire's stress on the curiosity of the flâneur, while Gertrude's throbbing joy reflects the sensual pleasure derived from flânerie. Although Gertrude experiences such moments only briefly, they reveal both her enthusiasm for flânerie and her wish to become a woman of affairs; the city is presented as a site of potential liberation for women rather than a 'dreadful night'. As such, Levy's novel adds to the complexity of decadent flânerie: unlike Baudelaire's flâneur who remains 'on the threshold' of urban modernity, Levy's flâneuse seeks both to observe the modern city *and* to participate in it. *The Romance of a Shop* clearly shows that not all forms of fin-de-siècle flânerie expressed scepticism towards the modern urban scene.

Dandy

While flânerie had close ties to the decadent milieu, the fin-de-siècle sensibility most closely associated with decadence is embodied by the dandy. In 1913, Jackson highlighted the centrality of dandyism to the writers of the 1890s and stressed that 'while the essential dandyism of the decade lasted it needed an urban background' (1950: p. 111). Dandyism was widely discussed during the 1890s itself: dandiacal figures were frequently the subject of both visual caricature by, for example, George du Maurier in *Punch*, and literary satire, including Max Beerbohm's 'Dandies and Dandies' (1896), which outlined three essential elements of dandyism: 'physical distinction, a sense of beauty and wealth or, if you prefer the term, credit' (Beerbohm, 1922: p. 15). Of course, dandyism was by no means an exclusively fin-de-siècle phenomenon; the sensibility had been described in the first half of the nineteenth century, notably by Jules Amédée Barbey d'Aurevilly in 'On Dandyism and George Brummell' (1845) and by Thomas Carlyle in *Sartor resartus* (1833–1834), where the dandy is characterized as a 'clothes-wearing man' devoted to 'self-worship' (Carlyle, 1896: pp. 247, 250). But while dandyism was not restricted to the fin de siècle, it came to be closely associated with the decadents and was perceived, by some, as a key feature of their depravity. Olive Schreiner, for instance, lampooned the dandy in her essay, 'The Woman Question', characterizing him as inactive and emblematic of societal decadence. She writes that 'the curled darling, scented and languid, with his drawl, and his delicate apparel, his devotion to the rarity and variety of his viands whose severest labour is the search after pleasure' is 'repulsive', because he represents 'a yet further product of decay' (quoted by Ledger, 1997: p. 76).

Schreiner's assessment of the idle, pampered 'darling' as illustrative of social degeneration raises a question that has divided critics in recent decades: to what extent was the dandy a threat to the social order? Various nineteenth- and twentieth-century critics have put forward contrasting conceptions of dandyism and its relationship to society, with some perceiving the dandy as fundamentally opposed to societal norms and keen to undermine them, and others regarding the figure as far less threatening. Taken together, these assessments reveal both the complexity and elusiveness of the dandy sensibility, while also demonstrating how dandyism, like flânerie, helped support ambivalent decadent engagements with urban society.

For some theorists of dandyism, the dandy posed a threat to bourgeois progress by undermining its fundamental ideologies. In 'The Painter of Modern Life', for example, Baudelaire highlights the various ways that the dandy sensibility opposed bourgeois norms, one of which was its embrace of the aristocracy. In contrast to Elaine Crowell, who notes that the dandy was recognized as 'a non-aristocratic man who gained access to upper-class circles through artifice, arrogance, and a meticulous attention to fashion and manners' (2007: p. 12), Baudelaire defines the dandy as a figure born into wealth: a man who 'has been brought up amid luxury and has been accustomed from his earliest days to the obedience of others' (1995: p. 26). This desire to maintain (or, in Crowell's framing, to develop) the air of the aristocrat is necessary, in Baudelaire's eyes, to resist a key aspect of modernity: democracy. Baudelaire notes that the dandy is especially hostile to the rise of democratic modernity: 'Dandyism appears above all in periods of transition, when democracy is not yet all-powerful, and aristocracy is only just beginning to totter and fall' (p. 28). Dandyism is portrayed as an aristocratic sensibility re-energized in the face of democracy's rise. As such, Baudelaire's dandy is in step with many decadent writers, including George Moore, who defended art on the basis that it is 'the direct antithesis to democracy' (1917: p. 100). Baudelaire's dandy, however, is not simply resistant to political and economic democracy but to uniformity more broadly. Baudelaire does not limit the dandy's advocacy of the aristocracy to money: indeed, he asserts that an alternative aristocracy can be established, one that is 'all the more difficult to shatter as it will be based on the most precious, the most enduring faculties, and on the divine gifts which work and money are unable to bestow' (1995: pp. 28–9). By possessing 'divine gifts', Baudelaire romanticizes the dandy and draws upon the language of militarism to do so: dandyism is characterized as the 'last spark of heroism' (pp. 28–9) in modern society, with dandies becoming 'stupendous warriors' against democracy, which 'flattens all' (p. 29).

The militant heroism of the dandy therefore lies in his 'characteristic quality of opposition and revolt' to the uniformity of modernity. Several features, many of which are akin to those of the flâneur, define this sensibility of 'opposition and revolt'. Among the 'divine gifts' possessed by the dandy that Baudelaire outlines are his being 'idle' or bored; he is one 'whose solitary profession is elegance' (p. 26). He is also described as a 'spiritualist' and a figure who may be capable of love but does not regard it 'as a special target to be aimed at', for without money or leisure, love 'becomes a repulsive utility', a 'conjugal duty' (pp. 27–8). Excessiveness is also crucial to the dandy's rejection of uniformity: Richard Dellamora characterizes the dandy as a figure who is 'too relaxed, too visible, [and] consumes to excess while producing little or nothing' (1990: p. 199). Like the flâneur, Baudelaire's dandy elevates aimlessness, beauty, and immoderate sensation over utility and democracy.

While Baudelaire draws several parallels between the sensibilities of the dandy and the flâneur, he also juxtaposes the two. For instance, Baudelaire highlights that the dandy does not interact with the crowd in the same manner as the flâneur: the dandy 'aspires to insensitivity, and it is in this that Monsieur G., dominated as he is by an insatiable passion – for seeing and feeling – parts company decisively with dandyism' (1995: p. 9). The implication here is that the dandy cultivates a sense of disinterestedness within society, a 'haughty exclusiveness, provocative in its very coldness' (p. 28), while the flâneur is deeply receptive to the people around him. The flâneur rejoices in his immersion in the crowd but 'the dandy is blasé' (p. 9); the dandy instead joys in 'astonishing others' (p. 27) through his oppositionalism. On this point, Baudelaire's characterization of the dandy is similar to Albert Camus' later treatment of the sensibility as an 'aesthetic of negation'. Camus' dandy is even more of a vacuum than Baudelaire's – 'perpetually incomplete, always on the fringe of things, he compels others to create him, while denying their values' (2000: p. 48) – but they both obtain their meaning through a negation of the society that surrounds them. In these framings, the dandy sensibility, in essence, exists to oppose and disrupt societal norms.

In contrast to the oppositionalist dandy that Baudelaire and Camus present, Michael Patrick Gillespie has argued that the fin-de-siècle dandy, especially in Wilde's hands, was not a renegade figure. Gillespie goes so far as to state that dandies 'assiduously offer nominal submission to principles of public respectability [. . .] they serve as mediators between independence and conformity' (2006: p. 167). Invoking Ellen Moers's foundational study, *The Dandy: Brummell to Beerbohm* (1978), Gillespie notes that dandies helped 'stretch the limits of public tolerance' rather than resist the public; they were hardly 'iconoclasts' in his view (p. 168). From Gillespie's perspective, the dandy sensibility may be subversive, but it is not subversive in a way that undermines society. The dandy instead carefully acknowledges certain boundaries, refusing to fully disrupt bourgeois norms. Examining *The Importance of Being Earnest,* Gillespie finds Wilde's dandies emblematic of this point, highlighting the mastery of paradox as a device that allows the dandy's symbiosis with society. Paradox, being 'the first step toward the cultivation of ambiguity' (p. 170), makes the social positioning of Wilde's dandies unclear; they are never fully opposed to anything. Indeed, the paradox at the core of the play – the importance of being earnest (sincere and committed) or Ernest (a mask) – is sustained until the final line. Gillespie's analysis also reveals a further way that Wilde complicates the notion of the dandy as a rebel, by giving almost every character in the play dandiacal attributes. Indeed, it is a female character, Gwendolyn, who states the most typically dandiacal line in the drama: 'in matters of grave importance, style, not sincerity is the vital thing' (Wilde, 2008: p. 295). Dandy and society become indecipherable in the play – dandies can and do exist in *The Importance of Being Earnest*, but they do not have to reject their society to live in it. As Lady Bracknell, another female dandy figure, reminds Algernon: 'Never speak disrespectfully of Society [. . .]. Only people who can't get into it do that' (p. 299). Both Baudelaire and Gillespie highlight the symbiosis between dandyism and society in their assessments, but while Baudelaire finds that the dandy's existence hinges on his warring against bourgeois norms and asserting his superiority, Gillespie finds far more reciprocity between them.

The multiplicity and ambiguity of the Wildean dandy that Gillespie elucidates underpins a further aspect of fin-de-siècle dandyism – sexual fluidity. The multiplicity of fin-de-siècle dandy figures allowed them to move fluidly between sexualities and genders; the dandy sensibility was a space where 'marginalized sexual identities were given room to develop' (Denisoff, 2001: p. 9). Indeed, the double lives and 'bunburying' that feature in *The Importance of Being Earnest* have been read as allusions to Algernon's fluid sexuality (Craft, 2006: pp. 136–66). This focus on sexuality became prominent at the fin de siècle, when 'the dandy's connotations changed: this once-refined apologist for aristocracy developed into an overdetermined embodiment of cultural disintegration'. This 'cultural disintegration', Crowell argues, was rooted in the 'suspicious effeminacy' of fin-de-siècle dandies such as Wilde (2007: p. 12). Like the New Woman, whose perceived masculinity and rejection of marriage and motherhood were styled as dangerous, the fin-de-siècle dandy's camp sensibility was also seen as a threat to patriarchal norms. Schreiner's characterization of the dandy as 'delicate' and depraved reminds us of just how acutely the figure's uncertain gender and fluid sexuality constituted a threat to social norms at the fin de siècle.

The complexity surrounding decadent engagements with urban society, via flânerie and dandyism, is embodied by a quotation from Wilde's *An Ideal Husband.* In the first act, after Lord Caversham expresses his jadedness with London, Mabel Chiltern responds, 'Oh, I love London society! I think it has immensely improved. It is entirely composed now of beautiful idiots and brilliant lunatics. Just what Society should be' (2008: p. 167). Mabel Chiltern's concerted ambivalence towards urban modernity reflects a broader response to city life across the decadent writing of the fin de siècle, and the sensibilities examined in this chapter were embraced to help express this ambivalence. The metropolis may have been filled with idiots, lunatics, and 'improvement', but urban life was equally alluring to decadent writers, who often placed themselves in proximity to urban crowds and society to observe, oppose, and even participate in them. At once entranced by and foreign to urban modernity, the flâneur embodies decadent ambivalence towards urban life, while his counterpart, the flâneuse, displays a greater enthusiasm for modernity. These complications are equally evident with dandyism, whose practitioners generally rely on urban society for their existence but also choose to subvert and undermine the uniformity society demands. In short, the various sensibilities discussed in this chapter were increasingly adopted at the fin de siècle to negotiate both the fascination and the abhorrence the decadent felt towards an increasingly urbanized modernity.

References

Baudelaire, Charles (1995). *The Painter of Modern Life and Other Essays*, Jonathan Mayne, ed. and trans., London: Phaidon.

Beerbohm, Max (1922). *The Works of Max Beerbohm*, New York: Dodd, Mead and Company.

Benjamin, Walter (2006). *The Writer of Modern Life: Essays on Charles Baudelaire*, Michael W. Jennings, ed., Cambridge, MA: Harvard University Press.

Bernstein, Susan David (2006). Introduction. In Susan David Bernstein, ed., *The Romance of a Shop*. Peterborough, ON: Broadview, pp. 11–41.
Boyiopoulos, Kostas, and Mark Sandy (2016). Introduction. In Kostas Boyiopoulos and Mark Sandy, eds., *Decadent Romanticism: 1780–1914*, Abingdon: Routledge, pp.1–14.
Camus, Albert (2000). *The Rebel*, Anthony Bower, trans., London: Penguin.
Carlyle, Thomas (1896). *Sartor resartus*, Archibald MacMechan, ed., London: The Athenæum Press.
Craft, Christopher (2006). Alias Bunbury: Desire and Termination in The Importance of Being Earnest. In Michael Patrick Gillespie, ed., *The Importance of Being Earnest*, New York: W. W. Norton & Company, pp. 136–66.
Crowell, Ellen (2007). *The Dandy in Irish and American Southern Fiction*, Edinburgh: Edinburgh University Press.
Dellamora, Richard (1990). *Masculine Desire: The Sexual Politics of Victorian Aestheticism*, Chapel Hill: University of North Carolina Press.
Denisoff, Dennis (2001). *Aestheticism and Sexual Parody 1840–1940*, Cambridge: Cambridge University Press.
Dijkstra, Bram (1986). *Idols of Perversity: Fantasies of Feminine Evil in Fin-de-Siècle Culture*, Oxford: Oxford University Press.
Elkin, Lauren (2016). *Flâneuse: Women Walk the City in Paris, New York, Tokyo, Venice, and London*, London: Chatto & Windus.
Fritzsche, Peter (2015). The City and Urban Life. In Michael T. Saler, ed., *The Fin-de-Siècle World*, Abingdon:Routledge, pp. 29–44.
Geddes, Patrick (1895). The Sociology of Autumn. *The Evergreen*, 2, 27–38.
Gillespie, Michael Patrick (2006). From Beau Brummell to Lady Bracknell: Re-viewing the Dandy in *The Importance of Being Earnest*. In Michael Patrick Gillespie, ed., *The Importance of Being Earnest*, New York: W. W. Norton & Company, pp. 166–82.
Jackson, Holbrook (1950). *The Eighteen-Nineties*, Harmondsworth: Penguin.
Ledger, Sally (1997). *The New Woman: Fiction and Feminism at the Fin de Siècle*, Manchester: Manchester University Press.
Levy, Amy (2006). *The Romance of a Shop*, Susan David Bernstein, ed., Peterborough, ON: Broadview.
Moore, George (1917). *Confessions of a Young Man*, London: William Heinemann.
Nord, Deborah Epstein (1995). *Walking the Victorian Streets: Women, Representation and the City*, Ithaca, NY and London: Cornell University Press.
Parsons, Deborah (2010). *Streetwalking the Metropolis: Women, the City, and Modernity*, Oxford: Oxford University Press.
Symons, Arthur (1896). At the Alhambra: Impressions and Sensations. *The Savoy*, 3, 75–83.
Thomson, James (1892). *Poems, Essays and Fragments*, John M. Robertson, ed., London: A. & H. Bradlaugh Bonner.
Vadillo, Ana Parejo (2005). *Women Poets and Urban Aestheticism: Passengers of Modernity*, Houndmills: Palgrave Macmillan.

Wilde, Oscar (1890). Amy Levy. *The Woman's World*, 3, 51–2.
Wilde, Oscar (2008). *The Importance of Being Earnest and Other Plays*, Peter Raby, ed., Oxford: Oxford University Press.
Wilde, Oscar (1891). *Lord Arthur Savile's Crime and Other Stories*, London: James R. Osgood, McIlvaine and Co.
Wilson, Elizabeth (1992). The Invisible Flâneur. *New Left Review*, 191, 90–110.

CHAPTER 6

Decadence and the Critique of Modernity

Jane Desmarais

> It is stupid to live in a time of growth; the soul is as uncomfortable as a body in a damp new house.
>
> (Goncourt, 1937: p. 93)

Between 1850 and 1890 the concept of decadence develops – principally through the work of the poet Charles Baudelaire (1821–1867), the critic Théophile Gautier (1811–1872), and the novelist Joris-Karl Huysmans (1848–1907) – as a critique of urban modernity. Living at a time when political, cultural, and scientific revolutions had swept across Europe, these writers were disgusted by overcrowding, poverty, and rampant commercialism, what Huysmans described as 'the caliphate of the counter' (1998: p. 179). Cultural anxiety about urbanization was not exclusive to decadence – the romantics had contemplated the city in its hellish forms, and realist writers like Honoré de Balzac, Gustave Flaubert, and Émile Zola had dissected the city's ills in their novels about French society – but in the work of French decadent writers we encounter a profound scepticism about modernity and progress. The Haussmannization of Paris in the mid-nineteenth century circumscribed a booming metropolitan culture, but it exiled its bohemian inhabitants and, in the view of decadents, pandered to the vulgar and philistine tastes of the bourgeoisie.

The banalization of culture was a 'trap to catch fools' (Gautier, 1903: vol. XXIII, p. 43) and not only created social fragmentation and new forms of mental illness but also threatened to stifle the faculties of judgement and feeling. Fulminating against the 'purely material developments of progress' in his essay 'Le Salon de 1859' ['The Salon of 1859'], Baudelaire declared that '[p]oetry and progress are two ambitious men that hate each other, with an instinctive hatred, and when they meet along a pathway one or other must give way' (1972: p. 296).

Decadent writers were not entirely hostile to modernity, however. While Baudelaire found the accelerated rate of urban change deeply disconcerting, he took pleasurable advantage of the new fashions and manners of metropolitan life. In his essay 'Le peintre de la vie moderne' ['The Painter of Modern Life'] (1863), he celebrates 'the eternal beauty and the amazing harmony of life in the capital cities' through the sketches of Constantin Guys, a little-known artist who 'gazes upon the landscapes of the great city – landscapes of stone, caressed by the mist or buffeted by the sun' and delights in 'universal life' (Baudelaire, 1995: p. 10). Baudelaire's ambivalence – his ability to be both attracted to and repulsed by his experiences of modern urban life and his fascination with modern man (inspired by his reading of Poe) – is championed by Gautier and by the 1880s becomes a decadent standard. His depiction of modern neurosis finds its fictional consummation in Huysmans's *À rebours* [*Against Nature*] (1884).

This essay examines the development of the concept of decadence as a critique of modernity through the work of French writers who, while horrified by progress, especially of the inflated status and importance granted to the bourgeoisie, were fascinated by the exigencies, distortions, and chaos of modern life, particularly as it impacted on the individual. The first part is a consideration of Baudelaire as a foundational figure, whose poetry evoked both the thrilling spectacle of the modern cityscape and the social alienation that came about through Haussmannization. In Baudelaire's poetry, the city is 'the domain of the momentary, the accidental, the heterogeneous and incomplete', and our vision is, as one critic notes, 'restricted to a fragmentary and often hallucinated perception' (Burton, 1980: pp. 88, 87). The second part focuses on those French writers who responded to Baudelaire or, if not directly to his work, to the modern malaise he gave expression to. In Zola's novels, for example, the concepts of decadence and degeneration are depicted as the twin political and economic consequences of a rapacious and corrupt capitalism. The third and final part of the essay tracks the concept of decadence as it develops in the fin de siècle to suggest a sense of psychological alienation. In Huysmans's *Against Nature* the decadent attitude to urban life is mediated through the subjective impressions of the main character, Duc Jean Floressas Des Esseintes, who is disturbed and sickened by what he sees as the fall of French 'syphilization'. Ailing and spiritually rudderless, he is unable to sustain himself on art and artifice alone and is forced to return to the 'depredations of the Parisians [. . .] their pointless ostentation and their obsolete arrogance, which [they] debased with [their] lack of good breeding' (1998: p. 179). As modernity advances and intensifies, so the concept of decadence becomes reclusive and solipsistic. The triumph of modernity signals the end of decadence.

i

The economic expansion and development of European cities led to rapid urbanization, but by far the greatest transformation occurred in the city of Paris. Rebuilt and reorganized to glorify the achievements of Louis-Napoléon Bonaparte (Napoléon III), it was remodelled as a consumerist paradise and became by the fin de siècle the cultural capital of Europe. In the 1850s and 1860s, Baron Georges Eugène Haussmann, appointed Prefect of the Seine, transformed Paris by destroying much of the medieval city for Louis-Napoléon, who sought systematic and ruthless urban renewal. Haussmann himself estimated that 350,000 people were displaced to the outskirts of the city during this period; people were uprooted as houses and shops were demolished for the building of new commercial sites like the market complex of Les Halles and the Rue de Rivoli. Among the many welcome innovations were new sewers, gas lighting, public parks, freed-up road traffic, and wide avenues and boulevards, but the poor were marginalized, creating discernible boundaries between wealthy neighbourhoods and slum districts.

The demolition of the old parts of the city and the rebuilding of central Paris gave the city the sparkle of confection, and people flocked to enjoy the vibrant shop-fronts and the new leisure spaces. Popular impressionist images of Paris between 1860 and 1890 depict the changing cityscape with new rooftop viewpoints created by multi-storey apartments that looked over the widened and straightened boulevards. Impressionist paintings of modern life show a secular middle-class culture on the move and on display: people eating, drinking, picnicking, strolling, playing, watching the world: 'In the new homogenized metropolis from which traditional civic roles have disappeared, to be is to be perceived' (Burton, 1980: p. 43). Nature is a backdrop to the theatre of human leisure, crowded into the new urban spaces – race courses, pavement cafés, railway stations, winter gardens, and public parks. In Édouard Manet's painting, *Musique aux Tuileries* [*Music in the Tuileries Gardens*] (1862) (fig. 6.1) two children in their best clothes play with buckets and spades in the centre foreground, and a well-dressed gentleman doffs his hat to a group of women on the right. Behind the woman in the blue bonnet on the left we can just make out the blurred figure of Baudelaire, top-hatted in a frock coat, his face smudged, striking in its foregrounded indistinctness. He cuts an anonymous figure; he is a fleeting and featureless element. Gathered informally in small groups under the trees, these people are clearly at leisure, but in spite of their proximity to one another, there is little interrelationship.

Fig. 6.1 The vagueness of Baudelaire's outline in Édouard Manet's *Music in the Tuileries Gardens* (1862) suggests the anonymity of the flâneur observing the urban scene [Getty Images / DEA Picture Library].

Unlike the bucolic *fêtes* of Pierre-Auguste Renoir (e.g., *Le déjeuner des canotiers* [*Luncheon of the Boating Party*] (1880–1881)), there is no physical activity, no dancing or flirting.

Haussmann's interventions reconceptualized Paris as a theatrical spectacle of renewal and refurbishment, health and beauty. For many, the newly gentrified Paris was exciting. The writer Georges Rodenbach found it more stimulating than his native Belgium, writing to Émile Verhaeren in 1878 that 'in Paris, one lives at twice the pace, [. . .] suddenly the sap rises and thought flowers' (quoted in Hollinghurst, 2009: p. 13). For others, however, urban development came at a price. The historian and philosopher Hippolyte Taine described the renovations of Paris as having created 'an overheated hothouse, aromatic and tainted' (quoted in Weber, 1982: 13).

The modernization of Paris captivated Baudelaire. In his famous collection of poems *Les fleurs du mal* [*The Flowers of Evil*] (1857) and his critical essays, notably 'The Painter of Modern Life' (1863), he conveys the thrill of being incognito in the midst of a crowd. 'For the perfect flâneur, for the passionate spectator', he avers, 'it is an immense joy to set up house in the heart of the multitude, amid the ebb and flow of movement, in the midst of the fugitive and the infinite' (Baudelaire, 1965: p. 11). *The Flowers of Evil* introduces us to a variety of urban spaces, from the public domain of labyrinthine streets and wide boulevards to the private realm of the attic *chambre*. Our senses are invited to contract and expand.

Unlike the attempts of earlier poets, like Alfred de Vigny ('Paris') and Gautier ('Le sommet de la tour' ['The Top of the Tower']), to take in the new urban reality from lofty aerial vantage points, Baudelaire's vision is both classical and romantic. He surveys the urban panorama from high up, but he also conveys the street-level experiences of the ordinary citizen. The first line of Baudelaire's poem, 'Les sept vieillards' ['Seven Old Men'], for example – 'City of swarming, city full of dreams' – offers an image of narrow spaces proliferating with colonies of ant-like crowds in the city streets (1993: p. 177), while the love poem 'Une charogne' ['A Carcass'] describes life at gutter level. Two strolling lovers happen upon an animal carcass laid out on the pavement in the summer heat, prompting the speaker to remind his companion that she in her turn will suffer the same fate, become '[h]orrible, filthy, undone' with 'legs spread out like a lecherous whore, | Sweating out poisoning fumes' (p. 59).

The chance encounters of urban life are perhaps best encapsulated, however, in the sonnet 'A une passante' ['To a Woman Passing By']. The German critic Walter Benjamin certainly thought so. He regarded

Baudelaire as the first poet to capture the transformations of the modern city, and he praised this poem for its expression of ambiguity. 'What this sonnet communicates', he asserts, 'is simply this: Far from experiencing the crowd as an opposed, antagonistic element, this very crowd brings to the city dweller the figure that fascinates' (Benjamin, 1968: p. 169). Here is James McGowan's translation of the poem in full:

> Around me roared the nearly deafening street.
> Tall, slim, in mourning, in majestic grief,
> A woman passed me, with a splendid hand
> Lifting and swinging her festoon and hem;
>
> Nimble and stately, statuesque of leg.
> I, shaking like an addict, from her eye,
> Black sky, spawner of hurricanes, drank in
> Sweetness that fascinates, pleasure that kills.
>
> One lightning flash . . . then night! Sweet fugitive
> Whose glance has made me suddenly reborn,
> Will we not meet again this side of death?
>
> Far from this place! too late! never perhaps!
> Neither one knowing where the other goes,
> O you I might have loved, as well you know!
>
> (Baudelaire, 1993: p. 189)

A woman dressed in mourning attire emerges from the surrounding city crowd. The poet is immediately smitten by her appearance, '[n]imble and stately' and the promise of tempest in her eyes, but as quickly as she materializes she dematerializes back into the crowd, and the poet is left to meditate on the fugitive phenomenon of love: 'Far from this place! too late! never perhaps!' Unlike Pygmalion who creates and possesses his ideal love object, Baudelaire's desires are thwarted by the city. His street idol, 'statuesque of leg', transmutes into a mere symbol (of the great love that might have been between them), and the poet is left pondering the cruel elusiveness of the city.

Transience and transformation are recurring themes in Baudelaire's work. In the prose poem 'La chambre double' ['The Double Room'], the bailiff's knock on the door suddenly rouses the drugged poet from his 'somnambulistic life'. The 'perfume of another world' is replaced in an instant with 'a fetid odour of tobacco mixed with some indescribably nauseating mustiness', and a depressing sense of Time's passing prevails, forcing the poet to return to a 'world so narrow and yet so full of disgust' (Baudelaire, 1988: p. 17). It is as if the poet's struggle to give shape to the world is denied not only by the transience of modern reality itself but also by the moves made in and by the poet's mind. For Baudelaire there is no Wordsworthian 'recollection in tranquillity', but a series of confrontations with a rapidly metamorphosing world.

Baudelaire found the flux of modern life exhilarating but also overwhelming and dehumanizing. In his descriptions of modern Paris, Baudelaire's rapid visual shifts in perspective and sense of psychological instability reflect his ambivalence about the rate and scale of social and cultural change. In order to prevent assimilation into the crowd's 'immense reservoir of electrical energy' (Baudelaire, 1995: p. 10), he asserts, the dandy-poet – 'the last spark of heroism amid decadence' (pp. 28–9) – must maintain an aristocratic aloofness in an effort to distinguish himself from the 'seething ferment of mediocrities', a society 'in thrall to material perfection' and 'greedy for wonder' (p. 94): 'the rising tide of democracy, which invades and levels everything, is daily overwhelming these last representatives of human pride and pouring floods of oblivion upon the footprints of these stupendous warriors' (p. 29).

Forced to negotiate the crowds and the dazzle of materialist bourgeois culture, Baudelaire became a self-declared exile in Paris. He laments the razing to the ground of the old Carrousel neighbourhood (between the Louvre and the Tuileries palace) and the demise of the shabby-chic social life there. What once had been a haven for bohemians and dissident artists among local tradesmen and entertainers was now a 'new ersatz imperial reality' replacing the old economy of 'merchandising, theatre and prostitution' (Terdiman, 2000: p. 120). In his magisterial poem, 'Le cygne' ['The Swan'], from the 'Tableaux Parisiens' ['Parisian Tableaux'] section of *The Flowers of Evil*, Baudelaire mourns the demise of old Paris. The poem opens with the tears of recently widowed Andromache and closes with the image of a negress on a desert island, but its central section focuses on the renovation of Paris, a barren modern cityscape, in which an escaped swan 'scuffling his splayed feet along the paving stones, | [. . .] trailed his white array of feathers in the dirt' (Baudelaire, 1993: p. 175). Baudelaire describes the poet's isolation and loss and imagines the past, present, and future as a flow of repeated experiences, conjoining the fall of ancient Troy with the desecration of modern Paris by Louis-Napoléon. He creates a layered and restless vision of urban renewal and human displacement. Images of flooding and drought run through the poem and suggest the contingent processes of memory. The image of the 'fraudulent Simois' augmented with Andromache's 'bitter tears' activates the poet's 'fertile memory' about old Paris in the second stanza, but by the third the contrasting river images of majesty and poverty leave only 'puddle-stain'. Water gives way to the dry earth of an emergent but desolate modern cityscape, populated by labourers who 'push their storms into the silent air'. Covered in dust, neck outstretched, the bird rails against an ungenerous God. The impression we are left with is one of dislocation and bathos:

> Flapping excitedly, bathing his wings in dust,
> And said, with heart possessed by lakes he once had loved:
> 'Water, when will you rain? Thunder, when will you roar?'
> I see this hapless creature, sad and fatal myth. (p. 175)

Baudelaire describes modern Paris as an *other* place, a city haunted by aspects of its demolished past, but he also conveys a powerful sense of the city as a transitional space. As Richard Burton argues, the city changes according to the law of diminishing returns: 'Cities rise and fall, yet each new foundation is somehow inferior to its predecessor; [. . .] Paris bears the same relation to Rome as "little Troy" to Troy and so on. This tragi-comic diminuendo is Baudelaire's counter to the historical crescendo predicted by the believers in Progress' (Burton, 1980: p. 50).

That such drastic urban development should engender a sense of grievance and neglect in Baudelaire was typical of the romantic poet, who regarded contemporary civilization as hostile to art and the moral values associated with it. Modern civilization seemed to him ugly, cheap, colourless, soulless, mechanical, vulgar, lacking in high ideals, inhumanly calculating, and debased by cynically materialistic priorities. But unlike the romantics who because of these attributes regarded modern civilization as un-poetical, Baudelaire was more experimental and open-minded. In modern life he saw the potential for great art. Strolling along the new boulevards and wandering in the refurbished districts of central Paris, he discerned qualities of beauty, grace, refinement, humanity, spirituality, social cohesion, idealism, and heroism that had prevailed in previous ages, arguing that 'for any modernity to be worthy of one day taking its place as "antiquity", it is necessary for the mysterious beauty which human life accidentally puts into it to be distilled from it' (Baudelaire, 1965: p. 13). Unlike the romantic poet who wrote with, and in a sense from, a direct sense of abandonment, Baudelaire's attitude to change was complex. His ambivalence, often expressed in his poetry by contrasts, dualities, and strange pairings, is typically decadent; he was disgusted by the materialism of modernity, yet he also took pleasure in its alluring and decorative aspects, particularly in relation to the poorest members of society. Here is Baudelaire on fallen womanhood:

> She advances towards us, glides, dances, or moves about with her burden of embroidered petticoats, which play the part at once of pedestal and balancing-rod; her eye flashes out from under her hat, like a portrait in its frame. She is a perfect image of the savagery that lurks in the midst of civilization. (p. 36)

The poet's pictorialization of the streetwalker is both critique and compliment. By drawing our attention to the cracked veneer of civilization, Baudelaire elevates the woman in her 'perfect [. . .] savagery' to the status of muse.

ii

Baudelaire's contradictory attitudes towards modernity, his wonder and disgust at so much change, were shared by many others, including the brothers Edmond and Jules de Goncourt who described the new boulevards in their *Journal* as 'some American Babylon of the future' (1937: p. 93) and the anarchist Pierre-Joseph Proudhon who found the new city 'monotone and tiring [. . .] with its railway stations which, replacing the gates of the ancient city, destroyed its raison d'être' (quoted in Burton, 1980: pp. 90, 91). Contemporary historians and philosophers, like Taine, regarded modern 'civilized' man as the embodiment of a broader social decadence that would lead to national decline. There was a growing fear in the mid-nineteenth century that France was losing its dominant position in the world and was heading for ruin. This was the view of C. M. Raudot whose *De la décadence de la France* [On the decline of France] (1849) was so well received that it went through four editions in its first year. Raudot's concern with demographic weakness (he was particularly concerned about the height of army recruits) was to some extent a nostalgic plea for a return to a pre-industrial golden age, but he was not alone. As the century wore on, cultural anxieties about female sexuality, falling birth rates, scientific progress, evolution, colonial expansion, disease, and immigration reached crisis point in France and across Europe, filling the pages of newspapers, magazines, and learned journals. The concept of decadence became intertwined with social and cultural discourses about racial degeneration and national decline.

By the 1860s, the concept of decadence – principally through the work of Baudelaire – acquires a new intensity. Baudelaire briefly reflected on social decadence in his essay 'L'art philosophique' ['Philosophic Art'] (1858–1860), but he was not much interested in formulating a theory of decadence or indeed being classified as decadent. Declaring the idea of decadent literature a 'gigantic yawn' (Baudelaire, 1995: p. 93), he eschewed labels and neat categorizations of his writing and resisted the pull of schools and traditions. Rather like the figure of the swan in his poem, Baudelaire was a loner. Gautier duly acknowledges the poet's singularity in his posthumous 'Notice' (1868) to *The Flowers of Evil*, in which he describes Baudelaire as an interstitial figure working a passage between romanticism and modernism. In the 'Notice', he strips the term of some of its opprobrium and epitomizes 'decadence' as the condition of modern man. This type was 'wan, overstrung, writhing, tortured by the fictitious passions and the genuine weariness of modern days', and Baudelaire pursued him 'through the sinuosities of the vast madrepore that is Paris; to watch him in his troubles, his anguish, his wretchedness, his prostration, his excitement, his nervousness, and his despair (Gautier, 1903; vol. XXIII, pp. 45–6).

The concept of decadence gathers momentum in the years following Gautier's 'Notice' as critics and social theorists try to find an explanation for the state of French culture and society, especially after the humiliating defeat of France to the Prussians in 1870–1871. In his essay on Baudelaire, written for a series on 'Contemporary Psychology' in 1881, the positivist critic Paul Bourget reflects on the poet's Parisian libertinism, his ability to distil a 'lubricious ruthlessness that verges on mania' into his poems, his 'sadness and intrinsic humanity' (Bourget, 2009: pp. 93, 94). 'Did not Baudelaire see things more clearly' he asks,

> when he considered a certain brand of melancholy the inevitable product of a divide between our needs as civilized beings and the reality of external causes and conditions? Proof that he did is that, from one end of Europe to the other, contemporary society exhibits the same symptoms, varying according to race, of this melancholy and this dissonance. (p. 95)

In a comparison between the social and moral bankruptcy of contemporary France and imperial Rome, Bourget concludes that their inevitable decline is testament to both the deficiencies and the advantages of a society built around inherited notions of individualism.

Baudelaire's interest in the degenerate individual – road sweepers, prostitutes, absintheurs – derived essentially from his reading of the American poet, critic, and storyteller Edgar Allan Poe, with whom he felt an enormous affinity. Baudelaire first read Poe in 1846 or 1847, and between 1852 and 1865 made extensive translations of his work, including three volumes of short stories, a novel (*The Narrative of Arthur Gordon Pym of Nantucket*), and an essay (*Eureka: A Prose-Poem*). Poe's depictions of a new realm of self-contained psychological obsessions fascinated the

French poet, and in 'The Painter of Modern Life' he makes reference to his story 'The Man of the Crowd' (1840) in which a 'convalescent [...] hurls himself headlong into the midst of the throng, in pursuit of an unknown, half-glimpsed countenance that has, on an instant, bewitched him' (Baudelaire, 1995: p. 7). As Gautier observes in the 'Notice' to *The Flowers of Evil*, Baudelaire described Poe in terms that applied equally to himself:

> He looked upon progress, the great modern idea, as no better than a trap to catch fools, and he called *improvements* in human dwellings rectangular cicatrices and abominations. He believed in the unchanging alone, in the eternal, in the self-same, and he enjoyed the cruel privilege of possessing, in a society in love with itself, that Machiavellian common-sense which goes before the wise man through the desert of history like a pillar of light. (1903: vol. XXIII, p. 43)

Both Poe and Baudelaire regarded their own cultures as barbarian and materialistic, but while Poe focused on the timeless and macabre sensational aspects of madness – a popular theme among readers of the short story – Baudelaire fixated on the complexities and contradictions of modernity.

Baudelaire's splenetic visions of modern Paris find their more satirical counterpart in the novels of Émile Zola (1840–1902), whose Rougon-Macquart series of novels documents the social, political, and economic life of France under the Second Empire. In Zola's novels, Paris is a city where the currencies of sex and money flow fast and furious, where desire for financial gain is synonymous with sexual adventure and conquest. From the wheeling and dealing in the financial areas of the city bustling with investment to the avaricious consumerism in thriving commercial areas lined with *grands magasins* selling luxury goods, Zola depicts the city as fermenting with libidinal energy and greed. At the centre of Zola's novel *La curée* [*The Kill*] (1872), for example, the hothouse in which Renée and Maxime commit incest is a metaphorically powerful symbol of modern decadence in Paris. It is an ambiguous space where roles reverse. In the hothouse Renée adopts a masculine role ('It was above all in the hothouse that Renée was the man') while the effete Maxime is forced to submit to her overpowering animal advances ('She gloated over Maxime, her prey lying beneath her'). In the lush and overheated atmosphere Renée assumes monstrous proportions. She is 'swollen with desire', and her violent and virile kisses 'bloomed and faded like the red flowers of the great mallow, which last scarcely a few hours and are endlessly renewed, like the bruised, insatiable lips of a giant Messalina' (Zola, 2004: pp. 160, 161).

iii

The modern metropolis generated new triumphant artist-types of urban sensibility, notably the flâneur and the dandy (see Chapter 5), but, as Zola and Baudelaire revealed, it also created monsters and victims, individuals with insatiable appetites for luxury and perversion. The figure of '*l'homme moderne*' [modern man] was a symbol of the vitality and exhaustion of modern French life, and Baudelaire, so Paul Verlaine and other contemporary writers attested, was the first writer to render him accurately. 'By this type', Verlaine claimed, 'I mean the physical, modern man, as fashioned by the refinements of an excessive civilisation, the modern man, [. . .] with his finely-honed and vibrant senses, his painfully subtle mind, his tobacco-soaked brain, his blood stewed with alcohol, in a word, the *bilious-neurotic* par excellence, as H. Taine would put it' (1926: vol. II, pp. 8–9; my translation).

This 'bilious-neurotic' type is the main protagonist of Huysmans's *Against Nature*, a compartmentalized and interiorized novel (like many decadent works), structured around a series of well-formed, self-contained scenes that occur to Des Esseintes in the form of memory and recollection. Originally titled *Seul* [Alone], it is the story of a sick, splenetic, world-weary Des Esseintes, the last scion of a noble family who secretes himself away in the Parisian suburb of Fontenay-aux-Roses. Huysmans made several trips to Fontenay with his mistress Anna Meunier in the early 1880s, and in 1881 spent three months there convalescing. It was not his intention to write a decadent novel. Indeed, like Baudelaire, he distrusted the sobriquet for the most part, but his aim was to write an anti-naturalist work of fiction, in which he could meditate on the moral and cultural wasteland that was modern French life. Like Poe, Baudelaire, and Gautier, Huysmans regarded the materialism of modern culture and the rise of the financier and the self-made man as a serious detriment to civilized values, 'blazing, like some ignoble sun, over the idolatrous city which grovelled as it chanted vile canticles of praise before the ungodly tabernacle of the Bank!' (1998: pp. 179–80). Huysmans was appalled by the 'modern aristocracy of wealth', and in a letter to Stéphane Mallarmé, championed Des Esseintes as '[t]he last representative of an illustrious race' (p. ix). Huysmans modelled his hero on various real-life eccentrics, including King Ludwig II of Bavaria, Edmond de Goncourt, Jules Barbey d'Aurevilly, Francis Poictevin, Baudelaire, and most famously, the dandy and aesthete, Robert de Montesquiou. Their homes were monuments to baroque personal fantasies adorned with living reptiles, relics of prehistoric times, and souvenirs of faraway places. Ludwig II owned mechanical lizards that travelled about the painted forests of his rooftop Winter Garden in Munich, while Montesquiou unsuccessfully tried to accommodate a live giant tortoise in his Parisian apartment.

Against Nature opens with the theme of debility and decline. Feeling worn out and attributing his ennui to hereditary degeneracy, Des Esseintes retires from a hectic life of debauchery and dandyism and retreats into a life of luxurious solitude. He goes 'against the grain' – as John Howard translated the French phrase *à rebours* in the first English-language edition of the novel in 1922 – and cuts himself off from the bourgeois masses who he regards as the epitome of philistinism and greed. He surrounds himself with human artistry as he despises all that is natural in the world, preferring instead to live within his designer house, each room decorated to give a sense of limitless adventure and sensation. The static narrative proliferates with paradoxes and ironies. Des Esseintes lives on the outskirts of Paris, 'at a sufficient distance for the tide of Paris to no longer reach him, yet still close enough to the capital to ensure his solitude' (p. 9), and by way of taking nourishment without the mess and bother of oral gratification, he feeds himself *à rebours*, by means of a peptone enema three times a day.

Des Esseintes' disgust for the bourgeois class is vehement and sustained. '[C]onfident and jovial', Des Esseintes reflects to himself, the bourgeois 'was lording it through the power of his money and the contagion of his stupidity' (p. 179). Unlike the flâneur who inhabits the city streets and is a part of the crowd, Des Esseintes incarcerates himself in a museum-house of art and pleasure, a decadent sensorium. He renounces all notions of normal physical wellbeing and basks in the alternating conditions of self-indulgence and self-denial. Unlike Baudelaire who in his ambivalence was, according to Gautier, the decadent poet of a decadent age, Huysmans denounces modernity outright. In *Against Nature*, as Natalie Doyle suggests, 'the hero's sexual impotence becomes the symbol of his *social* impotence. His attempt to transform this death into a total aesthetic experience [the Black Feast in Chapter 1] gives in a nutshell the meaning of the decadent project': *décadence* is 'an attempt to sublimate the artist's social alienation' (Doyle, 1992: 19). No longer able to stomach indigestible modernity, Des Esseintes withdraws and fosters a *culte de moi*.

The concept of decadence embodied by Des Esseintes acquires the attributes of a perverse pathology. Rather like a sufferer of anorexia, who is caught in the dilemma of living without participating fully in life, Des

Esseintes is alienated from society and a sense of healthy self. He is careful and obsessive about what enters his home and his ailing body, creating personal spaces within the rooms of his house that resemble a set of interlocking Japanese boxes that fit one inside the other. He eats his meals 'on a table in the centre of a small room which was separated from his study by a passage-way that was hermetically sealed and also padded, allowing neither odours nor sounds to penetrate the two rooms it served to connect' (Huysmans, 1998: p. 17). As the novel progresses, Des Esseintes' appetites decrease and waves of physical and mental nausea overtake him. While sorting through his beloved books, he is overcome by excessive sweating: 'the sight of the meat which had just then been placed on the table made his gorge rise' (p. 134). The solitude he craves becomes a source of anguish: the 'silence which he used to think of as compensation for the inanities he had listened to for years, now weighed him down like an intolerable burden' (p. 104).

Des Esseintes' resistance to modern life is not passive, however. On the contrary, he actively curates his life, collecting rare books, art, and flowers in an attempt to surround himself with elite pleasures and sensations that drown out the din of urban existence. Like the 'meticulously selected [literary and artistic] works distilled from tormented and subtle intellects', his collection of hothouse plants shows his horticultural connoisseurship. Not content with collecting species of flowers native to France, he purchases 'flowers of high lineage such as orchids, delicate and charming and quiveringly sensitive to cold, exotic flowers exiled in Paris' (p. 72). His collecting takes three forms. He buys rare specimens from the specialist greenhouses in the Avenue de Châtillon and in the Aunay Valley, artificial flowers made from a list of materials found in a theatrical costumier ('gums and threads, percalines and taffetas, papers and velvets'), and 'real flowers that mimicked artificial ones' (p. 73). The plants are unloaded into the house at Fontenay like armies of savages rounded up from colonial outposts. There is the Anthurium from Columbia, the Amorphophallus from Cochin China, the orchid from India, the Fly-trap from the Antilles, and the Cattleya from New Granada. Collected together in Des Esseintes' vestibule, with their 'crossed swords, kris', and 'spear-heads', the plants appear as a barbarian invasion, but it is clear from Des Esseintes' delight in the scene that these plants represent something hopeful. As Eugen Weber comments, 'the increasingly democratic society with its engulfing masses and [...] intellectual limitations' sometimes prompted a 'yearning for liberation sometimes expressed in rebarbarization, but more often against the surrounding "barbarians"' (1982: 15).

Huysmans alludes to a number of cultural crises associated with modernity in *Against Nature*, including declining birth rates, the spread of venereal disease, and immigration, particularly the threat of reverse colonization. He condenses these anxieties in the images of hothouse flowers. The flowers of the Echinopsis, for example, are described as 'the vile pink of amputated stumps', while the Nidularium, has 'saber-shaped leaves opening to reveal flayed, gaping flesh'. Surveying the assembled collection, Des Esseintes reflects on 'the magnificent horrors of their gangrened limbs' (Huysmans, 1998: pp. 75–7). Relishing the thought of the human susceptibility to disease, he concludes 'It all comes down to syphilis':

> And he was struck by a sudden vision of a humanity eternally tormented by the virus of bygone days. Since the beginning of the world, from father to son, all creatures passed on to one another the everlasting legacy, the eternal disease which ravaged the ancestors of man, which actually hollowed out the bones of the old fossils now being exhumed. (p. 77)

The rich dualities that we find in Baudelaire's writings, his ability to accommodate a sense of both exile and belonging in his depictions of the city transform in Huysmans's writings into the denunciation of the hypocrisy and corruption of modern life. Urban life leaves the decadent artist isolated and inward looking, a relic of an ancien régime and an exile of time and place. Ruminating on Gustave Moreau, one of Huysmans's favourite artists, Des Esseintes is reminded of the great art of earlier ages. He is full of admiration for Moreau's pagan mysticism: he was an 'Illuminatus who could sufficiently dissociate himself from the world to see blazing gloriously, in the very heart of Paris, the cruel visions and magical apotheoses of an earlier age' (p. 49). Des Esseintes' self-quarantine in the house at Fontenay, his attempt to enshroud himself in his collections of rare and ancient texts and artworks, keeps the tide of humanity at bay but is a lifestyle that is, ironically, incompatible with life itself. As Patrick McGuinness comments, 'the ascension of the artist to the fabled *tour d'ivoire* [. . .] expresses, in its self-referentiality, a sort of exhaustion-point of poetic subject. This is not the ancient idea of contemplation as learning or enlightenment, but the cannibalistic self-contemplation of world-banishing introspection' (2015: p. 83).

iv

The decadent attitude towards modernity is essentially sceptical and rejecting – it is a 'badge of honour in the war against the soulless materialism of the modern world' (Drake, 1982: 72) – but surveying the attitudes of different French decadents in the second half of the nineteenth century we can detect some significant variation, particularly between the sense of social alienation in Baudelaire and psychological alienation of Huysmans. Whereas for Baudelaire the task of the poet is to straddle the romantic and the modern sensibilities, continually working a passage between the two – 'to distil the eternal from the transitory' (1995: p. 12) – for Huysmans the great artist is continually in retreat from modernity. The Baudelairean concept of decadence is a contradictory world-view labile enough to accommodate the chaos and change of the modern metropolis. Gautier recognized this. In his 'Notice' he credits Baudelaire with having the right aesthetic credentials, arguing that his 'nature was more subtle, complex, logical, paradoxical, and philosophical than that of poets in general' (Gautier, 1903: vol. XXIII, p. 55). For Huysmans, however, while decadence is the only rational response to a modern world hell-bent on the worship of cheap commercialism, it is an unsustainable intellectual gambit impossible to follow through to a satisfactory conclusion.

References

Baudelaire, Charles (1965). The Painter of Modern Life. In *The Painter of Modern Life and Other Essays*, Jonathan Mayne, trans., London and New York: Phaidon, pp. 3–41.

Baudelaire, Charles (1972). *Charles Baudelaire. Selected Writings on Art and Literature*, P. E. Charvet, trans., London: Penguin.

Baudelaire, Charles (1988). *Twenty Prose Poems*, Michael Hamburger, trans., San Francisco: City Lights.

Baudelaire, Charles (1993). *The Flowers of Evil*, James McGowan, trans., Oxford: Oxford University Press.

Benjamin, Walter (1968). On Some Motifs in Baudelaire. In *Illuminations*, Hannah Arendt, ed., New York: Harcourt, Brace, & World, pp. 155–200.

Bourget, Paul (2009). The Example of Baudelaire. Nancy O'Connor, trans., *New England Review*, 30(2), 90–104.

Burton, Richard (1980). *The Context of Baudelaire's 'Le Cygne'*, Durham: University of Durham.

Doyle, Natalie (1992). Against Modernity: The Decadent Voyage in Huysmans's *À rebours*. *Romance Studies*, 21, 15–24.

Drake, Richard (1982). Decadence, Decadentism and Decadent Romanticism in Italy: Toward a Theory of Decadence. *Journal of Contemporary History*, 17(1), 69–92.

Gautier, Théophile (1903). Charles Baudelaire. In vol. XXIII of *The Complete Works of Théophile Gautier*, S. C. de Sumichrast, ed. and trans., New York: George D. Sproul, pp. 17–126.

Goncourt, Edmond and Jules de (1937). *The Goncourt Journals, 1851–1870*, Lewis Galantière, ed. and trans., London, Toronto, Melbourne, Sydney: Cassell.

Hollinghurst, Alan (2009). Introduction. In Georges Rodenbach, *Bruges-la-morte*, Mike Mitchell and Will Stone, trans., Sawtry, Cambs.: Dedalus, pp. 11–19.

Huysmans, Joris-Karl (1998). *Against Nature*, Margaret Mauldon, trans., Oxford: Oxford University Press.

McGuinness, Patrick (2015). *Poetry and Radical Politics in fin de siècle France: From Anarchism to Action française*, Oxford: Oxford University Press.

Terdiman, Richard (2000). Searching for Swans: Baudelaire's 'Le Cygne'. In Laurence M. Porter, ed., *Approaches to Teaching Baudelaire's The Flowers of Evil*, New York: Modern Language Association of America, pp. 115–22.

Verlaine, Paul (1923–1929). *Œuvres posthumes*, 3 vols., Paris: Messein.

Weber, Eugen (1982). Introduction: Decadence on a Private Income. *Journal of Contemporary History*, 17(1), 1–20.

Zola, Émile (2004). *The Kill*, Brian Nelson, trans., Oxford: Oxford University Press.

CHAPTER 7

Decadence and Aesthetics

Sacha Golob

The relationship between decadence and aesthetics is an intimate and complex one. Both the stock figure of the aesthete and the aestheticism of 'art for art's sake' are classic decadent tropes with obvious sources in figures such as Théophile Gautier, Walter Pater, and Joris-Karl Huysmans. Yet the connections between aesthetics and decadence are more conflicted than might first appear: historically, aesthetics has served both as a site for the theorization of decadence and as the basis of an attempt to limit it. The purpose of this chapter is to examine these intricate ties.

Such an examination must begin with Kant's formulation of the aesthetic space, a formulation which, whether evaluated positively or negatively, came to dominate modern discussion. An analysis of the effects of Kant's legacy on writers such as Gautier and Pater necessarily ensues, followed by discussion of the philosopher who placed perhaps the greatest emphasis on decadence and on the importance of art in responding to it: Friedrich Nietzsche. A brief conclusion sketches out some possible lines for further development, lines running though the thought of Martin Heidegger, Theodor Adorno, and Georges Bataille.

Kant and Modern Aesthetics

Nietzsche once mocked Kantian aesthetics for manifesting the 'naïvety of a country parson' and Kant's foundational role in the theorization of decadence is, unsurprisingly, a largely unintentional one (Nietzsche, 1994: p. 79). Kant's writings certainly contain a recognizable model of decadence, embedded within concerns about conflicts between theoretical reason and practical, or moral, reason. The danger, as Kant saw it, was that our intelligence incites and extends desires beyond their natural limits, particularly through acts of comparison (1991: pp. 223–4). Operating in a clearly Rousseauist vein, Kant notes that modern civilization exacerbates this trend, allowing a ceaseless, artificial multiplication of wants: this tendency reaches its peak in the demand for *Üppigkeit* [luxury], a demand that can never be completely satisfied (2011: pp. 96, 117–18). This threat is characterized by Kant in terms familiar from the later rhetoric of decadence: luxury produces 'softness and tenderness' of sense (p. 150). The immediate solution he offers is a form of asceticism: it would be better 'to get free of inclinations and to learn how to do without them' (p. 118).

These remarks on decadence, whilst important for mapping Kant's debts to Rousseau, are not, however, his principal contribution to the development of the concept. That distinction lies rather with his theory of aesthetics. Kant's use of the term 'aesthetics' simultaneously builds on and utterly radicalizes earlier work by the neo-Leibnizians Alexander Baumgarten and Georg Friedrich Meier. Baumgarten understood 'aesthetics' as both '*scientia cognitionis sensitivae*' [the science of sensitive cognition] and '*Wissenschaft des Schönen*' [the science of the beautiful] (Baumgarten, 1986: §1; Baumgarten and Meier 2013: §533).[1] For Kant, the relationship between these two definitions was a delicate one. Indeed, the first *Critique* explicitly takes Baumgarten to task for using the term to 'designate that which others call the critique of taste': Kant's objection, at this point, was that there are no a priori rules governing beauty and thus no possible science of 'aesthetics' so understood (1998: p. 173). Kant therefore initially reserves the term for the a priori study of sensibility, and it is in this context that the first *Critique* introduces the anti-rationalist 'Transcendental Aesthetic' (p. 173). By the time of the *Critique of Judgement* in 1790, however, Kant had reversed course and was now willing to use 'aesthetics' in something very close to the second Baumgarten/Meier definition, to designate the analysis of taste and beauty. It is 'Kantian aesthetics' in this sense which is important in the present context.

Fundamental to Kant's aesthetics is an attempt to separate judgements of taste from other forms of judgement, focusing on the case of beauty. First, judgements of beauty are neither objective nor cognitive: to say that an object is beautiful is not to attribute a property to it, but rather to articulate something of my reaction upon encountering the object.[2] Such judgements thus: '[G]o beyond the concept of the object, and even beyond the intuition

[1] The second remark is Meier's German reformulation of Baumgarten's Latin; the exact relationship between the two authors is contested, but for present purposes we can treat them as one.

[2] The underlying metaphysics here are delicate. It is clear how Kant understands the contrast between judgements of taste and ascriptions of primary qualities such as extension; it is much less clear how judgements of taste differ from, say, colour ascriptions and their objectivity or lack thereof. A closely linked issue arises with respect to non-conceptualism: on the one hand, he declares that 'beauty is not a concept of the object' (Kant, 1987: p. 290); on the other he states that it is an 'indeterminate concept' (Kant, 1987: p. 341).

of the object, and add [. . .] [a] feeling of pleasure (or displeasure)' (Kant, 1987: p. 288).[3] Second, judgements of beauty differ from both instrumental and moral assertions, understood by Kant as claims that something is good for some end or that it is good in itself. This is because a predication of beauty, unlike these other two, requires no concept:

> In order to consider something good, I must always know what sort of thing the object is [meant] to be, i.e., I must have a [determinate] concept of it. But I do not need this in order to find beauty in something. Flowers, free designs, lines aimlessly intertwined and called foliage: these have no significance, depend on no determinate concept, and yet we like [*gefallen*] them. (p. 207)

Third, judgements of beauty are distinguished from judgements based on desire or interest, judgements that I 'like' something, that it 'gratifies' me, that it is 'agreeable' (pp. 205–7). Kant draws this boundary in several ways, but what is clear is his aim in doing so: such judgements lack any claim to universality, since there is no reason that what pleases me should do the same for you:

> As regards the *agreeable* [*des Angenehmen*] everyone acknowledges that his judgement, which he bases on a private feeling and by which he says that he likes some object, is by the same token confined to his own person. Hence, if he says that canary wine is agreeable he is quite content if someone else corrects his terms and reminds him to say instead: It is agreeable to *me*. (p. 212)

In contrast, judgements of taste have a '*subjective* – i.e., aesthetic – *universal* validity, which does not rest on a concept': in asserting that something is beautiful, I demand that others ought to agree with me (pp. 215, 237). One of Kant's great challenges will be to explicate how such 'subjective universality' is possible (p. 214): if a claim is neither factual nor moral nor conceptual, how can it demand assent from others? In doing so, he appeals centrally to what he calls the 'free play' of imagination and understanding, the pleasurable reaction we experience as our faculties respond to the way in which beauty eludes standard conceptual classification (p. 240). In Kantian terms, beauty thus correlates with a particular form of 'synthesis', of mental combination.

Kant Among the Decadents

Kant's analysis is without doubt the dominant moment in modern aesthetics. It is also, much more specifically, one of the key texts in

[3] I use the standard *Akademie* pagination for this text.

understanding the view that has become known as 'aestheticism', a theory whose development was closely aligned with decadence by opponents and supporters. This is not to deny that individual supporters of aestheticism might reject both the term 'decadence' and the views associated with it; for example, Regenia Gagnier seeks to distinguish and valorize Victorian 'aesthetes' (including John Ruskin, William Morris, and Oscar Wilde) precisely by contrasting them with mere 'decadents' (1994: p. 265). My point is rather that aestheticism created the intellectual space for decadence as a concept to develop; as we will now see, it was an intellectual space whose architecture was remarkably Kantian.

First, and most obviously, Kant's view licenses a separation of art from utilitarian or didactic concerns. The Kantian aesthetic defines a distinctive zone of pleasure lacking any external purpose: in Kant's terms, beauty is defined by 'purposiveness' in the absence of any particular purpose (1987: p. 221). There is a clear resonance between this view and the aestheticist doctrine that art is not properly subject to moral or instrumental evaluation. Indeed, in its strongest form, aestheticism treats moral appraisal as radically inappropriate, akin to a category mistake such as asking the colour of the number six: as Wilde put it, '[t]here is no such thing as a moral or an immoral book' (2006: p. 36). Gautier had earlier launched a similar attack on the idea that art should serve some kind of social purpose: 'Nothing is really beautiful unless it is useless; everything useful is ugly, for it expresses a need, and the needs of man are ignoble and disgusting, like his poor weak nature. The most useful place in a house is the toilet' (1981: p. 39). Sloganized, such aestheticism yields the familiar rallying cry of 'art for art's sake'. As Carol Armstrong neatly puts it, Gautier's position amounted to a 'perverse twist on the Kantian notion of the autonomy of the "beautiful"' (2002: p. 402).

Second, Kant's system embeds taste and beauty within a story revolving around our reactions to objects and our awareness of ourselves as sites of a distinctive form of pleasure, a distinctive form of synthesis irreducible to the conceptual. This strand of Kantianism is clearly visible in thinkers such as Pater: as Elizabeth Prettejohn observes, it is thus vital to see Pater's work as supported 'not casually but rigorously by the German tradition of philosophical aesthetics that proceeded from Kant's *Critique of Judgement*' (2007: p. 3). It is thus natural for Pater to begin his *Studies in the History of the Renaissance* by privileging the following questions about art:

> What is this song or picture, this engaging personality presented in life or in a book, to *me*? What effect does it really produce on me? Does it give me pleasure? and if so, what sort or degree of pleasure? How is my nature modified by its presence, and under its influence? (2010: p. 3)

The infamous conclusion to that text likewise showcases the emphasis on synthesis characteristic of Kant's account: objects are 'loosed into a group of impressions, – colour, odour, texture, – in the mind of the observer' (p. 119). The result is a system that combines aestheticism with an emphasis on the fragmentary experience of pleasure through a combination that is neither fully free nor fully determined, one that is 'playful' in Kant's terms. Similar themes are evident in Wilde when, in 'The Critic as Artist', he has Vivian make a deeply Kantian-sounding appeal to: '[T]he aesthetic sense alone, which, while accepting both reason and recognition as stages of apprehension, subordinates them both to a pure synthetic impression of the work of art as a whole' (2001: p. 242). Indeed, Benjamin Morgan has recently suggested that:

> Perhaps what is aesthetic about aestheticism is not just its obsession with 'convulsed sensuousness' or purified ideals, but rather its recognition that physical beauty dramatizes the dilemma of the modern subject who is immersed in the material world, but striving to be free of material contingency. (2010: 749)

Kant's free play of the imagination, an escape from logical stricture, but one necessarily grounded in a dynamic response to sensory input, provides a natural model for such thinking. Kantian aesthetics thus provides some of the central intellectual architecture for aestheticism and so for the theorization of decadence.

Yet Kant's links to decadence are ironic; it is vital to appreciate just how far removed someone like Pater was from Kant's own position. This distance holds even outside the obvious questions of hedonism and morality. As Kate Hext neatly observes, Pater 'valued Kant as a sceptic' (2013: p. 55). The result is that his understanding of the texts is often staggeringly unorthodox. For example, his 'Prosper Mérimée' declares that: 'After Kant's criticism of mind, its pretensions to pass beyond the limits of individual experience seemed as dead as those of old French royalty' (Pater, 1910: p. 1). This fits exactly with the solipsism Pater toys with in the Conclusion to his *Renaissance*. But it is an extraordinary reading of a philosopher whose every effort was dedicated to seeking universal forms of experience – be they the first *Critique*'s categories of the understanding or the third's '*sensus communis*', 'a sense shared [by all of us], i.e., a power to judge that in reflecting takes account (a priori) [...] of everyone else's manner of judging' (Kant, 1987: p. 294).

By far the most important decadent distortion of Kant's philosophy, however, concerns the relationship between aesthetics and morality.

Whilst Kant did indeed seek to distinguish the beautiful from the moral, he also envisaged a vast web of incentives and intimations linking the two. Most obviously, he holds that the divide between beauty and desire allows the beautiful to prepare us for the moral obligation to set aside our mere interest, as he says: 'the beautiful prepares us for loving something, even nature, without interest' (p. 267). The converse also holds: developing and reflecting on moral ideas is the preliminary condition or 'true propaedeutic' for taste (p. 356). To put the point another way, Kant's 'purposiveness without a purpose' is very far removed from Gautier's 'uselessness': for Kant, the awareness of beauty suggests, albeit without proof, that the world is essentially hospitable to us and to the realization of an aim 'independent of all interest', namely morality (p. 167).

Perhaps the deepest explanation for these divergences inheres in Kant's effort in the third *Critique* to unify the various parts of his philosophical system. Kant's successors widely assumed this attempt at unification to be a failure, and, as a result, the carefully calibrated links which Kant had envisaged between domains such as the beautiful and the moral separate. What succeeded them was either the type of full-blown unificatory project beloved of German Idealism on the one hand, or the blunter distinction between aesthetics and morality found in aestheticism on the other. In this sense, what decadence thrives on is not so much the body of Kant's project, but, fittingly, its corpse.

Nietzsche and the 'Decadence Problem'

Nietzsche plays several roles in what one might call the 'genealogy of modern decadence'. He was accused by Max Nordau in his 1892–1893 *Entartung* [*Degeneration*] of supplying its theoretical underpinnings:

> The deification of filth by the Parnassians with ink, paint, and clay; the censing among the Diabolists and Decadents of licentiousness, disease, and corruption; the glorification, by Ibsen, of the person who 'wills,' is 'free' and 'wholly himself' – of all this Nietzsche supplies the theory, or something which proclaims itself as such. (1895: pp. 415–16)

Nordau is cautious about positing an actual line of influence, not least because of some obvious issues of chronology, but he opts instead for a diagnosis on which Nietzsche exemplifies a deep, common malady:

> At the same time it is unquestionable that Nietzsche could not have known the French Decadents and English Æsthetes whom he so frequently approaches, because his books are in part antecedent to those of the latter;

> and neither could they have drawn from him, because, perhaps with the exception of Ibsen, it is only about two years since they could have heard as much as Nietzsche's name. The similarity, or rather identity, is not explained by plagiarism; it is explained by the identity of mental qualities in Nietzsche and the other ego-maniacal degenerates. (p. 444)

This diagnosis is followed by a laughably crude survey of Nietzsche's ideas, held together by Nordau's trademark bluster: Nietzsche is 'a madman, with flashing eyes, wild gestures, and foaming mouth' who 'has not thought out one of his so-called ideas' (pp. 416, 432).

Nietzsche's role in Nordau's text is of interest because it exemplifies the close linkage between cultural decadence and biological degeneration defended therein: Nietzsche, the mad invalid, is the poster boy of a broader, social sickness. But it is, unsurprisingly, Nietzsche's own treatment of decadence that has been of far greater philosophical and cultural import.

Decadence, typically in the French spelling *décadence*, is one of the central targets throughout Nietzsche's work: as he puts it in *The Case of Wagner*, 'the thing I have been most deeply occupied with is the problem of decadence [*das Problem der décadence*]' (2005: p. 233). In *Ecce Homo*, he saw himself as a potential turning point, both the scion of a decadent culture and an alternative to it, someone who 'know[s] both' because 'I am both [. . .] simultaneously decadent and *beginning*' (p. 75). He continues:

> My task, preparing for humanity's moment of highest self-examination, a *great noon* when it will look back and look out, when it will escape from the domination of chance and priests and, for the first time, pose the question 'why?', the question 'what for?' *as a whole* –, this task follows necessarily from the insight that humanity has *not* put itself on the correct path, that it has absolutely *no* divine governance, that instead, the instinct of negation, of corruption, the decadence-instinct [*décadence-Instinkt*], has been seductively at work, and precisely under humanity's holiest value concepts. (p. 121)

As is suggested here, Nietzsche fundamentally understands decadence in terms of life-denial:

> The wisest men in every age have reached the same conclusion about life: *it's no good* . . . Always and everywhere, you hear the same sound from their mouths, – a sound full of doubt, full of melancholy, full of exhaustion with life, full of resistance to life. Even Socrates said as he died: 'living – that means being sick for a long time: I owe Asclepius the Saviour a rooster.' – What does this *prove*? What does it *demonstrate*? [. . .] 'There has to be some *sickness* here' – is what *we* will reply: these wisest men of all ages, let us start

> looking at *them* more closely! Perhaps they had become a bit unsteady on their feet? Perhaps they were late? doddering? decadent? (p. 162)

As Michael Silk summarizes, '[f]or Nietzsche, decadence is any kind of saying no to life' (2004: p. 594). Indeed, Nietzsche undertook to map the threat of decadence in both Greek and Christian culture in immense detail.

In the case of Greek culture, for Nietzsche the key to decadence is Socrates: he sees both Socratic rationalism and the disdain for life expressed in the dying words of the philosopher as symptomatic of a declining, weary instinct: 'My readers might know the extent to which I see dialectics as a symptom of decadence [*Décadence-Symptom*], in the most famous case of all, for instance: the case of Socrates' (2005: p. 75). The first accusation here is that Socratic dialectic arose out of an inability to embrace and tolerate the tragic nature of life, instead seeking refuge in an illusion of control where virtue, knowledge, and happiness neatly align:

> Conversely, those things which gave rise to the death of tragedy – Socratism in ethics, the dialectics, smugness and cheerfulness of theoretical man – might not this very Socratism be a sign of decline, of exhaustion, of sickness, of the anarchic dissolution of the instincts? [. . .] For the virtuous hero must now be a dialectician; there must now be a necessary, visible connection between virtue and knowledge, faith and morality[.] (Nietzsche, 1999: pp. 4, 70)

Platonic idealism provides the metaphysical accompaniment to this weakness by sanctifying another world sanitized of the imperfections of this one: Socrates and Plato are thus 'agents of Greek disintegration' (Nietzsche, 2005: p. 162).[4] A second charge is that Socratic methods allowed 'the rabble', particularly those unable or unwilling to engage in open combat, to subvert and ultimately 'humiliate' a noble culture, one in which '[n]othing with real value needs to be proved first' (p. 164). Socratic rationalism is thus an (all too) human power play, a triumph of one set of instincts over another, a victory for 'plebeian *ressentiment* [resentment]' (p. 164).

The advance of decadence is famously established for Nietzsche with the coming of Christianity: 'From the very outset Christianity was essentially

[4] Depending on the context, Nietzsche alternately emphasizes Socrates' agency in bringing about this degeneration or his status as a symptom of an already ongoing decline. For example, in the early period, *The Birth of Tragedy* commends Aristophanes for 'scent[ing] the characteristics of a degenerate culture' in Socrates, Euripides, and 'the music of the new exponents of the dithyramb' (Nietzsche, 1999: p. 83). Similarly, *Twilight of the Idols* describes Socrates as recognizing his own decadence as mirrored in society at large: '[H]e understood that *his* case, his idiosyncrasy of a case was not an exception any more. The same type of degeneration was quietly gaining ground everywhere: old Athens was coming to an end' (Nietzsche, 2005: p. 165).

and pervasively the feeling of disgust and weariness which life felt for life' (1999: p. 9). Christ is thus 'this most interesting decadent' (Nietzsche, 2005: p. 28) and the task of the priest is to cultivate these nay-saying, anti-life instincts (p. 122) – for example, by encouraging the slave revolt chronicled in *On the Genealogy of Morality*. One sees here a central aspect of Nietzsche's model of decadence: it identifies an unavoidable set of instincts – weariness, *ressentiment*, weakness – which are present in all cultures and yet which have come to dominate in some.

> Decadence belongs to all epochs of mankind . . .
>
> Decadence itself is nothing to fight against. It is absolutely necessary, and belongs to every age and every people. What should be fought with all one's might is the creeping contagion of the healthy parts of the organism . . . (Nietzsche, 1968: pp. 184–5)

Silk elegantly captures the main point: 'For Nietzsche, decadence exists in any age, but in the modern age it is dominant, and in the modern age, accordingly, any positive move must involve constructive confrontation with it' (2004: p. 595).

Nietzsche: Aesthetics and the Response to Decadence

How is such a 'constructive confrontation' to occur? Nietzsche employs a huge range of tools, from genealogy to the deliberate creation of new values, in his attempt to reverse the dominance of decadence. But the present context demands discussion of art, particularly art understood within a broadly aesthetic framework.

There are two examples that are particularly important here. The first is the appeal in *The Birth of Tragedy* to Greek theatre and ultimately to the Wagnerian *Gesamtkunstwerk* [total work of art] as a means of combating decadence. Nietzsche frames his project as an exercise in 'the science of aesthetics' that promises to offer an 'aesthetic' justification for life, a way of reconciling ourselves to it and embracing it, rather than distorting and denying it as Socratic tradition supposedly does (1999: p. 14); in short, 'our highest dignity lies in our significance as works of art – for only as an *aesthetic phenomenon* is existence and the world eternally *justified*' (p. 33). The details of Nietzsche's original argument here are deeply interwoven with a Schopenhauerian metaphysics that he later came to satirize for treating music as a 'telephone to the beyond' (1994: p. 78). But what is vital for current purposes is that art, once one has grasped its twin Apollonian and Dionysiac aspects, is the key means to reversing the decline instituted by Socrates and allowing a justification of the world that avoids his rationalism.

The second and related case is Nietzsche's later emphasis on self-creation: by this point, aesthetic justification is no longer a matter of music or theatre specifically but of a broader self-stylization: 'As an aesthetic phenomenon existence is still *bearable* for us, and art furnishes us with the eyes and hands and above all the good conscience to be *able* to turn ourselves into such a phenomenon' (Nietzsche, 2001: p. 104). This project is framed in terms that would have been eminently recognizable to aesthetes in both London and Paris: we must become 'poets of our life' (p. 170). Again, art is the key vehicle for escaping decadence, although it is also a risky one. There is always a danger that '[t]he ceaseless desire to create on the part of the artist, together with his ceaseless observation of the world outside him, prevent him from becoming better and more beautiful as a person, that is to say from creating *himself*' (Nietzsche, 1996: p. 236). There is a highly aestheticist ring to this. Yet it is vital to see that Nietzsche cannot subscribe to the 'art for art's sake' slogan: the cultural mission he ascribes to art is too important to allow that; its task is to recreate a 'yea-saying' culture in the face of Socratic and Christian denial: 'Art is the great stimulus to life: how could it be understood as purposeless, pointless, *l'art pour l'art*?' (Nietzsche, 2005: p. 204)

So far, a relatively simple model of the relationship between aesthetics and decadence is evident in Nietzsche's philosophy: crudely put, the former is a potential mechanism for fighting the latter. Yet, as throughout his work, Nietzsche's full position is both more conflicted and more interesting than such a summary would suggest. The best way to understand just how complex Nietzsche's view of decadence was is to examine his analysis of the man he came to call a 'typical decadent', the man who 'has made music sick' – Richard Wagner (Nietzsche, 2005: pp. 241, 242).

Nietzsche, Wagner, and the Ambiguous Status of Art

In *The Birth of Tragedy*, Wagner was very much a part of the solution to the problem of decadence. By *The Case of Wagner* in 1888, however, Nietzsche had come to see the composer as the highpoint of contemporary decadence; as we will see, this shift also illustrates the multi-faceted nature of that concept for Nietzsche.

Nietzsche sees Wagner as gradually aligning himself with precisely the decadent life-denial found in Christianity. *Parsifal* is the most obvious case, and the degeneration on display there is considered so extreme by Nietzsche that he toys with the idea of its being deliberately ironic:

> We might be tempted to assume[,] even to wish, – that Wagner's *Parsifal* was meant to be funny, like an epilogue, or satyr play with which the tragedian Wagner wanted to take leave of us, of himself and above all of *tragedy* in a manner fitting and worthy of himself, namely by indulging in an excessive bout of the most extreme and deliberate parody of the tragic itself, of the whole, hideous, earthly seriousness and misery from the past, of the finally defeated, *crudest form* of perversion, of the ascetic ideal. [. . .] it would be nice to think so: because what would an *intentionally serious* Parsifal be like? [. . .] A curse on the senses and the mind in one breath of hate? An apostasy and return to sickly Christian and obscurantist ideals? (Nietzsche, 1994: p. 74)

Such, Nietzsche suggests, is indeed the case: late Wagner possesses 'a secret desire' to 'preach a straightforward reversion, conversion, denial, Christianity, medievalism' (p. 75).

The Wagner case illustrates the full range of Nietzsche's understanding of the concept of decadence. First, he presents it in physiological and psychological terms. '*Wagner est une névrose*': Wagner is a neurosis, whose 'art is sick' (Nietzsche, 2005: p. 242). In line with this diagnosis, Wagnerian music spreads decadence through 'convulsions' and a theatrical excess that uses 'music to stimulate tired nerves' (p. 242). This assessment echoes Nietzsche's diagnosis of the priest in *On the Genealogy of Morality* as manipulating an 'excess of feeling' to simultaneously anaesthetize and exhaust his subjects (1994: p. 101). Second, decadence is a stylistic phenomenon:

> For the moment, I am only going to look at the question of style. – What is the hallmark of all *literary* decadence? [. . .] Life, *equal* vitality, the vibration and exuberance of life pushed back into the smallest structures, all the rest *impoverished* of life. [. . .] The whole does not live at all any more: it is cobbled together, calculated, synthetic, an artifact. (Nietzsche, 2005: p. 245)

Wagner, as the perfect decadent, was thus the perfect 'miniaturist' (p. 246). Third, decadence is inescapably a political issue. Faced with the 'anarchy' of his own instincts, Socrates sought to tyrannize them through rationality; resentful of the Athenian nobles and conscious of his own ugliness, he sought revenge by dialectic (p. 163). Similarly, Wagner is '[a] typical decadent, who has a sense of necessity in his corrupted taste, who uses it to lay claim to a higher taste, who knows how to enforce his corruption as a law, as progress, as fulfilment' (p. 241). Wagnerian decadence for Nietzsche is thus a profound physiological, stylistic, and political threat: in it, one of the key means to combat decadence, art, has become subordinated to it. Yet while Wagner comes to exemplify this threat, it is one with important parallels in Nietzsche's own thought. There is a persistent concern in Nietzsche that, by beautifying life, art serves simultaneously as incentive to embrace it and as a way of escaping its realities. Crudely put, is it truly affirmation if what one affirms is whitewashed? In *The Birth of Tragedy*, this anxiety is managed by appeal to the supposedly metaphysical insights granted by the Dionysiac and preserved within Greek theatre's fusion of Dionysiac and Apollonian moments. Without such a fusion, without the Dionysiac dimension, art itself risks degeneration into:

> an amusing sideshow [. . .] – where music is deprived of its true dignity, which consists in being a Dionysiac mirror of the world, so that all that remains to music, as the slave of the world of appearances, is to imitate the forms of the world of appearances and to excite external pleasure in the play of line and proportion. (Nietzsche, 1999: pp. 14, 93)

As noted, the Schopenhauerian metaphysics of the 'Dionysiac mirror' are rapidly abandoned by Nietzsche, but the basic problem remains.

On the one hand, he wants to applaud art as that in which '*lying* sanctifies itself and the *will to deception* has good conscience on its side' (Nietzsche, 1994: p. 121). This illusion is vital in a situation where 'honesty would lead to nausea and suicide' (Nietzsche, 2001: p. 104). As he puts it in a famous note, we thus 'possess art lest we perish of the truth' (Nietzsche, 1968: p. 435). On the other hand, however, such 'rounding off' of reality is closely linked to its denial (Nietzsche, 2001: p. 107):

> Perhaps there is even an order of rank for these wounded children, the born artists, who find pleasure in life only by intending to falsify its image, in a sort of prolonged revenge against life –. We can infer the degree to which life has been spoiled for them from the extent to which they want to see its image distorted, diluted, deified, and cast into the beyond – considered as artists, the *homines religiosi* [religious men] would belong to the highest rank. (Nietzsche, 2002: p. 53)

In short, Nietzsche alternately presents art as both the solution to decadence and as just another of its guises. It is the former moment which leads him to question whether Wagner 'was even a musician' as opposed to a mere actor or a physiologist, practising the 'corruption of the nerves' (Nietzsche, 2005: pp. 247, 257). It is the latter which leads him to warn of 'the artists of decadence, who fundamentally have a *nihilistic* attitude toward life [and] take *refuge* in the *beauty of form*' (Nietzsche, 1968: p. 450).

Three Lines of Development

The focus on Kant, Pater, and Nietzsche is justified because their systematic aesthetics is profoundly interconnected with the conceptual development of decadence. Conceivably, the rich matrix of decadence and aesthetics might be further understood by extension along three separate but potentially related vectors of development.

The first would be to pressure the notion of the 'aesthetic': what precisely marks an 'aesthetic' theory in contrast to a philosophy of art more broadly construed? After all, a number of twentieth-century thinkers offer detailed philosophies of art that actively reject the term: Heidegger, for example (1981: pp. 80–4). This is a deeply complex question and the answer will depend on whether one starts from a Kantian or a Hegelian conception of aesthetics. But one option would be to align aesthetics with a spectatorial approach, an emphasis on the viewer, rather than the creator of an artwork. The choice between an aesthetics of decadence as opposed to a more broadly decadent philosophy of art might then be developed in dialogue with the idea of self-curation, touched on above, that one sees in Nietzsche and in authors such as Wilde.

The second option would be to retain the term 'aesthetics' and explicitly insert the 'decadence problem' and its history into the work of those twentieth-century authors whose 'decadence' is no longer a central explanatory category, even if it still carries some of the old rhetorical force. Adorno is an obvious candidate: at the most basic level, 'decadence' and 'decadent' occur only a few times in his *Aesthetic Theory*, less than on many of Nietzsche's single pages. It would be interesting, in particular, to see how the complex social role which Adorno allows for autonomous art might ground a resistance to decadence or serve as a site for its development and play.

The third possibility would be to go back to Kantian aesthetics and to focus on those aspects left out of the narrative above, aspects such as the sublime. That concept played a relatively limited role in Kant's unintentional contributions to nineteenth-century work on decadence. But some of the thinkers one could easily align with decadence in the twentieth century rely on something close to a 'transgressive sublime': Bataille would be a natural case to focus on – provided, of course, one preserves the full range of ambiguities in both 'natural' and 'case'.

The aim of this chapter has been to chart the relationship between decadence and aesthetics, beginning with a kind of Kantian paternity that Kant himself would certainly have disavowed. This Kantian inheritance is at once appropriated and deformed in writers such as Gautier and Pater. By the time of Nietzsche, both the philosopher and art itself are deeply implicated in the ambiguity of decadence: each is simultaneously a product of it and the potential solution to the problem it poses. Finally, as any of the three additional approaches sketched out above shows, the relationship between decadence and aesthetics remains both intimate and conflicted.

References

Armstrong, Carol (2002). Art Criticism and Aesthetic Ideals. In Martin Kemp, ed., *The Oxford History of Western Art*, Oxford: Oxford University Press, pp. 400–3.

Baumgarten, Alexander (1986). *Aesthetica*, Hildesheim: Olms.

Baumgarten, Alexander, and Georg Friedrich Meier (2013). *Metaphysics*, Courtney D. Fugate and John Hymers, trans., London: Bloomsbury.

Gagnier, Regenia (1994). Critique of Practical Aesthetics. In George Levine, ed., *Aesthetics and Ideology*, New Brunswick, NJ: Rutgers University Press, pp. 264–82.

Gautier, Théophile (1981). *Mademoiselle de Maupin*, Joanna Richardson, trans., New York: Penguin.

Heidegger, Martin (1981). *Nietzsche: Volume One*, David Farrell Krell, trans., London: Routledge and Kegan Paul.

Hext, Kate (2013). *Walter Pater: Individualism and Aesthetic Philosophy*, Edinburgh: Edinburgh University Press.

Kant, Immanuel (1987). *Critique of Judgement*, Werner S. Pluhar, trans., Indianapolis: Hackett.

Kant, Immanuel (1991). *Political Writings*, Hans Reiss, ed., H. B. Nisbet, trans., 2nd edn, Cambridge: Cambridge University Press.

Kant, Immanuel (1998). *Critique of Pure Reason*, Paul Guyer, trans., Cambridge: Cambridge University Press.

Kant, Immanuel (2011). *Observations on the Feeling of the Beautiful and Sublime and Other Writings*, Patrick Frierson and Paul Guyer, eds., Cambridge: Cambridge University Press.

Morgan, Benjamin (2010). Aesthetic Freedom: Walter Pater and the Politics of Autonomy. *ELH*, 77(3), 731–56.

Nietzsche, Friedrich (1968). *The Will to Power*, Walter Kaufmann and R. J. Hollingdale, trans., New York: Random House.

Nietzsche, Friedrich (1994). *On the Genealogy of Morality*, Carol Diethe, trans., Cambridge: Cambridge University Press.

Nietzsche, Friedrich (1996). *Human, All Too Human*, R. J. Hollingdale, trans., Cambridge: Cambridge University Press.

Nietzsche, Friedrich (1999). *The Birth of Tragedy*, Ronald Speirs, trans., Cambridge: Cambridge University Press.

Nietzsche, Friedrich (2001). *The Gay Science*, Josefine Nauckhoff, trans., Cambridge: Cambridge University Press.

Nietzsche, Friedrich (2002). *Beyond Good and Evil*, Judith Norman, trans., Cambridge: Cambridge University Press.

Nietzsche, Friedrich (2005). *The Anti-Christ, Ecce Homo, Twilight of the Idols, and Other Writings*, Aaron Ridley and Judith Norman, eds., Judith Norman, trans., Cambridge: Cambridge University Press.

Nordau, Max (1895). *Degeneration*, New York: Appleton.

Pater, Walter (1910). *Miscellaneous Studies*, London: Macmillan.

Pater, Walter (2010). *Studies in the History of the Renaissance*. Oxford: Oxford University Press.

Prettejohn, Elizabeth (2007). *Art for Art's Sake: Aestheticism in Victorian Painting*, New Haven, CT: Yale University Press.

Silk, Michael (2004). Nietzsche, Decadence, and the Greeks. *New Literary History*, 35, 587–605.

Wilde, Oscar (2001). The Critic as Artist. In Linda Dowling, ed., *The Soul of Man Under Socialism and Selected Critical Prose*, London: Penguin, pp. 213–79.

Wilde, Oscar (2006). *The Picture of Dorian Gray*, Oxford: Oxford University Press.

PART II

Developments

CHAPTER 8

Decadence and the Visual Arts

Laura Moure Cecchini

A gloating woman in a red dress with a bodice that exposes her breasts triumphantly raises a broken marionette in one hand while holding a dagger in the other (fig. 8.1). She has used the dagger to slice open the torso of the puppet, dressed in the finery of an upper-class gentleman of the fin de siècle – tuxedo, top hat, monocle, and cane. The disembowelled torso oozes golden coins, which fall into a fountain decorated with a snake – a biblical image associated with female temptation. A jester holding a skull-topped marotte sits at her feet, at the edge of the pedestal on which she stands; his wings indicate that he is actually Eros, the god of love, transformed into an agent of death rather than passion. On the front of the pedestal, representatives of traditional masculine occupations – a painter, a musician, an intellectual, a soldier – are depicted as marionettes, like the one she is holding. In 1885 the Belgian artist Félicien Rops painted this watercolour, titled *The Woman with the Puppet*, as a response to the question 'Ubi mulier?' [Where is the woman?] chiselled on the pedestal. Here she is, Rops responds, manipulating man and exploiting him for his money. Sexual desire has led to humiliation and death.

Another image: a self-portrait etching by Julio Ruelas, a Mexican painter and printmaker, shows a male head cropped at the neck (fig. 8.2), looking downward, with dark bags under his eyes, a furrowed brow, and lips slightly parted. His forehead is about to be pierced by the sharp beak of a grotesque winged creature wearing a top hat, with bird feet clad in garters but with human hands and breasts. Spouting from its hat are what appear to be foul secretions or flames. In one of its hands, this strange creature holds a ruler, with which it is about to measure Ruelas' cranium. Titled *Criticism* (1906–1907) and made in the last year of Ruelas' life, after he had moved to Paris, the etching gives form to the torment of any artist or intellectual who has ever felt misunderstood but cannot afford to ignore the views of those who have the power to influence public opinion.

Fig. 8.1 Félicien Rops's watercolour *The Woman with the Puppet* (1885) presents the decadent image of woman as a femme fatale who uses sex to manipulate and destroy men [Musée Rops, Namur].

Fig. 8.2 Julio Ruelas' *Criticism* (1906–1907) is a self-portrait conveying the pain endured by the artist whose work is judged without being understood [Museo Nacional de Arte in Mexico, Mexico City].

Femmes fatales and tortured artists: two iconographies that suggest decadence. Corruption, degradation, perversion, decline, degeneration – all these terms belong to the conceptual constellation of 'decadence', a word 'annoyingly resistant to definition' (Weir, 1995: p. 1) that often connotes dissolute behaviour but is also used to characterize literature and visual arts that defy bourgeois conventions. Amado Nervo's description of the work of Ruelas – 'an inspiration that takes pleasure in the shadow, the anguish, the torment [. . .], a phantasmagorical world of torture' (1903: 82; my translation) – could be applied to that of many other artists working during the fin de siècle on both sides of the Atlantic. The word 'decadent' – 'at once allusive and elusive' (Flint, 1980: p. 4) – defies precise definition but is an ineluctable descriptor of a wide range of visual productions at the fin de siècle.

Despite the importance of fin-de-siècle conceptualizations of decadence in literature, intellectual consideration of what the term might mean in the visual arts was rare during the period. Although there were many contemporaneous commentaries on what was implied by the notion of decadence in literature – a genealogy that began with Désiré Nisard's *Études de moeurs et de critique sur les poètes latins de la décadence* [Cultural-critical studies of the Latin poets of the decadence] (1834), continued with the writings of Théophile Gautier (1835 and 1868), Charles Baudelaire (1857), and culminated in Paul Bourget's *Essais de psychologie contemporaine* [Essays on contemporary psychology] (1883) – an equivalent examination of decadence in relation to the visual arts was not clearly articulated.

In *Esthètes et magiciens* (1969; translated 1971 as *Dreamers of Decadence*), one of the few books explicitly devoted to the idea of decadence in the visual arts, Philippe Jullian discussed fin-de-siècle artists who painted images of 'satanism, dandyism, exoticism, and above all eroticism – in fact everything the bourgeois regarded as decadent' (1975: p. 28). This broad understanding of decadence enabled Jullian to analyse artists as different as Lawrence Alma-Tadema, William Bouguereau, and Pierre Puvis de Chavannes, as well as more canonical decadent artists such as Fernand Khnopff, Odilon Redon, Jean Delville, and Félicien Rops. However, at the same time as his book expands the meaning of decadence to include most artists working at the time, both Jullian's original subtitle – *l'art fin de siècle* – and the one used in the translation – *Symbolist Painters of the 1890s* – restrict it. Why exclude artists working beyond that time frame? And how might one differentiate between symbolism and decadence, terms that are very close but do not entirely overlap?

To understand decadence in art, one must consider three important ways in which the concept was used in relation to late nineteenth- and early twentieth-century visual culture: its application in art history; its association with specific styles, themes, and subject matter, especially in the iconography of women; and the rediscovery by decadents of mannerist and baroque artists whose work resonated with the fin-de-siècle worldview.

Art History and the Concept of Decadence

Notions of decadence, decline, and decay are intrinsically linked to the history of art. The discipline's three recognized forefathers – Giorgio Vasari, Johann Joachim Winckelmann, and Heinrich Wölfflin – all relied on the concept of decadence (and its antonym, progress) to make sense of the history of the visual arts and to evaluate the art of their times. A developmental model of art was central to the interpretative schemes of these art historians. In their organicist view, earlier developments prepare the stage for what comes later; and after a particular style flourishes for a time, its decline is inevitable as newer styles overtake it.

Vasari's *Lives of the Most Eminent Painters, Sculptors, and Architects*, the first edition of which was published in 1550, postulated an evolution of art from the thirteenth to the sixteenth centuries, from 'good' to 'better' to 'best' (or 'divine') – from Giotto to Michelangelo. For Vasari, art evolved until it reached the High Renaissance, after which it underwent a devolution through the undoing of ideal form. In the twentieth century, E. H. Gombrich addressed how this Renaissance idea of progress engendered a peculiar mentality in artists: no longer seeing themselves as mere tradesmen or craftsmen, they felt the need to experiment in order to solve certain aesthetic problems, and they addressed themselves to the small cultural elite who appreciated their talent (1966: p. 7). Still, Vasari's model expressed a pessimistic outlook: if artists born after him accepted the opinion that Michelangelo was the acme of artistic development, what could they aspire to?

In 'Thoughts on the Imitation of Greek Works in Painting and Sculpture' (1755), 'Essay on the Beautiful in Art' (1763), and *The History of Art in Antiquity* (1764), Winckelmann also employed the familiar narrative of origin, high point, and decline (or archaic, classical, and decadent periods) to articulate the evolution of art from the Greeks to the baroque and the rococo. Instead of focusing on patronage, political context, or the artist's biography, Winckelmann narrated the history of art as the story of the rise, fall, and recovery of the style that he believed to be superior to all the rest: classicism.

Applying the category of style in a systematic way to the entire history of Western art, Winckelmann divided Greek art into distinct periods and evaluated them on the basis of ahistorical standards of beauty. As Alex Potts has observed, Winckelmann was 'the first historian of art [. . .] to insist that all art produced by a tradition after its classical period would normally be inferior, that the logic of a larger historical imperative would inevitably override the efforts of individual artists and individual patrons to revive a flagging tradition, however well intentioned' (1994: p. 39). Although Winckelmann's outlook was more optimistic than Vasari's because it left open the possibility that good art would be produced again, such art could not be original: for Winckelmann, good art could only be the art that imitated the Ancients.

Notions of decadence and decay appear prominently in the preface to the first edition of Heinrich Wölfflin's *Renaissance and Baroque* (1888), a book that catalysed the study of art as an academic discipline worthy of occupying a space in the nineteenth-century university. Describing his subject as 'the disintegration of the Renaissance' and his goal as being to 'investigate the symptoms of decay', Wölfflin's book seems, at first glance, to continue the negative assessment of the period after the Renaissance, which was key to both Vasari's and Winckelmann's narratives (1964: n.p.). However, Wölfflin's analysis of the relationship between the classical and the baroque, between form and its undoing, is much more complex. Indeed, although he seems to consider Renaissance architecture as more orderly, human, and perhaps morally superior to baroque architecture, for Wölfflin the latter is as artistically important as the former.

To explain why the baroque followed the Renaissance, Wölfflin famously relied on a history of styles, rather than a history of individual artists. Using stylistic observations, he attempted to extrapolate a form of cultural psychology that analysed the specific ways in which, through time, societies related to the world around them and experienced space. For Wölfflin, the baroque coincided with the liberation from classical rules and mandates. Unlike the Renaissance, the baroque eschewed regularity and loved variation. Shunning rationality, it sought emotional engagement and immediacy. Rather than stillness and serenity, baroque architecture looked for movement and dynamism. And instead of seeing itself as dependent upon and inevitably inferior to tradition, the baroque was aware of the value of its own time.

Unlike Winckelmann, Wölfflin regarded the baroque as the style of his time: the music dramas of Richard Wagner were for him an example of the baroque love for the fleeting, the rejection of tradition, and the appeal to emotions (p. 87). Periods associated in the past with decadence were no longer to be rejected, but rather recognized as having the strongest affinity with the fin de siècle.

In 1894, the Italian literary critic Enrico Nencioni formulated this idea in a more extensive way (without, in all likelihood, having read Wölfflin's book). In a lecture given in Florence he argued that the baroque 'is essentially *modern* in its passionate search for novelty at all costs'. Though not an art historian, Nencioni organized his argument using art-historical references and according to an art-historical mode of thinking; and his final assessment overturned the notion of decadence as a form of shame about the present that Vasari and Winckelmann had put forward. 'Forget for a moment the *Manuals,* the lessons, the *Guides,* and what one *should* say and what one *should* admire', Nencioni urged. 'Look with your own eyes, think with your own head, and feel with your own heart. And *maybe* you'll feel closer to Bernini's Daphne than to the Juno in Villa Ludovisi; to Saint Theresa than to the Capitoline Venus' (1897: p. 297; my translation).

Nencioni carefully organized his arguments to persuade his readers to reassess their opinion of the baroque. He emphasized the ambivalence inherent in the baroque style, noting that the love for novelty associated with it had led artists into a state of delirium but had also produced truly original artworks. He then asked readers to reflect on the constructed nature of their aesthetic preferences: if the public freed itself from the prejudices ingrained by centuries of classical education, would they not appreciate baroque art? He explained the 'naturalness' of this appreciation, as opposed to the 'cultural' origin of the love for the classical, by pointing out the similarities between the baroque and the modern period. Nencioni concluded: 'We are all today quite barbaric, quite Byzantine, quite baroque', because 'our life is always artificial and always agitated: the nervous organism is continuously overexcited and is always restless and eager for new, strange, and excessive sensations' (p. 297; my translation). Decadence is, inevitably but proudly, the style of the present.

This brief narrative from Vasari to Nencioni shows how art history – as an academic discipline and a mode of evaluating visual culture – required the idea of decadence. Assessments of value and judgements of taste relied on the biological model of birth/growth/decay to distinguish between worthwhile and unworthy art forms. What changed during the fin de siècle, however, was that certain art historians and critics ceased to consider decay as something negative that should be overcome. They did not regard the present as necessarily inferior to the past and, contrary to Winckelmann, argued that it was useless to fight against contemporary trends by imitating the Greeks. Rather, like their counterparts in the arts and literature, art historians proudly appropriated an anti-classical, anti-rational taste as a mark of the originality and distinctiveness of contemporary styles.

Decadence and Fin-de-Siècle Artists

While visual artists were cultivating an aesthetic that was antithetical to inherited norms, art historians rediscovered and revalued periods of decadence by challenging what decadence meant and by asking whether it should always be rejected. Which should be considered the determining criterion for decadence – form or subject matter? 'There are no historical contents that can be characterized as decadent "in themselves"', wrote Vladimir Jankélevich in 1950, 'Decadence is not *in statu* but *in motu*' (quoted in Calinescu, 1987: p. 155). The same could be said of the formal features of decadent art: because notions of decadence appeared in the visual arts over a long period of time and in multiple geographic contexts, it is almost impossible to pinpoint stylistic markers that are specifically decadent. Yet certain aesthetic traits are commonly associated with notions of decadence: an excessive formal richness, the portrayal of depraved and hedonistic pleasures, an overall sense of corruption and erotic charge.

An emphasis on precious details at the expense of the whole was regarded in the 1880s as the mark of the 'style of decadence' in literature: 'the fact that life does not reside in the totality any more', as Friedrich Nietzsche observed (2005: p. 245), and the work does not have a cogent, rational, and unified organization. The text becomes fragmented, dominated by an aesthetics of decomposition. Nietzsche's assessment, elaborated in relation to literature, applies to decadent visual arts as well.

Huysmans's novel *À rebours* [*Against Nature*] (1884) articulated a set of tropes that gave visual form to the idea of decadence, identifying it with morbidity, precious detail, and carnality. The protagonist of *Against Nature,* Duc Jean Floressas Des Esseintes, lives a life of refined aestheticism, cultivating only those pleasures that stimulate his senses in contrarian fashion by going against the grain of anything perceived as normal or natural. Des Esseintes' dissatisfaction with contemporary times is emphasized by his physical removal from urban life, his pursuit of solitude, and his cultivation of tastes that run counter to the mainstream of nineteenth-century bourgeois society.

To identify the characteristics of decadent style, one has only to refer to the real-life late nineteenth-century artists named in the text of *Against Nature.* Huysmans has Des Esseintes say that he found in Odilon Redon and Gustave Moreau the fulfilment of decadent sensibility; and Chapter VI of *Against Nature* contains lengthy descriptions of Moreau's *Salomé Dancing before Herod* and *The Apparition* (both painted between 1874 and 1876). Des Esseintes finds in Moreau's 'architectonic mixtures, his

Fig. 8.3 Gustave Moreau's *Salomé Dancing before Herod* (1874–1876) may be the one painting most closely associated with nineteenth-century decadence [Hammer Museum, Los Angeles].

sumptuous and unexpected combinations of dress materials and his hieratic allegories [a] sinister quality [. . .] heightened by the morbid perspicuity of an entirely modern sensibility' (Huysmans, 2003: p. 56). The jewel-like *Salomé* (fig. 8.3), in particular, became a stylistic prototype of decadence in the visual arts. The encrusted surface of the painting is rich with detail; the objects in Herod's palace – the lamps, throne, columns – as well as the figures' clothes are painted in minute detail. Herod and the servant tasked with executing John the Baptist are hieratic, their facial expressions cast in shadows. The light plays on Salomé's ashen skin, especially on her face and outstretched arm. Her body, however, despite being the source of temptation for both John and Herod, is almost evanescent, but appears weighted down by strangely substantial veils. Although some objects are painted with vivid colours (the red in Salomé's sleeve and parts of her dress, the lapis lazuli adorning the column at the right), the overall impression is that of looking at the interior of a temple dimmed by incense.

The extensive descriptions in *Against Nature* make Moreau's paintings vivid in the mind of the reader. The two paintings were purchased by private collectors shortly after being exhibited in Paris at the Universal Exposition of 1878, making them unavailable to viewers except through Huysmans's *ekphrasis* (Bernheimer, 2002: p. 111). Moreau's work, with its hyper-refined details, encouraged viewers to get close to the canvas, as Peter Cooke has observed (2008: 404). Close looking is rewarded: the more attention is paid to the canvas, the more details are noticed – the pet panther in the shadows on the right, the servants hiding behind Salomé, the masterful draughtsmanship of the mosaics on the walls, and so on.

Such intimate engagement with the work of art is a feature of other visual manifestations of decadence as well. Unlike the social gaze encouraged by academic painting, or the cursory glance endorsed by impressionism, artists who addressed decadence wanted the experience of art to involve a protracted, solitary, and deep connection between the artwork and the viewer. Aubrey Beardsley's arresting erotic images, for example, belong to a middle ground between writing and drawing, inspired by Japanese *shunga* art, fin-de-siècle French posters, eighteenth-century pornographic engravings, illustrated novels, plays, and magazine fiction (as well as magazine covers and other sources).

The social critic and physician Max Nordau in his 1892–1893 book *Entartung* [*Degeneration*] (originally published in German but soon circulated in translation throughout Europe and America), condemned the widespread celebration of decadent art as false art. He employed the term 'degeneration' rather than 'decadence', as the former was currently used in neurology and psychiatry, the disciplines in which Nordau aimed to intervene. With his scientific authority, Nordau condemned most modern fashions in art and literature as evident manifestations of insanity. What is more, he interpreted the literary and visual arts as privileged realms in which to investigate what decadence, decline, and degeneration stood for. Nordau elevated the realm of visual and literary culture as the most important repository of a society's worldview: 'Books and works of art exercise a powerful suggestion on the masses. It is from these productions that an age derives its ideals of morality and beauty' (1895: p. viii). At the same time, he also put them on trial as proof of the era's corruption.

Nordau believed that authentic creativity cannot arise from disease, and he found symptoms of degeneration in many of his most highly praised contemporaries – including those closely associated with decadence, such as Huysmans, Wagner, Paul Verlaine, and Stéphane Mallarmé, as well as those who were not, such as John Ruskin, Leo Tolstoy, and George Bernard Shaw. For him, recent developments in the visual arts, as in the work of the impressionists and the Pre-Raphaelites, were evidence of social degeneracy – both in the choice of a non-edifying subject matter and a style that emphasized subjective experience over empirical observation. As Nordau argued in his dedication to the Italian psychiatrist Cesare Lombroso, 'If [books and works of art] are absurd and anti-social, they exert a disturbing and corrupting influence on the views of a whole generation' (p. viii). Such attitudes persisted, and perceptions of the dangers criminals represented were extended to artists and writers, so that they came to be perceived as 'corrupt and corrupting' (West, 1993: p. 29), a threat to the entire social fabric of late nineteenth-century society.

According to Matei Calinescu, 'The decadents cultivated the consciousness of their own alienation, both aesthetic and moral' (1987: p. 162). In the visual arts, representations of uncontrollable desire, overheated hallucinations, and escapist fantasies were modes of marking the artists' polemic against the dominant political and social forces of nineteenth-century bourgeois culture – without, however, addressing its capitalist foundations. Their rejection of democratic values and their nostalgia for an aristocratic existence that underscored their difference from 'the vulgar businessmen and the vile mob' (Drake, 1980: p. 221) translated into the cultivation of an over-refined sensibility.

During the late nineteenth century, artists throughout Europe and America aspired to illustrate the pessimism of their time, a sense of impending doom, and the pervasiveness of social corruption. Edvard Munch's *Spring Evening in Karl-Johann Street* (1892), for example, represents bourgeois culture as a catalyst for social alienation; the vacant gazes of the strollers and their lack of interaction exemplify common fears about the breaking down of social relations in cities at that time. Hallucinatory images such as Alfred Kubin's *Angst* (1903) and Munch's *The Scream*

(1893), were typical of numerous works of art that gave visual form to anguish, evoking the phantasmagoria of an age racked with cultural pessimism and anxiety.

Temptresses and Virgins: Decadent Representations of Women

The dominant iconography of decadence in the visual arts was the representation of women. All over the Western world – in countries as varied as France, England, Belgium, Spain, Austria, and Mexico – both threatening and disempowered women were prominent visual clichés of decay, degeneration, and decline. As Patricia Mathews has shown, avant-garde artists of the fin de siècle questioned patriarchal notions of masculinity. Because of their reliance on sensitivity, intuition, and spirituality, artists such as Moreau, Rops, Ruelas, Beardsley, and Kubin, among many other 'decadentists', might be seen as 'feminized'. Yet these counter-cultural artists, as well as scientific writers such as Nordau and Lombroso, agreed that genius was intrinsically male and that women were uncreative and unintellectual. As Mathews has observed, 'The control of women ideologically and socially was an essential strategy to assure the masculinity of genius' (1999: p. 70). Despite the decadent artists' critique of bourgeois values through formal components and subject matter, Mathews has pointed out that they reproduced, in their artistic practice, the social order they apparently despised, with its misogyny, racism, and classism.

No visual component conveys this better than what Bram Dijkstra has termed the 'iconography of misogyny', which dominated the visual production associated with decadence (1986: p. viii) and was evident in every artistic style current at the time: academic, late-impressionist, post-impressionist, symbolist, and so on. The widely accepted idea of the inherent perversity of women and the need to prevent them from overpowering men through sexual desire – i.e., turning them into the disembowelled marionette in Ángel Zárraga's *The Woman and the Puppet* (1909) or the abject pig in Félicien Rops's *Pornokrates* (1878) – were depicted through several recurring tropes. Corrupt women and their sexual power were meant to signify the imminent decline of fin-de-siècle culture.

On the one hand, portrayals of women as the sphinx, the vampire, the snake, or the medusa, combined with the fin-de-siècle obsession with representations of Judith, Circe, and Salomé, conveyed the threat represented by the changes in gender relations at the turn of the century. Gustav Klimt's famous *Judith and the Head of Holofernes* (1901) presents an unapologetic castrating woman; the opulent frame and gilding of the painting, along with the brazen expression of the model, reveal that she is no longer a paragon of female virtue, as she had been in traditional representations of that biblical figure. Jean Delville's *Medusa* (1893) is a medium in a trance, shown with upturned eyes and her head crowned by serpents, which have released their poison into two shallow bowls that she is holding to either side of her head. The poison has contaminated the delicate pomegranates at the bottom of the composition, and the toxic fumes emanating from them anticipate the whiplash line of art nouveau. The equivalency of eroticism and death was embodied in Judith and other femmes fatales.

On the other hand, depictions of female literary figures such as Ophelia, Isabella, Elaine of Astolat; and of virginal nymphs, 'angels in the house', self-sacrificing mothers, and consumptive beauties represented women as essentially helpless, immolating themselves for the salvation of the male soul. In works such as Elihu Vedder's *Soul in Bondage* (1891–1892), internal spiritual conflict is personified by a restrained angelic female figure. By depicting women as vulnerable and desiring to be controlled, this peculiar iconography catered to the bourgeois male's aggressive energies and feelings of mastery at a moment when women's rights movements were acquiring more and more visibility.

Finally, frequent portrayals of lesbianism and suggestions of female masturbation gave form to male fears that women might not need men at all. Artists as diverse as Beardsley, in his sinuous illustrations for *Lysistrata* (1896), the Brazilian impressionist Eliseu Visconti, in *In Summertime* (1891), or Egon Schiele, in his many drawings of raw female desire, represented women as dangerously self-sufficient, with the ability to achieve sexual gratification on their own. The fin de siècle was truly, as Nicole G. Albert has pointed out, an era in which 'sapphism [became] an overwhelming, even obsessive, topic' (2016: p. xix). The iconography of Sappho, Gomorrah, cross-dressers, and homo-social female spaces (bars, cabarets, tearooms, and department stores) became favourite subjects for artists such as Rops, Georges de Feure, and Tadeusz Styka, as well as illustrators in international mass publications such as *Gil Blas, L'assiette au beurre, Wiener Illustrierte Frauenzeitung,* and *La vie parisienne.*

El Greco and Gian Lorenzo Bernini as Decadent

One of the key ideas of fin-de-siècle decadence is the sense that the perception of decline and decay, of being at the end of history, is not a completely novel experience. Rather, decadent artists and intellectuals very often equated their own time with prior periods of decadence: the Roman Silver Age, the Byzantine Empire during Late Antiquity and the Middle Ages, the late Renaissance, the baroque period, or eighteenth-century France on the eve of the Revolution. As Huysmans has Des Esseintes say,

> [W]hen the period in which a man of talent is condemned to live is dull and stupid, the artist [. . .] bursts out of the prison of his century and roams about at liberty in another period, with which, as a crowning illusion, he imagines he would have been more in accord. (2003: p. 166)

Thus, it is not surprising that Des Esseintes, in addition to collecting work by artists of his time such as Moreau and Redon, 'had hung in his bedroom an extravagant sketch by Theotocopuli [El Greco], a study of Christ in which the drawing was exaggerated, the colouring crude and bizarre, the general effect one of frenzied energy [. . .]. This sinister picture, with its boot-polish blacks and cadaverous greens', resonates with 'certain ideas' Des Esseintes has about furnishing a bedroom: in order to put his past life and its 'nocturnal delectation' behind him, he chooses to make his living quarters into 'a place for sleep and solitude, a setting for quiet and meditation, a sort of oratory', but without 'the austere ugliness that characterizes all penitential prayer houses', choosing instead 'to employ cheerful means to attain a drab end, [. . .] a certain elegance and distinction' (pp. 61, 62). His inclusion of the painting by El Greco fits with Des Esseintes' penchant for luxury and hedonism while also providing another occasion for the evocation of sacrilege.

El Greco experienced a sort of revival in the second half of the nineteenth century. The opening of the Spanish gallery at the Louvre in 1838 had made nine El Greco paintings available to the French public. Yet most visitors at the time overlooked El Greco in favour of baroque painters such as Bartolomé Murillo or Zurbarán. It was Théophile Gautier, a central figure in the conceptualization of decadence, who re-examined El Greco, describing him as the precursor of romantic painters in his *Voyage en Espagne* (1843). Gautier interpreted El Greco's work as embodying the alleged madness of its author and his paintings as having been misunderstood by his contemporaries. Hence El Greco became the prototype of the marginalized and insane romantic artist.

It was this interpretation that became interesting for Huysmans and his generation: El Greco was quintessentially anti-classical – his figures wilfully deformed, his subject matter dark and morbid. As Mario Praz pointed out in *The Romantic Agony* (1933), decadentism could be interpreted as the heightened successor to romanticism. El Greco's distortions, his preference for lurid hues, and his purported desire to encourage new forms of vision could not fail to interest Des Esseintes, an aesthete who scorned aesthetic conventions. The association of El Greco with decadentism was to have a long-lasting influence. As late as 1965, Arnold Hauser compared mannerism with decadentism, identifying their affinity for 'the pleasure taken in fluency and suppleness of statement' and for 'the cult of form and articulated expression for its own sake' (1965: pp. 28–9).

Another anti-classical artist who, largely due to Gabriele D'Annunzio, came to be understood in decadent terms was the baroque sculptor and architect Gian Lorenzo Bernini. D'Annunzio was, as Richard Drake has declared, 'the cynosure of [Italian] decadence' (1982: 78). His carefully constructed persona evinced all the traits of the decadent aesthete: the careful attention to dress, the scandalous behaviour, the construction of a living environment filled with works of art, and the cultivation of aristocratic hobbies. But D'Annunzio's consecration as the most visible example of Italian decadentism was the publication of *Il piacere* [*Pleasure*] (1889), modelled on *Against Nature* in its detailed descriptions and its evocation of a purely sensuous existence. The protagonist, Andrea Sperelli, a rich and egocentric member of the aristocracy, leads an idle existence in Rome. The novel narrates his tormented love affair with two women: Elena Muti, the incarnation of the femme fatale; and Maria Ferres de Capdevila, the embodiment of an ideal of purity and salvation. Like Huysmans, D'Annunzio employed extremely refined language in his meticulous descriptions of environments and moods.

Although the political events of 1887 appear in the novel, D'Annunzio emphasized his hero's contempt for modern life by characterizing him as a baroque prince who longs to live in the seventeenth century, and who inhabits an opulent mannerist house, the Palazzo Zuccari (fig. 16.1). D'Annunzio's novel includes few precise references to seventeenth-century paintings and sculptures, but the baroque atmosphere of Rome pervades *Pleasure.* Sperelli is more at ease in this imagined past than in his own time, and his leisure is modelled on the pastimes of a young nobleman of the seventeenth century: the composition of poems and paintings, the pursuit of beautiful women, the moody contemplation of the meaninglessness of life (Cottini, 2017: 9).

This atmospheric evocation of seventeenth-century Rome is not the only connection between Sperelli and the baroque. When he is wounded in a duel, he retires to his cousin's house and plans to dedicate his convalescence to writing. His contemplated projects include 'a form of modern

Poem'; 'a book of art on the Primitives, the artists who foreran the Renaissance'; 'a book of psychological and literary analysis on the poets of the thirteenth century'; and, finally, 'a third book on Bernini, a great study of decadence, assembling around this extraordinary man, the favourite of six Popes, not only all the art but also all the life of his century' (D'Annunzio, 2013: p. 145).

The mention of Bernini in a novel published in 1889 is historically important, for D'Annunzio's evocation of seventeenth-century Rome as decadent was a calculated rejection of earlier critical assessments of the period among intellectuals and artists (Simonato, 2018). Although Wölfflin had defended the baroque's historical legitimacy in *Renaissance and Baroque* the year before, it is almost certain that D'Annunzio did not know about this book when writing *Pleasure* because Wölfflin was translated into Italian only in 1928 and D'Annunzio did not read German. It appears, then, that his evocation of Bernini and baroque Rome as 'decadent' was simply the result of his overturning prior criticism of the period. Since the decadentists accentuated their differences from the rest of bourgeois society and broke from their literary predecessors, it was appropriate for them to rediscover and re-evaluate the style most reviled by the previous generation of writers (Drake, 1980: p. 221).

Furthermore, D'Annunzio's descriptions of baroque Rome are also part of his polemic against the new political, social, and economic forces that were conspiring to dismantle the aristocracy and its way of life, demolishing many of the Roman villas and gardens to build modern housing. In one scene in the novel, when Andrea Sperelli is looking for Maria Ferres' house on Rome's Via Nazionale, D'Annunzio deliberately ignores two major new structures on the street – the neoclassical Palazzo delle Esposizioni (1883) and the neo-Renaissance Banca d'Italia (1886–1892). D'Annunzio's evocation of the destruction of baroque Rome under the demolition hammer was thus not only an expression of the refined taste of the decadent aesthete but also a condemnation of the mercantile values endorsed by post-unification Italy.

D'Annunzio's references to the baroque were not historically accurate but referred instead to what the baroque artist and the late nineteenth-century intellectual were presumed to have in common: both were ignored by the political regimes of their day and sought refuge in a world of unorthodox beauty. The baroque, together with other historical periods associated with decline, became identified with decadent aesthetics because they both evoked the search for artificial stimuli to enhance sensual pleasure.

Conclusion

What can the term 'decadence' do for the analysis of the visual arts that 'fin de siècle', 'symbolism', or 'aestheticism' cannot? Rather than signifying an organized and coherent movement or a particular style in the long fin de siècle leading up to the year 1900 and beyond, 'decadence' referred to a state of mind, a peculiar sensibility, one that was not limited to the 1880s and 1890s or to any single geographic region. The term refers to art and literature that displays sophisticated formal innovation as well as to the flamboyant, hedonistic lifestyle of many of its practitioners and suggests a moral appraisal of the exhaustion of culture. Ramón Casas' *Jove decadent (Després del ball)* [Young decadent woman (after the ball)] (1899) illustrates this idea. Dressed in sober black and holding what looks to be a *carnet de bal* [dance card], the languid woman seems to have collapsed onto a sofa, the presumed result of some kind of degenerate activity on the dance floor.

Calling an artwork 'decadent' implies that it is morally corrupting: the decadent work of art is the means whereby the degenerate artist exercises his pernicious influence over the viewer, and by extension, the whole of society. Thus, the decadent artwork not only expresses the decline of an entire culture but also actively contributes to its corruption. Art is seen as acting on the viewer's mind and imagination; yet 'decadent' artists were not using this influence for the benefit of society. Indeed, they were perceived by many as having renounced any educative purpose and eschewed edifying subject matter. They seemed to only aspire to convey a sense of beauty, but one that was not harmonious, instructive, or natural.

As artists proudly cultivated their independence from the leading social, cultural, and political forces of their own time, they defended their right to produce art for art's sake. They did not think of their art as spiritually elevating. Rather, as Frederic Harrison argued in his essay 'Decadence in Modern Art' (1893) – in which he studied the French artists who exhibited with the Société des Artistes Indépendants in the 1880s and at the Salon de la Rose+Croix in the 1890s – the decadent artist thinks of himself as 'an angelic being who is a law unto himself' (1893: 436), yet he also cultivates notoriety and relishes scandal.

By mocking aesthetic standards and moral rules, and defying any form of convention, artists who address the idea of decadence are also profoundly anti-democratic. Their art precludes universal appreciation, and proudly so. It assumes an elite audience that shares the inward-looking, anti-utilitarian, and escapist worldview of the artist. Decadent artists and decadent audiences are estranged from their society and feel disdain for those who are scandalized by decadent art's innovative form and immoral subject matter. Decadence, in sum, offers a harsh critique of the fin-de-siècle moral and aesthetic status quo – yet in its elitism and nostalgia for a bygone aristocratic way of life, it intentionally refuses to address the flaws of its own ideological position.

References

Albert, Nicole G. (2016). *Lesbian Decadence: Representations in Art and Literature of Fin-de-Siècle France*, New York: Harrington Park Press.

Bernheimer, Charles (2002). *Decadent Subjects: The Idea of Decadence in Art, Literature, Philosophy, and Culture of the Fin de Siècle in Europe*, Baltimore, MD: Johns Hopkins University Press.

Calinescu, Matei (1987). *Five Faces of Modernity: Modernism, Avant-Garde, Decadence, Kitsch, Postmodernism*, Durham, NC: Duke University Press.

Cooke, Peter (2008). Gustave Moreau and the Reinvention of History Painting. *Art Bulletin*, 90(3), 394–416.

Cottini, Luca (2017). D'Annunzio, Bernini, and the Baroque Prelude of *Il piacere*. *Forum Italicum*, 51(2), 1–20.

D'Annunzio, Gabriele (2013). *Pleasure*, Lara Gochin Raffaelli, trans., New York: Penguin.

Dijkstra, Bram (1986). *Idols of Perversity: Fantasies of Feminine Evil in Fin-de-Siècle Culture*, Oxford: Oxford University Press.

Drake, Richard (1980). *Byzantium for Rome: The Politics of Nostalgia in Umbertian Italy, 1878–1900*, Chapel Hill: University of North Carolina.

Drake, Richard (1982). Decadence, Decadentism and Decadent Romanticism in Italy: Toward a Theory of Decadence. *Journal of Contemporary History*, 17(1), 69–92.

Flint, Richard (1980). 'Fin de Siècle: The Concept of Decadence in French and English Art during the Late-Nineteenth Century'. Doctoral Dissertation, Indiana University.

Gombrich, E. H. (1966). *Norm and Form: Studies in the Art of the Renaissance*, London: Phaidon.

Harrison, Frederic (1893). Decadence in Modern Art. *Forum*, 15, 428–38

Hauser, Arnold (1965). *Mannerism*, New York: Knopf.

Huysmans, Joris-Karl (2003). *Against Nature*, Robert Baldick, trans., London: Penguin.

Jullian, Philippe (1975). *Dreamers of Decadence: Symbolist Painters of the 1890s*, New York: Praeger.

Mathews, Patricia Townley (1999). *Passionate Discontent: Creativity, Gender, and French Symbolist Art*, Chicago: University of Chicago Press.

Nencioni, Enrico (1897). Barocchismo. In Guido Falorsi, ed., *La vita italiana nel seicento: conferenze tenute a Firenze nel 1894*, Milan: Fratelli Treves, pp. 269–98.

Nervo, Amado (1903). Máscaras: Julio Ruelas. *Revista moderna: arte y ciencia* 6 (6), 81–2.
Nietzsche, Friedrich (2005). *The Anti-Christ, Ecce Homo, Twilight of the Idols, and Other Writings*, Judith Norman, trans., Cambridge: Cambridge University Press.
Nordau, Max (1895). *Degeneration*, New York: Appleton.
Potts, Alex (1994). *Flesh and the Ideal: Winckelmann and the Origins of Art History*, New Haven, CT: Yale University Press.
Simonato, Lucia (2018). *Bernini scultore: il difficile dialogo con la modernità*, Milan: Electa.
Weir, David (1995). *Decadence and the Making of Modernism*, Amherst: University of Massachusetts Press.
West, Shearer (1993). *Fin de Siècle: Art and Society in an Age of Uncertainty*, London: Bloomsbury Press.
Wölfflin, Heinrich (1964). *Renaissance and Baroque*, Kathrin Simon, trans., London: Collins.

CHAPTER 9

Decadence and Music

Emma Sutton

> Very modern, isn't it? Very Parisian. Very *decadent*.
>
> (Nietzsche, 1967: pp. 175–6)

Friedrich Nietzsche's famous account of decadent music, exemplified for him by Wagner's music dramas, unequivocally associates decadent art with modernity. The conditions of the modern metropolis – urban crowds, technological innovations, commerce, consumerism, publicity, mass education, mechanical reproduction, new sexual identities and social mores, and ethnic diversity – that Nietzsche evokes by alluding to Paris are fundamental to his analysis of decadent music. Discourse about decadent music was profoundly entwined with the social, intellectual, political, and economic conditions of modernity – with commerce, mass education, publicity, the global movement of people and goods, and changing ideas of nationhood. Nietzsche's writings demonstrate too that decadent art was shaped by and conceptualized in the terms of modernity's new disciplines and modes of thought. If Wagner was a 'sickness', a '*névrose*', a guide to the 'labyrinth of the modern soul' (Nietzsche, 1967: pp. 166, 156) whose music produced indigestion and sore throats (Nietzsche, 1982: p. 664), this was because his art seemed to Nietzsche and to many contemporaries to illustrate the need for the new mental and physical sciences (some regarded as pseudo-sciences today) and theories: psychology, sexology, evolution, degeneration, racial theories, and eugenics.

Music was absolutely central to late nineteenth- and early twentieth-century discourses about decadence, decadent art, and modernity. Some of the most influential texts that offered extended theories and classifications of cultural and artistic decadence – Nietzsche's work, Max Nordau's 1892 *Entartung* [*Degeneration*] – discussed music in more depth and at more length than any other art. For these authors, decadent music was a synecdoche of contemporary society: Nordau called it the 'monument' 'by which posterity will be able to measure the whole breadth and depth of the degeneration and hysteria of the age' (1993: p. 213) while Nietzsche observed '[t]hrough Wagner modernity speaks most intimately, concealing neither its good nor its evil' (1967: p. 156). It was also frequently held up as the most illustrative or extreme example of decadent art in criticism and theory that focused primarily on other media, as in Tolstoy's *What is art?* (1897). Recent analyses of decadence, however, have paid relatively little attention to music, a fact that is all the more surprising given music's 'driving position [. . .] in the decadent imagination' whether realized in music, literature, aesthetic theory, visual art, or other media (Downes, 2010: p. 57).

But, of course, decadent music wasn't all new. Nietzsche's reliance on the terms Apollonian and Dionysian in his binary model of ideal and decadent art reveals his debt to models from classical antiquity, a debt shared by many. Nineteenth-century European discourses about music were often shaped by examples from other cultures and historical periods. The Sirens, for example, had a busy afterlife in representations of decadent music, as did Sappho (a crucial figure for the aunt-niece co-authors, Michael Field (Katharine Bradley and Edith Cooper), in the 1880s and 1890s) and other figures from ancient history. Suetonius' account of Nero as an archetypally tyrannical and bombastic artist-composer, forcing women in labour to hear out his performances while other listeners leapt from the walls in attempts to escape (Suetonius, 2000: p. 206), was for some an evocative predecessor of the 'despotic' Wagner (Baudelaire, 1992: p. 332), imprisoning his audience for hours of opera or, as André Gill's 1869 cartoon depicted, hammering a giant ear drum with his enormous orchestra. The idea of decadent music – for which read aesthetically inferior, formally flawed, hyper-affective, morally 'bad', enervating, or corrupting in some way – has a long history, and examples of proto-decadent music can be found across cultures and historical periods. Socrates opposed 'purged' music with a model of ideal 'philosophical' music, Plato the 'virile' Doric mode with the 'relaxed' Lydian, early Buddhism and Sunni Islam proscribed music altogether, and biblical examples contrast the raucous music of idolatrous worship with the ameliorative music of figures such as David in 1 Samuel, whose harp-playing restores both the individual listener (King Saul) and wider society (since David is credited with the introduction of music into Jewish worship).

Later, similar oppositions can be seen in the tussle between the 'capricious' rhythmic variation of *Ars nova* and 'modest' *Ars antiqua* in the middle ages, between English staged music and Italian opera (suspect because of its associations with Catholicism, castrati, and commerce) in the eighteenth century, and between Joseph Goebbels's promotion of Nazi-sanctioned 'German music' and its counterpart, 'degenerate' music, in the 1930s. Innumerable examples suggest that music has frequently been perceived to require aesthetic, religious, or even state scrutiny and control. At times this control has been articulated via a binary model of music – 'decadent' vs. 'good' music (whether the latter was perceived to exist or had only the status of an imagined ideal) – and at others via wholesale proscriptions against music. Decadent music, we may be tempted to conclude, is an idea as old as music itself.

i

Classical examples are instructive because of the ways that decadent music is characterized and because of their influence on Nietzsche and, via him, much subsequent thought on decadent music. Two myths of Apollo evoke the richness and mutability of the term. In the first, narrated by Melanippedes of Melos in his comedy *Marsyas* and by Ovid in the *Metamorphoses*, the satyr Marsyas picks up the flute invented but discarded by the goddess Athena. She thrashes Marsyas for his presumption in taking up her instrument, but he is not deterred and becomes so accomplished that he challenges Apollo to a musical contest. Losing the contest, Marsyas is flayed alive by Apollo (Morford and Lenardon, 1999: pp. 178–9). The inferiority or proto-decadence of Marsyas' music resides in several qualities. First, his music is characterized as 'inauthentic', even ventriloquized: Marsyas may be technically proficient as a player but he lacks the imagination to have created the instrument, so his aesthetic achievement is secondary, dependent on and shaped by Athena's invention. Additionally, he has defied the explicit instructions of a figure symbolically positioned as a potential teacher and as representative of aesthetic predecessors and tradition. What we might call the social function of his playing also characterizes Marsyas' music as decadent: rather than existing for some individual or social good (the pleasure or edification of the listener or player, for instance), the purpose of Marsyas' playing is self-aggrandisement and competitive display. It contrasts sharply with the lack of self-interest apparent in Athena's casual discarding of the instrument. Moreover, his music defies cultural regulations governing the right to produce art: in presuming to play an instrument specific to the goddess, the male, half-bestial, mortal satyr transgresses gender, social, and even species hierarchies and taboos. Fundamental to the moral lesson of the myth is the idea that the music (the work of art) inevitably embodies the qualities of its creator: the unanimous verdict of the listeners reinstates social hierarchies, suggesting that Marsyas' music must fail if only because he is a lesser creature than a goddess. The extremity of the punishment carried out by Apollo furthers the implication that this is an important, if unstated, part of the lesson; the apparently simple but nebulous assumption that music expresses or contains something of its creator (whether composer or, as here, improvising performer) was to be one of the most contentious and problematic elements in nineteenth- and twentieth-century debates about musical decadence.

Apollo's second musical contest revealingly augments Ovid's representations of proto-decadent music. The contest is with Pan (Nietzsche's Dionysus), who 'dared to belittle the music of Apollo compared to his own'. Ovid tells us that, in the contest, Pan 'plays a dainty tune' on his 'rustic pipes' made of reeds and wax but is trumped by Apollo, whose lyre 'captivated by [its] sweetness'. Because King Midas of Phrygia is alone among the listeners in refusing to grant victory to Apollo, as punishment his ears are turned into those of a 'lumbering ass' (Morford and Lenardon, 1999: pp. 179–80). Here, the opposition is played out through the differing instrumentation and formal qualities of the music (pipes vs. lyre, 'daintiness' vs. irresistible 'sweetness') and – crucially – through the behaviour and qualities of the listeners: Midas' obtuseness compromises the status of the music he favours.

ii

Ovid's and Nietzsche's examples outline a model of decadent music that coexists and indeed competes (literally or symbolically) with 'healthy' or permissible music. Accounts that place music on a historical continuum likewise often involve oppositional definitions of decadent music, either as a type of music that represented a decline from some earlier ideal or as a term applied to music that was new, unfamiliar, 'modern'. Somewhat ironically, what Wagner had heralded in the 1850s as *Zukunftsmusik* [the music of the future] quickly became exemplary of decadence. In 1893, Valery Bryusov, editor of the Russian Symbolist journal *Vesy* [The scales], articulated this interdependence of modernity and apparent decline rather differently: 'the future belongs' to decadence because it denotes 'the attempt to bring poetry close to the contemporary' (Grossman, 1985: pp. 104–5). Decadent music, that is, was at once archaic, derivative, and secondary, yet somehow modern, avant-garde, and generative. And the instability of its historical placement was partly the result of the attitude of decadent music towards its aesthetic past – its use of quotation, pastiche, and established forms.

The explosion of the term in the late decades of the nineteenth century is particularly intriguing given that it followed shortly after the placement of music at or near the top of the hierarchy of the arts in a number of aesthetic and philosophical works and in the writings of the 'musical idealists'. Hegel's influential hierarchy relies on the elevation of mind over matter: music is a 'subjective' and 'romantic' art that may be seen to 'celebrate [. . .] its triumph over the external world' through attempts to surpass the constraints of form (1964: p. 436). In Hegel's model, music relies on feeling and is inferior only to poetry (which need only be thought, rather than heard) among the arts. Schopenhauer's writing on music was also influential, not least on Wagner who famously recast the plot and argument of the *Ring* following his conversion to Schopenhauer's theories in 1854. In *Die Welt als Wille und Vorstellung* [*The World as Will and Representation*] (1818; rev. 1844), Schopenhauer had afforded music a privileged position because of its ability to represent the 'Will': music 'differs from all the other arts by the fact that it is not a copy of the phenomenon [. . .] but is directly a copy of the will itself, and therefore expresses the metaphysical to everything physical in the world'. In his account, music is 'independent of the phenomenal world'; other arts 'speak only of the shadow but music of the essence' (1969: vol. II, pp. 262, 257). Even aesthetic theory that in other ways was read as a manifesto for decadent art continued to elevate music: in 'The School of Giorgone' (1877; added to the third edition of *The Renaissance: Studies in Art and Poetry* in 1888), Walter Pater reflects on the relationship between 'form' and 'matter', 'subject' and 'expression' in different arts, proposing that music is the 'true type or measure of perfected art' because 'it most completely realises this artistic ideal, this perfect identification of matter and form' (1986: p. 88). The 'constant effort of art' is 'to obliterate' the distinction between matter and form; thus, as the famous dictum proposed, '*All art constantly aspires towards the condition of music*' (p. 86). Such writings suggest that music might be particularly resistant to being characterized as decadent. The placement of music at the apex of the arts implied that it was aloof from and superior to its immediate context and to politics – decadent music was understood to be just the opposite. Decadent music problematically failed to 'transcend' (a key word) its immediate context, whether that context was understood biographically (in terms of a composer's personal traits), aesthetically (as a product of inferior artistic traditions), or socially (as reflecting a debased social or political context). There was, then, a great deal at stake in characterizing music as decadent by the late nineteenth century since it implicated an art perceived as the most elevated and ideal and as representative of art more widely. Decadent music denoted not just musical but also wider aesthetic and cultural decline.

iii

From the late nineteenth to the early twentieth century, the definition of decadent music underwent a number of changes. Following Nietzsche (and recalling Ovid), various commentators attempted to understand precisely where decadence might be located – whether in the composition, the performance, or the reception of music, or, most problematically, in the notes themselves. Considerations of the role of decadence in music necessarily included questions related both to collective contexts (nation, performance venue, audience) and to individual ones (listener, performer, composer), not to mention the artwork itself (form, style, genre, and so on), all of which led to both generic and specifically musical characterizations of musical decadence.

Given the political history of mid-nineteenth-century Western and Eastern Europe, it was inevitable that decadent music would be iterated in terms of national or ethnic identity – portrayed as inevitably the product of the composer's nation or ethnicity; as shaped by the aesthetic heritage, performance traditions, and contemporary society of that nation; and as a matter that denotes the 'taste' and, by implication, the aesthetic and socio-cultural wellbeing of that nation and its status in a global hierarchy. The intersection of the term 'decadent music' with contemporary geopolitical conflicts – ideological, economic, aesthetic, and military – is overt.

Wagner's essays, particularly those on Jewish music but also his writings on French music and his own *Zukunftsmusik*, were and remain the most notorious examples. His definitions not only influenced discourse that followed but also set up terms that would later be turned against him – by Nietzsche, most famously, in his characterization of Wagner's works as stylistically French, his 'heroines' as 'almost indistinguishable from Madame Bovary!' (1967: p. 176). French grand opera in *Eine Mitteilung an meine Freunde* [*A Communication to My Friends*] (1851) had served as the antithesis of everything Wagner wished his own music dramas to be: showy and materialistic, its 'sickly unsubstantiality' cloaked in 'a glittering show' in a capital city described as the 'modern Babylon' (1993: pp. 302, 383). *Opéra comique* fared no better: characterized as a 'coquette' in *Oper und Drama* [*Opera and Drama*] (1851), its debased music is used to characterize his own duplicitous Gutrune (1995b: p. 112). Wagner's opposition of his own German art to proto-decadent French music relied, as did much contemporary criticism and philosophy, on the term *Volk*; its connotations ('people', 'folk', 'nation', and, particularly in Johann Gottfried Herder's writing, a collective with a *Seele* (soul or essence)) were complex and nuanced, but in the lead-up to the unification of German-speaking states in 1871 it increasingly became synonymous with the term 'nation'. At the conclusion of *Die Meistersinger von Nürnberg* [*The Mastersingers of Nuremburg*] (1868), Hans Sachs invites the Nuremberg *Volk* to honour '[o]ur sacred German art' and to defend it against 'foreign rule and foreign ways' (1983: p. 125). This self-referential moment defines 'good' and proto-decadent music in terms of national and arguably, via the anti-Semitic representation of Beckmesser, ethnic identity.

In his account of Jewish music in *Das Judentum in der Musik* [*Judaism in Music*] (1850 anonymously; reissued 1869 under Wagner's name), the terminology and characteristics Wagner attributes to Jewish music are unequivocally proto-decadent. Jewish music is characterized as emotionally superficial, commercialized, and imitative, qualities that Wagner attributes to the cultural and linguistic marginalization of Jews within Europe. He argues that Jewish music will inevitably remain derivative because the only cultural and aesthetic tradition available to Jewish composers is 'sullied', 'senseless and distorted' synagogue chant: 'The Jew has never had an Art of his own' (Wagner, 1995a: p. 90). One of the most revealing elements of Wagner's definition of proto-decadent music is his assertion that musical style is particularly open to imitation or mimicry (the 'easiest to learn' of the arts (p. 88)), making music vulnerable to Jewish appropriation. Telling too is his claim that Jewish music enjoys contemporary commercial success because of the weakness of 'German' culture: the 'success' of Jewish composers, he argues, denotes the '*ineptitude of the recent musical epoch*' (p. 98). In metaphors nearly as striking for their decadence as their virulent anti-Semitism, he terms the 'Judaic period' of modern music 'stability gone to ruin' (p. 98), its art 'a worm-befretted carcass' (p. 99).

The legacy and proliferation of these metaphors and ideas are apparent in much late nineteenth- and early twentieth-century writing. Nietzsche's critiques not only portray Wagner's music dramas as 'French' but deploy larger geographical oppositions of southern and northern European cultures. His polarization of Wagner and the French Georges Bizet mobilizes clichés about perceived northern European pedantry, mysticism, and religiosity in contrast to the 'naturalness', grace, physicality, and ebullience of southern Europe. In musical terms, this opposition had often been articulated via the comparison of the 'playing north' and the 'singing south', the opposition of northern 'intellectual', polyphonic, keyboard, and symphonic music with the 'emotional', vocal, and lyrical music of the south, exemplified by *bel canto* (Zuckerman, 1964: p. 78). In *The Case of Wagner*, Nietzsche observes: 'With [*Carmen*] one takes leave of the *damp* north, of all the steam of the Wagnerian ideal' (1967: p. 158). The tendency to define decadent music in terms of nations or national traditions is also striking in Russian and Polish critical debate where decadence was frequently explained as an 'ailment' or '[f]oreign mania' (Bartlett, 1995: p. 82). Sergei Diaghilev's 'World of Art' exhibitions prompted a nationalist diatribe against decadence in 1899 from Vladimir Stasov (Downes, 2010: p. 55); the logic was deployed for the opposite effect by the president of the Hamburg Musical Society who implored Tchaikovsky to leave Russia so that he might overcome the inevitable 'shortcomings' of his national context and education (Bullock, 2016: p. 146). Yet the most vitriolic discourse that defined a national music in opposition to its 'degenerate' foil is evident in Nazi propaganda and policy in the late 1930s. In 1936, the *Jüdischer Kulturbund* [Jewish Cultural League] (the theatrical, musical and cultural programme run exclusively by and for Jews) was forbidden to play repertoire claimed by the Nazis as exclusively, ethnically, 'German': Beethoven and, by 1938, Mozart (Potter, 2007: p. 98). In 1938, the first *Reichsmusiktage* [Reich Music Days] took place in Düsseldorf alongside the *Entartete Musik* [Degenerate Music] exhibition. In his keynote lecture, Goebbels opposed 'German' to 'degenerate' music – a category loosely defined through a mélange of allusions to jazz, Jewish, 'Bolshevist', and commercialized music. Schoenberg and Webern were subject to anti-Semitic attacks, and the exhibition catalogue included caricatures of Jewish musicians. The exhibition paid relatively little attention to formal matters, but atonality was targeted: the catalogue accused Schoenberg of attacking the triad, 'the essence of German musical expression' (Potter, 2007: pp. 92–3). The cover of the exhibition catalogue depicted a caricature of an African-American saxophonist wearing a Star of David, concisely evoking the convergence of racial, national, and aesthetic terms in Nazi definitions of degenerate music.

iv

In contrast to analyses of decadent music informed primarily by national or racial theories, some definitions attributed decadence to the mass audiences of the late nineteenth century. Much discourse about decadent art registers discomfort with the newly enlarged scale of musical audiences, enabled by new forms of transport, larger theatres, and the technologies of advertising, publicity, and celebrity (whether of performers or composers, about whom documentary studies such as biographies and correspondence were burgeoning). Nietzsche proposed:

> One leaves oneself at home when one goes to Bayreuth [...] solitude is lacking [...]. In the theater one becomes people, herd female, pharisee, voting cattle, patron, idiot – *Wagnerian*: even the most personal conscience is vanquished by the levelling magic of the great number. (1982: pp. 665–6)

Nietzsche's revulsion fuses anxiety about the apparent threat that mass experience presents to individual (aesthetic) autonomy with distaste for commercialized art and that available to a wider audience. Despite the social exclusivity of the Bayreuth audience, Nietzsche unequivocally attributes the decadence of Wagner's work to its commercial success and calculated popular appeal, a definition reflecting the rise of 'middle-brow' art and the bifurcation of high and popular art at the fin de siècle. Nietzsche's alignment of women with mass, 'middle-brow' – in this case, decadent – art and consumerism has parallels in contemporary crowd theory. Gustave Le Bon's *La psychologie des foules* (1895; English translation in 1896 as *The Crowd: A Study of the Popular Mind*), for example, asserts that crowds are especially susceptible to 'theatrical representations' and are remarkable for their sentimentality and absence of critical discernment – traits found particularly in 'women, savages, and children' (1960: pp. 68, 35–6). Accounts of decadent music that define it through the scale of its performance or reception thus register changes in the performance conditions of some contemporary music as well as the conditions of modernity. Similar concerns were expressed about specific venues such as Berlin cabarets in the late 1930s (Steinweis, 1993: pp. 142–4), perceived as a synecdoche for the character and quality of the work performed there. Anticipating Theodor Adorno, decadent music signals the wider commodification of art.

V

Musical decadence was defined not only in terms of nations, 'races', and mass audiences or markets but also through the attributes of individuals. Defiantly 'perverse', idiosyncratic individual listeners commanded scrutiny in attempts to define decadent music through its formal qualities and conditions of performance and reception. The trope of the enervated, 'pathological' listener relishing his (and it was more often his) suffering as he listened to or recalled music became a familiar element of decadent fiction and critical debate. Baudelaire's declaration in 'Richard Wagner et *Tannhäuser* à Paris' (1861) that his 'rapture had been so strong, so awe-inspiring that [he] could not resist the desire to return to it again and again' (1992: p. 332) was formative, characterizing his listening as an addiction, a compulsion, a psychological symptom. Ludwig II's widely reported private performances of Wagner's operas, at which he was the sole audience member, also fuelled attention to decadent musicians. Such accounts and appraisals of aesthetic experience in pathological, clinical terms were highly influential; in particular, they shaped contemporary perceptions of gender and sexuality that became entwined with definitions of decadence. By the 1890s, decadent fiction was populated with masochistic listeners: the composer Magnus in a short story by Vernon Lee (Violet Paget) is emblematic, overwhelmed by music that paralyses his creativity and which affects him through highly sexualized images of penetration (2006: pp. 179–80); the protagonist in *Under the Hill* (1896), Aubrey Beardsley's erotic take on *Tannhäuser*, conducts a masturbatory reading of the score of *Das Rheingold* (1966: pp. 55–6); and Wilde's Dorian Gray listens in 'rapt pleasure' to *Tannhäuser* which he hears as a 'presentation of the tragedy of his own soul' (1994: p. 135). The assumption that musical tastes were a secure index of a subject's sensibility and even sexuality is evident from Magnus Hirschfeld's 1899 questionnaire intended to allow homosexuals to self-diagnose (it asked, 'Are you particularly fond of Wagner?' (Sutton, 2002: p. 54)) and in Havelock Ellis' observation in his seminal *Studies in the Psychology of Sex* (1900) that '[i]t has been extravagantly said that all musicians are inverts' (1921: vol. II, p. 295). Interrogated in the terms of the new mental sciences, these figures contributed to the converging fin-de-siècle typology of 'the decadent' and 'the homosexual'. Individual aesthetes whose behaviour or tastes were perceived to be idiosyncratic or 'perverse' became barometers of the aesthetic value of the works they admired; consequently, works or artists might be characterized as decadent through the perceived qualities of their admirers.

In certain contexts, performers too were identified as exhibiting proto-decadent elements. The claim was not unprecedented: castrati in British discourse about eighteenth-century Italian opera, for instance, and characterizations of Liszt and Paganini portrayed their virtuosity as compromising the repertoire they performed through their proto-decadent simulation and stylistic exaggeration (Bernstein, 1998: pp. 12, 112–13).

(Marsyas' mimicry is an even earlier example.) But this concern became prominent in the fin de siècle: works such as Offenbach's *Les contes d'Hoffmann* [*The Tales of Hoffmann*] (1881) or George du Maurier's best-seller *Trilby* (1894) use female automata and mesmerism to explore anxieties about the role of the performer in mediating, embodying, and 'voicing' music. These performers signal the decadence of a particular performance and are themselves characterized as decadent artists, offering inferior, 'insincere', or ventriloquized forms of aesthetic expression. But perhaps the most tenacious trope in writing on musical decadence was the assumption that something of the composer's 'character' and qualities were present in – and contaminated – their work.

The acute scrutiny of the composer was shaped by the mass media and publicity industry of the late nineteenth century but the perceptions underpinning such attacks suffused critical writing and aesthetic theory as well as biographies and popular discourse. Frequently, these discourses took the form of pathological images of the composer as an invalid displaying 'symptoms' of psychological or physical degeneration, or of depictions of the composer as the racial or sexual other. Nietzsche was one among many who pointed to Wagner's own personality to 'explain' the decadence of the music: from their titles onwards, *Der Fall Wagner* [*The Case of Wagner*] and *Nietzsche contra Wagner: Aktenstücke eines Psychologen* [*Nietzsche contra Wagner: Out of the Files of a Psychologist*] (1888) characterize Wagner in medicalized tropes. Nordau, too, portrays Wagner as the representative 'degenerate': 'The stigmata of this morbid condition are united in him in the most complete and most luxuriant development' (1993: p. 171). Wagner's consumption of silks and perfumes, his affairs, his homoerotic relationships with figures including his patron, Ludwig II, and his perceived 'mania' for attention and publicity were stock elements in caricatures and popular writing that contributed to constructions of his pathologized, decadent 'character'.

Several composers were retrospectively co-opted into the decadent canon via similar strategies. Beardsley's 1892 drawing *Frederic Chopin* [*sic*] depicts the composer seated with his hand hovering as if outstretched to an absent piano keyboard; his slumped posture, paleness, and tubercular frame represent him in the iconography of 'the decadent'. Similarly, in Thomas Mann's *Tristan* (1903) the fragile female inmate in a sanitorium plays his *Nocturnes* – the performance contributing to her collapse and death – and Albert Giraud's 'Chopin's Waltz' (1884) describes the music itself as the consumptive composer's own bloody spittle. Late nineteenth-century writing on the syphilitic Schubert, on Schumann, on Wolf, and even on late Beethoven (whose A-minor Quartet, Op. 132, with its movement inspired by illness and recovery, was prominent) deployed similar tropes. One of the most strident examples was the reception of Rachmaninov's work – particularly the *First Symphony* (1895) – that relied heavily on accounts of the composer's apparent neuroses and their inevitable expression in the music. (The work was destroyed by the composer after its disastrous première and was a factor in the writer's block for which he sought treatment through hypnosis.) César Cui influentially described it as containing 'sickly perverse harmonization' and 'a complete absence of simplicity and naturalness', while in 1927 the composer and his work were described as displaying 'volitional impotence' and a 'semi-conscious mood characteristic of a "hashish stupor"' (Downes, 2010: p. 98). These tropes shaped perceptions of Rachmaninov's work well into the twentieth century and were crucial to critical distinctions between romantic (exemplified by Rachmaninov) and modernist (exemplified by Scriabin) styles. Tchaikovsky, whose *Manfred Symphony* (Op. 58, 1885) and *Pathétique Symphony* (Op. 74, 1893) were frequently read as autobiographical, confessional narratives, particularly as 'covert narrative[s] of homosexual psychopathology', acknowledged the pressures of contemporary publicity and of romantic investment in the idea that a work authentically expressed the composer's personality or emotions: 'I hate it when people try to peer into my soul . . . In my music I claim extreme sincerity' (Bullock, 2016: pp. 142, 176). Such equations of artist and work have a long philosophical history, but these fraught fin-de-siècle accounts were inflected by new psychological ideas about character.

vi

We turn last to attempts to define decadent music within the musical text itself. In the case of opera and programme music, these attempts were relatively straightforward: operas that set texts by known decadent authors or that dealt with decadent topics, or programme music that represented decadent subject matter, were readily identified as decadent works. Thus, for all his divergence from Wilde's text, Strauss's *Salome* was a prominent example – the final scene notoriously described as 'the most disgusting ever to be shown on stage' (Kristiansen, 2011: p. 114), earning Strauss the dubious honorific 'the genius of bad taste', in Romain Rolland's words (1913: p. 407). Strauss's revisions to Wilde's play drew out the work's affinity to contemporary theories of (female) hysteria, asexuality, and pubescent insanity (Hutcheon and Hutcheon, 2000: pp. 209–14).

(Nietzsche had of course characterized Wagner's characters, particularly Amfortas and Parsifal, in similar terms.) Alban Berg's 1907 *Lulu*, based on Frank Wedekind's plays, was also a much-discussed example: its subject matter, encompassing femmes fatales, murder, prostitution, and popular spectacle such as the circus, placed the work securely in the canon of decadent opera, notwithstanding considerations of its formal qualities. Equally, the decadence of Debussy's *Pelléas et Mélisande* (1902) lay in both the subject matter of Maurice Maeterlinck's play and the musical fetishization of Mélisande's spectral, posthumous voice (Abbate, 2001: pp. 176–9). Some of Bartók's early works, such as *Bluebeard's Castle* (composed 1911) and *The Miraculous Mandarin* (1926), qualified on similar grounds: their thematic focus on prostitution, criminality, and violence was matched by a stylistic and expressive emphasis on the grotesque. In Eastern Europe, the pessimism of Mieczysław Karłowicz's symphonic poems – the *Rebirth Symphony*, Op. 7 (1902), *Returning Waves*, Op. 9 (1904), *Stansław and Anna Oświecimowie*, Op. 9 (1908), and *A Sad Story*, Op. 13 (1908) – were read as 'debilitations' of Dionysian energy, undermining narratives of heroism or redemption (Downes, 2010: pp. 84–96).

But the greatest critical challenge for fin-de-siècle writing on music was the question of whether music itself could be decadent. The assertion was certainly made insistently but, on the whole, with little formal rigour. These accounts locating decadence in formal questions of genre, tonality, melody, rhythm, and so on have been given renewed critical purchase in the last twenty years by critical musicologists who have pursued these insights via detailed formal analyses, documenting the significance of decadent music to the syntax and structures of modern(ist) music. Structural 'inferiority' – typically classified as miniaturism or as an excessive attention to 'surface' at the expense of structural coherence and 'depth' – was a common charge. Works that were perceived to be particularly self-referential, hybrid, or piecemeal in their structure were vulnerable to the charge of decadence. Thus Nietzsche derogatively classes Wagner as a '*miniaturist*' unable to master teleological form (1967: p. 171) while Karłowicz's *Returning Waves* was reviewed at its première as a 'whole [that] consists merely of pieces' (Downes, 2010: p. 87). More recently, Lawrence Kramer has drawn attention to the miniaturism evident in *Salome*'s temporal suspension – her monologue flaunts music's capacity to elongate time through 'luxurious nonaction' (2004: p. 141). Similarly, Tchaikovsky's *Queen of Spades* (1890) uses multiple pastiches (from Mozart to salon song) to create temporal ambiguity (Bullock, 2016: pp. 156–9). *Lulu*'s palindromic structure was widely critiqued as too artificial and reliant on a form of unity inferior to an organic, overarching structure (Berg's allusions, via the character Alva, to the hostile reception of his own earlier work likely did not help) (Perle, 1985: pp. 68–84, 69). Pierre Boulez later memorably described the opera as exemplifying 'an aesthetic of parody', reliant on 'a whole repertory of *objets trouvés*' (1986: p. 387). But these examples should not imply that decadent music is synonymous with structural weakness or attention only to surface:

> The relationship of decadence to formal organisation is a neglected field of enquiry. And in music this is especially vital: formal processes of intensification and dissolution [. . .], deformation, miniaturism and the preoccupation with 'ending' all possess powerfully decadent potential. (Downes, 2010: p. 17)

Thus, the very techniques of repetition and 'intensification' that seemed to some contemporaries evidence of structural inadequacy regenerated (through apparent perversion or dissolution) 'classical' musical forms. Relatively few critics noted this at the time; George Bernard Shaw's *The Perfect Wagnerite* (1898) was unusual in observing the structural tightness and formally conservative elements of Wagner's *Ring*. More often decadent structures were described in metaphors of degeneration or cultural otherness. Thus Wagner's *Unendliche Melodie* [infinite melody] not only lacks structure but also takes us back into the primordial soup: for Nietzsche it was 'the polyp in music' (1967: p. 157); for critic Edmund Gurney the music was like 'invertebrates', 'jellyfish', and 'seaweed' (1883: 441); to others it resembled an opium haze or Turkish mysticism. Wagner's deferred resolutions and ambivalent cadences, for example, were more often heard as decadent than as generative innovations. Yet Brunnhilde's two closing cadences in the last scene of *Götterdämmerung* [*Twilight of the Gods*] – musical symbols representative of polarized decadence and Dionysian revitalization – themselves shaped the two C-sharp cadences in the closing section of Salome's monologue and the double ending of *Elektra* (1909), propelling the proto-modernist syntax and symbolism of these works (Downes, 2010: p. 55).

Tonality and melody were also interrogated as sites of decadence. *Salome*'s decadence was attributed not only to its subject matter but also to its chromaticism and harmonic experimentalism: as an early listener complained, 'the pure triad is administered – like medication – only one teaspoonful every half hour' (Kristiansen, 2011: p. 115). More recently, the tonal struggle between Jochanaan (C major) and Salome (C-sharp major) has been widely read as expressing the polarization of 'normal' and 'perverse', masculine and feminine, saint and sinner at tonal level; it is given an extra twist as Salome's key enharmonically recalls the love duet of Camille

Saint-Saëns's *Samson et Dalilah* (Kramer, 2004: pp. 156–8). Certain motifs and harmonies – such as the flat/minor sixth – occur with frequency in, for example, Scriabin's Third, Fourth, and Fifth Piano Sonatas and in both Rachmaninov's; their unstable structural position contributes to the works' concerns with, respectively, Dionysian ecstasy and a sense of apocalyptic finality (Downes, 2010: p. 58). Such uses build on the popularity of the flat/minor sixth in romantic music but intensify it for pessimistic or decadent use: it is vital, for instance, to both the melodic descent and the harmonic character of Tristan and Isolde's longing at the start of the Prelude. The falling melodic minor seventh was another common decadent motif.

Even instrumentation and rhythm could be heard as expressions of decadence. The choice of a specific instrument might connote decadent concerns via intertextual allusion: Karłowicz's *A Sad Story* looks back to Tchaikovsky's *Manfred Symphony* in which the tam-tam signals Manfred's death. In doing so, it also signals Karłowicz's affiliation with Tchaikovsky's critiques of heroism and, specifically, of Germanic musical models associated with the masculine sublime (Downes, 2010: pp. 77–81, 92). It is worth noting too how often instruments themselves are figured as objects of erotic fetishization or as malevolent, seductive agents in decadent writing. Following Huysmans's *À rebours* [*Against Nature*] (1884), Dorian Gray takes 'curious delight' in the 'hideous voices' and 'bestial shape' of Amerindian instruments, the 'monsters of Art' (Wilde, 1994: p. 135), while in John Meade Falkner's *The Lost Stradivarius* (1895), instruments embody the uncanny, the haunted, and the taboo. Rhythm, perhaps because of its critical elasticity and lack of precision, was a particularly vivid term in definitions of musical decadence. In *Nietzsche contra Wagner*, Nietzsche characterized *Unendliche Melodie* as 'a rhythmic paradox and blasphemy', 'the complete degeneration of rhythmic feeling, *chaos* in place of rhythm' (1982: p. 666). Too little, and a work was vulnerable to accusations of an absence of 'vigour', regarded as enervated and effeminate. Too much, and it signalled primitivism: the English composer and educator Hubert Parry, for instance, rebukes Tchaikovsky for his 'barbaric rhythm and unrestrained abandonment to physical excitement which is natural to the less developed races' (1905: p. 119). Rhythm – especially 'decadent' rhythm – exemplifies the inextricability of apparently apolitical matters of musical form from fin-de-siècle anxieties about ethnicity and gender.

Whether in critical, philosophical, and aesthetic discourses or in popular metaphors and cultural tropes, music's centrality to decadence and to the gender, national, and racial discourses of the fin de siècle is irrefutable.

Modernity was frequently conceptualized via the idea of decadent music – a rhetorical move that persists in analyses of our own twenty-first-century versions of modernity. Nietzsche's perception of the necessity of studying this '*metropolitan*' (1967: p. 176) music is, we might conclude, no less pressing for critics across disciplines now.

References

Abbate, Carolyn (2001). *In Search of Opera*, Princeton, NJ: Princeton University Press.

Bartlett, Rosamund (1995). *Wagner and Russia*, Cambridge: Cambridge University Press.

Baudelaire, Charles (1992). *Selected Writings on Art and Literature*, P. E. Charvet, trans., Harmondsworth: Penguin.

Beardsley, Aubrey (1966). *Under the Hill*, London: New English Library.

Bernstein, Susan (1998). *Virtuosity of the Nineteenth Century: Performing Music and Language in Heine, Liszt, and Baudelaire*, Stanford, CA: Stanford University Press.

Boulez, Pierre (1986). *Orientations: Collected Writings*, Jean-Jacques Nattiez, ed., Martin Cooper, trans., Cambridge, MA: Harvard University Press.

Bullock, Philip Ross (2016). *Pyotr Tchaikovsky*, London: Reaktion.

Downes, Stephen (2010). *Music and Decadence in European Modernism: The Case of Central and Eastern Europe*, Cambridge: Cambridge University Press.

Ellis, Havelock (1921). *Studies in the Psychology of Sex. Volume II: Sexual Inversion*, Philadelphia: F. A. Davis.

Grossman, Joan Delaney (1985). *Valery Bryusov and the Riddle of Russian Decadence*, Berkeley: University of California Press.

Gurney, Edmund (1883). Wagner and Wagnerism. *Nineteenth Century*, 13, March, 434–52.

Hegel, Georg Friedrich Wilhelm (1964). Selections from *The Philosophy of Fine Art*. In Albert Hofstadter and Richard Kuhns, eds., *Philosophies of Art and Beauty: Selected Readings in Aesthetics from Plato to Heidegger*, Chicago: University of Chicago Press, pp. 382–445.

Hutcheon, Linda, and Michael Hutcheon (2000). Staging the Female Body: Richard Strauss's *Salome*. In Mary Ann Smart, ed., *Siren Songs: Representations of Gender and Sexuality in Opera*, Princeton, NJ: Princeton University Press, pp. 204–21.

Kramer, Lawrence (2004). *Opera and Modern Culture: Wagner and Strauss*, Berkeley: University of California Press.

Kristiansen, Morten (2011). Strauss's Road to Operatic Success: *Guntram*, *Feursnot*, and *Salome*. In Charles Youmans, ed., *The Cambridge Companion to Richard Strauss*, Cambridge: Cambridge University Press, pp. 105–18.

Le Bon, Gustave (1960). *The Crowd: A Study of the Popular Mind*, Harmondsworth: Penguin.

Lee, Vernon (2006). A Wicked Voice. In *'Hauntings' and Other Fantastic Tales*, Catherine Maxwell and Patricia Pulham, eds., Ontario: Broadview, pp. 154–81.

Morford, Mark D. and Robert J. Lenardon (1999). *Classical Mythology*, 6th edn, New York and Oxford: Oxford University Press.

Nietzsche, Friedrich (1967). The Case of Wagner. In *'The Birth of Tragedy' and 'The Case of Wagner'*, Walter Kaufmann, trans., New York: Vintage, pp. 145–92.

Nietzsche, Friedrich (1982). Nietzsche contra Wagner. In *The Portable Nietzsche*, Walter Kaufmann, trans., Harmondsworth: Penguin, pp. 661–83.

Nordau, Max (1993). *Degeneration*, Lincoln: University of Nebraska Press.

Parry, C. Hubert H. (1905). *Summary of the History and Development of Medieval and Modern European Music*, rev. ed., London and New York: Novello, Ewer.

Pater, Walter (1986). *The Renaissance: Studies in Art and Poetry*, Adam Phillips, ed., Oxford: Oxford University Press.

Perle, George (1985). *The Operas of Alban Berg: Volume II, 'Lulu'*, Berkeley: University of California Press.

Potter, Pamela M. (2007). Music in the Third Reich: The Complex Task of 'Germanization'. In Jonathan Huener and Francis R. Nicosia, eds., *The Arts in Nazi Germany: Continuity, Conformity, Change*, New York and Oxford: Berghahn, pp. 85–110.

Rolland, Romain (1913). *Jean-Christophe*, Gilbert Cannan, trans., New York: Henry Holt.

Schopenhauer, Arthur (1969). *The World as Will and Representation*, E. F. J. Payne, trans., 2 vols., New York: Dover.

Steinweis, Alan E. (1993). *Art, Ideology, and Economics in Nazi Germany: The Reich Chambers of Music, Theater, and the Visual Arts*, Chapel Hill: North Carolina University Press.

Suetonius (2000). *Lives of the Caesars*, Catharine Edwards, trans., Oxford: Oxford University Press.

Sutton, Emma (2002). *Aubrey Beardsley and British Wagnerism in the 1890s*, Oxford: Oxford University Press.

Wagner, Richard (1983). *The Mastersingers of Nuremberg / Die Meistersinger von Nürnberg*, London: John Calder; New York: Riverrun.

Wagner, Richard (1993). *'The Art-work of the Future' and Other Works*, W. A. Ellis, trans., Lincoln: University of Nebraska Press.

Wagner, Richard (1995a). Judaism in Music. In *'Judaism in Music' and Other Essays*, W. A. Ellis, trans., Lincoln: University of Nebraska Press, pp. 75–122.

Wagner, Richard (1995b). *Opera and Drama*, W. A. Ellis, trans., Lincoln: University of Nebraska Press.

Wilde, Oscar (1994). *The Picture of Dorian Gray*, Isobel Murray, ed., Oxford: Oxford University Press.

Zuckerman, Elliott (1964). *The First Hundred Years of Wagner's 'Tristan'*, New York: Columbia University Press.

CHAPTER 10

Decadence, Parody, and New Women's Writing

Kate Krueger

The conception of decadence as an equivocal but artistically rich self-consciousness in relation to urban modernity is traditionally figured in and through a distinctly male perspective. After Baudelaire's exploration of the urban voyeur in his 1857 collection of poetry, *Les fleurs du mal* [*The Flowers of Evil*], and his essay two years later, 'Le peintre de la vie moderne' ['The Painter of Modern Life'], the flâneur quickly became identified with the male decadent artist who conceptualized his role in and control over the urban panorama (see Chapter 6). The flâneuse, on the other hand, could not exist because, as Janet Wolff argues, she could not move freely through the city; an unaccompanied woman in public would be assumed to be a prostitute (1985: pp. 37–45). Removal from the public realm would seem to exclude the possibility of women becoming decadent artists. If one cannot gather impressions and explore chance encounters, one cannot experience either the freedom the modern city offers or the sense of alienation modernity itself entails. However, many women writers did, indeed, deploy the aesthetics of decadence to offer their own contributions to decadent conceptions of modernity.

At the fin de siècle, New Women writers blended the self-conscious aesthetics of decadence with the progressive gender politics of the New Woman movement in order to produce parodies that resituated women as creators within an expanding literary conversation. The New Woman, a term conceived in a debate between the Irish feminist Sarah Grand and the anti-feminist Ouida (Maria Louise Ramé) in 1894, was a label for women who challenged traditional social and economic constructions of gender roles, but it caught the public's imagination and was soon broadly applied to a variety of unconventional women, both real and imagined. From eschewing marriage to riding bicycles, women refused to have their roles designated for them by men. Modernity offered women the promise of autonomy if they could surmount outmoded social and economic barriers to independence.

New Woman writers concentrated on the struggles of women who grasped at self-determination. Decadent New Women writers were more concerned with critiques of bourgeois values through a lens of failure. They depicted the breakdown of aesthetic and social values, exposing hypocrisy and enduring inequality despite the promise of modern social progress. Decadent New Woman writers shared with male decadents an awareness that progress created new horrors and masked old manners. They embraced the decadent criticism of the bourgeoisie and the fluid identities that the fin-de-siècle city enabled, but women also showed that such acts of redefinition were not to be solely dictated by the gazes of modern men. Michele Hannoosh explains that decadent writers such as Baudelaire depicted two types of women: the ideal 'beauty incarnate' or 'the Eternal Feminine' who was sometimes a creature of instinct and occasionally a viciously destructive femme fatale (1989: p. 40). The work of decadent New Women writers emphasizes the breakdown of these conceptions of femininity and masculinity through a parodic mode of critique.

Parody became a powerful aesthetic tool for women who chose to write themselves into a distinctly male conception of urban modernity. It provided a productive third space that allowed New Women writers to demonstrate mastery of decadent aesthetics and position themselves as legitimate members of the movement by challenging decadent conceptions of modernity dependent upon tropes of the male gaze. Consequently, the parodies they created were less concerned with genre and more concerned with the representative motifs of decadent creation. Notable parodies by Ada Leverson, Ella D'Arcy, and Victoria Cross combine the reformist social politics of New Woman fiction with the attentiveness to artificiality and ambivalence central to decadence, conveying the subjectivity of women rather than depicting their objectification.

Parody is a complex form that requires sophisticated mastery of original material as well as a clear sense of variation. Linda Hutcheon offers a foundational definition of parody as 'repetition with critical distance, which marks difference rather than similarity' (1985: p. 6). Parody requires both the writer and the reader to be aware of the source material; certain codes must be shared 'between encoder and decoder in order for parody to be recognized' (p. 27). Hannoosh effectively argues that parody in the hands of decadents becomes a progressive strategy:

> parody must [. . .] mock itself, and in proposing something different, it must, by the logic of its own structure, allow for the reworking, reinterpretation, or even parody, of what it has itself proposed. Parody lets nothing

> rest secure, including what it seems to endorse, and thus is theoretically inconsistent with conservatism. (1989: p. 7)

Decadent women parodists were adept masters of the recognizable aesthetic codes of decadence even as they rewrote those codes to create their own art. As women, they were simultaneously insiders and outsiders, addressing decadent readers and (male) writers even as they rewrote that literary history to critique the objectification of femininity.

In parodic short stories by D'Arcy, Leverson, and Cross, the emphasis on sexualized femininity becomes much more complex than its decadent source material. Rather than a de facto catalyst for the development of the male artist, female bodies instead become women as subjects who have desires, wills, and creative potential of their own. D'Arcy recodes the male genius, making him a critical failure as a fantasist and creator, dependent upon women for their creative potential but extremely unskilled at reading them and their performances. Leverson's short fiction parodies the cruel objectification of women that was rampant in decadent posturing. She pillories the male decadent's presumption of difference from the late-Victorian masculine norm that is belied by the misogyny he shares with his forebears. Cross's androgynous heroine uses parodic gender performances to show how women adroitly assert their shifting subjectivity. Their parodies were not merely derivative deconstructions of misogyny. These artists were synthetic, a combination of decadent aesthetics and New Woman politics through which they created a new, coherent whole. Hannoosh explains that parody 'contributes to the ongoing history and tradition of literature by reworking the original into a new form' (1989: p. 17). For D'Arcy, Leverson, and Cross, this was certainly the case: parody offered an opportunity to assert themselves in the present.

The Yellow Book's Aesthetic Intersections

Decadent New Woman parodists found a crucial venue in *The Yellow Book*, which notably published daring and controversial short fiction by both men and women. From its inception, *The Yellow Book* (1894–1897) played up to its reputation as a notorious fin-de-siècle periodical that carved out a unique place in the market through its attention to innovative form and content. *The Yellow Book* vividly allied itself with decadence by way of its first four cover designs by Aubrey Beardsley, who earned his reputation as a decadent artist partly because of his focus on sexually suggestive androgynous bodies. The journal's impact was immediate:

Holbrook Jackson claims that the first number of *The Yellow Book* was 'in the nature of a bombshell thrown into the world of letters' (1913: p. 54).

The position of women within *The Yellow Book* coterie is both central and complex. The magazine certainly supported the New Woman, giving numerous women writers a much-needed outlet. *The Yellow Book* promoted controversial writing by both women and men, all dedicated to the exploration of modernity. Women no longer had to rely on publishing their work in women's periodicals in the English literary marketplace that demanded content appropriate for family-oriented middle-class readers. While some critics recognize the ways in which *The Yellow Book* gave women writers both access and autonomy (see Ledger, 2007, and Hughes, 2004), others argue that *The Yellow Book* also trafficked in well-worn stereotypes that objectified women, making its sexual politics largely misogynistic (Brake, 1995). However, the contents of *The Yellow Book* were never monolithic. Misogynistic decadent works were published alongside politically progressive New Woman short stories.

The Yellow Book capitalized on the most compelling and controversial figures of the moment: namely, the dandy, the decadent, and the New Woman. The dandy registered his superiority over the bourgeoisie through his aesthetic performance of dress and manner. In that sense, he overlapped with the decadent and the New Woman, who also set themselves against middle-class values, mores, and appearances. However, the decadent's break from the established order was reactionary, misogynist, and ambivalent in its attitude towards modernity. The New Woman was socially progressive and feminist, largely embracing modernity. Despite these differences, the conflation of these terms was commonplace during the period: the conservative press condemned all these figures together. While the dandy was mocked because of the fastidiousness and sometimes effeminacy of his dress as well as the sharpness of his wit (see Chapter 5), the New Woman was ridiculed for her masculinity, her strident demands for equality, and the depiction of female psychology, even as the decadent was demonized for his crass depiction of social ills and his fetishization of decay. For instance, Hugh E. M. Stutfield's essay 'Tommyrotics' (1895) indicts 'the debased emotionalism' of degenerate and decadent writers, the 'modern literature' that includes the dandy's 'inane paradoxes which the vulgar mistake for wit' and the 'emancipated woman' who depicts 'erotomaniacs' (2001: pp. 236–7). While in practice not all writers embraced them simultaneously, these figures often intersected in their rejection of established mores, engagement with modernity, and alternative femininities and masculinities. Each of these terms became loosely attached to many of the writers who contributed to *The Yellow Book*.

The kaleidoscopic narrative landscape of *The Yellow Book* provided a particularly fruitful outlet for parodic decadent New Woman fiction. D'Arcy mocked the presumption of the decadent 'man of genius', Leverson exposed the patriarchal power of courtship wielded by both conservative and decadent dandies, and Cross explored the transformative potential of androgyny while asserting female subjectivity. All three assert their centrality to *The Yellow Book* through the mastery of decadence in parodic fiction. At the same time, they embrace New Woman politics by using the parodic possibilities of *The Yellow Book* as a form of feminist critique.

D'Arcy's Failed Male Genius

Critics have taken Ella D'Arcy's portrayals of dysfunction seriously and, consequently, interpret her work as profoundly anti-feminist. Literary criticism of D'Arcy is replete with assessments of destructive female characters and male victims; the women are described as 'low-minded' and 'scheming' in their attempts to trap 'decent, sensitive' men with their 'feminine wiles' (Fisher, 1992: p. 184). Winnie Chan registers an 'ambivalent attitude', arguing that despite D'Arcy's designation as a New Woman, her short story 'Irremediable' depicts a 'promising writer' who weds a 'coarse and manipulative but sexually irresistible woman who ruins his life'. This character, according to Chan, is a 'misogynistic caricature of the harpy whose negligent housekeeping exacerbates her illiterate, incurious mind' (2016: p. 128). Chan rightfully points out that 'Irremediable', D'Arcy's contribution to the first volume of *The Yellow Book* in April 1894, effectively combines the decadent 'tortured-genius plot' with the New Woman 'marriage-problem' plot. And yet, all of these critics seem to be thoroughly convinced by the biases and various blindnesses of the male character, Willoughby.

D'Arcy chooses to focus the third-person narrative through the perspective of the 'tortured genius', and yet, in this case, he is only a genius in his own mind. The parodic power of D'Arcy's work lies in mimicking so completely the facile self-pity of the mediocre fin-de-siècle man (who is actually employed as a bank clerk, not an artist). He is tortured, yes, but he can be considered a genius only if 'genius' and 'man' are synonymous. This equivalency, of course, is the thrust of D'Arcy's powerful parody of this common decadent narrative.

'Irremediable' parodies a prominent origin-story of decadent art – the male artist receiving inspiration from his ability to see and translate the beauty and transient mystery of a prostitute in the street. This scenario is most obvious in Arthur Symons' poem 'Stella Maris', published alongside 'Irremediable'. In this poem, Symons recalls his chance encounter with a prostitute. The object of his poem, like a sea nymph, calls to him, so the poet 'comes to claim | My share of your delicious shame'. Symons' poetic persona claims that he remembers 'That joy, not shame, is ours to share' (1894: 130, 131). The encounter is essentially a one-night-stand that the male narrator immortalizes as a memory of a mutually satisfying sexual experience with an enigmatic woman who inspires his poetry. In 'Irremediable', however, Willoughby's kisses are not a momentary encounter; instead, he marries the mysterious déclassée woman he encounters by chance, and his entrapment in marriage destroys rather than elevates his art. Her presence does not provide flashes of understanding or brilliance; on the contrary, she reveals the way in which his own egotistical sense of self warps his understanding of her and of his own emotions.

In 'Irremediable', Willoughby actively courts his own destruction, driven by self-delusion into critically misreading the female object of his gaze and the nature of his own desires. On vacation, he meets a woman who is also on a holiday recovering from her work as a seamstress. Willoughby immediately registers Esther's class position and her accent, and because he has 'dabbled a little in Socialism and at one time had wandered among the dispossessed' (D'Arcy, 1894: 89), and because he has also recently been rejected by a woman of his own class, he initiates a kiss. When they reunite, 'he kissed her again, he kissed her many times, and pushed all thoughts of consequences far from him' (98). He offers her marriage, 'although such conduct to the mediocre man must appear incredible or at least uncalled for' (98). The ironic tone of the narration indicates a broad scepticism regarding Willoughby's sense of himself as more than mediocre; he is selfish and deluded, driven by his own vanity. The power in the relationship remains squarely his. The kisses and the marriage are his idea.

The narrative as a whole thoroughly mocks the decadent pose of the male gaze as genius-translator of the prostitute-as-muse. Willoughby's subsequent suffering is entirely self-created: 'In December he found himself the husband of a girl who was entirely dependent upon him not only for food, clothes, and lodging, but for her present happiness, her whole future life; and last July he had scarcely been more than a boy himself' (100). The first mention of Willoughby as potential writer occurs after an argument when Esther asks whether he is going to 'write those rubbishy stories of his', but Willoughby is too irritated by the idea that 'Esther never did any one mortal thing efficiently or well' enough to write (104). Willoughby recognizes his unreasonable hatred of her habits, which include standing, walking, sitting in a chair, and folding her hands. He belatedly realizes that he no longer feels 'the mistaken chivalry and flattered vanity' that originally drew him to marry her (107). His consuming hatred of her becomes his life-defining passion. Willoughby is the architect of his own destruction.

D'Arcy's parody recodes the decadent 'man of genius' as one who critically fails at fantasy. The prototypical sexually available muse created by his vision is a real person who resists his definitions. Although Willoughby would like to imagine himself as an artist and a sensitive rescuer of the woman he seduces, he is, in fact, just a bank clerk with delusions of grandeur. D'Arcy's hapless central character becomes so invested in fantasies of masculine ego that he corrupts his self-awareness. D'Arcy revisits the theme of the deluded man who ruins either his life or the life of the woman, or both, as in several other notable short stories in *The Yellow Book*, including 'A Marriage' and 'The Pleasure-Pilgrim'. Her short stories indicate just how damaging these decadent fantasies are, not only for the women objectified by them but also for the men who project them.

Ada Leverson's Patriarchal Dandy

While D'Arcy was associated with *The Yellow Book* through her work as sub-editor and her stories about people who make themselves miserable, Oscar Wilde described Ada Leverson's short stories in *The Yellow Book* and other venues as 'wonderful, witty, delightful sketches' (quoted in Denisoff, 2006: p. 104). Leverson was one of the most admired parodists of the fin de siècle, widely acknowledged within Wilde's literary circle as a skilful, sharp, and humorous writer who often targeted her male contemporaries. Yet, she was also famously sympathetic: when Wilde had nowhere to live between his two trials, she took him into her own home (Ledger, 2007: p. 20). While she supported Wilde, she also mocked the dismissive misogyny of decadent dandy-aesthetes. Multiple critics have recognized this tension in Leverson's work. Dennis Denisoff, for example, explains that 'Leverson's sympathy is coupled with a vehement disrespect for the misogynistic bent of aestheticism's self-representation' (2006: p. 10; see also Debelius, 1999: p. 193). But to define Leverson's work as solely reformist is to overlook its creative power, since parody is 'not [solely] a matter of nostalgic stylistic imitation of past models; it is a stylistic confrontation, a modern recoding which establishes difference at the heart of similarity' (Hutcheon, 1985: pp. 7, 8). In her short story 'Suggestion', published in the fifth number of *The Yellow Book* in April 1895, Leverson mocks the generational confrontation between the young decadent and the disapproving older generation he is so eager to reject. He and his father both callously use women in much the same way. Leverson's parody actively creates a new image of the decadent as someone more retrograde in his own attitudes than his transgressive poses would otherwise have us believe.

In 'Suggestion', Leverson captures the playful and convincing artificiality of the decadent. Simultaneously an homage to Wildean wit and a corrective to the decadent dismissal of female subjectivity, she creates a more complex characterization of the young man's part in perpetuating patriarchal mores and the traditionalism that he seems at first to attack. Leverson's first-person narrator Cecil describes his act of retaliation against Lady Winthrop, a Mrs. Grundy-like figure who seems to be an indispensable support to the narrator's father and a 'highly suitable' potential wife. She is 'prosaic, fond of domineering, and an alarmingly excellent housekeeper', but she also makes the mistake of calling the narrator an 'intolerable, effeminate boy'. The narrator takes credit for orchestrating, by suggestion, his father's subsequent marriage to his daughter's school friend Laura Egerton, 'a beautiful girl of twenty' (Leverson, 1895: 249). After encouragement from the narrator, including hints of his father's 'secret affection for her', she marries his father for love. The narrator expresses a momentary twinge of conscience: 'Poor girl! She little knew what an irritating, ill-tempered, absent-minded person he is in private life; and at times I have pangs of remorse' (250). And yet, Cecil profits from Laura's misery by thwarting an older, more staid woman who insulted him and by gaining a devoted member of the household.

Leverson adeptly parodies the decadent worship of artificiality and appearance through her representation of Cecil, who is excessively fond of his own face and is attentive to aesthetic objects and social performances. He also regularly acts out of selfishness and manipulates women as objects on the marriage market in order to secure money and access to people who please him. He pushes his sister Marjorie into marrying Lady Winthrop's nephew for his money and also to irritate his old nemesis (255). And, supposedly in order to improve Laura's depression after she is trapped in a loveless marriage with his father (who now spends much of his time with a mistress), but actually to keep a fascinating man within his sphere, he encourages Adrian Grant to seduce Laura into having an affair, advising him on the best way to manipulate her emotions (256). The reader is left with little doubt that the attempt will succeed. After all, Cecil has already wielded power through suggestion once.

Cecil's bored, casually dismissive pose recasts the Wildean stance as potentially catastrophic rather than solely witty. Reminiscent of Wilde's play *The Importance of Being Earnest*, first performed in February 1895, the story's comic tone mockingly depicts the way in which courtship is predicated on concealing one's character from one's romantic partner. Wilde's play, whose characters provide a model for Cecil's wit, was a highly successful satire of Victorian mores. In it, one man invents a brother Ernest in order to avoid familial obligations and instead pursue pleasure in London (taking on that alternative persona when in the city). His friend later pretends to be that brother in order to trick a woman into marrying him. When they discuss honesty, one claims: 'My dear fellow, the truth isn't quite the sort of thing one tells to a nice, sweet, refined girl. What extraordinary ideas you have about the way to behave to a woman!' (Wilde, 1990: p. 16). Both of Wilde's central male characters manipulate female objects of desire through their subterfuge and their (male) ability to move freely between the country and the city. They can become whomsoever they choose, while the women are fixed in their identities and locations. They are vulnerable to subterfuge because Victorian courtship rituals depend upon the performance of gentility, financial status, and social reputations to vouchsafe the worth of one's partner. In Leverson's send-up of Wildean comedy and the courtship rituals he mocks, she forces acknowledgement of a darker truth. Laura is a victim of manipulation, first falling into a callous marriage with a philanderer and then very likely into an extramarital affair. All these circumstances serve the desires and whims of men.

Cecil displays the hallmarks of the decadent dandy made famous through Wilde's comedy. Yet, Leverson's protagonist is conscious of his own patriarchal power. Aware of the choices he is making, he occasionally hesitates. He is given the opportunity to reject the manipulative and misogynistic use of Laura's body as a pawn for his own economic and social benefit. In the last moment, he reconsiders his allegiance to Laura and his father and, for a short while, wonders whether he should discourage Adrian from seducing Laura (an act that, if discovered, will permanently ruin her life). Yet, when he witnesses his father visiting his mistress yet again, Cecil reverts to his original choice. Cecil is adept at manipulating social performances and is therefore uniquely suited to register the inequities of power in marital relations. That he recognizes the potential damage of his acts is damning. Well aware that he can be an agent of change for the benefit of Laura and others within his sphere, he chooses instead to shore up pre-existing inequities. Leverson depicts the way in which shallow courtship rituals leave women vulnerable to husbands who at best misrepresent themselves and at worst treat them with callous disregard. Here, however, Leverson also indicates the ways in which such alliances are open to manipulation by decadent men.

Victoria Cross's Androgynous Subject

Victoria Cross is one of the pen names used by Annie Sophie Cory (1868–1952). Born and raised in India, she became well-known for her novel *The Woman Who Didn't* (1895), published by The Bodley Head, the firm founded by John Lane, who also published *The Yellow Book*. *The Woman Who Didn't* is a story of unconsummated love between a married man and a woman on a ship returning from India and is often assumed to be a response to Grant Allen's *The Woman Who Did* (1895), though the relationship of the two novels is not so clear-cut as the similarity of the two titles suggests. In January 1895 Lane also published Cross's 'Theodora: A Fragment' in the fourth volume of *The Yellow Book*, possibly the most transgressive and potentially progressive story to appear in the periodical. It became part of her novel *Six Chapters of a Man's Life* (1906), which follows the New Woman Theodora and the dandy Cecil as they travel in the East. The novel employs a number of Orientalist tropes, and its tragic and violent ending fails to sustain the promise of an androgynous and progressive relationship suggested by the 1895 story, which may be 'the most challenging exploration of sexual desire and eroticism to be found in the pages of *The Yellow Book*', according to Sally Ledger: 'it echoes Gautier's cross-dressing heroine, Théodore, in *Mademoiselle de Maupin*, with Cross's short fiction centring on a sexually ambiguous erotic encounter between a New Womanish figure and a male aesthete' (2007: 22). Characterized by critics as 'supposedly racy' (Chan, 2016: p. 127), casting an 'atmosphere of ambiguous sexuality' (Showalter, 1993: p. xi), and plotting 'a seduction game' (Boyiopoulos, Choi, and Tildesley, 2015: p. 19), what is most apparent about Cross's fragment is its engagement with gender and sexuality through the expression of frank desire by both characters.

The parodic power of Cross's fragment does not result from its sardonic tone; instead, Cross's acknowledgement of the performative nature of gender presages contemporary critical conceptions of parody in the form of drag (see Chapter 23). 'Theodora: A Fragment' presents characters who parodically inhabit the very forms that the fin-de-siècle mainstream press feared. Cross takes aim at the commonly expressed anxiety about the blurring of femininity and masculinity in 'manly' women and effeminate men. For instance, in her 1894 rejoinder to Sarah Grand in the debate that coined the term 'New Woman', the socially conservative Ouida declares that 'everything which tends to obliterate the contrast of the sexes [. . .] tends also to destroy the charm of intercourse, the savor and sweetness of life' (2001: p. 159). Eliza Linn Linton had made a similar claim in her 1891 article 'The Wild Women: As Social Insurgents': '[The Wild Woman] does all manner of things which she thinks bestow upon her the power, together with the privileges, of a man; not thinking that in obliterating the finer distinctions of sex she is obliterating the finer traits of civilization' (1995: pp. 198–9). While women tended to be the targets of such popular critiques of feminist agitation for more economic, political, and social autonomy, these socially conservative critics saw the move towards greater freedoms for women as collapsing the distinctions between masculine and feminine norms and, consequently, weakening both men and women. Fears about masculine women were coupled with critiques of feminine men. Linton characterized the situation of 'effeminate' men who must be rescued from women 'who are neither man nor woman'. If they ally themselves with traditional women who embrace their femininity, they might yet '[return] to the ranks of masculine self-respect, and leave off this base subservience to folly which now disfigures and unmans them' (p. 205). According to these critics, the New Woman is self-consciously androgynous, and it is her pursuit of masculine prerogatives that is at fault for the feminization of the men who support her. Both figures disrupt the advancement of British society.

Cross's 'Theodora: A Fragment' depicts the mutual longing the decadent dandy Cecil and the New Woman Theodora have for each other. Theodora constantly plays with her own appearance, embraces her own physical androgyny, and expresses frankly her own sexual desires. When she is first described by Cecil to his friend Digby as 'peculiar' (Cross, 1895: 157), Cecil resists any suggestion that he is sexually interested in her and hints at his homosexuality when he says, 'I think I have heard men remaining celibates before now, especially men with my tastes' (157). When he calls upon her, however, he cannot help but appraise the 'harmonious lines of her figure' and the 'great care' bestowed upon her face; 'the eyes were darkened' and 'the hair arranged with infinite pains' accompanied by a 'smile that failed to dispel the air of fatigue and fashionable dissipation that seemed to cling to her' (161). Theodora's masterful control of her dress, makeup, and hair, along with her 'fashionable dissipation', casts her as one of the modern women Max Beerbohm satirically praised in his *Yellow Book* article 'A Defence of Cosmetics'. Beerbohm's witty decadent essay mocks the supposed purity of Victorian femininity and instead praises the artificial beauty created by makeup: 'Artifice is the strength of the world, and in that same mask of paint and powder, shadowed with vermeil tinct and most trimly pencilled, is woman's strength!' (1894: 68). Beerbohm humorously calls attention to the way in which femininity itself is a pose that women perform. Cross plays upon the associations of femininity and artificiality that Beerbohm satirically observes, recasting his cynical tone in a more serious light. Her parody reconsiders the power inherent in embracing the failure of gender norms. While Beerbohm is wryly satirical, Cross's narrative casts these adaptations of appearance as particular skills worthy of respect.

As adept as Theodora is at the artificial performance of femininity, in her next meeting with Cecil she shows herself equally adept at cross-dressing, deepening her allure to Cecil. He invites her into his own home to view the treasures he has collected on his travels in the Orient. Her appearance, already physically androgynous (she is slim and has a 'curious masculine shade upon the upper lip' (Cross, 1895: 177)), is made more so when she dons a zouave (a man's military jacket) along with a fez and smokes a cigarette as she laughs. At this point, Cecil decides that he cannot deny his sexual desire for Theodora. In putting on each costume – first the feminine dress of the modern London woman and then the exotic Algerian garb of the military man – she clearly bends gender norms. She is sexually desirable to Cecil in both guises, and it is perhaps the very slippage between them that is the source of his attraction to her. Theodora's parodic performances of both identities call attention to the falsity of any claim that there is anything 'natural' about either femininity or masculinity, thus aligning with Beerbohm's earlier critique, yet doing so in a parody that celebrates artificiality rather than mocking it.

Yet, even as Theodora's parodic performance mocks the gender essentialism of the socially conservative press, her playful awareness of becoming an exotic object of desire for Cecil simultaneously challenges the colonialist consumerist impulse of decadence. Cecil's home full of objects from 'the East' is reminiscent of Dorian's collection in Wilde's *The Picture of Dorian Gray* (1891). Both are indebted to Joris-Karl Huysmans's *À rebours* [*Against Nature*] (1884), a novel in which the main character, Des Esseintes, faces madness after creating what Symons in 'The Decadent Movement in Literature' calls an 'artificial paradise' of pictures, books, and other art objects that 'satisfy his sense of the exquisitely abnormal' (2014: p. 180).

Wilde reimagines Des Esseintes' 'perverse pathology' and alienation from society as an exercise that deepens his moral break from humanity. For Dorian Gray, the consumerist impulse reflects a psychopathic narcissism and a desire for escape through a fixation on beauty and sensuality that fails to provide a way to reach back to humanity (Wilde, 2000: p. 134).

Cross's parody of these recognizable progenitors turns this decadent theme around yet again. Instead of elevating art objects as the epitome of human mastery (and serving autoerotic pleasure), Theodora uses Cecil's collection to confront a history of male consumption as a form of sexual objectification. Cecil's trophies become the tools with which Theodora asserts her modern sexuality in the present. His investment in collecting and his obsession with Oriental objects presage a similar desire to possess Theodora in the light of his potentially abnormal desires for the artificial. When she adorns a small statue of 'the Hindu equivalent of the Greek Aphrodite' with her own ring, she laughingly restores the goddess's reign, calling attention to the resonance of the figure's female power (Cross, 1895: 179). When Theodora dons the costume Cecil has brought back from the East, she literally becomes an object he has collected, like the drawings of the male and female lovers he has sketched, and yet she returns his gaze.

When she demands his sketchbook, Cecil confronts his discomfort with seeing Theodora as a mutually desiring subject. He begins to understand that his subjectivity, too, can be owned by another, as his memories are traced in the sketchbook she now possesses (186). Cecil admits an 'overwhelming desire to take her in [his] arms and hold her, control her, assert [his] will over hers, this exasperating object who had been pleasing and seducing every sense for the last three hours and now was leaving them all unsatisfied' (187). Nonetheless, Theodora continually challenges him with her desire; he cannot possess her without being possessed in turn. When their passion is finally consummated by their aggressive kiss, there is 'no confusion nor embarrassment in [her eyes], they were full of the hot, clear, blinding light of passion' (187). Through parodic gender performance, Theodora breaks down both the polarity of the gender binary and the one-directionality of desire in decadent texts that focus on possession and accumulation. While Cecil and Theodora's erotic encounter over a collection of Oriental objects brings Wilde's Dorian and Huysmans's Des Esseintes to mind, here there is a more conscious confrontation with the productive nature of mutual desire occurring between two subjects. Theodora resists objectification in part because she is androgynous. She cannot be pinned down.

Cross's 'Theodora: A Fragment' is driven by longing and desire, not ownership. Cecil does not wallow in what he possesses, but rather confronts what he lacks. Theodora's parodic performance of femininity and masculinity simultaneously critiques conservative notions of gender essentialism and decadent male narratives of the consumption of objects as a retreat from, or assertion of superiority over, the rest of humanity. Cross opens up a third space wherein androgyny becomes a pose through which one can assert subjectivity and erotic desire. The story, a fragment, gestures towards the possible, the unfinished, and the future that such playfulness has introduced but that readers of the fin de siècle had yet to fully imagine.

Conclusion

Parody remains a significant contribution to the productive possibilities of decadent literature in the hands of women writers of *The Yellow Book*, a primary discursive space for the exploration of decadent themes. The transgressive potential of decadence in Great Britain was cut short by the arrest, trial, and subsequent imprisonment of Oscar Wilde in April and May of 1895, with *The Yellow Book* ceasing publication shortly thereafter, in 1897. In assessing the lasting impact of decadence, we must also attend to the women writers who carved out a niche in the movement through their mastery of the source material that they parodied with sharp aesthetic skill. In doing so, these writers attempted to create a productive third space. As decadents, they too explored ambivalent attitudes towards modern progress and acknowledged the artificiality of gender performance. While decadence as a phenomenon remains largely understood as the provenance of male writers, these decadent parodies indicate that women did see something valuable in its exploration of ambivalence and actively contributed to decadence as a phenomenon of the British fin de siècle. As parodists and critics, they exposed the limitations of the misogyny of male decadence and demonstrated the ways in which one could use the decadent aesthetics of failure to interrogate gender norms. D'Arcy, Leverson, and Cross consequently placed themselves within literary history while also daring to redefine their present.

References

Beerbohm, Max (1894). A Defence of Cosmetics. *The Yellow Book*, 1, 65–82.

Boyiopoulos, Kostas, Yoonjoung Choi, and Matthew Brinton Tildesley, eds. (2015). *The Decadent Short Story: An Annotated Anthology*, Edinburgh: Edinburgh University Press.

Brake, Laurel (1995). Endgames: The Politics of The Yellow Book or, Decadence, Gender, and the New Journalism. *Essays and Studies*, 48, 38–64.
Chan, Winnie (2016). *The Yellow Book* Circle and the Culture of the Literary Magazine. In Dominic Head, ed., *The Cambridge History of the English Short Story*, Cambridge: Cambridge University Press, pp. 118–34.
Cross, Victoria (1895). Theodora: A Fragment. *The Yellow Book*, 4, 156–88.
D'Arcy, Ella (1894). Irremediable. *The Yellow Book*, 1, 87–108.
Debelius, Margaret (1999). Countering a Counterpoetics: Ada Leverson and Oscar Wilde. In Talia Schaffer and Kathy Alexis Psomiades, eds., *Women and British Aestheticism*, Charlottesville: University Press of Virginia, pp. 192–210.
Denisoff, Dennis (2006). *Aestheticism and Sexual Parody, 1840–1940*, Cambridge: Cambridge University Press.
Fisher, Benjamin Franklin IV (1992). Ella D'Arcy: A Commentary with a Primary and Annotated Secondary Bibliography. *English Literature in Transition 1880–1920*, 35(2), 179–211.
Hannoosh, Michele (1989). *Parody and Decadence: Laforgue's Moralités légendaires*, Columbus: Ohio State University Press.
Hughes, Linda K. (2004). Women Poets and Contested Spaces in *The Yellow Book*. *Studies in English* Literature, *1500–1900*, 44(4), 849–72.
Hutcheon, Linda (1985). *A Theory of Parody*, New York: Methuen.
Jackson, Holbrook (1913). *The Eighteen Nineties*, New York: Mitchell Kennerley.
Ledger, Sally (2007). Wilde Women and The Yellow Book: The Sexual Politics of Aestheticism and Decadence. *English Literature in Transition, 1880–1920*, 50(1), 5–26.
Leverson, Mrs. Ernest [Ada] (1895). Suggestion. *The Yellow Book*, 5, 249–57.
Linton, Eliza Linn (1995). The Wild Women: As Social Insurgents. In Susan Hamilton, ed., *'Criminals, Idiots, Women, and Minors': Victorian Writing by Women on Women*, Peterborough: Broadview Press, pp. 198–207.
Ouida (2001). The New Woman. In Carolyn Christensen Nelson, ed., *A New Woman Reader*, Toronto, ON: Broadview Press, pp. 153–60.
Showalter, Elaine, ed. (1993). *Daughters of Decadence: Women Writers of the Fin-de-Siècle*, Rutgers, NJ: Rutgers University Press.
Stutfield, Hugh E. M. (2001). Tommyrotics. In Carolyn Christensen Nelson, ed., *A New Woman Reader: Fiction, Drama and Articles of the 1890s*, Toronto, ON: Broadview Press, pp. 234–43.
Symons, Arthur (1894). Stella Maris. *The Yellow Book*, 1, 129–31.
Symons, Arthur (2014). The Decadent Movement in Literature. In *The Symbolist Movement in Literature*, Matthew Creasy, ed., Manchester: Carcanet Press, pp. 169–83.
Wilde, Oscar (1990). *The Importance of Being Earnest*, Mineola: Dover Publications.
Wilde, Oscar (2000). *The Picture of Dorian Gray*, London: Penguin Classics.
Wolff, Janet (1985). The Invisible Flâneuse: Women and the Literature of Modernity. *Theory, Culture, and Society*, 2(3), 37–45.

CHAPTER 11

The Philosophy of Decadence

Nicholas D. More

So far you have only been interested in decadents [. . .] – allow me to be uninteresting to you . . .

Friedrich Nietzsche to Malwida von Meysenbug, 8 December 1888 (*eKGWB*, BVN-1888, 1177a)[1]

More than any other philosopher of his era, Friedrich Nietzsche (1844–1900) conceptualized modern decadence on a grand and influential scale. While one could treat Martin Heidegger (1889–1976), Georges Bataille (1897–1962), Theodor Adorno (1903–1969), Gilles Deleuze (1925–1995), Michel Foucault (1926–1984), and Jacques Derrida (1930–2004) as philosophers who theorized aspects of decadence in the twentieth century, all of these thinkers pay explicit homage to Nietzsche – and trace their thinking about decadence to him.[2] Because Nietzsche is uniquely foundational to the philosophy of decadence as understood by these inheritors whose work still animates Continental philosophy today, this chapter will focus on that shared conceptual source.

Nietzsche held decadence to be any condition, deceptively thought good, which limits what something or someone can be. This concept informs his critical and affirmative projects, acting as a versatile tool to identify and overcome his own decadence, and to resist the decadence of Western culture. Decadence appears in five major areas of concern to Nietzsche: physiology; psychology; art and artists; politics; and philosophy.

[1] Nietzsche's works are abbreviated as follows: *A* (*The Antichrist*), *BGE* (*Beyond Good and Evil*), *CW* (*The Case of Wagner*), *EH* (*Ecce Homo*), *eKGWB* (*Digital Kritische Gesamtausgabe Werke und Briefe*), *GM* (*On the Genealogy of Morals*), *TI* (*Twilight of the Idols*), *UM* (*Untimely Meditations*), and *Z* (*Thus Spoke Zarathustra*). Chapter title abbreviation and section or aphorism number, not page number, follow the abbreviations. For all other works, standard citations are provided. Ellipses are Nietzsche's unless bracketed. Thanks to Teresa Knight for ideas on this essay's structure and tone.

[2] James Brusseau shows how French philosophy views decadence in a Nietzschean sense (*Decadence of the French Nietzsche*, 2005), and David Weir remarks that Nietzsche 'is the philosopher who has thought most deeply about the phenomenon of decadence' (Weir, 1995: p. 134). In *Minima Moralia*, Adorno writes that Nietzsche 'teach[es] the norm to fear its own perversity' (Adorno, 2005: p. 97).

Physical and mental phenomena provide the substrate of his understanding, but they manifest in cultural, political, and philosophical forms that, in turn, affect the body and mind. In each of the five areas that this essay will engage, the concept of decadence for Nietzsche serves (i) to unmask valued cultural phenomena as corrupt, (ii) to name and analyse degenerate effects, and (iii) to spur reflection on how to respond.[3]

The Physiology of Decadence

Before the advent of bacteriological science in the late-nineteenth century, human illness was poorly understood. Diseases were linked to a host of fictive causes and valences that drew upon social, moral, and religious ideas, and sufferers were subject to ineffective, often injurious treatment. In the most famous and widespread example, a painful and deadly illness was understood to signify artistic talent and to bring a 'good death'. Clark Lawlor has shown that in 'the Romantic formulation, consumption [*tuberculosis* after 1882] was aestheticized in a positive manner as a sign of passion, spirituality, and genius' (2006: pp. 1–2). People saw the disease itself as good.

Nietzsche resisted prevailing narratives of illness by emphasizing the corporeal meaning of disease. In living things, decadence for Nietzsche is fundamentally 'a physiological regression' (*A* 17). This follows from his naturalist philosophy. Nietzsche took reality to be encompassed by nature and shunned recourse to supernatural entities, immortal souls, or mystic casuistry. Thus, human beings are entirely bodies; human beings are animals, descended from other animals; human beings exist in time and die a permanent death. Human beings also *create* everything in the realm of thought and culture that we take to be significant, meaningful, and beautiful – and the obverse. Given his naturalist philosophy, decadence for Nietzsche is fundamentally material: the malfunction or breakdown of organic systems, leading to literal weakness and a lessening or loss of the power to organize and act. Yet while the necessary condition of decadence is somatic malfunction, the full concept requires the misinterpretation of that malfunction as good. As seen with tuberculosis, the decadent deceptively thinks the sickness itself marks the sufferer as good.

[3] The words *décadence* and *décadent* first appear (120 times) in the four short books of Nietzsche's last productive year, 1888 (*The Case of Wagner, The Antichrist, Twilight of the Idols*, and *Ecce Homo*), and three times more in the only new material for *Nietzsche Contra Wagner* (1888). The words also appear at least once in 133 sections of Nietzsche's notebook fragments, and in 22 of his letters. The present chapter treats only material Nietzsche prepared and intended for publication.

Modernity is an age of physical exhaustion caused by the well-known rise of industrial economies, urbanization, and *laissez-faire* capitalism, and Nietzsche often characterizes his era in bodily terms. A decadent organism is sick, exhausted, overexcited or nervous, shows an inordinate fear of pain, has insufficient strength to carry on activities for which it is otherwise capable, and finds it hard to fend off deleterious stimuli that prolong illness or maladaptation. 'The exhausted are *attracted* by what is harmful' (*CW* 5). Physiological decadence decreases or deadens perception, degrades one's taste, breaks down natural defences, and makes it difficult to discern one's own best interest or to take necessary steps for recovery. The rise in nicotine or alcohol addiction, for example, creates physiological decadence: in a chemical sense the body becomes trained to think of the substances as good, even as they inhibit our organic functioning. Thus, any kind of 'contempt for the body' is a 'recipe for decadence' (*EH* Daybreak 2).

Effective responses to physiological decadence are material cures and therapies, a general conservation of energy, and what Nietzsche calls 'good taste' in all the concrete realities of one's situation, that is, one's choice of diet, environment, recreation, relations with others and, in sum, how one reacts – in disciplined self-defence – to external stimuli (*EH* Clever 10). After a lifetime of his own physical suffering, for example, Nietzsche claimed that sometimes 'sickness can actually be an energetic *stimulus* to life, to being more alive' (*EH* Wise 2). In contrast to the decadent, however, Nietzsche is aware of his illness *as injurious* and seeks to overcome it. Still, in dire cases, sickness may require 'not reacting at all any more' in order to effect a slow return to health (*EH* Wise 6).

The Psychology of Decadence

Prior to Sigmund Freud (1856–1939), Alfred Adler (1870–1937), and Carl Jung (1875–1961), Nietzsche considered psychology 'the path to the fundamental problems' of human life and values, a difficult descent 'into the depths' blocked by moral prejudice and masked by human refinement (*BGE* 23, 270). His own forays led him to the view that human beings manifest a ubiquitous will to power, understood as the variable impulse of all living things to secure favourable conditions for life: to pursue the beneficial, to combat the injurious, to reproduce, to become what they are in the fullest sense possible. 'I consider life itself instinct for growth, for continuance, for accumulation of forces, for *power*: where the will to power is lacking there is decline' (*A* 6). His naturalism led Nietzsche to view psychology as 'morphology' and 'the development of the will to power'

(*BGE* 23). So considered, psychological decadence becomes any mental condition, deceptively thought good, which limits a subject's flourishing.

Psychological weakness appears most often as a type of suffering, a 'preponderance of feelings of displeasure over feelings of pleasure' that constitutes 'the *formula* for decadence' (*A* 15). In such condition, people commonly invent psychic compensation. 'Who alone has reason to *lie himself out* of actuality? He who *suffers* from it. But to suffer from actuality means to be an abortive actuality. . . . The preponderance of feelings of displeasure over feelings of pleasure is the *cause* of a fictitious morality and religion' (*A* 15). In *The Antichrist* and *On the Genealogy of Morals*, Nietzsche locates such psychological decadence, for example, in Jewish and early Christian resentment of Roman oppression. This long suffering of a people inspired an unconscious 'revolt in morality' (*GM* I, 10) whereby a psychological weakness found expression in a cultural revaluation of values. As evidence, Nietzsche identifies words in German, Persian, Slavic, Gaelic, Greek, and Latin that point to class descriptors as the origin of later moral evaluation terms (*GM* I, 4–5). Masters – strong, ruling, confident, proud, happy – applied self-descriptive concepts to establish what is *good*, while the rest of a population were found lacking and, as the not-masters, were either ignored or deemed bad. Slaves and other oppressed human beings, in contrast, reversed such values over time by looking first at the source of their unhappiness, the masters, and calling them *evil*. It followed that masterly traits were also evil, while the opposite of such traits were turned, by default, into virtues.

> Considered psychologically, Jews are the people with the toughest vital energy which, placed in impossible circumstances, voluntarily, from the most profoundly shrewd sense of self-preservation, took sides with all the instincts of decadence – *not* as being dominated by them but because they sensed in them a power by which to prevail *against* 'the world'. (*A* 24)

Through this oppressed optic, pride and worldly success became sins, and humility, meekness, and impoverishment a blessed condition (as the Sermon on the Mount would have it). It took hundreds of years, but 'slave morality' overtook ancient understandings of human happiness and wellbeing. Modern views of 'good and evil' retain this Judeo-Christian stance in religious and secular contexts, by which we castigate egoism and celebrate selflessness. For Nietzsche, such values point to psychological decadence writ large because they undermine human striving.

The effects of psychological decadence are debilitating to individuals and cultures and take many forms. Altruism, for example, constitutes psychological decadence for Nietzsche because it celebrates one's own loss of self. Altruism is 'the true sign of decadence, being *seduced* by what is harmful, not being *able* to find your advantage any more, self-destruction made into the sign of value in general' (*EH* Destiny 8). The result is depressive and weakening.

Pessimism is another prominent effect of psychological decadence. Nietzsche sees judgements against human life as 'stupidities' because we are never in a position to evaluate life in toto (*TI* Socrates 2). Condemnations of this world as a 'veil of tears' are neither true nor false, but symptoms of the evaluators' own decadent position. In a similar sense, all manner of idealism and the positing of other worlds or life after death constitute covert judgements against life on earth – elaborate compensations that indicate a psychological inadequacy for facing the world as it is.

Therapeutic responses to psychological decadence amount to the difficult task of comprehending and accepting the actual conditions of human life, resisting fictive compensations, understanding the value of one's own goals and ways of living, and embracing the past in *all* its complexity to overcome resentment and desire for revenge. Nietzsche's formula for this psychological health is *amor fati* – love of one's fate, affirmation of (without deception about) even the painful and questionable in life (*EH* Birth 2).

Decadence in Art and Artists

Like many intellectuals, Nietzsche considered the cultural production of thinkers and artists to constitute our human meaning. Unlike most intellectuals, however, he saw all truth and meaning as humanly created, not found. Thus our cultural calling embraces the continual project of value and meaning creation, and products of culture are neither timeless verities nor a tale of progress, but a contest of contingent notions of truth and value. Nietzsche evaluates such competing notions by the extent to which they help or hinder the enhancement of life. Given this stance, 'artistic creation' encompasses everything from painting to philosophy, science to politics. The health or sickness of art is therefore of paramount importance. Decadence in an artist, for Nietzsche, is the lack of power to organize one's material thematically and formally, and decadence in art works is the seduction that we are in the presence of something worthwhile when we are not.

In Nietzsche's aesthetics, the judgement of beauty is a human projection and species affirmation, redolent of our own health and vigour. In contrast, 'ugliness is understood as a sign and symptom of degeneration: anything vaguely reminiscent of degeneracy causes us to judge the thing "ugly"' (*TI* Untimely 19–20). Hence Nietzsche treats works of art as analogous to living things, with decadent art exhibiting an 'anarchy of parts' and a lifeless style (*CW* 7). The parts of living things work in concert, are intimately related, and exist to allow the whole to function as the thing that it is. Beautiful art mirrors the organic unity of living things by having parts well-arranged. In decadent art, parts instead take precedence over the whole – which confounds the artefact and breaks its analogy to the organic.

The effects of literary decadence appear, for example, when 'life no longer dwells in the whole. The word becomes sovereign and leaps out of the sentence, the sentence reaches out and obscures the meaning of the page, the page gains life at the expense of the whole – the whole is no longer a whole' (*CW* 7).[4] Here, the life of the writer's prose is its meaning. If words or phrases 'become sovereign', then meaning can be lost, even if individual elements shine with brilliance. Nietzsche cites the Goncourt brothers (Edmond de, 1822–1896; Jules de, 1830–1870), whose fragmentary novels inspire in the philosopher 'a kind of compassion for so much distress' (*CW* 7). The result for Nietzsche is ersatz art, mere pastiche, something that inevitably falls apart, becomes incoherent, even meaningless – thus lifeless and ugly, part and parcel of nihilism.

Because decadent artists have insufficient strength to command their material, they expend what energy they have in small-scale phrases and details strung together. Thus, decadent art is composite, calculated, artificial, and built for effects. Nietzsche sees 'excessive liveliness in the smallest parts; excitement at any price; cunning as the expression of *impoverished* life; more and more nerves in place of flesh' (*CW* Afterword). Such art conveys a sense of effort and strain, a paralysis of meaning, and 'torpidity *or* hostility and chaos': mere languor or a spasm of dark energy. In decadent music – German opera composer Richard Wagner (1813–1883) is Nietzsche's primary example – sonic phrases exist only to move the audience, creating a series of moods divorced from any coherent meaning of the putative dramas they accompany. Nietzsche concludes that Wagner is no dramatist at all; he lacks the skill and strength of a genuine artist because the knots of his operatic plots are absurd. Instead, Wagner uses *acting* and semblance in place of substance. Romantic author 'Victor Hugo [1802–1885] and Richard Wagner – they signify the same thing: in

[4] For thoughts on Nietzsche's notional debt to (and difference from) Paul Bourget's statement along quite similar lines, see Constable, Denisoff, and Potolsky, (1999: p. 16).

declining cultures, wherever the decision comes to rest with the masses, authenticity becomes superfluous, disadvantageous, a liability. Only the actor still arouses *great* enthusiasm' (*CW* 11). The nineteenth-century artist-as-actor arouses the crowd by the decadent simulacrum of import and consequence, by the appearance of meaning and significance, by the seduction of dramatic phrases and gestures.[5]

The effects of a modern decadent art are tailored to a modern decadent audience; as the art corrupts, the audience clamours for more. In art like Wagner's, 'all that the modern world requires most urgently is mixed in the most seductive manner: the three great *stimulantia* of the exhausted – the *brutal*, the *artificial*, and the *innocent* (idiotic)' (*CW* 5). This casts modernity as a physical condition of enervation; sufferers need an infusion of energy to be moved. *Brutal* stimulants are required because modern people have a dulled sensibility. Tired and sick, they need more volume, more violence, more notes, and more extremes if they are to react at all. An *artificial* kind of stimuli is required because reality takes psychic strength to engage. The modern soul lacks the requisite fortitude – it is too weak to think about the real. Finally, an *innocent* (idiotic) kind of stimuli is required because it makes no moral demands and presents no danger. Exhausted people cannot engage with complexity, rigour, or threat. Instead they need the cute, the nostalgic, the bombastic, the obvious, and the kitsch.[6]

The overall effect of decadent art for Nietzsche is to make 'an alliance of beauty and sickness' (*CW* Afterword), to seduce and corrupt our taste for the very things that weaken us. Decadent art creates artificial vehicles to carry ever more necessary and empty stimuli. It is now a parasite that we invite to feed upon us.

The therapeutic response to decadent art and artists for Nietzsche has three elements. The first is to unmask decadence in art as such. When people conflate commercial success and popular acclaim, or the merely critical, dark, and broken, with genuine artistic health and value, unmasking decadence becomes more difficult. Hence much of Nietzsche's writing is the calling out of diseased art. The second element is to resist decadent

5 Nietzsche has in mind the stylized acting of the nineteenth century. Prior to Konstantin Stanislavski (1863–1938), Western acting was flatly representational, focused on caricature, gesture, and the voice. Stanislavski inaugurated the physical and psychological realism in acting that we know today.

6 Nietzsche links innocence to the idiotic via Fyodor Dostoyevsky, reading *The Idiot*'s epileptic protagonist as a 'good man' in the decadent Christian sense, as naïve, optimistic, deceived, weak, and ill. See the *CW* Epilogue, and when Nietzsche regrets 'that no Dostoyevsky lived in the neighborhood of this most interesting decadent [Jesus]; I mean someone who could feel the thrilling fascination of such a combination of the sublime, the sick and the childish' (*A* 31).

art, to turn away. After writing a paean to Wagner in his first book (*The Birth of Tragedy*, 1872), Nietzsche broke from his friend in 1876 after witnessing the inauguration of the composer's Bayreuth Festival, a display of fake art and mass pandering to anti-Semitic reprobates, Christian idealists, and German nationalists. After being part of Wagner's inner circle, Nietzsche abandoned the cause. The third element of a therapeutic response to decadent art is to cultivate a healthy taste by listening to better music – Nietzsche praises Georges Bizet's (1838–1875) *Carmen*, for example, as having precision, lightness, organization, and salutary effects on thinking (*CW* 1–3) – and by reading realist authors far removed from modernity, people like Thucydides (Greek historian, c. 460–c. 400 BCE), Sallust (Roman historian, 86–c. 35 BCE), Horace (Roman poet and satirist, 65–68 BCE), and Machiavelli (Italian humanist and political philosopher, 1469–1527) (*TI* Ancients 1–2). Nietzsche views these authors as a 'cure' for all '"higher swindle" or, if you prefer, "idealism"'.[7]

Illuminating his own view of healthy art, Nietzsche praises the Horatian *Odes* in which 'every word, as sound, as locus, as concept, pours forth its power to left and right and over the whole, this minimum in the range and number of signs which achieves a maximum of energy of these signs – all this is Roman and, if one will believe me, *noble par excellence*' (*TI* Ancients 2). The concision and unity of Horace's poetry allow every word to resonate with meaning. Nietzsche himself admits a 'very serious ambition for Roman style, for the "*aera perennius*" in style [enduring like bronze]' (*TI* Ancients 1). Hence Nietzsche considered his own writing to be a therapeutic reply to modern decadence, an attempt at self-recovery.

Decadence in Politics

Nietzsche's naturalist philosophy of politics understands healthy social organization as akin to the order required for organic life. As in art and other human artefacts, the question involves a consideration of the best relations between parts and wholes. For Nietzsche, the best social organization serves the interests of culture, not economic or political aggrandizement. In the modern world, political decadence for Nietzsche is the disintegration of Europe and the weakening of a ruling principle that could otherwise unify people.

[7] Idealism in ethics refers to the view that universal principles should direct one's actions. Nietzsche alludes to the general habit of idealists to describe things as they ought to be instead of how they are.

The chief effect of political decadence in the West is nationalism and the rise of Otto von Bismarck's (1815–1898) modern state in particular. 'All our political theories *and* state constitutions, the "German *Reich*" certainly not excluded, are consequences, necessary effects of decline; the unconscious influence of decadence has gained ascendancy' (*TI* Untimely 37). As in other spheres, the problem is privileging parts (nations) over wholes (the people of Europe). For Nietzsche, the triumphant 'Wars of Liberation' aimed at France (1813–1815) were a disaster, and Germans now 'have everything that has happened on their conscience, everything that is the case today, the most *anti-cultural* sickness and unreason there is, nationalism' (*EH* CW 2). Nationalism harms culture first because it privileges origin over form in art. Nietzsche laments, for example, that Wagner '*condescended* to the Germans', he 'became *reichsdeutsch*' [faithful to the German state] (*EH* Clever 5). Nationalism also harms culture by disparaging the culture of others, limiting the spread and influence of ideas from outside one's experience, causing a narrow turning inward. Thus, Nietzsche calls nationalism a disease, deeming it the '*névrose nationale* [national neurosis] that Europe is sick from, this immortalizing of Europe's provincial character, of *petty* politics' (*EH* CW 2). While his fellow Germans celebrated their increasing self-importance, Nietzsche saw instead a haunting spectre. Germans, he wrote in 1888, 'have even robbed Europe of its sense, its *rationality* – they have steered it into a dead end' (*EH* CW 2).

The second major effect of political decadence is the weakening of the ruling principle, shown in the unwillingness to use power for meaningful cultural ends. Instead, 'whenever the word "authority" is so much as heard one believes oneself in danger of a new slavery. The decadence in the valuating instinct of our politicians, our political parties, goes so deep that *they instinctively prefer* that which leads to dissolution, that which hastens the end' (*TI* Untimely 39). Nietzsche sees this hatred of authority as an outflow from the decadent values of slave morality, especially the belief that power is evil. The historical result of this Judeo-Christian value triumph is the rise of democracy, the attempt to put everyone and no one in charge, to diffuse power into enough hands that its exercise would be unable to cause the pain and suffering that constitute the decadent's principal fear. This lack of organizing power Nietzsche identifies as decadent, both in art and politics, and it leads to further dissolution of life and life's meaning: culture.

Nietzschean responses to political decadence take three forms: a longing for the unification of Europe, cultural precedence in political philosophy, and the rejection of conservative attempts at reversion to earlier epochs. Nietzsche himself was officially stateless and championed the idea of thinkers being 'good Europeans' most of all (*BGE* Preface). Hence, he desired leadership 'strong enough to make Europe into a unity, a political *and economic* unity for the purpose of world governance' (*EH* CW 2). Nietzsche celebrated a vision of European solidarity and the continent's history of shared cultural exchange.

The second kind of response to political decadence is to imagine a society devoted to cultivating creators and to living by their vision. In contrast to an inherited class structure or plutocracy, this 'rule of the best' would be an 'aristocracy of intellect',[8] in which society is organized to further culture and artists, to aid those responsible for the continual recreation of human truths and values that Nietzsche counts as the meaning of human life (*UM* III 2). While the philosopher also imagined a future kind of person that might fit this ruling-artist model, an 'Overman' who would create new values and look upon contemporary human beings like we look upon primates (*Z* Prologue 3), Nietzsche never wrote anything like a treatise on political philosophy and believed that 'anything great in the cultural sense is apolitical, even *anti-political*' (*TI* Germans 4). He seems to have viewed only the Italian Renaissance, a few ancient Greek city states, and the late Roman republic as examples of political arrangements that did not obstruct cultural flourishing.

The third kind of response to political decadence is to reject any attempt at returning to previous forms of healthy social structures. Instead, Nietzsche says we have no choice but to walk further into decadence before we can inhabit a new kind of future. He writes:

> *In the ear of the Conservatives.* – What was formerly not known, what is known today or could be known – a *reversion*, a turning back in any sense and to any degree, is quite impossible. We physiologists at least know that. But all priests and moralists have believed it was possible – they have *wanted* to take mankind back, *force* it back, to an *earlier* standard of virtue. (*TI* Untimely 43)

Nietzsche rejects such value nostalgia. The perennial attempt to revert to former times of health and good character is unwise because we exist in time. The values of an age stem from a thousand contexts, conditions, contingencies, needs, interests, pressures, pleasures, and histories. We exist

8 The phrase is from an 1889 essay by Georg Brandes, in *Friedrich Nietzsche* (1914: p. 52). Brandes entitled the first part of his book on Nietzsche's philosophy, 'An Essay on Aristocratic Radicalism', a coinage that Nietzsche cites approvingly in correspondence (*eKGWB*, BVN-1888, 984).

now in the age of decadence, and there is no way to revert to another one. Nietzsche continues:

> Even politicians have in this matter imitated the preachers of virtue: even today there are parties whose goal is a dream of the crabwise *retrogression* of all things. But no one is free to be a crab. There is nothing for it: one *has* to go forward, which is to say *step by step further into decadence* (– this is *my* definition of modern 'progress' . . .). One can *retard* this development and, through retardation, dam and gather up degeneration itself and make it more vehement and *sudden*: more one cannot do. (*TI* Untimely 43)

Here Nietzsche rejects the myth of progress, moral or otherwise. We are different, and weaker, so our moral, cultural, and political virtues are different – and accord with our enervated state. The contemporaries of Italian noble Cesare Borgia (1475–1507) would 'laugh themselves to death at the comic spectacle of us moderns, with our thickly padded humanity, going to any length to avoid bumping into a pebble. In fact, and without meaning to be, we are boundlessly funny with our modern "virtues"' (*TI* Untimely 37). In a decadent condition we have no choice but to 'progress' deeper into our sickness. Nietzsche thinks we could 'retard this development' and 'gather up degeneration itself', but this would only intensify its effects. As to political decadence, in sum, we may dream of a healing unification and the rule of art, but there is no going forward – or back – until we see our current disease through to the end.

Decadence in Philosophy

Philosophy is the highest calling of profound and creative spirits, for Nietzsche, but also the hiding place of secret priests and diseased minds that poison humanity with fictive conceptual schemes and degenerate moral dicta. On the whole, decadence in philosophy is contempt for individual life and circumstance in favour of tyrannical abstraction disguised as 'rationality' and 'morality' – the degeneration of philosophy from a life guide to a pointless escape from and condemnation of life. Instead, philosophy should be suited to individual lives and differences, a 'spiritualizing' of our instincts, a thoughtful channelling of our passionate energies into shared cultural forms (*TI* Morality 3). 'To *have* to combat one's instincts – that is the formula for decadence: as long as life is *ascending*, happiness and instinct are one' (*TI* Socrates 11).

The effects of decadence in philosophy are extensive and far-reaching, and Nietzsche's works are replete with attacks on the sickness of philosophy.[9] He sees philosophies of modernity as exhausted and pessimistic, but they do not initiate philosophical decadence; it has deep roots in the West.

Nietzsche traces decadence in philosophy to Socrates (470–399 BCE), a man who took revenge on life by opposing it with concepts and 'rationality at any cost' (*TI* Socrates 11).[10] Observing that in every age the wisest of men have considered life worthless, Nietzsche recalls that 'even Socrates said as he died: "To live – that means to be a long time sick"'. If it makes no sense to judge life as worthy or worthless because we are in no position to judge it per se, Nietzsche writes that a negative judgement of life 'proves rather that they themselves, these wisest men, were in some way in *physiological* accord since they stood – *had* to stand – in the same negative relation to life'. Hence, he wonders: 'all these great wise men – they have not only been decadents, they have not even been wise?' (*TI* Socrates 2). This sets the stage in Nietzsche for discovering a long history of philosophical decadence.

Nietzsche identifies the Socratic love for argumentation as the primary sign of an already existing decadence. 'With Socrates Greek taste undergoes a change in favour of dialectics [. . .]. It is above all the defeat of a *nobler* taste; with dialectics the rabble gets on top' (*TI* Socrates 5). Nietzsche characterizes this nobler taste as confidence in one's position and ruling instincts. 'Wherever authority is still part of accepted usage and one does not "give reasons" but commands, the dialectician is a kind of buffoon: he is laughed at, he is not taken seriously. – Socrates was the buffoon who *got himself taken seriously*: what was really happening when that happened?' Nietzsche's answer: born of an abundance of health and destructive power, ancient Greek civilization had grown fearful of its instinctual, unconscious 'dark desires' and saw Socrates as a saviour. 'The fanaticism with which the whole of Greek thought throws itself at rationality betrays a state of emergency: one was in peril, one had only *one* choice: either to perish or – be *absurdly rational*' (*TI* Socrates 10).[11] Socratic philosophy thus

[9] I have indicated elsewhere that Nietzsche is primarily a satirist of philosophy; see More (2014). *Nietzsche's Last Laugh: Ecce Homo as Satire*. Cambridge: Cambridge University Press.

[10] Socrates appears in nearly all works by Plato; there is no consensus about where the philosophy of Socrates ends and Plato's begins.

[11] Nietzsche writes of the ancient Greeks: 'I saw their strongest instinct, the will to power, I saw them trembling at the intractable force of this drive – I saw all their institutions evolve out of protective measures designed for mutual security against the *explosive material* within them.' This force 'discharged itself in fearful and ruthless external hostility: the city states tore one another to pieces' (*TI* Ancients 3).

attempted to produce 'a permanent *daylight* – the daylight of reason. One must be prudent, clear, bright at any cost: every yielding to the instincts, to the unconscious, leads *downwards* . . . ' (*TI* Socrates 10). Greek dialectics was the attempt to counter powerful instincts that were already distrusted and in disarray. Dialectics is thus an unwise response to decadence; viewing the instincts of life as an enemy to be rooted out by reason, it only furthers such decadence.

After the long sickness of Christian philosophy, Immanuel Kant (1724–1804) stands for Nietzsche as another remarkable example of philosophical decadence, revealed by the Enlightenment philosopher's abstraction in ethics, a 'purity' that denies individual difference and circumstance. Referring to Kant's ethics that prescribes how moral action must be done from nothing but respect for universal moral law, Nietzsche contrasts his own view of philosophic health with Kant's dyspepsia:

> An action compelled by the instinct of life has in the joy of performing it the proof it is a *right* action: and that nihilist with Christian-dogmatic bowels understands joy as an *objection.* . . . What destroys more quickly than to work, to think, to feel without inner necessity, without a deep personal choice, without *joy?* As an automaton of 'duty'? It is virtually a *recipe* for decadence, even for idiocy. (*A* 11)

Here, Kant's philosophical decadence causes an un-selfing by urging people to distrust their own judgement in deciding how to act. Decadents want duties and principled rules to do their thinking for them – an abrogation of the individual's own interests and values. Nietzsche concludes: 'The erring instinct in all and everything, *anti-naturalness* as instinct, German decadence as philosophy – *that is Kant! –*' (*A* 11).

A neo-Kantian, Arthur Schopenhauer (1788–1860) championed pessimism as the only cogent response to human life. Yet he saw art as redemptive: by stilling the clamorous will, art can turn us into disinterested observers. While Nietzsche mocks Schopenhauer's philosophy and condemns his hatred for life, he does not regard the pessimist as a cause of decadence. Instead, Schopenhauer is only the latest sign of its appearance. Nietzsche lists the two principal insights of *The Birth of Tragedy* as recognizing Socrates and then Western morality as 'symptom[s] of decadence'. He continues:

> These two insights catapulted me high above any pathetic, idiot gossip about optimism *contra* pessimism! I was the first to see the real opposition: – the *degenerate* instinct that turns against life with subterranean vindictiveness (– Christianity, Schopenhauer's philosophy, and in a certain sense even

> Plato's philosophy, the whole of idealism as typical forms) and a formula for the *highest affirmation* born out of fullness, out of overfullness, an unreserved yea-saying even to suffering, even to guilt, even to everything questionable and strange about existence. (*EH*, Birth 2)

Nietzsche thus views Schopenhauer in a long-standing pattern of Western philosophy: the expression of degenerate life, stemming not from insight but from the sick condition of the philosopher expressing it. Nietzsche stands against this decadence, on the side of 'highest affirmation', as the philosopher who embraces life despite its painful and confusing aspect, an attitude only possible for the healthy and strong. Hence unlike the pessimistic decadent who condemns pain, Nietzsche understands life to include pain without thereby misreading life as worthless. And unlike the Romantic decadent who celebrates pain, Nietzsche understands life to include pain without misreading that pain as good.

In outline, Nietzsche first locates philosophical decadence in the extreme rationalism of Socrates and the idealism of Plato. He sees it spread through the Christian tenets of slave morality, infect the Enlightenment, and find its modern exponent in Schopenhauer. And Nietzsche?

> What does a philosopher demand of himself first and last? To overcome his time in himself, to become 'timeless'. With what must he therefore engage in the hardest combat? With whatever marks him as the child of his time. Well, then! I am, no less than Wagner, a child of this time; that is, a decadent: but I comprehended this, I resisted it. The philosopher in me resisted. (*CW* Foreword)

The response to decadence in philosophy is to unmask it as a disease, not an intellectual position; to accept it as endemic to our time, while understanding its causes and history; and to resist it with philosophical teachings that act as political and personal antidotes to decadent pathogens. Overall, Nietzsche considered himself a decadent to which his philosophy was a response. 'Apart from the fact that I am a decadent, I am also the opposite' (*EH* Wise 2). In *Ecce Homo*, he describes his philosophy as the result of striving to recover from the physical and psychic pain that haunted most of his life. 'I turned my will to health, to *life*, into a philosophy' (*EH* Wise 2). His philosophy is not a totalizing system, but a guide to living his particular life. As transposed autobiography, it became the means for Nietzsche to pursue and articulate the dangerous truths that constitute his legacy to the West. In this way, Nietzsche's philosophy is the transfiguration of his fight to recover health, an anti-decadent technique that, as we know, had its limits:

Nietzsche mentally collapsed at forty-four and died some eleven years later in 1900.

Conclusion

Nietzsche is the philosopher of decadence par excellence: its victim, its diagnostician, and its therapist. No niche phenomenon, decadence is any condition, deceptively thought good, which limits what something or someone can be. And while every human decadence has a physiological and psychological basis, such states are transfigured into cultural signs that seductively school the next generation in how to be sick. So understood, decadence in Nietzsche is nearly synonymous with the human condition in the West since Socrates. Twentieth-century and contemporary philosophers continue to explore this vexing legacy.

References

Adorno, Theodor (2005). *Minima Moralia: Reflections from Damaged Life*, E. F. N. Jephcott, trans., London: Verso.

Brandes, Georg (1914). *Friedrich Nietzsche*, A. G. Charter, trans., London: William Heinemann.

Brusseau, James (2005). *Decadence of the French Nietzsche*, Lanham, MD: Lexington Books.

Constable, Liz, Dennis Denisoff, and Matthew Potolsky, eds. (1999). *Perennial Decay: On the Aesthetics and Politics of Decadence*, Philadelphia: University of Pennsylvania Press.

Lawlor, Clark (2006). *Consumption and Literature: The Making of the Romantic Disease*, London: Palgrave Macmillan.

More, Nicholas D. (2014). *Nietzsche's Last Laugh: Ecce Homo as Satire*, Cambridge: Cambridge University Press.

Nietzsche, Friedrich (2005). *The Anti-Christ, Ecce Homo, Twilight of the Idols, and Other Writings*, Aaron Ridley, ed., Judith Norman, trans., Cambridge: Cambridge University Press.

Nietzsche, Friedrich (1961). *Thus Spoke Zarathustra*, R. J. Hollingdale, trans., Harmondsworth: Penguin Books.

Nietzsche, Friedrich (1967). *On the Genealogy of Morals: A Polemic. Ecce Homo: How One Becomes What One Is*, Walter Kaufmann, trans., New York: Vintage.

Nietzsche, Friedrich (1967). *The Birth of Tragedy. The Case of Wagner*, Walter Kaufmann, trans., New York: Vintage.

Nietzsche, Friedrich (1968). *Twilight of the Idols: or How to Philosophize with a Hammer. The Antichrist*, R. J. Hollingdale, trans., Harmondsworth: Penguin Books.

Nietzsche, Friedrich (1983). *Untimely Meditations*, R. J. Hollingdale, trans., Cambridge: Cambridge University Press.

Nietzsche, Friedrich (1986). *Beyond Good and Evil: Prelude to a Philosophy of the Future*. R. J. Hollingdale, trans., Harmondsworth: Penguin Books.

Nietzsche, Friedrich (2006–). *Digital Kritische Gesamtausgabe Werke und Briefe*. Paolo D'Iorio, ed., Paris: Nietzsche Source.

Weir, David (1995). *Decadence and the Making of Modernism*, Amherst, MA: University of Massachusetts Press.

CHAPTER 12

The Sexual Psychology of Decadence

Melanie Hawthorne

In 1882, Friedrich Nietzsche famously declared in *The Gay Science* that God was dead, summarizing in this one pithy pronouncement a century of far-ranging cultural change with regard to social questions about morality in general and sexual conduct in particular and signalling the direction that further social evolution would take. Nietzsche's formulation points to the fact that the decadent movement represents the culmination of over a century of social and political change that challenged the very foundations of moral philosophy and human behaviour. The libertine tradition of the eighteenth century laid the groundwork for this development, forging the connection between sexual taboos and other forms of social power. This questioning attitude combined with various scientific and pseudo-scientific approaches that developed in the course of the nineteenth century to produce a fertile and innovative literary movement at the end of the century. Inquiry in areas such as criminology, sexology, and psychology (including psychoanalysis) allowed and even encouraged the decadents of the fin de siècle to see sexuality as a laboratory for addressing various social and political questions in addition to pursuing the perennial literary question 'what is love?'

Nietzsche's peers at the fin de siècle were the heirs of the Enlightenment libertines of the previous century who claimed the freedom to explore ethics (among other things) in a world no longer dominated by religious dogma. In the Age of Reason, sexual freedom could be framed as part of political and moral philosophy: free thinking and free love went together. To challenge sexual mores was merely an extension of other challenges to the very fabric of society that included calling into question the belief in the divine right of kings and their power to exercise absolute rule. If fear of punishment in an afterlife (if not in this one) did not put a brake on human appetites, the thinking went, what could and should be the limits on human behaviour? The Marquis de Sade came to represent the libertine for the eighteenth century and embodied both aspects of this challenge to the social order: he gave his name to one notable form of sexual expression while serving as the prototypical victim of repressive absolutist rule through his incarceration in the reviled Bastille prison.

The Enlightenment engendered a series of problems that went on to beset large parts of the Western world in the nineteenth century. After nearly two millennia, unquestioning acceptance of Christian dogma was challenged, along with the perceived superstition and mysticism that accompanied it. Following the French Revolution (1789–1799), the power and reach of traditional authorities such as the church and the monarchy began to ebb, replaced by various institutions of the secular state that distanced itself from those sources of authority. In Britain, the ruling monarch remained the Supreme Governor of the Church of England, but in an increasingly ceremonial capacity. In the United States, on the other hand, the separation of church and state was enshrined in the Constitution from the nation's very inception. Between these two poles, other separations took longer, but came inexorably: in France, for example, the Third Republic (declared in 1870) aligned itself with anti-clericalism, culminating in the official separation of church and state in 1905. The new state powers faced a social challenge. If the basis of morality and of society more generally is not handed down by some transcendent, supreme being, where do values come from and who is authorized to formulate, interpret, and enforce them? In the course of the nineteenth century, a number of answers to these questions were derived from science (positivism, evolution, eugenics), from art (art for art's sake), and from various vestiges of religion as well as pseudo-religions, cults, and religious substitutes (theosophy, Satanism, Orientalism, Rosicrucianism). The upshot was to wrest power away from Christian authorities to dictate such public matters and to invoke the discourses of more modern experts to justify the state's interest in regulating interpersonal and family relationships, whether in the name of reducing crime (through prevention and punishment) or in the interest of the greater social good (such as protecting the welfare of children). Thus, as Michel Foucault has noted, the influence of the priest who regulated sexuality as a form of sin gave way to the authority of the police (such as criminologists), scientists (who developed subfields as sexologists and psychologists), and – increasingly – doctors (1990: p. 116).

i

The dominant paradigms driving nineteenth-century transformations of the social order derived, one way or another, from science. Free thought gradually melded with scientific positivism to shape the belief that the application of reason to human problems would bring about better social outcomes. Science became the new authority. A mania for objective metrics and taxonomy provided an alibi for investigating otherwise dubious topics, so that measuring the body parts of populations identified as criminal (murderers, pederasts, etc.) provided raw material for more far-ranging speculations. The work of Pierre Paul Broca (1824–1880) helped establish the discipline of anthropometry (the study of humans through measurement). While such projects as inferring brain capacity from the measurement of a person's head have been largely discredited, Broca was not the only one who believed that gathering human physical data had a predictive value. The biometric work of Cesare Lombroso (1835–1909) in Italy and of Alphonse Bertillon (1853–1914) in France also exemplifies this trend. Lombroso was a doctor turned criminologist (many credit him with inventing this branch of science) who built on emerging evolutionary theory. He believed that criminal actions had a physical basis, and that certain traits – congenital defects – found in the body expressed themselves in behavioural tendencies. Crime could be predicted and controlled by looking for these traits, which included features such as prominent jaws (prognathism) and sloping foreheads. Lombroso's definition of 'criminal' included sexual deviants and prostitutes. His and Guglielmo Ferrero's 1893 work on female prostitution, *La donna delinquente: La prostituta e la donna normale* [*The Criminal Woman: The Prostitute and the Normal Woman*], for example, argues that a disposition towards prostitution was an inborn tendency, not the result of social factors such as poverty or lack of other economic opportunities, a belief that justified treating prostitutes as inherently a criminal class. Émile Zola's *Nana* (1880) was a perfect fictional illustration of such contemporary attitudes. The novel echoed the theories of Alexandre Parent-Duchâtelet (1790–1836), a doctor by training, whose sociological survey *La prostitution dans la ville de Paris* [*Prostitution in the City of Paris*] (published posthumously in 1836) provided a great deal of raw material for later theories to draw on. *Nana* also illustrates the way literary works in other genres (in this case, naturalism) sometimes served as precursors of decadence.

Auguste Tardieu (1818–1879) was also a medical doctor trained in forensics who applied his knowledge to broader social problems. While his research into child abuse drew attention to an important social issue, his forensic approach to the 'problem' of male homosexuality, or 'pederasty', is responsible for propagating certain bogus myths. In his attempts to diagnose homosexuals by forensic means, Tardieu claimed to be able to detect (passive) homosexuals by the funnel shape of their anus. The third part of his *Étude médico-légale sur les attentats aux mœurs* [Medical-legal study of assaults on public decency] (1857), which includes homosexuality, had far-reaching influence (Tardieu's humiliating, invasive, and discredited test is still inflicted on men suspected of being 'sexual deviants' in various parts of the world today). Other tell-tale signs included a corkscrew-shaped penis or the inability to urinate in a straight line. Tardieu managed to make all this sound so scientific that his views were widely disseminated, creating stereotypes that would last for generations (Robb, 2004: pp. 46–47).

For decadents, the homosexual (as opposed to homosexual acts) was a fairly recent invention and provided a vehicle for numerous challenges to middle-brow culture. The label itself came into existence initially in German in 1869, when it was used by an Austro-Hungarian writer, Karoly Maria Benkert von Kertbeny (1824–1882), in a pamphlet addressed as an open letter to the Prussian Minister of Justice as part of a campaign for legal reform (Herzer, 1985; see also Steakley, 1975). The first attested usage of the French word 'homosexuel' was in 1891, with English 'homosexual' following in 1892. Until then, a number of other words held sway, such as 'pederast', 'sodomite', 'urning', and 'uranian'. But the advent of a new concept of an identity, or case history, defined by object choice crystalized around 1870, and, as Foucault (1990: p. 43) put it, a new type was born. Henceforth, a number of decadent authors made homosexuality central to their work. Examples include, perhaps most famously, Oscar Wilde's *The Picture of Dorian Gray* (1891), but other examples may be found in the work of Jean Lorrain (pen name of Paul Duval, 1855–1906), for example in his novels *Monsieur de Bougrelon* (1897) and *Monsieur de Phocas* (1901). The names of both eponymous characters encode their 'deviant' practices: 'Bougrelon' contains the word 'bougre', for example, the French cognate word for 'bugger', while 'Phocas' manages to sound particularly suggestive in English.

There was a significant divergence at the fin de siècle in the treatment of male and female homosexuality (lesbianism, or as more commonly termed during this period, 'sapphism'). While homosexuality was penalized in Germany (hence the need for the reform movement), neither male nor female homosexuality was criminalized in France, although the corruption of minors and the 'assault' on public morals were both still illegal and could be invoked as an excuse to limit activities like cruising and 'cottaging' (the slang term for sex in a public restroom). Lesbianism was often tolerated, especially when it could be subsumed into a heterosexual context. It was often framed as an extension of the general licentiousness (nymphomania) that gave rise to prostitution and was therefore part of a repertoire of sexual behaviours that included, rather than excluded, men. Famous courtesans were known to have lesbian (or 'sapphic') relationships, thus the *grande horizontale* Liane de Pougy (Anne Marie Chassaigne, 1859–1960) published a thinly veiled account of her affair with American heiress Natalie Barney (1876–1972) as *Idylle saphique* [*Sapphic Idyll*] (1901) that only enhanced her reputation and desirability (she married royalty and became a princess). Lesbians are frequently the subject of decadent literature, for example *Méphistophéla* (1890) by Catulle Mendès (1841–1909), where a black mass is celebrated and evil lesbians are referred to as 'succubi' (for a fuller treatment of lesbian themes in decadent literature, see Albert, 2016). Lesbianism, unlike male homosexuality, was never criminalized in Britain and so gave rise to less scandal; male homosexuality, however, was not only criminalized but also carried harsh penalties after passage of the Labouchère Amendment of 1885 (under which Oscar Wilde was prosecuted). Many gay men fled the repression of Victorian England, seeking out the tolerance of less puritanical countries such as France and Italy, a frequent trope in decadent fiction. Writing about what was sometimes later called 'the love that dare not speak its name' was thus an act of provocation because of legal prohibitions against same-sex love.

ii

In addition to criminology, the late nineteenth century also saw the invention of sexology, the systematic study of sex that presented itself as disinterested, scientific inquiry in order to keep at bay any suggestion of prurience. Sexologists such as Richard von Krafft-Ebing (1840–1902) and Havelock Ellis (1859–1939) varied widely in their theories. The Austro-German Krafft-Ebing was a psychiatrist by training who published the much-read *Psychopathia sexualis* in 1886. Subtitled 'a clinical forensic study' in the English translation of 1892, it focused on sexual behaviours as revealed in case studies and gave a prominent place to sadism and masochism, along with homosexuality. The book was quickly translated into other languages and became quite influential. While the sexologist approach still presented sexual deviance as something pathological (a form of illness), it recommended compassion and treatment rather than condemnation and criminal prosecution. In particular, Krafft-Ebing believed that homosexuality might have a biological basis, arising from anomalous conditions during the foetal gestation period. This gave rise to the concept of 'sexual inversion', a phrase that was to have a long life. Inversion was a popular theory among many who were sympathetic to gays because it de-stigmatized the behaviour: rather than being a criminal trait, it was a mistake of nature, and those suffering from such a condition deserved sympathy (though not total exculpation). In his memoirs, John Addington Symonds invoked Krafft-Ebing with a sense of relief as a way of understanding himself:

> I shunned the society of masculine boys, disliked physical exercises of a violent kind, preferred solitude and study to games, because subject at the age of puberty to excessive involuntary losses of semen, stammered for a period in my speech; in short I exhibited many of the symptoms which Krafft-Ebing and his school recognize as hereditary neuroticism predisposing its subject to sexual inversion. (1984: p. 64)

Having a diagnosis was a way to take control over one's sexual predispositions.

Havelock Ellis came by his interest in sexology through his work as a medical doctor and co-authored the first medical textbook in English on homosexuality in 1897. He formulated the intersex condition of Eonism, named after the French chevalier d'Éon (1728–1810) who transitioned midlife from being a man to a woman (Kates, 2001). Ellis' wife Edith Lees was a writer and suffragist who was openly lesbian; thus Ellis had a personal perspective on these issues, and reasons to be sympathetic. For some, in retrospect, Ellis' support for eugenics has tainted his work on sexology, but in his day he was considered a progressive voice. These various sexological theories competed among themselves for dominance, but taken collectively they established a serious medical subfield, albeit a sometimes controversial one.

The work of the sexologists was continued in Germany by Magnus Hirschfeld (1868–1935), who founded the Scientific Humanitarian Committee in 1897, and later (1919) the Institute for Sexual Sciences (Institut für Sexualwissenschaft) in Berlin. Here, Hirschfeld advocated for homosexual rights and pioneered transgender issues (often referred to as the 'third sex'). The first sex-reassignment surgeries were performed there in the 1930s, beginning with Lili Elbe in 1930 (Foerster, 2006). The Institute was an obvious target for the Nazis, who thought it represented exactly the kind of degeneration they associated with the decadent Weimar period (one of the core sites of decadence identified by Weir (2018); see also Chapter 17), and it was destroyed in 1933. Hirschfeld himself went into exile in France, where he died in 1935.

iii

The shift towards understanding sexual expression as a form of psychology (i.e., a behaviour shaped by the mind rather than a physical predisposition) was also a product of the fin de siècle. The study of the (sexed and gendered) mind was pioneered by doctors such as the Paris-based Jean-Martin Charcot (1825–1893), who began his career as a neurologist and anatomist. His work on hypnosis and hysteria, however, led him increasingly to explore the powerful workings of the unconscious mind. Psychology subsequently came to be dominated by the work of Sigmund Freud, many of whose paradigms – often in revised form – still prevail today. While Freud's work was sometimes slow to spread (his German connections were an obstacle to dissemination and acceptance of his work in France, for example), its pervasive influence now goes unquestioned. In general, psychoanalysis, while rooted in sexology, marked a development that went beyond the positivism that sexology inherited from criminological treatments of sexual variations and non-normative sexual behaviour. Freud (among others) continued to distinguish between 'normal' and 'pathological' developments (he suggested that homosexuality was merely an arrested form of normal development, for example), but since most people seemed to exhibit some form of neurosis or other, the frequency of such deviance contributed to its de-stigmatization: no-one was completely normal. Thanks to medical studies of the mind, decadent literature is often preoccupied with mental states, the workings of the unconscious, and the imaginative landscape, underscoring the relative lack of interest on the part of decadents in anything as banal as mere reality. Again, the roots of later movements such as surrealism can be detected in such decadent preoccupations.

Freud came to study with Charcot in Paris in 1885 and therefore was in Paris at the height of the decadent movement. His ground-breaking *Studien über Hysterie* [*Studies on Hysteria*], co-authored with his colleague Josef Breuer, was published in 1895. His own preoccupation with the kind of millennial thinking that fed into various fin-de-siècle movements is illustrated by his decision to give his foundational work *Die Traumdeutung* [*The Interpretation of Dreams*] the publication date of 1900, even though it was actually published in 1899. His work may not have influenced decadent literature as directly as it did later modernist works, but it is symptomatic of the new attitudes towards the role of mental factors shaping sexual expression that were so pervasive at the fin de siècle. Indeed, today the question of influence almost seems moot because Freud was so much a man of his time that he might fairly be characterized as a decadent author himself, and some of his case studies, such as *Dora: Bruchstücke einer Hysterie-Analyse* [*Dora: Fragments of an Analysis of a Case of Hysteria*] (1905), are sometimes studied as if they were novels.

iv

While same-sex eroticism is a dominant theme in the decadent literature of many countries, it is far from being the only sexual preoccupation. Decadents absorbed the legacy of the freedom to explore sexuality even as they confronted a century's worth of growing middle-class conservatism. On the one hand, then, the fin-de-siècle period saw an expansion of the sexual repertoire to admit not just the sadism of Sade but also its twin, the masochism of Leopold von Sacher-Masoch (whose *Venus im Pelz* [*Venus in Furs*] was first published in German in 1870) (Sacher-Masoch, 1999), and not just homosexuality and lesbianism, but even heterosexuality. That word was first coined to name a perversion (understood as a turning away from the 'correct' direction of a drive), as historian Ned Katz (1996) has shown, characterized by an excessive and 'unhealthy' lust for the opposite sex. So understood, heterosexual 'perversion' informs such novels as *Il piacere* [*Pleasure*] (1889) by the Italian decadent (and later fascist) Gabriele D'Annunzio (1863–1938). The protagonist of *Pleasure* is a decadent aesthete who pursues an ex-lover and comments on the aesthetic aura that their love-making imparts to the objects around him, 'animating' and endowing them with special value. In addition to these possibilities, the decadent period is characterized by the exploration of all manner of other sexual variations. What if the object of one's desires is not another adult person but rather a child (paedophilia) or even an animal (bestiality)? What if one's desire is for an inanimate object (fetishism)? What if one's desire is something *like* conventional forms of sexuality, existing, as it were, alongside it, but takes different forms (paraphilias)? Paraphiliac desires include voyeurism, for example, and a panoply of additional fixations, among them algolagnia (pleasure in pain), bondage, frottage (rubbing against a person or an object), onanism (including masturbation), priapism (abnormally prolonged periods of erection), transvestism, trichophilia (hair fetishism), and vampirism (sexual pleasure in drinking blood) – all of which came under the curious and courageous gaze of the decadent.

These topics were mostly explored through imaginative writing (novels, plays, poetry) rather than in lived experience – what philosophers might call 'thought experiments' – but such bold discussion of taboo subjects came to characterize decadent literature. Sade's exploration of the connections between sex and pain (and even cruelty) received an update in such works as *Le jardin des supplices* [*Torture Garden*] (1899) by Octave Mirbeau (1848–1917), a novel that presents all manner of exquisite sexual pain as attractions in a sort of theme park of cruelty, and *La cité des sourires* [*City of Smiles*] (1900) by Jane de la Vaudère (Jeanne Scrive, 1857–1908), in which Japanese female sex workers must continue to smile no matter what cruel treatment they receive. Works by A. C. Swinburne (1837–1909), Joris-Karl Huysmans (1848–1907), Oscar Wilde (1854–1900), and others were a laboratory for imagining different psyches. It is no coincidence that the classic 1884 novel of decadence *Monsieur Vénus*, by French decadent writer Rachilde (Marguerite Eymery Vallette, 1860–1953) is subtitled 'un roman matérialiste' [a materialist novel]; the exploration of the malleability of sex and gender roles takes for granted that ethics are determined by human beings who are limited only by physical (material), not spiritual, laws.

In this sense, decadence may be viewed as an extension of Zola's attempt to treat literature as a scientific experiment even though decadence and naturalism, viewed as literary movements, are often thought to be at odds. Unlike naturalism, however, fin-de-siècle writing is often at pains to go beyond what is perceived as natural or given. Simply recording what nature provides (the realist project of holding up a mirror to nature) is no longer a compelling goal; rather, testing the boundaries of human imagination is a more fitting ambition. As Wilde argues in *The Decay of Lying* (1891), any fool can tell the truth, but it takes creativity to invent something false – a quality that sets humans above the animals (though it turns out animals lie, too). According to Wilde, the proper activity of art is the telling of untrue things, and their value is determined by their beauty (though this remains to be defined). In this sense, the aesthetics of decadence represents a significant cultural break with movements such as realism and naturalism. Decadence takes a more experimental turn. Like post-impressionist painting that pushes aesthetics beyond the mere reproduction of reality, decadence asks more conceptual questions about the role of art, thereby laying the groundwork for later modernist forms.

This conceptual turn often lends a cerebral air to decadent explorations of sexuality. Celibacy, the complete abstention from sexual behaviour altogether, may be the ultimate sexual perversion, and the greatest sexual adventure may be one that takes place entirely in one's head. Huysmans's novel *À rebours* [*Against Nature*] (1884) is a classic of the genre, featuring an aesthete who barely leaves the country retreat where he relishes experiences that, for the most part, remain the product of memory and imagination. Rachilde, Huysmans's contemporary famous for her depiction of female libertines, made a specialty of inventorying the many forms of perversion in her numerous novels, and cerebral manifestations play a big part, ranging from *À mort* [To death] (1886), in which an adulterous lover promises his rival husband that he will never 'see' the man's wife again (which turns out to mean that he will simply keep his eyes closed), to the late novel *Le prisonnier* [The prisoner] (1928) that explores the possibility of two people having sex without ever touching. Perhaps the most famous of Rachilde's cerebral scenes, however, is the spectacle of the heroine Eliante Donalger making love to a pottery amphora in *La jongleuse* [*The Juggler*] (1900) in front of a non-plussed would-be lover who cannot decide if he should be jealous (which would validate the amphora's status as a rival) or not. Somewhat less well known but in the same vein is Belgian suffragist Marguerite Coppin's *Le troisième sexe* [The third sex], in which the heroine Sixte (the name seems a quasi-anagram of 'sex') repudiates sex and gender categories altogether (an early example of gender fluidity). Presenting as female, repulsed by heterosexuality, but equally unattracted to her own sex, Sixte flees into the third category of the title, a cerebral androgyny that resists being categorized by remaining purely intellectual. Alerted by the title, Belgian authorities at the time of publication were prepared to crack down on what promised to be a licentious novel, only to be disappointed by the dryness of what was actually being offered.

Cerebrality is also often explored in conjunction with religious speculations, especially Christianity. The traditional church position that non-procreative sex is sinful made it hard to reconcile physical sexual expression with doctrine, but there were a number of creative solutions to the problem. One was to refrain from sex altogether, or at least try to. For a number of gay men this meant that high-church Catholicism was not incompatible with an otherwise homosocial existence. Poet John Gray (1866–1934) and his longtime companion Marc-André Raffalovich (1864–1934) would be prime examples of men who managed their sexuality this way: Raffalovich penned several volumes on what he called, variously, 'uranisme' or 'unisexualité', while John Gray (1866–1934), long thought to be one of the defining inspirations of Wilde's Dorian, converted to Catholicism in 1890 and served – apparently without problem – as a priest in Edinburgh (he became a canon of the diocese of St Andrews in 1930). Aubrey Beardsley, the artist who arguably did more than any other to create a decadent visual style, was also a convert to Catholicism (along with many others of the decadent generation). Beardsley was often assumed to be homosexual, though according to his biographer Matthew Sturgis this was a common mistake (Beardsley was known to consort with prostitutes), but Beardsley, too, was far less sexually active than his work might lead one to think, though this may be due more to poor health than intellectual conviction.

A critical acceptance of so-called perversity was also heralded as a sign of intellectual independence from bourgeois conformism. Relative political stability in Europe in the latter half of the nineteenth century allowed the rise of a secure and comfortable middle class. In France, the consolidation of the Third Republic after the 1880 elections opened the door to social reforms and a sense of reprieve from the social upheavals that had dogged every generation for a century (1789, 1815, 1830, 1848, 1870). But bourgeois stability came to be seen as a stultifying trap. In 1886, Philippe-Auguste de Villiers de l'Isle-Adam (1839–1889) introduced the word 'android' to a popular audience in his speculative novel *L'Ève future* [*Tomorrow's Eve*]. Often labelled a symbolist, Villiers de l'Isle-Adam was already a champion of the decadents thanks to his mystical play *Axël* (first published posthumously in 1890, it circulated widely in manuscript prior to publication) and his stories *Contes cruels* [*Cruel Tales*] (1883). *Tomorrow's Eve* tackles the problem of disappointing reality and suggests that superior people need not be limited by what nature offers. If a woman's personality could not live up to her physical beauty, she could be replaced by a robot that would retain the appearance and substitute a superior nature that would make her a worthy mate.

This improbable scheme is realized in the novel when the American inventor Edison, a 'modern magician', creates a female robot companion for himself and proposes to make a similar android for his lovesick friend Lord Ewald. This refined English lord is in love with an actress, Alicia Clary, a paragon of beauty but whose body and soul do not match: 'her intimate being was in flat contradiction with the form it inhabited' (2001: p. 31). Despite Ewald's efforts to improve her, no amount of training can groom the essential crassness out of her soul (she is no 'fair lady' like Eliza Doolittle in George Bernard Shaw's *Pygmalion*). Ewald is careful to explain that Alicia is not 'wicked' (that at least would be interesting), but simply incorrigibly 'mediocre' (p. 42). What to do? He cannot give her up, but he cannot tolerate her inherent inferiority, either. One can read the novel as merely misogynistic (women are inevitably flawed but the heterosexual man is stuck with them), but a more nuanced interpretation is that technology (and imagination) can help correct the inevitable mediocrity of bourgeois culture. The novel opens the door to many successors, such as

Ira Levin's 1972 novel *The Stepford Wives* (the basis of the 1975 film of the same name) and more recent forays into the 'woman problem', such as Alex Garland's film, *Ex Machina* (2015). The greatest sin to the decadent mind is not any sexual (or moral) peccadillo, but the stifling complacency that emerges when the battles have been won and revolutionary fervour dissipates. It was a great disappointment to the decadents to confront the fact that after a century of promising political revolution and industrial innovation, most people returned to mediocrity when given the chance, settling down to dwell on petty concerns and simple pleasures rather than continuing with riskier social experiments. For decadents who wanted to signal their disdain for this compromise, a quick way to demonstrate their contempt was to espouse sexual non-conformity.

Courting disapproval was thus a badge of merit. Some decadents went further, arguing that acceptance of natural limitations was a trait found in animals; deliberately flouting nature was, therefore, a sign of human superiority. This argument formed the defence of homosexuality advanced by Russian aesthete Mikhail Kuzmin (1872–1936) in *Wings*, his roman à clef of 1906. Heterosexual reproduction merely obeys animal instincts, whereas acting 'contrary to nature' (a frequent euphemism for homosexuality) requires creativity, a uniquely human trait. The novel's hero Vanya Smurov gradually comes to embrace his homosexuality with pride, thanks to an older mentor, the part-English aesthete Larion Stroop. Vanya discovers Italy and the Classics, realizing that people who accept this perspective form a kind of super-race: they metaphorically grow wings (hence the title) and are uplifted, rising above their more blinkered peers. Kuzmin was representative of many Russian decadents who believed that resisting procreation was the path to conquering death. They turned to what Olga Matich calls 'erotic celibacy' (2005: p. 7) and experimented with various alternative sexual arrangements that fostered cerebral forms of erotic desire that did not take the form of physical intercourse. Matich traces these tendencies in the work of Zinaida Gippius (1869–1945) and Lidia Zinovieva-Annibal (1866–1907), among others. Zinovieva-Annibal's novella *Thirty-Three Abominations* in particular caused a scandal when it was published in 1907 because of its lesbian theme. The first-person narrator draws the attention of a famous actress named Vera on the eve of the narrator's wedding. Vera keeps her secluded and worships her body (physically, and not just intellectually), but almost immediately begins to fear that age will destroy this physical perfection. To prevent the loss, Vera arranges for an avant-garde group of painters (the 'thirty-three abominations' of the title) to paint her beloved, but each artist paints only his own vision and none captures the perfection that Vera sees, so she poisons herself in despair.

While Russian decadents may have turned to experiments with celibacy in order to reconcile different forms of sexual expression with lingering notions of Christian sin, other decadents turned to pre-Christian 'pagan' civilizations for ways to move beyond the judgement and guilt that often accompanied non-reproductive, non-heteronormative sexualities. Even the most conservative social forces recognized the greatness of classical societies such as the Greeks and the Romans, and so the practices of these civilizations could be invoked as a justification. These great models predated the advent of Christianity, so they could not be accused of 'choosing' sinfulness, and their values informed the core of what modern societies often claimed as their own inspiration. There were thus not only political reasons to invoke parallels with ancient democracies and republics (Desmarais and Baldick, 2012) but also important moral ones. For men with homosexual inclinations, the emphasis in ancient Greek society on the nobility of relations between older and younger men and the aesthetic value placed on youths who embodied physical perfection were invoked, and 'Greek Love' (sometimes termed 'Platonic') became a common euphemism for homosexuality. This discourse played a notable role, for example, in the trial of Oscar Wilde, where Wilde attempted (unsuccessfully, as it proved) to evade charges of improper relations with men by appealing to a higher level of morality. As Linda Dowling (1994) has demonstrated, there was a high-mindedness in the appeal to civilized values that was particularly compelling for a time, where it inspired a generation of Oxford men, but it was simply too radical to be acceptable to the Victorian mind in the long run.

Classical sources could also serve as an inspiration for women, particularly through the figure of the Greek poet Sappho (c. 630–c. 570 BCE), who not only legitimated women writers in general but also provided a strong precursor for female same-sex eroticism (Gubar, 1984). Sappho 'named' this behaviour twice, not only through her own name (sapphism), but through the place of her birth, the island of Lesbos that provides the modern term 'lesbianism'. Sappho was a notable source of inspiration for the turn-of-the-century Anglo-French writer Renée Vivien (Pauline Tarn, 1877–1909), who learned Greek in order to be able to translate the works of Sappho and other classical women poets. Vivien referred to Sappho frequently in her own work, invoked 'pagan' values that absolved her of guilt about her feelings for other women, and at one point contemplated trying to revive a school for women poets on the island of Lesbos with her lover Natalie Barney. While Vivien's rejection of Christian values has led some to label her a 'Satanist' (Faxneld, 2017), she was extremely ambivalent: like many decadents, she eventually converted to Catholicism, though since this was a last-minute, death-bed conversion, its sincerity has not gone unchallenged. Regardless of whether she embraced Christianity at the end, her life-long celebration of the pre-Christian world offered a way to escape the notion of 'sin' entirely and position herself beyond or outside such concepts, rather than simply in opposition to them.

The gravitas of classical sources also served as inspiration for the work of Pierre Louÿs (1870–1925), whose book of poetry *Les chansons de Bilitis* [*The Songs of Bilitis*] (1894) became a touchstone of both decadent literature and twentieth-century lesbian subculture (Schultz, 2014). The poet Bilitis, who pens tender poems to her lovers, was an invented character (though Louÿs claimed he was only 'translating' her work), but numerous other figures of classical antiquity inspired decadents, either through their exemplary love (Hadrian and Antinoüs), or their reputation for monstrous appetites (Heliogabalus, Messalina). Classical authors such as Plato (especially through his origin story of human sexuality in the *Symposium*), Juvenal, Catullus, and others became coded, but culturally authorized, ways to communicate that different sexual behaviours have always existed.

V

In summary, the fin-de-siècle period represents a pivotal moment in Western culture when a century's worth of moral philosophy coincided with a radical new aesthetic movement to pave the way for sweeping new paradigms that would dominate the twentieth century. After making the regulation of sexuality a secular issue, various Western societies struggled throughout the nineteenth century to articulate who (if anyone) should be entrusted with such authority and what exactly ought to be regulated and how. A broad range of thinkers and writers loosely associated with the decadent movement at the end of the century took up the effort, using literature as a medium to foster speculation and provoke reflection. Fictional experiments that explored the psychology of sexual behaviour probed the outer boundaries of what was acceptable (and why), and pushed readers to consider things that went beyond traditional comfort zones. At the same time, an aesthetic shift away from realism, as broadly understood, ushered in new, experimental forms that would take flight in the modernist mood of the twentieth century. While the representation of some kind of 'truth' was still a worthy artistic goal, this aim was no longer understood as a matter of some surface depiction of a person's clothes and immediate environment (the effects that seemed to matter in movements such as realism and naturalism). Striving for a deeper, psychological truth meant entertaining new forms of artistic expression that could capture things that did not manifest themselves in surface appearances. In this way, decadence offers not only a moment in which exciting new aesthetic possibilities begin to emerge, but also a re-conceptualization of human intellectual endeavours that place sexuality at the centre of modern questions about the exercise of power. Such questions are still being worked through today, a century later, and it is to understand the roots of some debates that still dominate current issues that inquiring minds continue to return, with insight and profit, to the work of the decadents.

References

Albert, Nicole (2016). *Lesbian Decadence: Representations in Art and Literature of Fin-de-Siècle France*, Nancy Erber and William A. Peniston, trans., New York: Harrington Park Press.

D'Annunzio, Gabriele (2013). *Pleasure*, Lara Gochin Raffaelli, trans., New York: Penguin.

Desmarais, Jane, and Chris Baldick, eds. (2012). Introduction. In *Decadence: An Annotated Anthology*, Manchester: Manchester University Press, pp. 1–11.

Dowling, Linda (1994). *Hellenism and Homosexuality in Victorian Oxford*, Ithaca, NY: Cornell University Press.

Faxneld, Per (2017). *Satanic Feminism: Lucifer as the Liberator of Women in Nineteenth-Century Culture*, New York: Oxford University Press.

Foerster, Maxime (2006). *Histoire des transsexuels en France*, Béziers: H&O Éditions.

Foucault, Michel (1990). *The History of Sexuality*, vol. I, Robert Hurley, trans., New York: Random House.

Gubar, Susan (1984). Sapphistries. *Signs*, 10(1), 43–62.

Herzer, Manfred (1985). Kertbeny and the Nameless Love. *Journal of Homosexuality*, 12(1), 1–26.

Kates, Gary (2001). *Monsieur d'Éon Is a Woman: A Tale of Political Intrigue and Sexual Masquerade*, Baltimore, MD: Johns Hopkins University Press.

Katz, Jonathan Ned (1996). *The Invention of Heterosexuality*, New York: Plume.

Kuzmin, Mikhail (2007). *Wings*, Hugh Aplin, trans., London: Hesperus Press.

Lombroso, Cesare, and Guglielmo Ferrero (2004). *The Criminal Woman, the Prostitute, and the Normal Woman*, Nicole Hahn Rafter and Mary Gibson, trans., Durham, NC: Duke University Press.

Lorrain, Jean (2015). *Monsieur de Phocas*, Francis Amery, trans., Sawtry, Cambs.: Dedalus Press.

Lorrain, Jean (2016). *Monsieur de Bougrelon*, Eva Richter, trans., Palm Springs, CA: Spurl Editions.
Louÿs, Pierre (2010). *The Songs of Bilitis*, Alvah C. Bessie, trans., Mineola, NY: Dover.
Matich, Olga (2005). *Erotic Utopia: The Decadent Imagination in Russia's Fin de Siècle*, Madison: University of Wisconsin Press.
Nietzsche, Friedrich (1974). *The Gay Science*, Walter Kaufmann, trans., New York: Vintage.
Parent-Duchâtelet, Alexandre (2008). *La prostitution à Paris au xixe siècle*, Alain Corbin, ed., Paris: Seuil.
Rachilde (1886). *À mort*, Paris: Monnier.
Rachilde (1990). *The Juggler*, Melanie Hawthorne, trans., New Brunswick, NJ: Rutgers University Press.
Rachilde (2004). *Monsieur Venus*, Melanie Hawthorne and Liz Constable, trans., New York: MLA.
Robb, Graham (2004). *Strangers: Homosexual Love in the Nineteenth Century*, New York: Norton.
Sacher-Masoch, Leopold von (1999). *Venus in Furs*, Harmondsworth: Penguin.
Schultz, Gretchen (2014). *Sapphic Fathers: Discourses of Same-Sex Desire from Nineteenth-Century France*, Toronto: University of Toronto Press.
Steakley, James D. (1975). *The Homosexual Emancipation Movement in Germany*, Salem, NH: Ayer.
Sturgis, Matthew (1998). *Aubrey Beardsley: A Biography*, London: HarperCollins.
Symonds, John Addington (1984). *The Memoirs of John Addington Symonds: The Secret Homosexual Life of a Leading Man of Nineteenth-Century Letters*, Phyllis Grosskurth, ed., Chicago: University of Chicago Press.
Villiers de l'Isle-Adam, Philippe-Auguste de (2001). *Tomorrow's Eve*, Robert Martin Adams, trans., Champaign: University of Illinois Press.
Vivien, Renée (2017). *A Crown of Violets*, Samantha Pious, trans., Sequim, WA: Headmistress Press.
Weir, David (2018). *Decadence: A Very Short Introduction*, Oxford: Oxford University Press.
Wilde, Oscar (2003). *The Decay of Lying*. In *Complete Works of Oscar Wilde*, Merlin Holland, ed., London: Collins.
Wilde, Oscar (2003). *The Picture of Dorian Gray*. In *Complete Works of Oscar Wilde*, Merlin Holland, ed., London: Collins.
Zinovieva-Annibal, Lydia (1975). *Thirty-Three Abominations*, S. D. Cioran, trans. In Carl R. Proffer, ed., *The Silver Age of Russian Culture*, Ann Arbor, MI: Ardis Press.
Zola, Émile (2009). *Nana*, Douglas Parmée, trans., New York: Oxford University Press.

CHAPTER 13

The Theology of Decadence

Matthew Bradley

In the last essay Walter Pater ever wrote, an unfinished piece on Pascal published posthumously in 1894, he described with some vigour what he saw as the impertinence, even the profanity, of 'the theologian by profession'. The theologian is, Pater says:

> [. . .] all too intimate in laying down the law of the things he deals with – the things 'which eye hath not seen' – pressing into the secrets of God's sublime commerce with men, in which, it may be, he differs from every single human soul, by forms of thought adapted from the poorest sort of men's dealing with each other, from the trader, or the attorney. (1909: p. 64)

Decadence, as both a cultural signifier and a literary mode, appears at first glance to be utterly inhospitable to the idea of theology, never mind *a* theology. Theology lays down the law, decadence seeks to subvert it. Theology looks to the universal pattern, decadence looks to the individual cell. Theology deals in abstractions, decadence resists them. Theology totalizes; decadence relativizes.

Yet as critics have noted, the claim – or accusation – of decadence always implies something about the relationship between the universal and the local, and the real and the ideal (Gagnier, 2010). At its most basic level, to raise the question of decadence is to raise the question of the relationship between what *is* and what *should be*; any conception of decadence is by necessity also a conception of some ideal state, or wider order, that such decadence is failing to live up to or go along with. To label an individual, a culture, or a piece of writing as 'decadent' is to consider the nature of what it is to be in a state of transgression, what the parameters of such a state are, and what such a state is being defined against. The notion of decadence also incorporates the shadow of possible consequences, implying as it does a state that is unsustainable, and thus that a wider crisis or end-point, even some sort of punishment, is to come. These preoccupations are aesthetically distinctive to the mode: symbolism, for example, one of the closest literary relatives of decadence, is interested in the way 'the Infinite is made to blend itself with the Finite' (Symons, 2014: p. 6), but it is not interested in what *should be*, or in ideas of transgression, still less of punishment. Neither transgression nor punishment, of course, are exclusively theological questions or concerns. But as decadence evolved as a literary movement over the course of the nineteenth century, it drew heavily on the ways in which theology (specifically Christian theology) had tried, and was still trying, to address these questions and concerns. There is a tangible but often uneasy relationship between nineteenth-century decadence and theology. Even Pater, for all his lifelong disparagement of the discipline, recognized that theological literature expressed most powerfully the absorption of individual spirit into literary style – what he called 'soul' (1889: pp. 22–3). In 1894, a theatre journalist reported that Oscar Wilde 'reads Theology every day; "the history of Theology is the history of madness"' (1979: vol. I, pp. 230–1).

The work of even partially sketching out 'a theology of decadence' is then perhaps most useful if it traces how particular theological ideas – principally those concerned with (i) transgression, (ii) punishment, and (iii) apocalypse – grew anew in the strange and modern hothouse of decadent literary form. I begin with the work of Baudelaire and his use of original sin as formulated by the conservative Catholic theologian Joseph de Maistre, and in particular one of his principal ideas about the nature of divine justice and punishment, *réversibilité*. I then trace the development of these strands into the work of Joris-Karl Huysmans, before moving to the apocalyptically charged flowering of decadence in England at the Victorian fin de siècle, particularly in *The Picture of Dorian Gray* where Wilde experiences the dual inheritance of an aesthetic relativism derived from Pater and theological ideas of sin and punishment as a form of apocalyptic crisis.

Transgression: Baudelaire, Joseph de Maistre, and Original Sin

Charles Baudelaire was the first to positively reclaim the idea of decadence as a potential space for strange modern experiences and radical literary experimentation. When modern critics accuse a literary work of decadence, Baudelaire writes in his 'Notes nouvelles sur Edgar Poe' ['Further Notes on Edgar Poe'] (1857), he knows he will find in its pages a degree of daring, excitement, and impeccable literary ability (1964: p. 93). After all, the multifarious colours of a dying sun are likely more interesting than the 'harsh white light of day' and will be where 'certain poetic spirits will discover new delights' (p. 93). Yet Baudelaire was also the writer responsible for simultaneously intertwining such delights with very specific ideas about evil – the discussion, results, and the 'flowers' of it – at the root of the decadent aesthetic.

Baudelaire's preoccupation with what is perhaps the most famous of all meditations on transgression against God – the doctrine of original sin – is well known. T. S. Eliot argued that Baudelaire's interest in the extremes of sinfulness in the Christian worldview, up to and including his apparent adoption of Satanism, was so unorthodox because it was conceived in a state of 'theological innocence' (1999: p. 422). In other words, Baudelaire developed a new, potentially subversive mode of Christianity in ignorance of orthodox Christian theology. Baudelaire, Eliot says, is 'discovering Christianity for himself' (p. 422). The elucidation of this tendency is a prominent feature of much critical commentary on religion as part of decadent writing in more general terms, where something like 'theological innocence', or the subversion of what little knowledge is possessed, is itself taken to form part of the transgression. This tendency can be found in poetic practitioners of decadence like Lionel Johnson, who in 1891 sends up the religion of the modern decadent by expressing a preference 'to dally with the enchanting mysteries, to pass from our dreams of delirium to our dreams of sanctity with no coarse facts to jar upon us' (1891: p. 157). Similarly, modern critics like Ellis Hanson see Roman Catholicism as primarily an exploratory space that decadent writers use mostly as 'a highly unstable field for sexual negotiation' in which theology is 'for the most part a distraction' (1993: pp. 26, 19).

Yet even to talk about an interest in original sin is to beg a theological question, and Baudelaire's interest in the doctrine was in any case highly theological. It derived originally from St. Augustine, an important figure to literary decadents (Oscar Wilde advised readers of the *Pall Mall Gazette* in 1886 that Augustine was the only Church Father worth looking at (2013: p. 62)). Arguing in a Pauline vein, Augustine stated that a man was not sinful as a result of this or that individual act; rather, man's very being, and in particular the sexual act that brought it forth, was inherently sinful, making all of humanity a *massa damnata* [condemned crowd], because human nature was itself determined after the Fall (2003: p. 547, 988–9). Sin in Augustine is raised to the status of a universal metaphysical condition and – crucially – the evidence for that condition is at least partly discoverable in nature and natural processes, i.e., sex and procreation.

This aspect of Augustine's thought had an obvious appeal to those like Baudelaire who were uncomfortable with the veneration of a 'state of nature' as the moral and spiritual panacea for mankind, the philosophical gospel preached by Jean-Jacques Rousseau. The very first statement in Baudelaire's *Les fleurs du mal* [*The Flowers of Evil*] is that 'Folly and error, stinginess and sin | Possess our spirits and fatigue our flesh' (2008: p. 5). Baudelaire's equally famous protest in his essay 'The Painter of Modern Life' (1863) goes even further:

> Everything beautiful and noble is the result of reason and calculation. Crime, of which the human animal has learned the taste in his mother's womb, is natural by origin. Virtue, on the other hand, is artificial, supernatural, since at all times and in all places gods and prophets have been needed to teach it to animalized humanity, man being powerless to discover it by himself. Evil happens without effort, naturally, fatally; Good is always the product of some art. (1964: p. 32)

Left to itself, says Baudelaire, nature will always tend towards selfishness and violence, so any appeal to it as a basis for human ethics or the source of all good and beauty (as eighteenth-century thinkers under the influence of Rousseau did) is utterly misguided. Morality requires concentrated thought and effort; selfishness and violence require none at all.

The writings of the ultra-conservative Catholic theologian Joseph de Maistre (1753–1821) were crucial in Baudelaire's development of these ideas. Maistre was a writer whom Baudelaire had read in earnest in the 1850s, and he once famously remarked that it was Maistre, along with Edgar Allan Poe, who had taught him to think (Pichois and Ziegler, 1987: p. 183). Maistre's theology is well-described by Françoise Meltzer as a kind of 'hyper-Augustinianism' (2011: p. 15), vastly expanding the animating role of original sin as the fundamental principle of the natural world as we experience it. His influence on 'The Painter of Modern Life' is obvious:

> There is nothing but violence in the universe, but we are spoiled by a modern philosophy that tells us that *all is good*, whereas evil has tainted everything, and in a very real sense, *all is evil*, since nothing is in its place. The keynote of the system of our creation has been lowered, and following the rules of harmony, all the others have been lowered proportionately. *All creation groans*, and tends with pain and effort towards another order of things. (Maistre, 1994: p. 31)

Virulently anti-Rousseauist, Maistre was equally virulent in his opposition to the valorization of human reason that Rousseau himself was arguing against: 'authority', for Maistre, 'should be the fundamental ground for decision' because 'human reason is manifestly convicted of impotence for guiding men' (p. 59). This scepticism is another clear legacy to Baudelaire, who was also extremely dubious about the power of human reason and the claims of secular progress. For Maistre, this principle of authority above all is also extended to God, whose actions are always experienced by mankind as authority, not reason; indeed, in Maistre's doctrine, the pain and suffering that the world inflicts on us is active retribution for human sinfulness, and also His way of keeping order. In that sense, Maistrean theology pushes Augustinianism to its limits by making the natural tendency of the world towards evil both humanity's sin *and* its punishment. Baudelaire delivers a version of this dark philosophy in his poem 'Châtiment de l'orgueil' ['Punishment for Pride'], a Faustian tale in which a thirteenth-century theologian claims that it is the brilliance of scholarly work that raises God to glory on earth, rather than any action of God's. 'Immédiatement sa raison s'en alla' [At once his reason's sentence had begun], we are told; the theologian is instantly blinded, becoming 'as useless and ugly as a worn-out thing', 'no better than a common beast' and, most chillingly, 'the jeering children's special treat' (2008: pp. 36–7), leaving him to all the decay and casual cruelty that nature – in its raw state of awfulness – can inflict.

Baudelaire's innovation, however, is to see the kind of *moral* effort which is needed to correct the rapaciousness and unthinking selfishness we find in nature as being part of fundamentally the same endeavour as an *aesthetic* effort, which is needed in order to correct the forms of nature and which appeals to the senses rather than the reason. Baudelaire was building here in part on Théophile Gautier's theories of beauty and uselessness in the preface to *Mademoiselle de Maupin* (1836), where Gautier, in a non-theological context, had expressed scepticism about the possibilities of human progress in any realm outside the imagination: 'What a foolishness it is, the supposed perfectibility of the human race, forever being dinned in our ears!' (2005: p. 24). But Gautier also informs Baudelaire's association of the idea of natural process with a kind of visceral horror: 'everything that is useful is ugly, for it is the expression of some need, and the needs of men are ignoble and disgusting, like his poor and infirm nature' (p. 23). For Baudelaire, the figures who overcome these horrors of nature with reasoned elegance and calculated artifice – the poet, the artist, and the dandy – are obeying an ethical imperative that bears comparison, he says, with the strictest monastic rule (1964: p. 28). Baudelaire's bringing together of the model of human sinfulness and transgression from Augustinian and Maistrean theology with Gautier's aesthetics thus produced one of the distinctive keynotes of the theology of decadence: an investigation of the role of art and the artist in a fallen world conditioned by original sin.

Importantly, although the aesthetic effort itself may be an attempt to redeem the original sin of human nature and of the natural world in much decadent writing, it also involves an adoption of that sin, and in ways that tend to blur the boundaries between the aesthetic effort and the sin it is supposed to redeem – as Baudelaire's title, *The Flowers of Evil*, demonstrates. The production of beauty rarely removes a sense of personal sinfulness or an escape from the horror; on the contrary, decadent writers continually brood on precisely this sense, re-living it repeatedly in their beautiful artificial dreams and their horrifying artificial nightmares. The impulse to art and artifice is thus figured as an attempt both to redeem the Augustinian *massa damnata* but also as a spectacular performance of that damnation visited on the artist themselves. As Jean Pierrot observed, 'the decadent consciousness was a suffering consciousness, one that lived its moral and esthetic experience in the mode of guilt' (1981: p. 90). And this tension is important because it suggests something about the way that *punishment* is organized within the theology of decadence: it is the would-be aesthetic redeemer who is most involved with sin and evil and – in accordance with Maistrean doctrine – who undergoes the most guilt, pain, and suffering.

Organizing Punishment: *Réversibilité* from Baudelaire to Huysmans

The doctrine of original sin is, in its Augustinian form, a doctrine fundamentally concerned with *heredity* – it transmits the sin of the (original) father to his descendants, who are held responsible for it, and who will face the potential consequences. Maistre argued passionately that this condition was analogous to physical illness: there is an 'original illness' (because we are all subject to malady simply by virtue of being physical entities), but there are also specific strains of illness which can be transmitted through the generations (1994: p. 34). Original sin operates likewise, so complaining about a lack of fairness is as pointless as complaining of the same in relation to physical maladies. This structure, whereby hereditary physical taint is brought together with ideas of sinfulness and transgression is self-evidently a structure that we can find in decadent writing, but Maistre's own theology pushes even this notion to extremes.

Maistre's doctrine of *réversibilité* is the idea that individuals, by taking on pain and suffering as punishment for sins they have not personally committed, can earn at least partial redemption for those sins: '*the righteous, suffering voluntarily, satisfy not only for themselves, but for the culpable, who, of themselves, could not expiate their own debts*' (1993: p. 264). In other words, if the theologian of Baudelaire's 'Punishment for Pride' had persuaded a willing and righteous friend to do so, he or she could have accepted the punishment on the theologian's behalf, and God's justice would have been satisfied. *Réversibilité* was a vital part of Maistre's whole theology – he reminds his reader in the *St. Petersburg Dialogues* that the Hebrew word for sin and sacrifice is one and the same (p. 268). Nevertheless, like much of Maistre's theology, the doctrine seems almost gleefully reactionary, not only because it appears to defy fairness and reason even more than Augustinian original sin already did, but also because it seemed to count redemption in the currency of human suffering; 'THE REMEDY FOR DISORDER WILL BE PAIN', as Maistre emphatically stated (p. 272). No doctrine seems to more strongly support Pater's view that the theologian brings transcendent matters down into the narrowly transactional language of the trader or the attorney: a doctrine where divine punishment can be exactly weighed and measured, even bought and sold.

Baudelaire touches directly on the doctrine in *The Flowers of Evil*, in a poem simply titled 'Réversibilité'. The speaker addresses his lover as the 'angel' of such qualities as gladness, kindness, health, and beauty, and then asks her whether she knows anything of their inverse ('do you know of anguish', 'do you know of hatred', 'are you aware of Fevers', 'do you know of wrinkles', and so on). The dying King David, says the poet, might well have asked under the principle of *réversibilité* for his pain and suffering to be transferred to the 'angel', thus giving her all-too-intimate knowledge of anguish, hatred, and wrinkles: the poet, by contrast, asks only that she give her prayers for him (2008: pp. 91–2). But the poem's barely suppressed wish to visit these horrors on unthinking virtue and contentment is a moment of experiment with the sadistic energies of a doctrine that can transfer punishment, inflicted through spiritual anguish and physical deformity, from a guilty person to a guiltless one.

Réversibilité, however, is more usually located in decadent writing in relation to masochistic than sadistic tendencies, with the decadent artist cast as sufferer. Both François Meltzer and Matthew Potolsky have recognized the importance of Maistrean *réversibilité* to Baudelaire, although both focus primarily on its importance to his cultural politics (Meltzer, 2011: pp. 33–6; Potolsky, 2013: pp. 35–41). Potolsky in particular looks at Baudelaire's characterization of Edgar Allan Poe and the literary community, where Poe is a martyr who sacrifices himself on the altar of public disapprobation in order to redeem the very public that has condemned him (2013: p. 36). This is an important insight, although it can be applied to Baudelaire's conception of the figure of the poet in much wider terms as one who is always cursed to take on pain and suffering in this way. In 'Bénédiction', the poet's mother curses him from birth, then his wife tries to tempt him into idolatry. Throughout, the poet resists these frustrations and attempts to embroil him in sin; instead, he looks to heaven and his lucid soul which block from his sight 'des peuples furieux' [the angry people], recognizing all the while that to endure such pain and rejection is part of his mission to reach 'de pure lumière' [the pure light] (Baudelaire, 2008: pp. 12–13; editors' translation).

The poet thus becomes a model of the Maistrean martyr to *réversibilité*: a figure who attempts to redeem his society by producing art, but where that redemption is measured in proportion to the pain he suffers at that society's hands. In fact, as the doctrine of *réversibilité* dictates, the greater the suffering and punishment inflicted on the 'righteous poet' by society, the greater the redemption of the world. This aesthetically inflected version of the theological model of *réversibilité* became a strongly marked feature of literary decadence, perhaps most clearly in the idea of the *poète maudit* or 'cursed poet'. Alfred Vigny first used the phrase in 1832 but Paul Verlaine made it an enduring term in French literature through his 1884 collection *Les poètes maudits* [*The Cursed Poets*] (which included work by Arthur Rimbaud, Stéphane Mallarmé, and Villiers de l'Isle Adam), writing in the foreword:

> Absolus par l'imagination, absolus dans l'expression,
> absolus comme les Reys Netos des meilleurs siècles.
> Mais maudits!
> Jugez-en.
>
> [Absolute by the imagination, absolute in the expression,
> absolute like the Reys Netos [pure kings] of the best centuries.
> But cursed!
> Judge for yourself!] (1884: p. 1)

Godlike in their embodying of the 'absolute', pure and kingly in their spiritual leadership, they are also the outcasts, the suffering, and the cursed, a dynamic for which Maistrean *réversibilité*, at least in part, provides the theological model.

Published in the same year as *The Cursed Poets*, Huysmans's iconic decadent novel *À rebours* [*Against Nature*] (1884) saw its anti-hero Des

Esseintes voluntarily exile himself from both nature and civilization in order to live an 'absolute' life of art and artifice. Huysmans indicates clearly that it is a combination of Des Esseintes' early fascination with medieval theology, a product of his Jesuit education, and the hereditary degenerative taint that has passed through the generations of his interbreeding family that is at the root of his adult penchant for artificiality and ardent longing for an ideal (2009: pp. 3, 65). But while Des Esseintes worships Baudelaire, and his project is rooted in a Baudelairean disgust for both nature and civilization, he is notably dismissive of 'the revolting dogma of original sin' (p. 69) and, moreover, calls Maistre 'an inflexible bigot', an 'overbearing, pompous, empty-headed bore' (p. 126).

This rhetoric would seem to indicate a weakening of the influence of Maistrean ideas on the theology of decadence at this point in the development of the movement, where Huysmans becomes influential. However, in his 1903 preface to a reprint of *Against Nature*, Huysmans remarked that 'the mystical works that succeeded it are not comprehensible without *Against Nature*, which is [. . .] the stock from which they all sprang' (p. 193). The 'mystical works' he refers to are generally known as the Durtal novels – *Là-bas* [*Down There*] (1891), *En route* (1895), *La cathédrale* [*The Cathedral*] (1898), and *L'oblat* [*The Oblate*] (1903) – a series in which the lead character Durtal, motivated by the same disgust for the world and passion for art as was Des Esseintes, explores the depths of evil to be uncovered in modern Parisian Satan-worship before making (at the beginning of the second novel, *En route*) an orthodox conversion to Catholicism, ultimately becoming a Benedictine oblate (i.e., someone who lives in a monastery and partakes in some monastic offices but is not under full vows of obligation). If we consider these novels, including *Against Nature*, as an evolving spiritual journey (as Huysmans recommends), the rejection of original sin in the earlier novel is very much a first stage, as it is expressed in the midst of a religious crisis for Des Esseintes in which he feels, uncomfortably, that 'his scepticism was beginning to be eroded' (p. 66). The final erosion of this scepticism is not overcome by Des Esseintes himself but *is* overcome by Durtal. Indeed, at the end of *En route,* Durtal undergoes a mystic dark night of the soul in which he is interrogated by a quasi-Satanic sceptical voice, who confronts him squarely with the doctrine of original sin and the unfairness of the way it punishes the innocent for the sins of the guilty; nonetheless, Durtal boldly asserts its truth: 'What are heredity and atavism, save, under another name, the terrible sin of the beginning?' (Huysmans, 2002, p. 237).

It is no coincidence, then, that Durtal becomes increasingly obsessed with the idea of sacrificial substitution, albeit in a very specific context: the theological justification of monastic orders. Maistre had long recognized the vital importance of the role of monastic orders within his theological framework for *réversibilité*:

> Sometimes it is asked, of what use are these terrible austerities, which are also *self-sacrifices*, practised by certain religious orders? It would be precisely the same thing to ask of what use is Christianity, which rests entirely on an enlargement of this same dogma *of innocence paying for crime.*
>
> The authority that approves these orders chooses certain men and women and insulates them from the world in order to make them *conductors.* (1993, p. 267)

In *En route*, holy orders are described in similar terms: they are 'the lightning conductors of society' because 'they draw on themselves the demoniacal fluid, [...] absorb temptations to vice, [and] preserve by their prayers those who live, like ourselves, in sin' (Huysmans, 2002: p. 40). But they are also, in Huysmans, deeply aesthetic spaces. It is Durtal's passion for plainchant and for the architecture of church symbolism (particularly of Chartres in *The Cathedral*) that lead him to the Church, then to a temporary retreat at La Trappe monastery. Unlike *les poètes maudits*, Durtal chooses an entirely voluntary exile that allows aesthetic correction of the world to take place alongside theological orthodoxy.

In the monastery, the principle of *réversibilité* is then divided between the spiritual travails of Durtal, who battles with his doubts and his scepticism, and the bodily anguish that he locates within the hagiographical tradition. Durtal becomes obsessed with the physical martyrdom of saints like St. Lidwine (of whom Huysmans himself wrote a biography), such as the worms in her flesh. Huysmans describes Durtal's response to the physical damage St. Lidwine's privations cause as an almost sensual ecstasy and wonder (p. 39). In this way, *réversibilité* provides a theological justification for the decadent obsession with, and delight in, decay and trauma. Salvation comes through the spectacle of pain and suffering, and thus becomes something to delight in. Thus, a strict adherence to aesthetic principles can co-exist with an obsession with decay under the shelter of theological doctrine.

Huysmans is explicitly attempting in the Durtal novels to grant significant parts of the decadent aesthetic a theological legitimacy. The mistake, he explains, is to consider that aesthetic impulses, particularly the kinds of transgressive ones that combine strong impulses to venerate beauty with a strong sense of sinfulness, are not compatible with Christian orthodoxy. Durtal, by the final novel, adopts what he calls 'art for God's sake' (1996: p. 17). The Church has foolishly let people forget that theology has already explored what are now seen as the exclusively secular preoccupations of modern art:

> All the great movements of our day, one after the other – romanticism, naturalism – had been effected independently of her [the Church], or even against her will. [. . .] The Catholic force, *which might have been thought better prepared than any others to contest the ground which theology had long since explored*, retired in good order, satisfied to cover its retreat by firing from a safe distance, with its old-fashioned match-lock blunderbusses, on works it had neither inspired nor written. (1997: p. 211)

The thrust of the Durtal cycle is an attempt to show that the 'theology of decadence', with its veneration for art as the solution to a fallen world, has not been a displacement, or even a heretical modification of existing theological ideas; rather, it was within the framework of orthodox theology all along.

Apocalypse: The Relative Spirit and Divine Authority

The Christian Apocalypse and Christian eschatology (the branch of theology dealing with the end of things) are equally important as structural models for literary decadence as the doctrine of original sin. *The Flowers of Evil* begins with the apocalyptic threat that Ennui, the master-monster of the modern condition, will 'dans un bâillement avalerait le monde' [in one yawning swallow all the world] (2008: pp. 6–7). In his *Journaux intimes* [*Intimate Journals*], Baudelaire went further and proclaimed the coming end of the world, a whimpering finish that will see mankind fully mechanized in spirit and be located in 'the degradation of the human heart' (2006: pp. 56–7). Arthur Symons reported that the poet Gérard de Nerval once returned his author's advance because he thought the apocalypse had come (2014: pp. 10–11). A world or a culture at the end of things, a sense of transgression, a trembling of the veil that seems to promise condemnation, even punishment, from some unknown authority, are preoccupations at the heart of the decadent aesthetic.

In one way, such apocalyptic thinking is a deviation from the general adherence to Augustinianism in decadent theology. No-one did more than Augustine to purge from Christian orthodoxy the idea that the end of the world as described in the Book of Revelation referred to an imminent material reality, arguing that it should be understood only in spiritual terms

(2003: pp. 517, 906–7). But in another way, decadent experiments with apocalyptic thinking are simply a natural enlargement of previous experiments in the mechanics of divine punishment, like *réversibilité* – because the Apocalypse is the ultimate revelation of both the final sweep of God's punishment on all sinners and the divine judgement by which the rationale for those punishments is decided (the word 'apocalypse' itself, of course, means a revelation or an unveiling).

Max Nordau's infamous *Entartung* [*Degeneration*] (1892–1893) begins with an analysis of 'fin de siècle' as the backdrop to modern decadent art. The term is, Nordau says, just a slightly misguided modern expression of 'the horror of world-annihilation', a response to the 'sound of rending in every tradition, as though tomorrow would not link itself to to-day' (1895: pp. 2, 5). Yet in *The Picture of Dorian Gray* (1891), we find one of the most explicit desires for tomorrow *not* to link itself to today in the whole decadent canon:

> '*Fin de siècle*,' murmured Lord Henry.
> '*Fin du globe*,' answered his hostess.
> 'I wish it *were fin du globe*,' said Dorian, with a sigh, 'Life is a great disappointment.' (2006: p. 151)

David Weir has identified what he calls a 'paradoxical nostalgia for the millennium' as a feature of decadent writing, a sense of disappointment that the cleansing power of some kind of apocalypse to re-shape the world will never come (1995: p. 202). A feeling of disgust with the world, a sense of its sinfulness, and the belief that it needs urgent and immediate correction naturally leads to contemplation of the models for that correction.

Yet English decadent writing, so heavily implicated in eschatology by its association with ideas of fin de siècle, is also one of the parts of the decadent tradition that seems most comfortable with embracing artifice and strangeness *without* recourse to theological ideas of sin, punishment, or apocalypse. In part, this is because many of Baudelaire's ideas were mediated for English readers by A. C. Swinburne, who in his influential 1862 review of *The Flowers of Evil* was happy to compare Baudelaire to a 'medieval preacher' but characterized this as a pose, part of the French poet's aesthetic disinterestedness (2006: p. 346). Pater, in one of the first significant usages of the term in England, called for 'a refined and comely decadence' in his Preface to *Studies in the History of the Renaissance* (2010: p. 5). Notions like original sin or divine punishment are not meaningful in a modern world whose prevailing spirit is *relativism*, or what Pater had as early as 1866 called the 'Relative Spirit' – a condition where nothing 'can be rightly known, except relatively and under conditions', and a pursuit of the 'eternal outline' of 'the absolute' is an outmoded and sickly thought (1889: p. 65). This relativism is fundamental to Pater's thought: it is at the root of his hostility to theology, and it acts to dissolve theological concepts like original sin and make them meaningless. Indeed, Kate Hext has rightly argued that Pater is drawn to ideas like the Lockean *tabula rasa* precisely because they dispense with a vision of humanity conditioned by original sin and allow us to 'create and recreate ourselves as we wish' (2013: p. 36). In Pater's novel *Marius the Epicurean* (1885), Marius is strongly drawn to Christianity, but always in a spirit, we are told, that is 'faithful to the spirit of his early Epicurean philosophy' (1985: p. 235). Christian belief in the resurrection of the dead at the apocalypse, for example, is simply for Marius a beautifully extreme manifestation of 'a chivalrous refusal to forget or finally desert the helpless' (p. 230): it is certainly nothing to do with the revelation of God's judgement and the system of His punishments.

The double emphasis on an aesthetically disinterested and avowedly non-theological devotion to the supremacy of *l'art pour l'art* and a highly theologically inflected emphasis on sin and punishment had been a tension in the decadent tradition since Gautier and Baudelaire – and it is precisely this tension that Huysmans attempted to resolve in the Durtal novels. But as Walter Benjamin recognized, the doctrine of *l'art pour l'art*, or art for art's sake, was essentially apophatic or theologically negative in character:

> At this time, art reacted with the doctrine of *l'art pour l'art*, that is with a theology of art. This gave rise to what might be called a negative theology in the form of the idea of 'pure' art, which not only denied any social function of art but also any categorizing by subject matter. (1970: p. 226)

The profound discord between a doctrine that tried to define art by what it was *not* (whether ethical, political, religious, or moral), and a doctrine that explored art's role within a specific theological framework of sin and punishment, had always lain close to the surface of the decadent aesthetic; in English decadence, particularly the work of Wilde, it is especially palpable. The apocalyptic character of the decadent mode at this time may play its part. Even toying imaginatively with *fin du globe* (never mind wishing for it), cannot easily co-exist with an impulse to a thoroughgoing aesthetic relativism; precisely because the Apocalypse, if it comes, will be the ultimate debunking of that relativism, a confirmation that we *cannot* re-define these terms, nor re-make ourselves as we wish. Among the many other things it will be, the Apocalypse will be final confirmation that theological terms like sin or grace are *not* relative, that the resurrection of the dead will not be open to beautiful re-interpretation, and that the terms of our punishment will not be in our hands. This certainty, the lifting of the burden of relativistic ambiguity, is one of its attractions.

The Picture of Dorian Gray is the work in which this long-simmering theological tension in literary decadent writing most clearly emerges. Wilde's apophatic statements of what art should or should not be and his refusal to make temporal claims on it – most famously the refusal of all moral claims on art in the preface to the novel – co-exist with a punitive theological economy that specifically exacts a measured punishment for human sinfulness in the currency of physical suffering and decay. Wilde had written in 'The Critic as Artist' that 'What is termed Sin is an essential element of progress', an increase of the race, and 'at one with the higher ethics' (2007: p. 148). But this transvaluation of the idea of sin, the relativizing of its meaning and scope, fails to compete with a wider Augustinian theology of sin as decided by a higher and hidden authority. While still alert to the fascination and excitement of the rebellion inherent in sinfulness ('For all sins, as theologians weary not of reminding us, are sins of disobedience' (Wilde, 2006: p. 160)), sin in the metaphysical fabric of *Dorian Gray* is defined objectively, not relatively: each sin can be catalogued, and each sin carries a punishment.

But it is also a novel of *réversibilité*, albeit *réversibilité* written in a startling new way, because the punishment for Dorian's sins is, in the novel's famous conceit, transferred *to the domain of art itself*. As Dorian reflects at the end of the novel:

> Ah! in what a monstrous moment of pride and passion he had prayed that the portrait should bear the burden of his days, and he keep the unsullied splendour of eternal youth! All his failure had been due to that. Better for him that each sin of his life had brought its sure swift penalty along with it. There was purification in punishment. Not 'Forgive us our sins' but 'Smite us for our iniquities' should be the prayer of man to a most just God. (p. 185)

The still-recognizable Maistrean theology of sin and punishment invades the apophatic space; art is given redemptive power because it is made to take on the stain of human sin. Dorian is not a suffering outcast from society, or a monastic aesthete, or a *poète maudit* – art has been made to take the burden of sin from him. The domain of aesthetic relativism is colonized by authority, punishment, and a sense of inevitable – and measurable (to God) – sinfulness. Against the apocalyptic backdrop of the end of the nineteenth century, Wilde memorably dramatizes in *The Picture of Dorian Gray* what is perhaps the central dilemma of the theology of decadence: the role of art in redeeming a world that appears irrevocably conditioned by transgression and sin, so much so that it seems to cry out for some sort of punishment or correction.

References

Augustine, St. (2003). *City of God. Henry Bettenson*, trans., London: Penguin.

Baudelaire, Charles (1964). *The Painter of Modern Life and Other Essays*, Jonathan Mayne, trans., London: Phaidon Press.

Baudelaire, Charles (2006). *Intimate Journals*, Christopher Isherwood, trans., New York: Dover Publications.

Baudelaire, Charles (2008). *The Flowers of Evil*, James McGowan, trans., Oxford: Oxford University Press.

Benjamin, Walter (1970). *Illuminations*, Hannah Arendt, ed., Harry Zohn, trans., London: Jonathan Cape.

Eliot, T. S. (1999). *Selected Essays*, London: Faber and Faber.

Gagnier, Regenia (2010). *Individualism, Decadence and Globalization: On the Relationship of Part to Whole 1859–1920*, Basingstoke: Palgrave Macmillan.

Gautier, Théophile (2005). *Mademoiselle de Maupin*, London: Penguin.

Hanson, Ellis (1993). *Decadence and Catholicism*, Cambridge, MA: Harvard University Press.

Hext, Kate (2013). *Walter Pater: Individualism and Aesthetic Philosophy*, Edinburgh: Edinburgh University Press.

Huysmans, Joris-Karl (1996). *The Oblate of St. Benedict*, Edward Perceval, trans., Sawtry, Cambs.: Dedalus Books.

Huysmans, Joris-Karl (1997). *The Cathedral*, Clara Bell, trans., Sawtry, Cambs.: Dedalus Books.

Huysmans, Joris-Karl (2002). *En route*, W. Fleming, trans., Sawtry, Cambs.: Dedalus Books.

Huysmans, Joris-Karl (2009). *Against Nature*, Margaret Mauldon, trans., Oxford: Oxford University Press.

Johnson, Lionel (1891). The Cultured Faun. *The Anti-Jacobin*, 7 (14 March), 156–7.

Maistre, Joseph de (1993). *St. Petersburg Dialogues*, Richard A. Lebrun, ed. and trans., Montreal: McGill-Queen's University Press.

Maistre, Joseph de (1994). *Considerations on France*, Richard A. Lebrun, ed. and trans., Cambridge: Cambridge University Press.

Meltzer, Françoise (2011). *Seeing Double: Baudelaire's Modernity*, Chicago and London: University of Chicago Press.

Nordau, Max (1895). *Degeneration*, London: William Heinemann.

Pater, Walter (1889). *Appreciations: With an Essay on Style*, London: Macmillan and Co.

Pater, Walter (1909). *Miscellaneous Studies*, London: Macmillan and Co.
Pater, Walter (1985). *Marius the Epicurean*, Michael Levey, ed., London: Penguin.
Pater, Walter (2010). *Studies in the History of the Renaissance*, Matthew Beaumont, ed., Oxford: Oxford University Press.
Pierrot, Jean (1981). *The Decadent Imagination*, Derek Coltman, trans., Chicago: University of Chicago Press.
Pichois, Claude, and Jean Ziegler (1987). *Baudelaire*, Graham Robb, trans., London: Vintage.
Symons, Arthur (2014). *The Symbolist Movement in Literature*, Matthew Creasy, ed., Manchester: Carcanet Press.
Verlaine, Paul (1884). *Les poètes maudits*, Paris: Léon Vanier.
Weir, David (1995). *Decadence and the Making of Modernism*, Amherst, MA: University of Massachusetts Press.
Wilde, Oscar (1979). *Oscar Wilde: Interviews and Recollections*, E. H. Mikhail, ed., 2 vols., New York: Barnes and Noble.
Wilde, Oscar (2006). *The Picture of Dorian Gray*, Joseph Bristow, ed., Oxford: Oxford University Press.
Wilde, Oscar (2007). *Criticism: Historical Criticism, Intentions, The Soul of Man*. Vol. IV of *The Complete Works of Oscar Wilde*, Josephine M. Guy, ed., Oxford: Oxford University Press.
Wilde, Oscar (2013). *Journalism Part I. Vol. VI of The Complete Works of Oscar Wilde*, John Stokes and Mark W. Turner, eds., Oxford: Oxford University Press.

CHAPTER 14

The Science of Decadence

Jordan Kistler

The study of decadent literature reveals a complicated relationship between science, nature, and decadence. Many writers of the fin de siècle appeared to reject the natural world in favour of an 'artificial paradise' of their own making (Symons, 1893: 866). Arthur Symons, for example, defended the artificiality of decadence by asking, '[I]s there any "reason in nature" why we should write exclusively about the natural blush if the delicately acquired blush of rouge has any attraction for us?' (1896: p. xiv). Yet, decadence itself is an organic metaphor, extending the natural processes of decline and decay to societies and the arts. Rather than a rejection of nature, decadent art can be seen to readily embrace new scientific theories that changed the way people thought about the natural world.

The relationship between literature and science is not, however, one-sided. As Gillian Beer has suggested, there is 'two-way traffic' in 'not only ideas but metaphors, myths, and narrative patterns' that moves between scientists and non-scientists (2000: p. 5). The pessimism of nineteenth-century science stemmed from the brutal world of industrial capitalism in which it was developed. Decadent writers then incorporated both scientific ideas and language into a literary style obsessed with decay and decline. Finally, science returned to decadent literature to pathologize certain modes of artistic expression as yet another sign of the impending degeneration and death of the human species.

Three key scientific theories of the nineteenth century underpin the decadent fixation on decline, decay, and degeneration: uniformitarianism, evolution, and the conservation of energy. All three theories identify impermanence in natural structures previously believed to be permanent and stable.

i

Uniformitarianism caused a seismic shift in the way people understood their relationship to the earth. Charles Lyell's *Principles of Geology*

(1830–1833) popularized the theory of uniformitarianism, which suggested that the changes observed within the geologic record occurred slowly over long periods of time. This view contrasted with the previously accepted theory of catastrophism (propounded by scientists like Georges Cuvier), which posited that geologic changes were caused by sudden, catastrophic events, like the flood described in the book of Genesis. In contrast to a biblical understanding of the age of the earth, which suggested the planet was 6,000 years old, uniformitarianism introduced the concept of 'deep time', or the idea that the world had existed for millions or billions of years (scientists did not agree on figures during this period). Thus, the nineteenth-century public was confronted for the first time with the idea that the earth had existed long before humanity's arrival – and would continue to exist long after its demise.

Humanity's belief in its own centrality was further shaken by the mounting evidence for evolution, or the transmutation of species. The concept of deep time allowed for the possibility of gradual change within species. The theory of evolution was widely popularized in England by Robert Chambers in his 1844 *Vestiges of the Natural History of Creation* (published anonymously). In *Vestiges*, Chambers presented evidence for the evolution of species, but did not suggest the mechanism by which evolution occurred. This explanation was provided fifteen years later, in Charles Darwin's *On the Origin of Species* (1859), which introduced the theory of natural selection. Pre-Darwinian evolution was often viewed as progressive, with species evolving towards ever 'better' versions of themselves, and could be reconciled with the idea of a benevolent Creator. Darwin's theory of natural selection, which pointed to random mutation and competition for limited resources as the mechanism of change, could not. Evolution by way of natural selection was as likely to lead to degeneration (evolution to a less complex form) or extinction as to ascent up the evolutionary 'ladder'.

While uniformitarianism and evolution forced humanity to confront its own impermanence, new ideas in physics raised the possibility of the impermanence of the universe itself. The first law of thermodynamics, developed in the 1850s, demonstrated that energy is constant: it can be transformed, but never created or destroyed. This discovery quickly led to the formulation of the second law of thermodynamics by William Thomson (Lord Kelvin), which stated that 'although mechanical energy is *indestructible*, there is a universal tendency to its dissipation which produces gradual augmentation and diffusion of heat, cessation of motion, and exhaustion of potential energy through the material universe'

(Thomson, 1862: 388). At its core, this law means that nothing lasts forever – everything eventually succumbs to entropy. In the *Origin,* Darwin deliberately avoided discussing the application of his theories to humanity. Lord Kelvin had no such qualms. He extrapolated the inevitable outcome of the processes of entropy in the physical world: the heat death of the universe. The earth was not a 'perpetual motion machine' that could 'go on forever as it is illuminated by the sun from infinity of time past to infinity of time future' (Thomson, 1892: 321). The sun, like any other body subject to the laws of physics, is in the process of cooling and contracting, 'running down like a clock' until it eventually stops forever (Thomson, 1862: 388).

Thus, uniformitarianism demonstrated that humanity had not always been in existence; extinction suggested that humanity would not always exist; and thermodynamics insisted that the earth itself would cool, slow, and stop, destroying all life. The term 'decadence' suggests the end of an age or a civilization. Kelvin's work revealed the certainty of the coming end of the world. Though the heat death of the universe was many millions of years away, these scientific theories seemed directly applicable to nineteenth-century life and society. Herbert Spencer, for instance, was quick to appropriate Darwin's theory of natural selection to a Malthusian celebration of laissez-faire capitalism. Just one year after *Origin* appeared, in 'The Social Organism' (1860), Spencer extended Darwinian theory to the social structures of society, developing an extended analogy between 'the body politic' and 'a living individual body' in order to naturalize nineteenth-century class divisions and the exploitation of the working classes by the elite (1860: 93). Thus, he argued that as bodies have different parts that serve different functions, so too do societies; it is therefore natural that the 'inferior class' becomes 'exclusively occupied in providing the necessaries of life for the community at large' (105) while an elite few gain 'supreme power' (116). Spencer adroitly manipulated this organic metaphor to demonstrate that the economic structures of Victorian society, centred on competition and profit, were mandated by nature itself.

Spencer elaborated on his theory of natural competition in *The Principles of Biology* (1864), in which he insisted that Darwin had given the world 'unmistakable proof that throughout all past time, there has been a perpetual preying of the superior on the inferior – a ceaseless devouring of the weak by the strong' (1864: p. 340). Spencer argued that since competition for limited resources is the mechanism through which a species evolves, modern charity disrupts the natural processes of evolution and inhibits the species from improving. His progressive reading of evolution as a means of advancement, then, was made to serve a eugenicist vision in which the 'diseased and feeble' were destroyed in order to 'keep up the average fitness' of the species (p. 445). Darwin attempted to curtail a eugenicist application of his theories by insisting that sympathy and altruism were signs of advanced evolution in *The Descent of Man and Selection in Relation to Sex* (1871). Despite this, Darwin was indelibly associated with the new morality of Spencer in the form of Social Darwinism.

ii

The Social Darwinist fear of 'unfit' members of society interrupting the progress of the species is reflected in the newly emerging fields of criminology, sexology, and sociology. These fields incorporated Darwinian theory in an attempt to police the 'fitness' of the species in the face of apparent degeneration.

In his 1880 work *Degeneration: A Chapter in Darwinism,* E. Ray Lankester delineated the three possible outcomes of natural selection: 'balance', or the maintenance of the status quo, 'elaboration', or increasing complexity, and 'degeneration', or diminishing complexity (1880: p. 29). Here Lankester reflects the realization that a species' 'fitness' to its environment does not necessarily lead to a 'better' version. Simplified structures might just as often ensure the survival of the species. The possibility of degeneration was encapsulated for many naturalists in the barnacle, an animal that begins its life mobile, but as it reaches maturity 'takes to a perfectly fixed, immobile state of life', in which 'its organs of touch and of sight atrophy [and] its legs lose their locomotor function' (p. 35). This state ensures the barnacle's survival, but not its intellectual advancement, and thus counters any progressive understanding of Darwinism. Degeneration occurs when conditions of the environment 'render [an animal's] food and safety very easily attained' (p. 33). Applied to humanity, degeneration may occur *because* of advances in civilization which mean the average man does not need to struggle for his survival. Lankester makes the application of these ideas to mankind explicit by pointing to the end of the Roman Empire, when possession of 'the riches of the ancient world' led to degeneration. The fate of the barnacle, then, could be the fate of humanity.

One of the most famous accounts of the degeneration of the human species came from the Italian criminologist Cesare Lombroso. His magnum opus, *L'uomo delinquente* [*Criminal Man*] was first published in 1876, but was revised and expanded over five editions and twenty years. No English translation of this work was available in the nineteenth century (the first English edition that appeared was by Lombroso's daughter Gina Lombroso-Ferraro, published in 1911, and was a summary of Lombroso's work rather than a translation). Yet, Lombroso's theories, particularly the physical characteristics of the 'born criminal', permeated popular culture throughout Europe. Lombroso insisted that crime is not a matter of free will but rather the result of biological and social factors and thus believed that the penal system must focus on the criminal rather than the crime. In the first edition of *Criminal Man* he sought to taxonomize the criminal into various easily recognizable types. For instance, thieves have small eyes and thick eyebrows, while habitual murderers have hawk-like noses and thin lips (Lombroso, 2006: p. 51). Lombroso's theories hinged on the idea of atavism, or reversion to an earlier stage of evolution. This was made to serve classist and racist ideologies, which linked the lower classes and people of colour to earlier 'savage' stages of humanity.

The first edition of *Criminal Man* is aligned with Social Darwinism in its efforts to identify and isolate genetically inferior portions of humanity for the good of the species as a whole. By the final edition, however, pessimism had replaced progressive evolution. Having begun in the first edition by classifying the criminal as an unnatural atavistic throwback, at odds with the modern age, by the third edition (1884) Lombroso came to assert that crime is natural and exists among all living things: he pointed to the 'murder' of insects by carnivorous plants (brought to scientific attention by Darwin's 1875 *Insectivorous Plants*) to demonstrate 'the dawn of criminality' (2006: p. 168). Lombroso argues that in the earliest stages of humanity, and among nineteenth-century 'savages' (or the natives of non-European nations), there is no notion of crime. Thus, justice and sympathy are refigured as the artificial products of modern civilization. The pessimism of this view was extended even further in the fifth and final edition: not only was crime natural, and thus impossible to eradicate, but in order to reconcile modern crime rates with Darwinian law, crime must have 'a certain social utility' (p. 352). Lombroso thus suggests that crime is one of the traits actively *selected* by natural selection. Humanity can never be free of it.

Darwinism had a widespread influence on social scientists of the period, but Kelvin's theories, though not as obviously prominent, were also extremely influential. In many ways the opposite of Social Darwinism, social applications of thermodynamics suggested that decline was linked to *advances* in civilization rather than regression. Thus, in his 1895 *Civilization and Decay: An Essay on History*, Brooks Adams suggests decadence is the result of modernity and the intellectualism of an urban elite. The symptoms of a dying society, accordingly, are the ascendancy of the 'moneylenders' (with all its anti-Semitic undertones), the emancipation of women, and the separation of church and state (Adams, 1895: pp. 292–3). In this work, Adams applies the laws of thermodynamics to humanity and reads civilizations as analogous to suns: destined to contract until they begin to cool and die. Unlike fears of degeneration grounded in Darwinian biology, Adams viewed the decline of civilizations not as a possibility, but as a certainty. As the sun must eventually die, Adams argues, so too must all civilizations.

The sexologist Richard von Krafft-Ebing similarly insisted that abnormal sexuality was a side effect of advances in civilization. 'Periods of moral decadence', Krafft-Ebing writes, 'are always contemporaneous with times of effeminacy, sensuality, and luxury' (1894: p. 6). Where Lankester pointed to luxury as a sign that life had become too easy, which resulted in the degeneration of the species, Krafft-Ebing suggests that 'sensuality' and 'luxury' coincide not with ease of life but 'with increased demands upon the nervous system' (p. 6). The resulting nervousness leads to yet more sensuality, the destruction of traditional institutions of marriage and family, and eventually 'the destruction of the state [. . .] in material, moral, and political ruin' (p. 6). Thus, in his 1886 *Psychopathia Sexualis* (translated into English in 1894), Krafft-Ebing traced all perversions of sexual function to hereditary nervous disorders, displayed in one or both of the patient's parents. His study encompasses sadism, necrophilia, cannibalism, masochism, nymphomania, incest, and homosexuality, all linked to mental and physical illnesses. Though Krafft-Ebing's focus on heredity employs Darwinian rhetoric, much of his discussion of 'nervous energy' is based on Kelvin's thermodynamics. Krafft-Ebing applies 'conservation of energy' to human sexuality to argue that the demands of the fast-paced modern world lead to the dissipation of a limited source of energy. Thus, 'intense mental activity (hard study) [and] physical exertion' can diminish the natural sexual function (p. 47). The fast pace of modern life thus emasculates men, robbing them of their normal sexual virility or diverting it into perverse channels.

These ideas were equally applied to women in order to counter the demands for education and equality made by the New Woman in the final decades of the century. The psychiatrist Henry Maudsley pointed to the idea that 'the energy of a human body [is] a definite and not inexhaustible quantity' to support his assertion that 'educational strain' in young women would 'drain' the resources that would otherwise be expended on 'the physiological changes which constitute puberty' (1874: 199–200). By diverting the limited energy resources of the body to the brain rather than the uterus, women would be rendered unfit to be mothers. Female decadent writers were thus often accused of 'unsexing' themselves through their intellectual pursuits (209).

Ideas stemming from Kelvin's work in physics, such as the pessimistic certainty of decline, the belief that the fast pace of the modern world would more quickly dissipate human energy leading to effeminacy and sexual perversion, and fears that nervous disorders could be passed from parent to child, are all evident in decadent literature.

iii

In their attempt to find beauty in 'even of the loathsomest bodily putrescence and decay' (Swinburne, 1862: 999), authors of decadent literature explored the full range of sexual perversions outlined in Krafft-Ebing's work. Necrophilia, cross-dressing, lesbianism, hermaphroditism, and sadomasochism pervade Charles Baudelaire's *Les fleurs du mal* [*The Flowers of Evil*] (1857), A. C. Swinburne's *Poems and Ballads* (1866), and Oscar Wilde's *Salomé* (1891), as well as a host of other decadent works. A number of these 'perversions' come together in the figure of the femme fatale, an archetype constructed from the scientific belief that the modern age was blurring the line between the sexes, masculinizing women and emasculating men. As we have seen, doctors of the time insisted that female independence came at the direct expense of the feminine 'duty' of motherhood. Women who failed to conform to the sexual standards of British society were thus labelled as degenerate by medical and scientific discourses.

The femme fatale is beautiful, exotic, sexually aggressive, violent, and unmaternal. She is, in essence, the opposite of the ideal European woman of the nineteenth century. The perverse nature of a woman seeking sexual or economic independence was reified by science during this period. Krafft-Ebing and other medical professionals insisted that 'voluntary subjection to the opposite sex' came naturally to women (1894: p. 137). A desire for equality, then, was a sign of an unnatural nature. Sexual desire, too, was pathologized. Doctors like William Acton insisted that women did not naturally experience sexual desire (1862: p. 101), a position later 'confirmed' by Krafft-Ebing: 'Since woman has less sexual need than man, a predominating sexual desire in her arouses a suspicion of its pathological significance' (1894: p. 48). As a discipline, then, sexology considered female desire a symptom of disease.

Disease was linked to degeneration in the figure of the femme fatale by Darwin's theory of sexual selection, which suggested that pronounced sexual difference was a sign of advanced stages of evolution. In *The Descent of Man*, Darwin noted that sexual difference was more significant in man than in other primates (1871: p. 316) and suggested that the so-called lower races presented fewer sexual differences than were apparent in white Europeans (p. 321). Thus, he claims that among the natives of Australia there is very little difference between the height of men and women, while 'Eastward of India' and in Africa 'beards disappear' or are 'scanty or wanting' (p. 321). The femme fatale's masculine traits or behaviours thus marked her, in Darwinian terms, as racially Other and degenerate. The exoticizing and racializing of the decadent femme fatale is apparent in orientalist works like Gustave Flaubert's *Salammbô* (1862).

The decadent femme fatale, situated lower on the evolutionary ladder than the civilized modern woman, is insistently associated with the natural world and animal instincts. She is often a perverted or inverted Mother Nature, reflecting a nature that is 'red in tooth and claw' (Tennyson, 1994: p. 315). This is the figure that appears in Walter Pater's famous description of da Vinci's *Mona Lisa* in *Studies in the History of the Renaissance* (1873). 'La Gioconda' is the embodiment of 'the animalism of Greece, the lust of Rome' and like mother nature, she is older than time, 'older than the rocks among which she sits' (Pater, 2010: p. 70). She is morally corrupt, artificial, diseased, and perverts the maternal instinct. The femme fatale in Joris-Karl Huysmans's *À rebours* [*Against Nature*] (1884) is similarly described: she is 'the symbolic incarnation of undying Lust, the Goddess of immortal Hysteria, the accursed Beauty exalted above all other beauties by the catalepsy that hardens her flesh and steels her muscles, the monstrous Beast, indifferent, irresponsible, insensible, poisoning' (2003: p. 53). The Victorian femme fatale is built upon the model provided by gothic fiction of the late-eighteenth century and romantic poetry like John Keats's 'La Belle Dame Sans Merci' (1819) and Samuel Taylor Coleridge's 'Christabel' (1816), yet she is no longer a supernatural entity. She is entirely natural, or the embodiment of nature, reimagined through the pessimism of Darwinism and Kelvin's thermodynamics. She represents the long stretch of deep time, the animal, the savage, the degenerate, the end of civilization, and possibly even the end of the world.

Female decadent writers of the period often invoked the femme fatale, though to different effect. In Victoria Cross's 'Theodora: A Fragment', the New Woman and the femme fatale merge into an androgynous and sexually daring new breed of womanhood. Rather than suggesting that Theodora's masculine qualities mark her as degenerate, Cross aligns this new kind of womanhood with advances in civilization which have abstracted man from nature and his natural drives, allowing new tastes to develop. Here she echoes Symons' defence of cosmetics quoted at the beginning of this chapter. The narrator of 'Theodora' notes that scientific theories of the day suggest that love is 'merely the impulse [. . .] to select a fitting object which will help in producing a Third Life', but that this instinct is 'apt to be led astray' (Cross, 1895: 170–1). Theodora, with her narrow hips and small breasts is 'unfitted [. . .] in carrying out Nature's aim', but entirely 'fitted to give [the narrator] as an individual the strongest personal pleasure' (170–1). Here we see an inversion of Spencer's Social Darwinism. Cross acknowledges that civilization has strayed from nature, allowing the 'unfit' to flourish in society, but rather than framing this development as the source of the enfeeblement of the species, she introduces it as a form of liberation. The narrator is freed from the demands of nature to pursue sex for sex's sake, a 'gratification which has no claim whatever, in any sense, to be beneficial or useful' (171).

This celebration, like many of those championed by the New Woman, is complicated by the looming spectre of the species. Theodora, along with other heroines of New Woman writing, eschews motherhood; in the Darwinian understanding of progress, which is always linked to propagation, the failure to reproduce suggests that the new breed of woman will die out before she has a chance to impact the species. This is one example of the anxieties about heredity that haunt decadent writing. This preoccupation can be seen most prominently in Émile Zola's Rougon-Macquart series, twenty novels which trace degeneration inherited from the matriarch Adelaïde Fouque through four generations of her family. *La faute de l'Abbé Mouret* [*The Sin of Abbé Mouret*] (1875) traces the terminus of one branch of the family. Désirée Mouret is extremely healthy in body, representing all the fecundity of nature, but has the mind of a child. Her brother Serge is an intellectual, but suffers from a nervous disorder that manifests in religious mania. In the naturalistic language of Zola's novels, their diseases and disabilities are evidence of a tainted bloodline and mark the siblings as unfit to procreate, leading to tragedy. Like Zola, Henrik Ibsen and Thomas Hardy also translate 'the sins of the father' into scientific language, grounding the fatalism of their works in the science of heredity.

iv

The fatalism of decadent literature at times extended to the literal end of the world. The specific apocalyptic destruction of the heat death of the universe appeared in a number of literary works during the second half of the nineteenth century, like H. G. Wells's *The Time Machine* (1895). The eerie ending of Wells's novella imagines a desolate future, in which the stationary cooling earth is brooded over by a dying sun, and the only life left are monstrous, slow-moving mega fauna. A similar future is conjured by the poet Arthur O'Shaughnessy in 'The Line of Beauty' (1881). In this poem, O'Shaughnessy tackles the familiar trope of the immortality of art contrasted with human mortality, but couches it in scientific terms. Thus, he does not just imagine an individual death, or the end of an age, but rather the end of the earth as a whole:

> When mountains crumble and rivers all run dry,
> When every flower has fallen and summer fails
> To come again, when the sun's splendour pales,
> And earth with lagging footsteps seems well-nigh
> Spent in her annual circuit through the sky;
> When love is a quenched flame, and nought avails
> To save decrepit man, who feebly wails
> And lies down lost in the great grave to die;
> What is eternal? What escapes decay? (O'Shaughnessy, 1881: p. 106)

According to the scientific theories invoked here: nothing escapes decay. The usual optimism of poetry which locates immortality in art is undermined by the spectre of the dying sun.

The threat of decline and death that hovered over the century manifested in an aesthetics of decay in decadent literature. Thus, Swinburne praised and imitated the beauty that Baudelaire found in putrescence, and New Woman writers found liberation in 'unfitness'. Similarly, in works like Pater's *Marius the Epicurean* (1885), death, disease, and ruin lead quite naturally to the 'picturesque' (2008: p. 108): 'Turn thy body about, and consider what thing it is, and that which old age, and lust, and the languor of disease can make of it. [. . .] Consider that thy marbles are but the earth's callosities, thy gold and silver its *fœces;* this silken robe but a worm's bedding, and thy purple an unclean fish' (p. 134). Here the Emperor Aurelius ties what are usually symbols of the artificial in decadence – marble, silk, precious metals – to the natural world and insists that they are the result of death and decay.

A similar beauty in devastation manifests in the common decadent fantasy of nature reclaiming the earth from mankind, as in Zola's *The Sin of Abbé Mouret* or in Richard Jefferies' novel *After London, Or Wild England* (1885), which charts human life after the fall of modern civilization. In this post-apocalyptic world, natural law reigns, and thus 'men for ever trample upon men, each pushing to the front' (Jefferies, 1885: p. 47). Here we can see the Darwinian ideas which underpin a number of key elements of decadent literature: the new morality of Social Darwinism and the erasure of the line between man and beast.

One of the principal scientific theories incorporated into decadent literature was 'the survival of the fittest' (a phrase coined by Spencer, but later incorporated into Darwin's *Origin*). Spencer's application of natural selection to human society foregrounded competition, death, and extinction, leading Lombroso to assert that 'statistics as well as anthropological observation indicate that crime is a natural phenomenon – one that some philosophers would deem as necessary as birth, death, and conception' (2006: p. 92). These ideas were current in decadent literature well before the publication of Lombroso's *Criminal Man*, however. In his essay 'The Painter of Modern Life' (1863), Baudelaire insisted that 'crime, of which the human animal has learned the taste in his mother's womb, is natural by origin' (1965: p. 32). Here Baudelaire employs Darwinian language to argue that nature is the source of all that is violent and ugly, and thus aesthetics must be realigned around the veneration of the artificial. The new morality of Social Darwinism thus appears in decadent literature in the form of the mantra 'art for art's sake', which rejects the demands for moral and improving art, and instead foregrounds form and style as the only proper ways to judge art.

Morality based on Darwinian theory suggests that what is 'good' leads to survival, and thus what is 'right' brings the individual personal benefit and pleasure. Decadent hedonism, like that preached by Lord Henry and practised by Dorian in Oscar Wilde's *The Picture of Dorian Gray* (1891), is the direct descendant of Social Darwinism. In his novel Wilde explores the results of taking Darwinian morality to its logical extreme. Lord Henry parrots Walter Pater's famous 'Conclusion' to the *Renaissance,* in which he insists that 'to burn always with this hard, gemlike flame, to maintain this ecstasy, is success in life' (Pater, 2010: p. 120). Henry thus insists that man should 'live out his life fully and completely, [. . .] give form to every feeling, expression to every thought, reality to every dream' (Wilde, 2006: p. 19). Henry justifies his theories with contemporary science. Like Lombroso, who argued that crime was 'entirely lacking in primitive man', Henry insists that repression is unnatural: 'self-denial' is the 'mutilation of the savage', for which humanity is punished (p. 19).

The basis for the morality preached by Henry Wotton was the realization that human beings are taxonomically mere animals, and thus subject to animal instincts and desires. Alongside decadent hedonism, this knowledge manifests in gothic villains modelled on the degenerate savage described by Lombroso and his contemporaries. Thus, Robert Louis Stevenson's Mr. Hyde is 'troglodytic' and 'ape-like': smaller, hairier, and less well developed than his more human half, Dr. Jekyll (1886: pp. 25, 37). Bram Stoker's Dracula, with his 'peculiarly sharp white teeth' and 'aquiline' nose, is modelled explicitly on Lombroso's description of the 'habitual murderer' (1993: pp. 18). Richard Marsh's *The Beetle* (1897), Florence Marryat's *The Blood of the Vampire* (1897), and Guy Boothby's *Pharos the Egyptian* (1899), among many others, all employ this motif, embedding their monsters within contemporary scientific discourse.

V

If the authors of gothic novels invoked science in order to diagnose their characters, the reverse was also true: science looked to literature to diagnose the problems of the age. At the end of *Civilization and Decay,* Adams turns from economic theory to modern art, asserting that 'the history of art coincides with the history of all other phenomena in life', and thus, the art of a period can 'portend decay' (1895: p. 294). Science, therefore, used art and literature as proof of decline and degeneration. At its most superficial level, this took the form of the literary case study, in which fiction becomes evidence. Ignoring Wilde's warning that 'it is the spectator, and not life, that art really mirrors' (2006: p. 3), the literary case study accepts fiction as a mirror of reality. Thus, Lombroso employed Shakespeare to support his claim that criminal women 'far exceed men in their ferocity and cruelty': 'thus Shakespeare depicts Lady Macbeth as more cruel and cold than her male accomplice' (2006: p. 67). Krafft-Ebing, too, treats literature as analogous to patient testimony or statistical data. He points to the prevalence of sadism and masochism in 'the latest "decadent" literature of France and Germany' (1894: p. 123) as evidence that these perversions were on the rise in the general population. Rates of homosexuality, too, can be inferred from decadent literature: 'That inversion of the sexual instinct is not infrequent is proved, among other things, by the circumstance that it is frequently a subject in novels' (p. 230). Krafft-Ebing points to Honoré de Balzac, Denis Diderot, Théophile Gautier, and Flaubert as evidence.

In the literary case study, literature is accepted at face value, and made to serve a utilitarian purpose. More often, however, scientists viewed decadent literature as itself symptomatic of decline and degeneration. In the first case, fiction is literalized; in the second, it is pathologized. For many in the fields of criminology, sexology, suicidology, and the like, an artistic temperament was itself a sign of perversion, degeneration, or atavism. Krafft-Ebing defined 'brilliant endowment in art' as a 'psychical anomaly' evident of 'mental degeneration' (p. 225), while Lombroso suggested that criminals love poetry because it satisfies their 'boiling passions' (2006: p. 80). Pederasts, meanwhile, could be identified by their 'exquisite taste in the arts' (p. 73). This artistic temperament, combined with sexual perversion, was evidence that pederasts were atavistic throwbacks to Ancient Greece, when both flourished (p. 222).

The theory of literature as symptom was taken to its extreme by the physician Max Nordau in his work *Entartung* [*Degeneration*] (1892–1893). Couched as a medical text, *Degeneration* is a polemic against contemporary art, which Nordau views as a disease to be identified and eradicated by the physician (1895: p. 15). He insists that 'the originators of all the fin-de-siècle movements in art and literature' are 'degenerates', and further claims that the physician can study their art in the same way he would conduct a medical examination of the body (p. 17). This is possible, he argues, because disease is often mistaken for artistic genius. Thus, what the modern world calls imagination is simply the result of a weak and wandering mind (pp. 21, 56), while artists praised for their stylistic innovations are merely realists with faulty senses. Thus, impressionism is the result of 'visual derangements': 'the degenerate artist who suffers from *nystagmus*, or trembling of the eyeball, will, in fact, perceive the phenomena of nature trembling, restless, devoid of firm outline' (p. 26). Similarly, the symbolist school is populated by 'mystic imbeciles' suffering from diseased minds, for whom 'the activity of the organic nerves preponderates over that of the cerebral cortex', which results in an inability to express themselves clearly (p. 118). Nordau's diagnoses all stem from the assumption that a healthy mind expresses itself as directly, clearly, and literally as possible. Thus, the use of allegory or symbols must be a 'a diseased mental activity' and is indicative of imbecility, delirium, or paranoia (p. 396). Poetry is the chosen form of expression only of those suffering from 'weakness of mind' (p. 88), while rhyme is but a manifestation of 'echolalia' (p. 270). These artists, he implies, are attempting to express themselves realistically and objectively, but their perception of what is real has been warped by disease.

Nordau does not merely diagnose artistic movements and styles as degenerate; he diagnoses individual artists. Swinburne is of the 'higher degenerate type' (p. 94); Dante Gabriel Rossetti is an 'imbecile' (p. 94); Paul Verlaine is a 'paroxysmal dipsomaniac' and 'impulsivist' (p. 120); Gautier and Baudelaire both have 'mystically degenerate mind[s]'

(p. 300); Ibsen is an 'anti-social' egomaniac (p. 398); Friedrich Nietzsche is a 'frothing madman' (p. 415); and Zola is a 'sexual psychopath' (p. 500). Nordau's reach is so far that he is even able to medically diagnose anonymous readers. Those who read decadent literature are therefore 'abnormal subjects' with 'unbalanced minds': 'the neurasthenic, the hysteric, the degenerate, the insane' (p. 451).

Unlike the majority of scientific men considered in this chapter, Nordau believed in a progressive form of evolution. The history of art, he argues, gives evidence of mankind's progress. While literature of the past was entirely in verse, in the nineteenth century, poetry is 'only employed for purely emotional portrayal' (p. 543). This demonstrates that knowledge and judgement are conquering instinct and emotion. Thus, Nordau assures his readers, we may look forward to a future in which 'art and poetry will have become pure atavisms, and will no longer be cultivated except by the most emotional portion of humanity – by women, by the young, perhaps even by children' (p. 543).

Nordau's views suggest that art and science are fundamentally incompatible, yet in the nineteenth century the boundary between the two disciplines was especially fluid. Language and ideas moved freely between the sciences and the arts. Though some nineteenth-century literature evinces fears of the new reality revealed by uniformitarianism, evolution, and thermodynamics, many writers wholeheartedly welcomed this new world view. Decadent art, especially, can be seen to embrace scientific theories, using them to justify the tenets of the movement. The new morality of Social Darwinism thus underpins the amorality of art for art's sake, while the certainty of eventual decline and destruction revealed by the second law of thermodynamics justifies the search for beauty in putrescence and decay. Decadence is far from a rejection of the natural world. Rather, nature and the theories that articulate it are among the key building blocks of decadent art.

References

Acton, William (1862). *The Functions and Disorders of the Reproductive Organs in Childhood, Youth, Adult Age, and Advanced Life: Considered in Their Physiological, Social, and Moral Relations*, 3rd edn, London: John Churchill.

Adams, Brooks (1895). *Civilization and Decay: An Essay on History*, London: Swan Sonnenschein & Co.

Baudelaire, Charles (1965). The Painter of Modern Life. In *The Painter of Modern Life and Other Essays*, Jonathan Mayne, trans., London and New York: Phaidon, pp. 3–41.

Beer, Gillian (2000). *Darwin's Plots: Evolutionary Narrative in Darwin, George Eliot and Nineteenth-Century Fiction*, 2nd edn, Cambridge: Cambridge University Press.

Chambers, Robert (1844). *Vestiges of the Natural History of Creation*, London: John Churchill.

Cross, Victoria (1895). Theodora: A Fragment. *The Yellow Book*, 4, 156–88.

Darwin, Charles (1859). *On the Origin of Species by Means of Natural Selection*, London: John Murray.

Darwin, Charles (1871). *The Descent of Man and Selection in Relation to Sex*, London: John Murray.

Huysmans, Joris-Karl (2003). *Against Nature*, Robert Baldick, trans., London: Penguin Classics.

Jefferies, Richard (1885). *After London, or Wild England*, London: Cassell & Company.

Krafft-Ebing, Richard von (1894). *Psychopathia Sexualis, with Especial Reference to Contrary Sexual Instinct: A Medico-legal Study*, Charles Gilbert Chaddock, trans., London: F. J. Rebman.

Lankester, E. Ray (1880). *Degeneration: A Chapter in Darwinism*, London: Macmillan and Co.

Lombroso, Cesare (2006). *Criminal Man*, Mary Gibson and Nicole Hahn Rafter, trans., Durham, NC and London: Duke University Press.

Lyell, Charles (1837). *Principles of Geology*, 5th edn, London: John Murray.

Maudsley, Henry (1874). Sex in Mind and in Education. *Popular Science Monthly*, 5, 198–215.

Nordau, Max (1895). *Degeneration*, New York: D. Appleton and Company.

O'Shaughnessy, Arthur (1881). *Songs of a Worker*, London: Chatto & Windus.

Pater, Walter. (2008). *Marius the Epicurean: His Sensations and Ideas*, Kansas City: Valancourt.

Pater, Walter (2010). *Studies in the History of the Renaissance*, Oxford: Oxford University Press.

Spencer, Herbert (1860). The Social Organism. *Westminster Review*, 17, 90–121.

Spencer, Herbert (1864). *The Principles of Biology*, vol. I, London: Williams and Norgate.

Stevenson, Robert Louis (1886). *Strange Case of Dr. Jekyll and Mr. Hyde, London*: Longmans, Green, and Co.

Stoker, Bram (1993). *Dracula*, Ware, Hertfordshire: Wordsworth Classics.

Swinburne, A. C. (1862). Charles Baudelaire: *Les Fleurs du Mal. The Spectator*, 998–1000.

Symons, Arthur (1893). The Decadent Movement in Literature. *Harper's New Monthly Magazine*, 87, 858–67.

Symons, Arthur (1896). *Silhouettes*, 2nd edn, London: Leonard Smithers.

Tennyson, Alfred (1994). *The Works of Lord Alfred Tennyson*, Ware, Hertfordhsire: Wordsworth.

Thomson, William (Lord Kelvin) (1862). On the Age of the Sun's Heat. *Macmillan's Magazine*, 5, 388–93.

Thomson, William (Lord Kelvin) (1892). On the Dissipation of Energy. *Fortnightly Review*, 51, 313–21.
Wilde, Oscar (2006). *The Picture of Dorian Gray*, Oxford: Oxford University Press.
Zola, Émile (2017). *The Sin of Abbé Mouret*, Valerie Minogue, trans., Oxford: Oxford University Press.

CHAPTER 15

The Sociology of Decadence

Jeffrey K. Sachs

When we recognize decadence in society – say, in the 'Death by Chocolate' option on a dessert menu or in the 24k gold facial at a Dubai hotel – what are we recognizing? Wealth? Waste? Hedonism? Excess? To be sure, the lineaments of decadence precede sociology as an institutionalized discipline by a considerable time. 'Decadence' is a word, much like 'love' or 'authenticity', with such a range of meanings that it can function as a genre, type, form, or structure in which cultural elements fit. Common features of decadence in a general, social sense are recognizable in King Midas' bargain; Agamemnon's desire to keep Chryseis (despite this choice plaguing the Achaeans); or the loss of civic virtue Edward Gibbon identifies in *The History of the Decline and Fall of the Roman Empire* (1776–1789). We might define decadence loosely as a classifier for categorizing pathological social conditions that catalyse 'decline'; identifying sites of actual or theoretical contamination; or identifying harbingers of more widespread deterioration. While the term 'decadence' itself has not been explicitly used in much sociological scholarship, the structure of decadence has been deployed to situate related concepts like anomie and alienation in narratives of decline. The history of sociological thought shows decadence lurking behind those theories, concepts, models, and observations where sociological research seeks to mark out the current or downstream problems of society.

Historically, social theorists have shown a predisposition for the 'decline narrative': structurally, 'decline' presumes the weakening of social well-being relative to an earlier state. Sociological discourse has often been pessimistic about the current state of things and nostalgic about particular idealized social conditions. The decline narrative has frequently helped frame popular sociological foci such as the logic of capitalism, modernization, the rise of democracy or of authoritarianism, the development of industrial or post-industrial societies, the advent of neo-liberalism and globalization: each of which has been narrated, at one time or another, as institutions that strain, contaminate, or gradually deplete the healthy features of society. Sociologists have also found the narrative of decline, or, as we will call it in this chapter, the 'pathological decadent form', outside scholarship functioning as a label with which people mark out and make known the pathologies of their social worlds. For example, the legitimating complaint that 'the music currently being produced [...] is not *really* country music' has been shown to exist since the genesis of country music itself (Peterson, 1997: p. 7, my italics). In another example, the popular slogan of Donald Trump's 2016 Presidential Campaign – 'Make America Great Again' – seems to situate its foundational logic in nostalgia for a historic period of dubious origin, though the slogan still reflects on the idea that 'we' have since declined from that point.

Throughout the institutional history of sociology dating back to the late nineteenth century in the United States and Europe, different perspectives in social thought and schools of methodology have used the pathological decadent form in cases that both suppose the engagement of 'real' causal variables and as a mode of social critique. Basically, sociology engages with decadence (or societal decline) using two perspectives: one sees decadence as a real thing that can be studied, something highly empirical, structural, mechanistic, and capable of yielding a more prescriptive, nomothetic explanation; the other views decadence as a concept or label attached to a particular type of narrative commonly used for social critique. Such a narrative is culturally malleable and therefore often fragmented, but it is also patterned with certain recognizable features; that is, the narrative has the capacity to take on new attributes or alternative arrangements at different times and places.

From the perspective of cultural sociology, decadence is a stamp that marks a meaning-structure in a discourse about society. Regardless of its connection to real variables or to cultural frames, decadence can be examined sociologically, within different contexts, as explanations, or sets of narratives, that outline the causal linkage between social elements and decline. That said, decadence has been relatively one-dimensional in sociological thought. Interestingly, in everyday life, we find evidence that decadence is not always negative or, at least, need not be. While sociological discourse has commonly used decadence as a pathological label, there are social conditions where decadence takes on a positive charge: situations where the social world accepts and even embraces features that under different conditions would be viewed as pathological.

As shown in this chapter, the 'decadent role' in the production of art may be such that pathological attributes become accepted or expected to the point that they confer artistic legitimacy. The decadent role, in other words, becomes acceptable under a creative mandate; that is, individuals in certain fields of artistic production may present the pathological features of social decline so long as they connect those decadent attributes to creative output. When the decadent role satisfies the creative mandate, it can often improve artistic capital in the creative field. However, when the decadent role fails to live up to its creative mandate, the artist becomes re-classified as a glaring example of decline and is re-labelled as pathological. This sociological dynamic helps to explain why the work of certain nineteenth-century decadents – such as Oscar Wilde – are now held in high artistic regard. In the case of Wilde, his reputation as an artist has survived efforts to label him as pathological, so he has posthumously 'lived up' to the creative mandate his decadence entailed. More recently, in various areas of popular culture, including American stand-up comedy and rock and roll music, the decadent role is not necessarily so assured. Hence, the primary aim of this chapter is to illuminate the cultural capacity of decadence in society and explain the structural depth of decadence for sociological inquiry.

The Decadent Label

In 1871, J. B. Mayor wrote in the *Journal of Philology* that the word 'decadence' 'seems to have made little way in England until the last quarter of a century, when [. . .] it came into fashion, apparently to *denote* decline, and *connote* a scientific and enlightened view of that decline on the part of the user' (p. 348; my italics). Mayor's philological characterization of decline helps us understand decadence only generally, but the 'connotation' suggests that decadence signifies an intellectual contemplation: perhaps a currency of cultural distinction, inaccessible to non-scientific or unenlightened thinkers. Let us consider, then, a construction of this connotative form without the signifier but with a parallel structure. In an 1872 letter to Ivan Turgenev, Gustave Flaubert once lamented:

> The bourgeoisie is so bewildered that it has lost all instinct to defend itself; and what will succeed it will be worse. I'm filled with the sadness that afflicted the Roman patricians of the fourth century: I feel irredeemable barbarism rising from the bowels of the earth. I hope to be gone before it carries everything away. But meanwhile it's not very gay. Never have things of the spirit counted for so little. Never has hatred for everything great been so manifest – disdain for Beauty, execration of literature. (1982: p. 200)

Here, we find features of the decline narrative where Flaubert identifies certain pathological social conditions – bewilderment, barbarism, decline of spirit, decline of beauty, and so on. An interesting feature, however, is Flaubert's feeling of isolation. He appears to see the symptoms of decline in the same manner that early modern anatomists theorized pathologies: by linking bodily symptoms to internal lesions. The discipline of observation in anatomy maintains that symptoms link to lesions that are out of sight (inside the body), though not out of sight for those who know how to dissect and examine the mechanical functioning of the bodily system.

As an academic discipline in Europe and the United States, sociology began shortly after Flaubert's letter to Turgenev.[1] Interestingly, when sociology became institutionalized it took on a methodological perspective similar to that of the anatomist and constructed its practice to address sentiments not unlike those that Flaubert articulated.[2] Flaubert's notion of decline functions according to two implicit ideas:

(i) *Label:* The lesions on society are growing but are hidden to the everyday person who has become inured to pathological practices.
(ii) *User:* To recognize these lesions is to be a reflective outsider: to inquire, organize, and criticize the complexity of the system.

Institutional sociology emerges with these same suppositions about societal pathologies, but, like physicians trained in anatomy in contrast to those with no such training, sociologists distinguish themselves professionally from the instinctual methods of social critics, such as Flaubert, by foregrounding the strength (or objectivity) of their methodology.

Considering the social critic and the social scientist together, however, we can identify as a fundamental feature of decadence a 'judicial position' that allows someone to label an activity as pathological which also labels the participants in the activity, who, seemingly, do not recognize the pathological features of their behaviour. The decadent stamp carries with it an

1 In 1875, William Graham Sumner offered the first course titled 'Sociology' at Yale University; the first formal department of Sociology was established at the University of Chicago in 1892 by Albion Small; and, in Europe, Émile Durkheim established the first formal department of Sociology in France, coinciding with his publication of *Les règles de la méthode sociologique* [*The Rules of Sociological Method*] (1895).

2 The early methodological mode of many sociologists and social anthropologists, such as Durkheim and A. R. Radcliffe-Brown was *structural functionalism*, a methodological perspective that imagined institutions functioning like organs of the body; these organs keep the societal whole operating properly. Various destabilizations would cause certain institutional organs to weaken and others to compensate, which outlined a system of adaptability where the bodily system always seeks equilibrium through the dynamic feedback of its institutions.

implicit logic that the person who labels something as pathological can do so only by maintaining a disciplined footing in reality while the person or persons participating in and contributing to decline are detached from reality, and, as such, are not attending to the needs of the 'real' system (i.e., the system where concrete properties of inequality exist, with more problems emerging when people detach themselves from reality or disregard it without recognizing the compound effect of others doing the same).

Given this distinction, we can formulate a more systematic ideal type for the structural logic of the pathological decadent stamp:

(i) *The labelling group*: the source of the 'gaze' – usually situated outside the pathological space and machinery;
(ii) *The labelled group*: marked as the source of decline – usually labelled as an activity or an institution that determines or encourages an activity, its ritualization, or ethic; and
(iii) *The pathological/normal dynamic* (the binaries in conflict): reality (or positivism) is *normal* and conflicts with romance (or imagination), which is judged to be *pathological.*

The concepts of the 'normal' and the 'pathological' derive from Émile Durkheim's *The Rules of Sociological Method* (1895). These two concepts theorize the division between acceptable and unacceptable classes of acts, groups, and identities: 'those that are entirely appropriate and those that should be different from what they are' (1982: p. 85). Durkheim considers these terms in close relation to their biological connotations; that is, things that are *pathological* are meaningfully connected to notions of illness and pain, while things that are *normal* are considered healthy and progressive. From this perspective, the notion of decline in *decadence* is easy to connect with social *pathology* using Durkheim's terminology, given that pathological elements in society are sources of weakness and are therefore subject to be labelled as such. With these structural elements in place, we can account more systematically for the common pathological decadent form via some examples and comparisons.

The Common Pathological Decadent Form in Sociology

Flaubert presses an issue in his letters to Turgenev that is recognizable as the thematic centre of his earlier work, *Madame Bovary* (1857). In *Madame Bovary,* the main character, Emma, extends herself beyond the resource-capacity of her actual life by pursuing a more romantic existence that emulates fantasies of social conventions she has encountered in literature.

This pursuit is narrated as one ending in tragic decline: in Emma's case, with suicide.

In the late-nineteenth century, just prior to the institutionalization of sociology, a number of social critics provided less methodologically rigorous evaluations of social ills. In 1883, the novelist and social critic Paul Bourget interpreted *Madame Bovary* as a cautionary tale about the romantic ideal, which he described as 'an infinite need for intense passions' (2013: 14). From Bourget's perspective, *Madame Bovary* illuminated the problematic linkages between culture (which frames and encourages the romantic imagination), industry, and consumption. Bourget believed that individual-material interaction at the centre-point of these overlapping spheres would encourage *bovarysme* by generating social aspirations that would lead, invariably, to personal decline and, further, societal decline. As Bourget maintained, 'not only does [the ideal] lead man to find himself out of proportion with his surroundings, but it makes him incommensurate with himself' (p. 16).

Moving from fin-de-siècle social criticism into institutional sociology, if we look at one of Durkheim's explanations for social decline, we find that the substance of Bourget's and Flaubert's explanations, under the label of the romantic ideal, reappears relatively unchanged. In *Suicide* (1897), Durkheim introduced the sociological concept *anomie* [lawlessness, from Greek *a-* 'not' + *nomos* 'law']. Despite the different label, it is relatively easy to see that anomie is comprised of the same structural elements as the romantic ideal. For instance, Durkheim asserted that, under anomic conditions, 'reality seems valueless by comparison with the dreams of fevered imaginations; reality is therefore abandoned [. . .]. A thirst arises for novelties, unfamiliar pleasures, nameless sensations, all of which lose their savor once known' (1979: p. 256). Here, the same pathological elements are identified as those Bourget named in his criticism of the romantic ideal. The difference, for the most part, resides in the assumed theoretical underpinnings of action and order between the two social 'gazes'. For Durkheim, anomie results from institutional tensions under the theoretical premises of structural functionalism (see n. 3, above). Flaubert and Bourget, on the other hand, use a less systematic theory of organization; theirs is more intuitive, based on personal reflection and general perspectives learned from literature and history. Thus, we find that procedures for the user of the decadent stamp – the way of seeing – can vary significantly. Hence sociologists often dismiss the procedures of social critics as insufficiently scientific or rigorous, despite that both, as seen in this case, can locate the same mechanisms for social decline.

In another example contemporary with Durkheim, Thorstein Veblen introduced the concept of *conspicuous consumption* in *The Theory of the Leisure Class* (1899) by combining the ethos of the romantic ideal with an underlying logic similar to Karl Marx's concept of *Entfremdung* [alienation]. In effect, Veblen sought to illustrate how society had come to function on the radical presentation of social relations as our dominant mode of social engagement, or, more particularly, how the social world had become the expression of relative social positions between individuals through 'commodity fetishism' and consumption. As Marx asserted in *Das Kapital* [*Capital*] (1867), commodity relations in a capitalist system alienate individuals from their contributions to society (Marx, 1990). In a capitalist political economy, according to Marx, the real value of labourers becomes abstracted by way of relative-economic exchange relations between things. That is, the value of a thing is a measure of its ability to be exchanged for other things, not the value of the underlying labour that brought the thing into existence. In such an environment, Veblen asserted, the 'conspicuousness' or the public presentation of one's consumption serves as the definition of one's productive contribution to society: that is, 'social esteem' becomes signified by the things one openly consumes in relation to others. Decline, for Veblen, becomes inevitable within this system because the competitive environment of consumption-driven esteem pulls aspirations away from real or needed social contributions and motivates the consumption and production of things that have no use. In fact, Veblen pointed out, the most conspicuous form of consumption in this environment becomes waste, measured by time: 'Time is consumed non-productively (1) from a sense of the unworthiness of productive work, and (2) as an evidence of pecuniary ability to afford a life of idleness' (2009: p. 22). Thus, from Veblen we identify the same thematic elements of social detachment as those Bourget and Durkheim discovered, respectively, in the concepts of the romantic ideal and anomie. The difference, again, lies with the theoretical underpinnings of the social gazes observing how individuals in the system act and organize. Conspicuous consumption is founded on premises of distinction and systemic conflict. In this respect, Veblen's framework theorizes a social actor with more agency than Durkheim's; Veblen also presents a system that appears capable of undermining itself and degenerating, rather than adapting to tensions, as the structural functionalist perspective would contend.

The four examples we have just considered (Flaubert, Bourget, Durkheim, and Veblen) each reflect the more stable structural elements of the decadent stamp outlined earlier. Interestingly, the labelling groups in each case make an asymmetric accusation about society; that is, they set themselves apart from the location and mechanisms of decline: they are outsiders examining the pathological mechanisms of others. Their use of the decadent stamp foregrounds the qualities of reality, useful activity, and healthy contributions as positive dimensions. In contrast, each example also expresses the pathological dimensions as detachment, fantasy, and imagination as a positive-feedback loop. These features encourage decline via lawlessness, collective depletion, and waste.

Ethnographic Pathological Decadent Form

More contemporary, meaning-centred sociology, borrowing methods from ethnographic anthropology, acknowledges that the social scientist must be influenced by the same institutions and structural logics that he or she tries to observe 'objectively'. Because sociologists aim to 'make sense' of social order and action, some contemporary sociologists using ethnographic methods have begun to inquire as to how the everyday person plays 'sociologist'; that is, how do everyday people make sense of and mark out social pathologies? The significant shift to more meaning-centred approaches in the 1960s and 1970s in the social sciences and humanities marked a 'cultural turn', perhaps best exemplified by the work of Clifford Geertz (1973). For the study of decadence in sociology, meaning-centred approaches transfer the sociological gaze from recognizing 'real' mechanisms of decline in society (as we have just discussed) to observing how segments of social life interpret decline or pathologies and investigating what responses these meaning-structures reveal.

Gary Allen Fine provides a good example of this type of inquiry in 'The Goliath Effect: Corporate Dominance and Mercantile Legends' when he observes that many people react to decadence much as Bourget, Flaubert, Durkheim, or Veblen did. Fine identifies the similarity in patterns of folklore circulation that attach pernicious cautionary tales to large corporations; for instance, McDonald's 'uses worms in its burgers' (1985: p. 63). Fine observes that these stories emerge when a corporation establishes its dominance in a particular area and so becomes a 'goliath'. He asserts that 'these stories reflect conditions of modernity and raise the concerns of the age. They represent attempts by the public to deal with massive social dislocations affecting them' (63–4). The folk thus participate in the same work as sociologists, using the decadent stamp to label various social pathologies; that said, in the case of the folk, labelling tends to be pragmatic in devising schema for rejecting the labelled 'thing' as pathological; crucially, if the function of sociology is to participate in the same kind of intervention, the discipline, then, has a difficult time making itself distinct from social criticism. The perspective of the folk, however, highlights an important aspect of labelling in general: that it allows one group (defined or undefined) to view the activity of another group as contaminating; hence, the dynamics of power involved in group labelling cause some labels to gather stronger or weaker affiliations.

When everyday people label contamination in society, to some degree they do so while also wanting to account for their own proclivities as not pathological (or normal). In a fragmented society, such as our own, this self-interest introduces a great deal of complexity: normal and pathological dividing lines can often conflict in negotiations between different legitimating claims about needs, esteem, and desires. Along these lines, an example from Allison Pugh illustrates that there are more dimensions to interpreting decadence than what we have seen thus far in the standard narrative. Pugh explores the way individuals in different circumstances formulate consumption practices with regard to raising children. She finds that low-income parents will sometimes purchase certain non-essential items such as toys or fancy clothes for their children instead of purchasing essential things for themselves, like a suitable place to sleep or sufficient amounts of food (2009: p. 122). Pugh finds that parents who make these decisions recognize how certain possessions carry 'symbolic power' and serve as 'an essential component of dignity' for their children (p. 124). Thus, these parents deliberately choose 'decline' for themselves in exchange for the social and symbolic prestige non-essential purchases confer on their children. Pugh also illustrates how the more traditional notion of decadence linked to overconsumption, 'commodity fetishism', materialism, and the like is more consistently the concern of middle- to upper-middle-class parents who attempt to resist their children's 'consumer desires', fearing that not resisting could foster downstream decadent personality traits (p. 173). The important feature that Pugh illuminates in her ethnographic work is that people have the capacity to interpret the lineaments of decline, in terms of being a structural logic or symbolic boundary, as possibly acceptable or unacceptable depending on different social conditions.

The 'Normative' Decadent Form

We have already established that the activity of recognizing the pathological aspects in society is closely related to the label of deviance. Durkheim points out that we cannot actually prove that what we identify as 'normal' is healthy and as 'pathological' is unhealthy: 'Such a proof presumes that the problem has already been solved. The proof is only possible if the nature of the normal state has been determined beforehand and consequently the signs whereby normality may be recognized are already known' (1982: p. 90). Hence, the labels 'normal' and 'pathological' are somewhat like tastes, and (especially in a complex, modern society) such tastes likely show a great deal of variation as social worlds divide into different cultural circles of social engagement. For this reason, the 'normative' decadent form often coincides with cultural rifts whereby the cultural circle that accepts the decadence does so in relation to viewing one or a set of 'status quo' cultural circles as pathological; that is, the normative type often underlies some counter-cultural stance.

Howard Becker provides an apposite description of the normative form of decadence in *Art Worlds* (1982) when he connects this form to the exempting 'role' the artist plays: 'At an extreme, the romantic myth of the artist suggests that people with such gifts cannot be subjected to constraints imposed on other members of society; we must allow them to violate rules of decorum, propriety, and common sense everyone else must follow or risk being punished' (1982: p. 14). The exceptional classification given to the artist follows from the belief that innate talent situates the artist outside the common social world of being like everyone else; that is, adherence to normality does not create the exceptionality of the artist; thus, normal practices should not be used to constrain the artist: doing so would risk limiting his or her artistic capacity. Becker poses this common view in order to challenge the reality of it as the crux of his work; nonetheless, as a common view it presents an important frame that makes this normative decadent 'role' in society acceptable.

The 'sad clown' has been a cultural artefact for some time: a traditional example is the title character in Ruggero Leoncavallo's opera, *Pagliacci* (1892). In contemporary popular culture the 'sad clown' more commonly frames the prevalent cultural yoking of talent to decline in stand-up comedy.[3] Explanations of this relationship typically couple the 'role' of the stand-up comedian with personal pathology:

> It is a comedian's job to find humor in things that are not funny, and the way a good comedian does that is by being a naturally funny person who suffers

[3] For this chapter, we look at stand-up comedy only briefly and consider it particularly from the perspective of American stand-up comedy. In other areas of the world, stand-up comedy might take a wholly different form.

> those terrible, unfunny things. Other comedians, such as Artie Lange and David Cross, continue to tell jokes about using heroin, regardless of the pain it has caused knowing it's their job to keep talking about it. (Snipes, 2015)

In this example, the personal decline of the comedian functions not simply as an indicator of taste but appears to characterize the obligation of the comedian, serving as the pathway through which he or she gains legitimate access to content. We see the stand-up comedian connected to somewhat objectively pathological elements – addiction, depression, hedonism; however, in the case of the stand-up comedian, real features of decline can provide social capital that becomes exchanged in performance for authenticity. Within such a social framework for evaluating comedians one will not be surprised to find lists of 'all-time best stand-up comedians' populated with a high proportion of performers who are now deceased because of drug overdoses or suicides related to depression or dissipation.

The relatively coherent connection between 'good' comedy and authentic decline, in fact, has been salient enough to inspire a number of psychological studies. Below, one such study provides an explanation for why this connection exists:

> There appears to be an awareness on the part of the audience of the relationship between humor and anxiety. Consequently it would be reasonable to assume some awareness of the fact that comedians are very anxious and often depressed people. Some indication of the need to view humor as a release for tension can be seen in the increasingly sadomasochistic relationship between the comedian and his audience. (Janus, 1975: 169)

In this explanation, pathological features are described as a mode through which the connection between the comedian and the audience is made. The passage also describes common traits of the stand-up comedian as naturally tied to these attributes of decline. The classification of 'stand-up comedian' is described as marked by decadence somewhat naturally, as if decline were a constituent element of the label 'comedian' itself. In this manner, artistic production for the stand-up comedian becomes authentically intertwined with decline, which thus classifies the comedian as 'exceptional' or situated outside the normal rules. This status parallels the basic features of the normal decadent form already discussed.

Looking at artistic production more broadly, we can find the normal decadent form in many other artistic fields as well. Again, because 'pathological' and 'normal' labels are used relationally like 'deviance', the normal decadent form often appears as a perspective in cultural circles that view the 'status quo' conventions of other cultural circles as pathological.

Following World War I, such Lost Generation writers as Ernest Hemingway in *The Sun Also Rises* (1926) and F. Scott Fitzgerald in *The Great Gatsby* (1925) used their novels to frame the derangement of 'normal' society, representing both their characters and themselves as glaring non-participants in that society, thereby intermingling their fictional and real worlds. We see in their characters the purposeful appropriation of 'pathological' features brought on by their disenchantment with what they view as a grossly dehumanized modern world, and we know that the actions of these fictional figures are similar to narratives about the authors in 'real life'. This disenchantment encouraged the re-emergence of romantic pursuits as these authors' fictional life-worlds and real life-worlds are enmeshed to the point that the reality of their decadence becomes blurred and sensationalized. Hemingway artfully embraces the pathological features of his expatriate status (real and fictional) by means of a disenchanted character in *The Sun Also Rises*:

> "You're an expatriate. You've lost touch with the soil. You get precious. Fake European standards have ruined you. You drink yourself to death. You become obsessed by sex. You spend all your time talking, not working. You are an expatriate, see? You hang around cafés."
>
> "It sounds like a swell life," I said. (2006: p. 115)

As a narrative type, detachment often seems linked to goals of 'originality' and 'authenticity' in artistic production. As definitional claims, however, these classifications feel somewhat mutually exclusive. That said, this contradiction perhaps explains how decadence connects to artistic production; refusing to participate in society detaches the artist from norms, thereby increasing the perception of originality; at the same time, when decline is linked to production it can be viewed as sacrifice. These two dimensions associate 'authenticity' and 'legitimacy' with decline when conditioned through artistic production.

The performative type of the author in decline, which has perhaps taken Hemingway as its ideal type in subjective, confessional literary forms, can also be observed in several literary-cultural trends since World War II. The Beat Generation writers, for instance, strongly resisted status quo culture, or what they perceived as segments of stifling conservatism. Examples from this group include William Burroughs's *Naked Lunch* (1959), embracing drug use, and Allen Ginsberg's *Planet News* (1968), embracing sexual awakening. The ethos of the Beat Generation, both in artistic production and lived activity, encouraged experimentation and discovery; two classifications that associate quite strongly to a positive view of carrying an 'exceptional' status and being situated 'outside' of dominant cultural norms.

In a different literary circle, Charles Bukowski channelled the 'pathological' features of working-class culture to provide a logic for acceptable decadence in substances and prurience among 'down and out' labourers, perhaps best exemplified in the collected work of his underground newspaper column, *Notes of a Dirty Old Man* (1969). Here, the positive features of an 'outside the norms' identity become attached to the exceptional authenticity of the overlooked labourer: artistic and alienated. Interestingly, while the physical decadent activities of the Beat Generation and Bukowski were similar, such as over-indulgence in drugs, alcohol, and sex, the working-class perspective of 'normal' decline stands in stark contrast to the Beat perspective. Hence, the two groups likely would have viewed the impetus for the activity of the other as lacking artistic merit and therefore 'pathological'. To be sure, there are many examples of the decadent 'role' being played by writers: a few other examples include the 'gonzo' journalism of Hunter S. Thompson or the 'dirty realism' of Raymond Carver, Tobias Wolff, Jayne Anne Phillips, and Richard Ford. Outside these cultures, such writers as John Cheever and J. D. Salinger offered more accessible examples of social decadence in their narratives of disenchantment and dissipation among segments of upper-middle class society, which often featured 'slight rebellions' between protagonists and conservative social worlds (Salinger, 1946).

In modern American and European society, culture has become fragmented into social circles, some of which overlap, but there is often an effort within circles to emphasize an identity to keep their culture distinct and thus avoid overlapping with others. Where such opposition takes place at extreme levels, one circle often labels another, or a set of others, as 'pathological'. This is not to say that there are no longer norms or dominant normal communities; but identity affiliation has moved away from lines divided along distinctions of class and has adopted cultural labels and 'performativity' as its currency for distinction strategies (Butler, 1990). From this shift, a multitude of different 'interpretive communities' exist which often view themselves as normal but possibly view other communities as pathological, especially those accused of subverting the agency and identity of the labelling group (Fish, 1982). In an identity-centred environment, increased fragmentation allows for the meaning-structure of a normal decadent type to become more varied but also more frequently found. The linkages formed between the cultural circle, the artist, and decadence illuminate the motivations of a group to disclose and normalize itself, and be non-traditional. Given this structural logic, the normative decadent type can be found in most areas of artistic production – visual art, theatre, film, music, and others.

When sociologists examine structural logics, they also tend to seek out the conditions in which structures (especially those with 'roles') 'toggle' in order to determine where the sensitivity of structural binary relationship resides (as in the linguistics of Ferdinand de Saussure, the sociology of Durkheim, and the anthropology of Claude Lévi-Strauss). In this case, I want to see what attributes of the artistic 'role' will make the decadent form toggle between normal and pathological. For the normative decadent form, we have found that the cultural circle that labels the artist as creative also finds the artist's decadent features acceptable because they associate with sacrifice for artistic production (which also amounts to sacrifice for the cultural circle), and also because the decadent features can position the artist as 'outside' or 'original', which helps legitimize the non-status quo identity as 'authentic'. The dynamic between authenticity and originality seems to obtain in cultural circles where decadence has a stronger fit to the cultural identity (such as the culture of misery and humour in stand-up comedy); cultural fit, with regard for decadence, seems to be in line with the degree of opposition the cultural circle expresses to dominant norms; for example, the normative decadent 'role' fit the cultural circle of the Rolling Stones during the 1960s and 1970s and thus helped confer artistic capital on the band through the ties between the decadent 'role' and counter-cultural aspects of their fan base.

In general, the decadent role fits the counter-cultural milieu of rock and roll music. Trashing hotel rooms, sexual promiscuity, and excessive drug use all served to spite status quo society, which the rock and roll circle regarded as 'pathological' because of its political support of the Vietnam War and its general ambivalence about advancing peace, civil rights, and personal autonomy. However, it is important not only that the artist occupying the decadent role fit with the cultural circle, but also that he or she continue to be artistically productive and satisfy the creative mandate of originality and authenticity within the circle. Without these attributes, the artist no longer has value within the circle. Once decadence can no longer be linked to an authentic sacrifice for artistic production, the artist becomes re-classified as 'pathological' under explanations that the artist has become 'cheap' or 'factory-produced'. Once such re-classification occurs, the counter-cultural circle situates the artist within status quo culture as a 'sell-out'. In such cases, cheap artists and the articulated elements of their weaker performances often function as inflection points that mark the distinction between the tastes of the cultural circle and the commercial tastes of the mass outside the cultural circle. We see examples of this when, for instance, writers churn out mass-market, fast-paced novels that appear unrelated to their complex, cerebral, and reflective earlier work; when rock musicians switch to disco; when an acclaimed method actor appears in commercials for pay-day loans; or when an indie singer becomes a regular judge for a television talent show. In such cases, the artist fails to maintain membership within the cultural circle under the creative mandate.

Finally, we should consider at least one other dimension of the normal decadent type as an object of sociological inquiry. The ideas and examples considered in this chapter have involved white (American or European) men; thus, a good question might be, 'How often does the normal decadent type obtain for artists with variations in gender, sexual orientation, or racial background?' Consideration of such variations would likely generate a broader view of how cultural circles overlap despite not identifying as such; for instance, if fans of rock and roll view the decadent role as 'pathological' when occupied by a female, such as Janis Joplin or Joan Jett, this cultural circle might share more overlap with status quo culture than it believes. We also might find that cultural circles become more fragmented along these lines if, for instance, women in the rock and roll cultural circle endorsed Joplin in the decadent role but men did not. Whatever the case may be, further explorations of decadence as a sociological inquiry should pursue conditions that possibly reveal new dimensions of the decadent role in society, exposing irregular and culturally significant forms of normal or pathological decadence given variations in a structural arrangement.

References

Becker, Howard S. (1982). *Art Worlds*, Berkeley: University of California Press.

Bourget, Paul (2013). On Flaubert. Nancy O'Connor, trans., *New England Review*, 33(4), 10–30.

Bukowski, Charles (1969). *Notes of a Dirty Old Man*, San Francisco: City Lights Books.

Butler, Judith (1990). *Gender Trouble*, New York: Routledge.

Durkheim, Émile (1979). *Suicide: A Study in Sociology*, George Simpson, ed., John A. Spaulding, trans., New York: Free Press.

Durkheim, Émile (1982). *The Rules of Sociological Method*, Steven Lukes, ed., W. D. Halls, trans., New York: Free Press.

Fine, Gary Alan (1985). The Goliath Effect: Corporate Dominance and Mercantile Legends. *The Journal of American Folklore*, 98(387), 63–84.

Fish, Stanley (1982). *Is There a Text in this Class?* Cambridge, MA: Harvard University Press.

Flaubert, Gustave (1982). *The Letters of Gustave Flaubert, 1857–1880*, Francis Steegmuller, trans., Cambridge, MA: Belknap Press.

Geertz, Clifford (1973). *The Interpretation of Cultures*, New York: Basic Books.

Hemingway, Ernest (2006). *The Sun Also Rises*, New York: Scribner.

Janus, Samuel S. (1975). The great comedians: personality and other factors. *The American Journal of Psychoanalysis*, 35, 169–74.

Marx, Karl (1990). *Capital: A Critique of Political Economy*, vol. I, London: Penguin.

Mayor, John E. B. (1871). Decadence. *Journal of Philology*, 3, 347–8.

Peterson, Richard A. (1997). *Creating Country Music: Fabricating Authenticity*, Chicago: University of Chicago Press.

Pugh, Allison J. (2009). *Longing and Belonging: Parents, Children, and Consumer Culture*, Berkeley: University of California Press.

Salinger, J. D. (1946). Slight Rebellion off Madison. *The New Yorker*, 21 December, 82–6.

Snipes, Lucas (2015). Why comedians are prone to addiction (and why comedy is the best medicine). *The Guff*, http://guff.com/why-comedians-are-prone-to-drug-addiction-and-why-comedy-is-the-best-medicine.

Veblen, Thorstein (2009). *The Theory of the Leisure Class*, Oxford: Oxford University Press.

PART III

Applications

CHAPTER 16

Decadence and Urban Geography

Theresa Zeitz-Lindamood

Most of the writers we now construe in the context of decadence created works of art defined by imaginative responses to the city. Baudelaire is perhaps the most celebrated case in point: although he did not care for the new Paris wrought by Napoléon III and Baron Haussmann, the advent of urban modernity led to an awareness that the pace and posture of modern life required new forms of artistic expression. He also observed in the flâneur the emergence of a new urban type, a person whose passive but perceptive attitude towards the urban scene makes him a close cousin to the more pessimistic but equally disengaged decadent. The sense of the city conveyed by decadent writers is often quite precise, keyed to the urban geography of specific neighbourhoods. The study of such geography has for some time now figured in the analysis of cultural developments, with Carl E. Schorske's now-classic book *Fin-de-siècle Vienna* (1980) serving as a kind of touchstone text for critics of various stripes intent on applying the sort of urbanist analysis Schorske applied to Vienna to different cities at different times. One of Schorske's most influential admirers is David Harvey, whose *Paris, Capital of Modernity* (2003) offers a model worthy of further emulation in the practice of reading literature less as a literary critic would and more as an urbanist thinker might. An urbanist reading of a decadent text must perforce pay attention not only to urban geography, including the plan of the city in which the work is set, its dominant architectural styles, socio-economic differences in neighbourhoods, and so on, but also to the cultural, social, and psychological meanings that the urban setting produces in a particular decadent text. In this essay, the urbanist approach will be brought to bear on three novels whose urban geography is especially significant to their respective narratives: Gabriele D'Annunzio's *Il piacere* [*Pleasure*] (1889), Oscar Wilde's *The Picture of Dorian Gray* (1891), and Thomas Mann's *Der Tod in Venedig* [*Death in Venice*] (1912). These three works illustrate, respectively, the special relationship of the urban scene to cultural, social, and psychological issues germane to the decadent narrative of each novel.

i

Like other European cities in the latter half of the nineteenth century, Rome underwent a significant process of urban transformation. After the unification of Italy in 1861 and the establishment of Rome as the capital, the programme of urban renewal was hardly on the scale of Baron Haussmann's renovation of Paris, but numerous streets were widened, new boulevards constructed, and old buildings demolished to make way for new ones. At the same time, the remarkable architectural heritage of Rome posed a challenge for city planners, who were faced with the problem of honouring that heritage while also superseding it under the double aegis of nationalism and modernity. This tension seems especially evident in the case of Giuseppe Sacconi's monument (1885–1911) to Vittorio Emanuele II, a structure that seems less an homage to the Roman past than a bombastic effort to outdo it, with its massive white marble colonnade atop the Capitoline Hill. Classical ruins and medieval churches had to be destroyed to make way for the Vittoriano, actions that prompted Primo Levi to criticize the project in 1904 by saying that the new Italy was 'under the obligation not to superimpose itself upon ancient Rome and papal Rome, seeking where it might succeed in erasing these images – it does not need to repeat the guilty error of Christianity against paganism – but it needs to elevate this third Rome above the other two' (quoted in Kirk, 2011: p. 105). The great antiquity of the city, in short, placed a burden on urban planners to pursue restoration as well as renewal: 'In Rome, progress was the investigation of the past' (Nilsen, 2016: p. 53).

This context helps to explain Gabriele D'Annunzio's attitude towards the urban geography of Rome and other Italian cities. A recent biographer describes D'Annunzio as 'an energetic conservationist' whose eventual prestige allowed him to intervene against modern threats to the architectural heritage (Hughes-Hallett, 2013: p. 116). In *Pleasure*, there is scant mention of urban modernization, but what little there is confirms D'Annunzio's aversion to it. At one point, Andrea Sperelli, the decadent hero of the novel, happens upon 'throngs of workmen returned from the new construction sites'. We are not told what these sites are, but Sperelli's disapproval of them is registered in the way the workmen are represented. They appear to Sperelli as 'ruddy and sinister figures', a group of 'bestial men' making their 'barbaric descent' from the Quirinal Hill into the Piazza

Barberini, where, in a kind of urban variation of the pathetic fallacy, Bernini's 'Triton was no longer spouting water' (D'Annunzio, 2013: pp. 74–5). Possibly, one of these 'new construction sites' is the Via Veneto, which opened in 1886, the year in which much of the present action of the novel is set. The widening of the Via Veneto, like other projects backed by Francesco Crispi, the nationalist statesman who was prime minister during the writing of *Pleasure*, led D'Annunzio to condemn urban modernization as '[a] wind of Barbarism blowing over Rome' (Hughes-Hallett, 2013: p. 117), a description consistent with the characterization of the 'barbaric' construction workers in the novel. In *Pleasure*, the barbarism of modernity is figured in different ways, but it is always destructive: 'Beneath today's grey democratic flood, which wretchedly submerges so many beautiful and rare things, that special class of ancient Italic nobility in which from generation to generation a certain family tradition of elect culture, elegance, and art was kept alive is also disappearing' (D'Annunzio, 2013: p. 33).

That expression of anti-democratic sentiment, with its corollary endorsement of the aristocratic class, is voiced by the narrator but identified with Sperelli. The protagonist's decadence is characterized not only by his aversion to the ascendance of the bourgeois class, one of the hallmarks of liberal modernity, but also by the combination of aesthetic refinement and moral corruption so typical of the decadent hero generally and exemplified by Joris-Karl Huysmans's Duc Floressas des Esseintes above all. Indeed, at this early stage of his literary career D'Annunzio held Huysmans in high regard, so it should come as no surprise that Sperelli should share certain traits with Des Esseintes, such as his aristocratic disdain for the masses, his arcane bibliophilia, and his mania for collecting precious objects generally. But Sperelli differs from Des Esseintes in so far as he indulges in normative sexual pleasures, and is, in fact, quite promiscuous, bedding more than one incidental demimondaine over the course of the narrative while engaged in the dual pursuit of his two contrary loves, the worldly Elena Muti and the saintly Maria Ferres. By contrast, Des Esseintes' libertine life is all in the past, as are the several less-than-normative encounters the character recollects, including one lasting several months with a young man. More important, none of Des Esseintes' erotic adventures call forth moral judgement from the narrator, whereas D'Annunzio goes to some length to point out the moral shortcomings of Sperelli: 'He had within himself the germ of all infections. Corrupting himself, he corrupted. [...] A base curiosity compelled him to choose the women with the worst reputations; a cruel taste for contamination compelled him to seduce the women who had better reputations' (pp. 98–9). In the end, the narrator conveys the unmistakable sense that Sperelli, suffering a mixture of '[p]hysical torture and moral anguish' (p. 326) after both lovers abandon him, has gotten exactly what he deserves.

The narrator's moral condemnation of the character is curiously reflected in the architectural style of the very house where Sperelli lives. The decadent keeps rooms in the Palazzo Zuccari, designed in the mannerist style by the painter Federico Zuccari and constructed at the end of the sixteenth century (1590–1603). The façade that opens onto the Via Gregoriano features a massive door flanked by two windows, all of which fuse decorative anthropomorphic and functional architectural elements to suggest grotesque human faces (fig. 16.1). The Palazzo Zuccari is near Trinità dei Monti, 'where the shadow of the obelisk of Pius VI marks the passage of time'. This location satisfies the character's urban preferences: 'Rome was his great love: not the Rome of the Caesars but the Rome of the popes; not the Rome of the arches, of the thermal baths, of the forums, but the Rome of the villas, of the fountains, of the churches' (pp. 36–7). Nonetheless, on at least one occasion Sperelli expresses some affinity for the Rome of the Caesars after all, when he refers to his home as 'Palazzo Zuccari: *domus aurea*', the reference to Nero's golden house revealing the character's kinship with that most decadent of Roman emperors. Sperelli further elaborates on the meaning that his neighbourhood holds for him when he says, 'Between the obelisk of the Trinità and the column of the Conception, my Catholic and pagan heart is suspended *ex voto*' (pp. 46–7). The avowal nicely captures the tension between Sperelli's two loves, the Catholic Maria and the pagan Elena, and, possibly, between his elevated aesthetic tastes and his base hedonistic desires.

Zuccari's grotesque doorway to the palazzo is monstrous by any architectural measure, a meaning that accords well with Sperelli's status as a moral monster. Later in the novel, Sperelli takes a carriage from a Mendelssohn concert with Elena Muti and another woman, the Princess of Ferrentino. The carriage is 'forced to proceed very slowly because the entire road was cluttered with rioting people' (p. 261). The riot Sperelli and his carriage-mates encounter is a protest related to the slaughter of several hundred Italian soldiers on 26 January 1887 at the village of Dogali in that part of Ethiopia that has since become the country of Eritrea. Nationalists in Parliament hoped to exploit the massacre to legitimize their colonialist ambitions, but they found scant support among the Italian public. As D'Annunzio puts it in the novel, 'in the ashen cold evening' of 2 February 1887 'the horror of the distant massacre was making the masses

Fig. 16.1 The monstrous anthropomorphism of the Palazzo Zuccari (1590–1603) seems to personify, architecturally, the moral shortcomings of Andrea Sperelli in D'Annunzio's *Pleasure* (1889) [Getty Images / David Soanes Photography].

yell'. Andrea looks out the carriage window and murmurs, 'All for four hundred brutes, who died brutally!' (p. 261). The comment shocks the Princess of Ferrentino, as it did D'Annunzio's publisher, who found the remark offensive and wanted to excise it, but D'Annunzio defended it as a necessary detail in the characterization of Sperelli: 'That phrase is spoken by Andrea Sperelli and not by Gabriele D'Annunzio, and it fits well in the mouth of that monster' (quoted by Stille, 2013: pp. xxi–xxii). Aside from the insensitive Dogali remark, Sperelli never acknowledges the relatively new fact of Italian nationhood. His only political allegiance is to the aristocratic class to which he belongs, a transnational – or antinational – characteristic consistent with decadence generally. This 'monstrous' aspect of Sperelli's character is confirmed by omission: the Palazzo Zuccari is at the top of the Spanish Steps, which commands a view of most of Rome, including the Capitoline Hill where the construction of the Vittoriano, begun in 1885, would have been clearly visible. But Sperelli never notices or acknowledges what would have been the most obvious evidence of the urban transformation of Rome in the late 1880s – and the most substantial architectural validation of the modern nation-state of Italy.

Sperelli's refusal to acknowledge what Levi called 'this third Rome' is curiously at odds with the character's romanticism, given that romanticism generally involves nationalistic sentiment, as in, for example, Lord Byron's 'The Isles of Greece' (1821). The vicarious Greek nationalism of the British Byron is oddly pertinent to Sperelli, not only because the character seems more like a latter-day incarnation of the Byronic hero than a true fin-de-siècle decadent, but also because there is something unmistakably English about Sperelli's Rome. His neighbourhood – the Trinità dei Monte, the Spanish Steps, the Piazza di Spagna – was the one most often frequented by British tourists in the nineteenth century (and probably today as well), as the presence of Babington's Tea Room at the base of the Spanish Steps shows. Although this landmark was not opened until 1893, four years after the publication of *Pleasure*, the fact that the need for such a distinctly British establishment existed in Sperelli's neighbourhood tells us something about that neighbourhood, as does the building at the bottom of the Spanish Steps where John Keats died in 1821, now known as the Keats-Shelley House because of both poets' love of Rome. Along with the Tea Room, the site certifies the area as one of the more 'English' places in Rome. In *Pleasure*, no poet is alluded to more frequently than Percy Bysshe Shelley; Sperelli loans Maria Ferres a volume of Shelley's poetry; and the lovers visit both Shelley's and Keats's grave in the English cemetery in the Testaccio district of Rome (about an hour south, on foot, from the Piazza di Spagna).

Sperelli's cultural attachment to the English romantics of an earlier age is matched by his affinity for the group of British poets and artists associated with the Pre-Raphaelite Brotherhood. His erotic conquests include the

Englishwoman Clara Green, who is staying, of course, '[a]t the Albergo d'Europa, [. . .] in Piazza di Spagna'. Sperelli is attracted to this woman, in part, because she 'had a light dusting of aesthetic cultivation, left to her by her love of the poet-painter Adolphus Jeckyll', a follower of 'John Keats in poetry and Holman Hunt in painting' (pp. 220, 221). This imaginary poet-painter is almost certainly a fictionalized version of Dante Gabriel Rossetti himself, a leading member of the Pre-Raphaelite Brotherhood. The late romanticism of the Pre-Raphaelites combines with Shelley's original version to suggest that Sperelli's decadent romanticism has replaced nationalistic ardour with aesthetic enthusiasm. Indeed, such aesthetic displacement is what makes his romanticism decadent. The author of *Pleasure* might not yet have become 'Mussolini's John the Baptist' (Woodhouse, 1998: p. 3), but the absence of nationalistic pride in the new Italy on the part of Sperelli is probably one thing that led D'Annunzio to call his creation a monster.

So, of course Sperelli would make his home in a monstrous house in that area of Rome that old Baedekers call 'the central point of the strangers' quarter' (Baedeker, 1900: p. 151). As if to underline just how thoroughly a stranger to his own country Sperelli has become, at the very end of the novel, as the character returns to his home in despair, he walks past the Palazzo del Quirinale, at the time the official residence of the King of Italy, where a brass band is playing in the twilight:

> The ample waves of that metallic music spread through the burning air. The obelisk, the fountain, the colossi, towered in the red glow and took on a purple tint as if penetrated by an impalpable flame. Immense Rome, dominated by a battle of clouds, seemed to illuminate the sky. (D'Annunzio, 2013: p. 327)

The passage affirms the immensity of Rome as the capital of the Italian nation, a Rome that Sperelli has so far refused to accept or acknowledge, as his present reaction makes clear: 'Andrea fled, almost out of his mind' (p. 327). All roads may lead to Rome, but for Sperelli, at least, those roads ultimately lead nowhere.

ii

Where the urban geography of *Pleasure* confirms Sperelli's cultural aversion to the new Italy, the London cityscape of *The Picture of Dorian Gray* (1891) conveys the characters' social awareness of the sort of extreme economic and moral contrasts that so preoccupied Wilde's contemporaries. In 1889, Charles Booth, the shipping magnate turned social reformer, published the first volume of his several surveys of working-class life. The initial instalment of *Life and Labour of the People in London* dealt exclusively with the problem of poverty in the East End, a problem very much in evidence in *The Picture of Dorian Gray*, which is really a tale of two cities, both of them London: the fashionable West End enclave of Mayfair and the troubled East End sector of Whitechapel. In the first chapter of the novel, the East End is evoked when Lord Henry Wotton recalls that his Aunt Agatha has 'discovered a wonderful young man' whom she is trying to recruit 'to help her in the East End' (Wilde, 2006: p. 15). The young man is none other than Dorian Gray, who will go on to pursue his own sordid pleasures in the East End rather than advance the philanthropic programme of social and moral improvement Lady Agatha supports.

Like all of the well-to-do figures who populate the novel, Dorian lives in the West End. His house is in the area of Grosvenor Square, just west of Hyde Park. The exact address is not indicated, but at a critical point in the novel as Dorian is walking home, he runs into the artist Basil Hallward '[a]t the corner of Grosvenor Square and South Audley Street' (p. 124). By this stage of the novel, Dorian is well removed from any possible interest in the sort of philanthropy Lady Agatha had earlier called on him to perform. And perform is the right word: what the well-meaning woman wants Dorian to do for the impoverished East Enders is play the piano for them. As Dorian tells Lord Henry, 'I am in Lady Agatha's black books at present [. . .] I promised to go to a club in Whitechapel with her last Tuesday, and I really forgot all about it. We were to have played a duet together – three duets I believe' (p. 16). Shortly thereafter Lady Agatha chides her nephew for trying 'to persuade our nice Mr. Dorian Gray to give up the East End', adding that 'he would be quite invaluable. They would love his playing'. Lord Henry responds with one of his typical paradoxes – 'I can sympathise with everything except suffering' – and when another character protests that 'the East End is a very important problem', he offers another witticism that contains a pointed critique of the practice of addressing social needs by cultural means: 'It is the problem of slavery, and we try to solve it by amusing the slaves' (pp. 36–7).

Later in the novel, after he has murdered his friend Basil and blackmailed Alan Campbell, another friend, into disposing of the body, Dorian feels 'keenly the terrible pleasure of a double life' (p. 147). The meaning of the phrase 'double life' is subject to a variety of interpretations: it might refer to the contrast of the respectable mask of manners that Dorian presents to fashionable society with the sordid life of pleasure that he leads, or to the difference between his appearance as a marriageable bachelor and the forbidden reality of same-sex relations. Numerous passages in the novel are quite suggestive of same-sex affection, but such passages seem to concern more the proclivities of Basil Hallward and Lord Henry Wotton rather than those of Dorian. While it is true that Basil asks Dorian why his 'friendship is so fatal to young men', he also tells him about one Lord Stavely's allegations that Dorian is 'a man whom no pure-minded girl should be allowed to know and whom no chaste woman should sit in the same room with' (p. 127). The remark clearly suggests some kind of heterosexual misconduct, and, after all, Dorian did express his love for the actress Sybil Vane and planned to marry her before her deliberately artless theatrical performance induced him to break with her. Of the several young men Dorian is said to have ruined, only one – Adrian Singleton – appears in the novel, but the context concerns opium addiction, not homosexuality.

The pleasure of the 'double life' that Dorian feels so keenly, then, may include an element of same-sex excess, but the novel is by no means clear on this point. Given the double geography of the novel, the division of action between the high-society pastimes of the West End and the lower-class activities of the East End, a more reasonable reading of the sordid elements of Dorian's life that are registered on the portrait hidden in the attic room of his Grosvenor Square residence might be as some generalized, composite set of actions more common to Whitechapel than Mayfair. This much is suggested by the rumours that Dorian 'had been seen brawling with foreign sailors in a low den in the distant parts of Whitechapel and that he consorted with thieves and coiners and knew the mysteries of their trade' (p. 120). In other words, the portrait is a representation of the moral and economic problems of the East End that have emerged as a threat to the privileged social world the West End aristocrats inhabit. This urbanist reading of the portrait is confirmed when Dorian suddenly decides to 'creep out of the house, go down to dreadful places near Blue Gate Fields, and stay there, day after day, until he was driven away'. Upon his return to his Mayfair mansion, 'he would sit in front of the picture, sometimes loathing it and himself, but filled, at other times, with that pride of individualism that is half the fascination of sin and smiling with secret pleasure at the misshapen shadow that had to bear the burden that should have been his own' (p. 119).

One measure of the contrast between the two neighbourhoods that Dorian Gray inhabits, the first as a resident, the second as a visitor, is

Henry B. Wheatley's *London Past and Present: Its History, Associations, and Traditions*, a three-volume guide published in 1891, the publication year also of the revised and expanded version of Wilde's novel. The guide offers a contemporary assessment of the social and economic extremes of the two Londons Wilde's novel explores. For example, Wheatley describes the general area of Mayfair as 'a fashionable locality between Piccadilly and South Audley Street' (1891: vol. 2, p. 515). He includes details that illuminate the property values in Dorian Gray's neighbourhood, mentioning one mansion sold in 1869 for £175,000 (vol. 1, p. 388), roughly £20.5 million in today's currency. Whitechapel, by contrast, is described as 'populous' and 'commercial, but as regards the bulk of its inhabitants, poor'. Wheatley says the construction of Commercial Street has helped the district somewhat, formerly

> one of the very worst localities in London; a region of narrow and filthy streets, yards and alleys, many of them wholly occupied by thieves' dens, the receptacles of stolen property, gin-spinning dog holes, low brothels, and putrescent lodging-houses – a district unwholesome to approach and unsafe for a decent person to traverse even in the daytime. (vol. 3, p. 500)

Despite removal of 'some of the worst of the rookeries' and an elevated police presence, Whitechapel 'is still one of the foul spots of London' (vol. 3, p. 500).

Even fouler is the area of Blue Gate Fields, where Dorian goes to feed his opium habit. Wilde uses the older name for the street Wheatley identifies as Ratcliff Highway or St. George's Street, the district Booth called 'the most desolate' in London, 'which appears to stagnate with a squalor peculiar to itself' (Booth, 1904: p. 66). Wheatley says the street is 'the favourite haunt of degraded Lascars, Malays, and Chinamen, who may in some of the dens be seen smoking opium in the fashion common in Eastern Asia' (vol. 1, p. 212). The den where Dorian accidentally encounters the sailor James Vane is 'a long, low room which looked as if it had once been a third-rate dancing-saloon':

> Shrill flaring gas-jets, dulled and distorted in the fly blown mirrors that faced them, were ranged round the walls. [. . .] The floor was covered with ochre-coloured sawdust, trampled here and there into mud, and stained with dark rings of spilt liquor. Some Malays were crouching by a little charcoal stove playing with bone counters, and showing their white teeth as they chattered. (Wilde, 2006: p. 157)

Wilde's account accords well with the fuller description Wheatley provides:

> From end to end the street has a maritime savour. In some way or other every shop and place of business or resort seems to be dependent on ships or sailors [. . .]; and, unfortunately, flaring drinking, dancing and music rooms, and haunts of a far worse order. Here, among other 'dens', are the Chinese opium-smokers' sties. (1891: vol. 3, p. 150)

Wheatley also comments on '[t]he terrible outrages on poor women in 1888 and 1889, known as the Whitechapel murders' (vol. 3, p. 501), murders now attributed to the still-unidentified criminal known as Jack the Ripper. Wilde would certainly have known about the Whitechapel murderer, whose victims were stabbed multiple times, as Dorian does Basil Hallward: 'He rushed at him, and dug the knife into the great vein that is behind the ear, crushing the man's head down on the table, and stabbing again and again' (2006: p. 134). Dorian's double life, then, involves the insinuation of Whitechapel criminality into Mayfair respectability.

In a way, what distinguishes Wilde's revision of the 1890 *Lippincott's Monthly Magazine* version of *The Picture of Dorian Gray* for book publication in 1891 is precisely the addition of the same sort of social material that Booth and Wheatley documented. Indeed, the magazine version makes no mention of Blue Gate Fields and opium dens, nor do Lady Agatha and other characters express social concerns about the life of the poor in Whitechapel. Possibly, the additions form part of Wilde's efforts to temper the same-sex implications of 'the terrible pleasure a double life' that are much more evident in the magazine – and in the manuscript – than in the book. At the very least, the fact that the two modalities of Dorian's behaviour are keyed to specific London locales means that Wilde was extremely sensitive to the social resonance of urban geography.

iii

Although Venice is widely associated with decadence, that identification is problematic if decadence is construed as a kind of malaise of modernity. After all, the Adriatic capital did not undergo the kinds of urban renovations that transformed Baudelaire's Paris, D'Annunzio's Rome, or Wilde's London. Of course, one might say that the absence of modernity is precisely the quality that makes the sinking city so appealing to the decadent sensibility, along with its vast troves of fine art and the architectural mixture of Byzantine, Gothic, Renaissance, baroque, and mannerist styles. That sequence of styles led John Ruskin, who took Gothic architecture as the standard of excellence, to settle on Venice as paradigmatically decadent. Moreover, the fact that the city was once the seat of a great empire adds immeasurably to its latter-day association with a long but luxurious decline. So, there are ample reasons for Thomas Mann's choice to set his decadent narrative of disease and desire in Venice. But why begin that narrative in Munich? Urban planners during the era of the Wittelsbach king Ludwig I (1786–1868) had transformed the Bavarian capital into a city of art, making it the cultural and intellectual counter to Berlin, the Prussian centre of commerce and finance. In his 1905 story 'Glaudius Dei', Mann emphasized the rational, planned nature of the city:

> Munich was luminous. A radiant blue-silk sky stretched out over the festive squares and white-columned temples, the neo-classical monuments and Baroque churches, the spurting fountains, the palaces and gardens of the residence, and the latter's broad and shining perspectives, carefully calculated and surrounded by green. (1998: p. 85)

This representation in large measure reflects the reality, and it is no great stretch to read this 'carefully calculated' northern city as a rationalistic, healthful contrast to the confused, sick southern city Mann imagines in *Death in Venice.*

At the same time, a darker sense of Munich pervades the early pages of the novella, perhaps indicative of a growing sense of social unease over the fate of Europe in 1912, but more directly explainable as a reflection of the psychological complexities of the novella's central character. *Death in Venice* begins when the celebrated author Gustav Aschenbach, a man past fifty, leaves his home on the Prinzregentenstrasse, a street in the northeastern sector of the old city originally planned to house the bourgeoisie. (Mann lived at several addresses in this area, the first of many clues that the middle-aged Aschenbach represents certain potentialities in the personality of Mann himself, who was in his mid-30s when he wrote the story.) Aschenbach takes a 'rather long walk' through the Englischer Garten, a city park, and pauses for a moment at the Aumeister beer garden (Mann, 1994: p. 3). Since the Prinzregentenstrasse spans the River Isar running alongside the Englischer Garten, Aschenbach may well have crossed the river on his walk. If so, that would be the first of several references Mann makes to the character passing over bodies of water. Later, Aschenbach will enter Venice by sea, travelling from east to west from Pola, and, once in Venice, he will travel by gondola from the dock at San Marco to the Lido. Both these journeys are highly unusual, since tourists from northern Europe usually took the land route by train and entered Venice from the west, and of course the usual passage from the city of Venice proper to the barrier island known as the Lido is by vaporetto, not gondola. Clearly, these irregularities are meant to suggest the mythological passage across the River Styx, a meaning that becomes obvious in the case of the gondola, 'painted the particular sort of black reserved for coffins' (p. 17), guided by a gondolier whose symbolic semblance to Charon is evident. In Munich, Aschenbach ends his walk 'at the North Cemetery stop for the tram' (p. 3), so the likelihood is that the character did indeed cross the River Isar, thereby forming the first, and most subtle, allusion in the text to the soul's mythological journey to the underworld of death.

The death imagery is abundant as Aschenbach, waiting for the tram, gazes at 'the stonemasons' shops, where the crosses, monuments, and headstones for sale formed a second, untenanted graveyard, and the Byzantine architecture of the mortuary chapel across the way' (pp. 3–4). Given the narrative arc of the story, such symbolic use of the cityscape is hardly surprising, but there are several additional elements of urban geography that are highly suggestive of underlying complexities and tensions in the character that are manifested more fully later on. As Aschenbach waits for the tram, 'Neither on the paved Ungererstrasse, stretched in glistening solitude toward Schwabing, nor on the Föhringer Chaussee was there a vehicle to be seen' (p. 3). The street name Föhringer Chaussee does not appear on period maps of this neighbourhood in Munich, but the use of the old term 'Chaussee', one meaning of which is 'lane' or 'country road', probably refers to that part of the Föhringer Road that runs through the Englischer Garten (the Ausmeister is on this 'Chaussee') and which intersects the Ungererstrasse, the modern, paved street with its 'glistening' tram tracks. If so, the reference is strange, since Aschenbach is more than two kilometres distant from the Föhringer Road. The observation that there is no 'vehicle to be seen' is therefore rather curious since it would be hard for the character to see whether there was a tram on the road or not. Mann seems to have gone out of his way to set up a contrast of the more overtly modern Strasse and the implicitly pastoral Chaussee.

The contrast is heightened and complicated by the reference to Schwabing, the district associated at the turn of the century with Munich's bohemian arts community. Among other artistic associations, Schwabing has resonance as the urban scene of Stefan George's celebrated *Kreis*, the circle of like-minded aesthetes led by George who advocated *l'art pour l'art* and cultivated same-sex desire in elevated, Platonic terms. Now Aschenbach, like Mann, is the very model of the responsible, civic-minded bourgeois artist, but over the course of the story he becomes more like the bohemian George, rationalizing his homosexual obsession with the Polish boy Tadzio as the highest form of Platonic *eros*, imagining himself as Socrates and Tadzio as Phaedrus. In a sense, the road to Schwabing leads all the way to the Lido and to Aschenbach's ecstatic, erotic death.

The more immediate manifestation of Aschenbach's future destiny is the appearance of the strange figure on the steps of the mortuary chapel across from the Nordfriedhof tram stop. With his red hair, straw hat, and snub nose, some version of the figure, identified as 'a foreigner, [. . .] a traveller from afar' (p. 4), will appear several times over the course of the story: as an old man made up to appear young on the ferry from Pola to Venice ('wearing a bright yellow, overly fashionable summer suit, red tie, and a panama hat with a cockily upturned brim' (p. 14)); as the red-haired street-singer who performs in the front garden of Aschenbach's hotel on the Lido ('His pale, snub-nosed face was beardless and did not permit an easy reckoning of his age' (p. 50)); and, finally, as Aschenbach himself, after having his hair dyed and his cheeks rouged ('His tie was red, and his broad-brimmed straw hat was encircled by a band of many colors' (p. 59)). The figure is understandably a focus of critical attention and is easily interpretable as a composite of social, philosophical, and mythological meanings. Socially, certain details of dress, such as the straw hat and red tie, identify the figure in his various guises as bohemian; philosophically, details of physiognomy, notably the snub nose, suggest traditional representations of Socrates; mythologically, other details, such as the association with music as well as the foreignness of the figure, suggest the god Dionysus, while the staff and the wide-brimmed hat are attributes of Hermes (Koelb, 2004: pp. 96–7). Some of these meanings are encoded into the urban geography that opens the story, with the Aumeister beer garden implying Dionysian revelry and the Nordfriedhof suggesting Hermes, the god who leads dead souls into the underworld. These Munich landmarks are, again, situated on intersecting streets, as if to suggest the interpenetration of conflicting psychological impulses in Aschenbach's character.

Once Aschenbach is in Venice, the impetus to the conflict is the boy Tadzio, the older man's attraction to him manifesting the dualism typical of turn-of-the-century thinking about homosexuality: as either pathological or Platonic – either a debased or elevated form of 'normative' sexuality, a sickness or a sublimation. Although the urban geography of the Venice section of the novella is not so detailed as the brief Munich section, for the most part when Aschenbach is on the Lido gazing at Tadzio playing on the strand or swimming in the sea he sees the boy as an idealized, Platonic figure: 'His eyes embraced the noble figure there on the edge of the blue, and in a transport of delight he thought his gaze was grasping beauty itself' (p. 37). By contrast, when Aschenbach stalks Tadzio through the labyrinthine streets of Venice the older man's sick desire for the boy is all but indistinguishable from the cholera that is killing him:

> Trailing the lovely boy one afternoon, Aschenbach had penetrated deep into the maze in the heart of the diseased city. [. . .] He was compelled to a disgraceful sort of discretion that involved clinging to walls [. . .], and he did not for some time become conscious of the fatigue, the exhaustion which a high pitch of emotion and continual tension had inflicted on his body and spirit. (p. 59)

Evidently, the physical illness and the metaphorical sickness of same-sex desire both have their origins on the Lido, when Aschenbach breakfasts on 'large, fully ripe strawberries he obtained from a peddler' a moment after gazing on Tadzio (pp. 25–6). Almost certainly, Aschenbach has contracted the physical disease of cholera from these strawberries, since we are told that 'the food supply [. . .] had been infected, for death, though denied and hushed up, devoured its way through the narrow streets' (p. 54).

Mann's psychological deployment of urban geography is clear: the streets of Munich and the stones of Venice both encode the character's sickness in such a way as to make certain particulars of each cityscape resonate with the decadent narrative. Something similar happens with the decadent narrative of *The Picture of Dorian Gray*: the double optic of Wilde's social perspective on the class differences of radically different London neighbourhoods reinforces the extreme contrast between Dorian's outward appearance and the inner depravity his portrait records. In the case of D'Annunzio's Andrea Sperelli, it is a building, not a painting, that captures the character's monstrous morality, but, like Wilde and Mann, D'Annunzio takes great care to situate his decadent narrative in a particular cityscape. All three cases show that it is not enough to read the novel: one must also read the city.

References

Baedeker, Karl (1900). *Central Italy and Rome*, 13th edn, London: Dulau.

Booth, Charles (1904). *Life and Labour of the People in London*, London: Macmillan.

D'Annunzio, Gabriele (2013). *Pleasure*, Lara Gochin Raffaelli, trans., New York: Penguin.

Harvey, David (2003). *Paris, Capital of Modernity*, New York: Routledge.

Hughes-Hallett, Lucy (2013). *Gabriele d'Annunzio: Poet, Seducer, and Preacher of War*, New York: Random House.

Kirk, Terry (2011). The Political Typography of Modern Rome: Via XX Settembre to Via dell' Impero. In Dorigen Caldwell and Lesley Caldwell, eds., *Rome: Continuing Encounters between Past and Present*, Farnham, Surrey: Ashgate, pp. 101–28.

Koelb, Clayton (2004). *Death in Venice*. In Herbert Lehnert and Eva Wessell, eds., *A Companion to the Works of Thomas Mann*, Rochester, NY: Camden House, pp. 95–113.

Mann, Thomas (1994). *Death in Venice*, Clayton Koelb, ed. and trans., New York: Norton.

Mann, Thomas (1998). *Death in Venice and Other Tales*, Joachim Neugroschel, trans., New York: Penguin.

Nilsen, Micheline (2016). *Architecture in Nineteenth Century Photographs: Essays on Reading a Collection*, New York: Routledge.

Schorske, Carl E. (1980). *Fin-de-siècle Vienna: Politics and Culture*, New York: Knopf.

Stille, Alexander (2013). Introduction. In Gabriele D'Annunzio, *Pleasure*, Lara Gochin Raffaelli, trans., New York: Penguin, pp. xvi–xxii.

Wheatley, Henry B. (1891). *London Past and Present: Its History, Associations, and Traditions*, 3 vols., London: John Murray.

Wilde, Oscar (2006). *The Picture of Dorian Gray*, Joseph Bristow, ed., Oxford: Oxford University Press.

Woodhouse, John (1998). *Gabriele D'Annunzio: Defiant Archangel*, Oxford: Oxford University Press.

CHAPTER 17

Socio-aesthetic Histories: Vienna 1900 and Weimar Berlin

Katharina Herold

A particular relationship between social class and cultural productivity defines the nature of German-speaking decadence in Europe around the turn of the twentieth century, one that generated fundamental innovations in music, art, science, and literature. The term 'decadence' in the German context oscillated in meaning between what Friedrich Nietzsche had understood as *Kunstprinzip* [artistic principle] and *Krankheit* [sickness]. These two extremes designate decadence as a literary movement as well as a socio-political condition equivalent to 'degeneration'. Nietzsche's reading of Paul Bourget's essay on Baudelaire (1883) suggested to the German reader a decadence defined by cultural fragmentation, an anarchy of parts or excessive individualism leading to social decline. In mid-century France and in the 1880s and 1890s in England, decadence developed as an artistic phenomenon associated with Bohemian circles. By 1900, decadence had reached German-speaking artistic circles, which in Vienna were centred in the heart of the middle classes. Vienna produced some of the household names of Continental decadence, including Gustav Klimt, Egon Schiele, Sigmund Freud, Ludwig Wittgenstein, Gustav and Alma Mahler, Arnold Schoenberg, Theodor Herzl, Arthur Schnitzler, Robert Musil, and Karl Kraus. About twenty years later decadence seized the imagination of the masses across society in Weimar Berlin. In the Berlin of the 1920s and 1930s artists and authors such as Otto Dix, George Grosz, Alfred Döblin, Oswald Spengler, Walter Benjamin, Kurt Tucholsky, and Christopher Isherwood re-shaped the aesthetics of decadence by responding to the social and political disintegration of old orders as something that affected the whole of society, transcending class boundaries.

A comparison of Vienna and Berlin, two of the important centres of German-speaking decadence, provides insight into the relationship of social class and aesthetic experience in the waning years of the Austro-Hungarian Empire (1897–1914) prior to World War I and during the tumultuous period of the Weimar Republic (1919–1933). To give a flavour of how the social history of Austria and Germany in the two periods under consideration shaped the aesthetics of decadence at the time, this chapter focuses on the decadent art and writing of Klimt, Freud, and Schnitzler in Vienna, followed by Dix, Döblin, and Isherwood in Berlin. The cultural and urban development of both cities, in their shared departure from nineteenth-century certainties, qualifies them for comparison in the context of decadence: Vienna's imperial decline clashed with a radical rethinking of tradition in art, and Berlin's expressionistic distortions brought forth a brutal modernity that conservative thinkers considered to be the expression of racial degeneracy. This chapter outlines the temporal and geographical progression of the 'bourgeoisification' (Weir, 2018: p. 81) of decadence from a concept descriptive of the vanishing dominance of aristocratic culture in nineteenth-century Europe to a mass movement in the early twentieth century. In both Vienna and Berlin, decadent artistic circles formed at the core of urban bourgeois society. In Weimar Berlin, decadence progressed even further. Crossing class divisions, Berliners from all walks of life were seduced by the decadent interwar frenzy of the 1920s. Conditioned by accelerated processes of economic, social, and cultural modernization, the concept of decadence thus underwent a transformation from the expression of a new direction in modern art in Vienna to an expression of the crisis of modernity evident in the cultural excesses of Weimar Berlin.

i

Vienna experienced decadence as a form of social segregation after the crisis and collapse of liberalism at the turn of the century. The 1870s had seen the rise of socialism in Austria and with it strong public support for the arts. The imperial ratification of the populist anti-Semite Karl Lueger, leader of the Christian Socialist Party, as Vienna's mayor in 1897 heralded the decline of the thriving liberalism of the middle classes. Coupled with the disintegration of the Austro-Hungarian Empire as a fragile, multi-ethnic society, the 'failure of liberalism' resulted in the retreat of intellectuals and artists from the public sphere of politics into aesthetic realms. Yet unlike in Paris or England where decadent artists operated from a deliberate, dandified distance, the Vienna Secession, led by its first president Gustav Klimt in 1897, at first did not result in a withdrawal of the bourgeois class. Rather, as Carl E. Schorske claims in his seminal study *Fin de Siècle Vienna: Politics and Culture* (1961), the breakdown of liberalism enabled the principle of art for art's sake to replace political action: that principle claimed 'the allegiance of virtually a whole class, of which the artists were a part. [...] [A]s civic action proved increasingly futile, art became almost a religion, the source of meaning and the food of the soul' (1981: pp. 8–9). Bourgeois participation in artistic culture set Vienna apart from several other German-speaking centres of decadence, notably Munich, Bayreuth, and Dresden. In Vienna, political alienation went hand in hand with cultural innovation. Social progress was explained less by historical circumstance than by psychological condition. Viennese bourgeois modernity, according to Schorske's panoptic view, is therefore characterized by its falling away from rationalism and the emergence of such conflicting tendencies as communitarianism and functionalism. The shift from political involvement to a retreat into the arts becomes explicit in the works of the period. They are preoccupied with psychoanalysis, impressionism, and the irrationality of mass movements, accommodating those as divergent as fascism and Herzl's Zionism. Many historians have seen in this failure of the bourgeoisie to assert itself one reason for the emergence of Nazism in Europe over the first quarter of the twentieth century.

Schorske identified as one major factor for this shift the urban renovation of Vienna as a visual register of the dialectic of principles that characterizes culture in fin-de-siècle Vienna. In the wake of this major renovation of medieval Vienna, emblematically embodied in the Ringstrasse [Vienna Ring Road], the opposed principles of functionality and beauty raised questions about the relation of decadence and modernity. The contrived ornamentation and historicism of the Ringstrasse came to be identified with decadence and increasingly competed with a more modern urban functionalism and the quickening pace of metropolitan life.

The Ringstrasse was conceived as a wide avenue framed by pompous bourgeois city houses, as well as an array of public buildings, including the Town Hall, the Stock Exchange, the University, and the State Opera. Extravagant shopping arcades and warehouses were also planted in the centre of the old town. From 1860 to the 1890s a vast programme of urban renovation sparked discussions on the purpose of art, which played a decisive role in the elevation of Vienna as one of the cradles of modern art in Europe. The Ringstrasse's eclectic historicism and emphasis on ornamental decoration freely mixing Renaissance, baroque, and classical styles defined the 'Ringstrassenstil' and ignited a heated debate about the purpose of art between advocates of *Schmuck* [ornament] and *Zweck* [functionality]. A group of architects led by Otto Wagner, Josef Hoffmann, and Adolf Loos came to object to such 'artistic chaos' in favour of a 'harmonization of art and purpose' (Schorske, 1981: p. 79). Wagner and

Loos championed utility and simplicity in the service of modern urban mobility. In his anti-historicist manifesto 'Ornament and Crime' (1908), Loos contended that overt historicist ornamentation bordered on public criminal offence. The use of ornamentation and artifice, as in, for example, the extremely decorative surfaces of Klimt's paintings, is unfit for the modern age, Loos claimed, because its eroticism invites degeneration and moral corruption.

Over the last forty years, Schorske's observations have been revised, most notably by Steven Beller's collection of essays *Rethinking Vienna 1900* (2001), which seeks to culturally specify and historically qualify Schorske's generalizing paradigm. The collection addresses, for example, the importance of the contributions of the Jewish bourgeoisie and the actual, more complex make-up of liberalism in Austria which was far from homogenous. However, the overall sense of a decadent disenchantment with the modern world, which Schorske identified in controversies about contemporary architecture, was also evident in the works of fine artists and authors of the same generation.

ii

Klimt's paintings capture the essence of Viennese bourgeois decadent aesthetics. His 'diseased' artworks demonstrate how overt ornamentation expressed a rejection of the political world and yet presented an open provocation to society. In contrast to the Secessionist architects who sought to define a progressive modernity through an increase in mobility for common welfare, Klimt searched for a modernity defined by psychological introspection. This tension, an indicator of bourgeois social disintegration, erupted in the 'Klimt Affair', which turned from a dispute about deviant aesthetics into a political scandal. In 1894, the Ministry of Education commissioned Klimt to redesign the University of Vienna's Great Hall, with an approved budget of what would today amount to 400,000 euros. Klimt's so-called *Fakultätsbilder* [Faculty Paintings], large-scale murals depicting allegories of Medicine, Jurisprudence, and Philosophy, were met with fierce criticism. In the eyes of the government, Klimt's shocking images showing reclining nudes, ghostly bodies interspersed with skulls, and grotesque infants represented too much of a departure from artistic conventions. In the government's view, Klimt perverted the purpose of the commission, which was intended to honour the university as a stronghold of bourgeois values and prestige. Klimt refused to hand over his work to the

Ministry of Education and in 1905 returned his commission, the last he would receive.

The failure to adjust his artistic vision to public tastes and historicist traditions of painting conditioned Klimt's late turn towards highly artificial portraiture. The sense of decadent opulence conveyed through the images of sublime eroticism in his numerous portraits of high-society women, such as the *Portrait of Adele Bloch-Bauer I* (1907), with its highly ornate, gold-leaf design, caused critics to declare Klimt's paintings evidence of 'pornography and perverted excess' (Nèret, 2000: p. 24). In line with Freud's developing theories on psychoanalysis, these paintings aimed to reveal the unconscious, deviant workings of sexual instinct and sensual experience.

Other artists such as Egon Schiele and Oskar Kokoschka, two of today's most acclaimed painters of Viennese modernism, were less invested in the elevation of artifice over nature yet were still criticized for their artistic attacks on public decency. Klimt's sumptuous, mythical allegories were produced as private commissions to flatter the rich, paying bourgeoisie. In contrast, Schiele's and Kokoschka's expressionist, angular nudes forged a new form of psychological portraiture highlighting the beauty of ugliness and everyday decay. As a result, Schiele faced his first trial in 1910, after fourteen of his drawings had been removed from an exhibition in Prague. In 1912 he was arrested for moral depravity.

iii

The aesthetic representation of depraved and morbid sexuality pervaded all genres of art in Viennese modernism. Indeed, the concept of decadence forged links between such disciplines as architecture, fine art, and literature. Narratives of uncontrollable instincts bringing about social decay dominated works by leading writers of the German-speaking fin de siècle: Frank Wedekind's plays uncovered the hypocritical bourgeois attitudes towards sexuality in *Frühlings Erwachen* [*Spring Awakening*] (1891); his Lulu cycle, formed of *Erdgeist* [*Earth Spirit*] (1892–94) and *Die Büchse der Pandora* [*Pandora's Box*] (1901), depict a society 'riven by the demands of lust and greed' (Banham, 1995: p. 1190); Robert Musil's *Die Verwirrungen des Zöglings Törleß* [*The Confusions of Young Törless*] (1906) explores the violent, homoerotic, and sadistic sexuality of pubescent boys rebelling against the power structures of educational systems; Stefan Zweig's memoirs and short stories (*Vergessene Träume* [*Forgotten Dreams*] (1900)) evoke the sense of Vienna as a forsaken dream displaced by a dystopian modern world; Thomas Mann's *Der Tod in Venedig* [*Death in Venice*] (1912) alludes to the detrimental powers of homoerotic desire, leading the novella's protagonist astray and to his death. But to stay with our focus on *Jung-Wien* [Young Vienna], no literature captures the tensions between social appearance and deviant sexual satisfaction behind closed doors better than Arthur Schnitzler's fiction and drama. A doctor by training and Freud's colleague, Schnitzler's works dissect and mirror the dialectical dynamics of *Eros* [life force] and *Thanatos* [death drive], which Freud's psychoanalytical case studies of hysteria in women proposed.

By 1900, the clash between tradition and decadent forms of modernity had transformed Vienna from a proud and open metropolis to a city troubled by uncertainty. The anxiety prompted by the decay of the old order and the as yet unknown future of 'the dead city' (or 'city of ruins' as Hugo von Hofmannsthal described Vienna in 1893) (Rasch, 1986: p. 33) is evident in the metaphor of sickness symptomatic of the collapse of Viennese society into a state of decadence starting from the heart of the bourgeois value system – the family. Freud's psychoanalytic studies are a case in point. In *Dora: Fragment of an Analysis of a Case of Hysteria*, published in 1905, five years after the ground-breaking *The Interpretation of Dreams*, Freud documents the bizarre sexuality of the bourgeois class in the case of 'Dora'. 'Dora' was the pseudonym for a young woman named Ida Bauer (1882–1945) who suffered from a nervous condition. Today this short account is regarded as a foundational text in modern psychoanalytic theory. However, the borders between science and fiction in Freud's case studies are fluid, as Freud himself acknowledged: 'I am aware that – in this city, at least – there are many physicians who (revolting though it may seem) choose to read a case history of this kind not as a contribution to the psycho-pathology of the neuroses, but as a *roman à clef* designed for their private delectation' (Freud, 1997: p. 3).

Freud believed that the reason for Dora's hysterical symptoms originated in a series of pathologically perverse relationships in her family and social circle – again a reflection of the network of social decadence affecting especially the middle classes. Dora's story unfolds as a *ménage à six*. Dora's father, in pursuit of an affair with Frau K., offers Dora to his lover's husband, Herr K. Herr K. makes advances on the fifteen-year-old Dora and even attempts to propose to her. Further complications ensue when Frau K. expresses homoerotic desires for Dora, who reciprocates. The Bauers' governess, having developed an attraction to Dora's father, uses Dora to be close to him. In turn, Herr K.'s own governess, with whom he has also had an affair, claims that Herr K. is trapped in a loveless marriage.

Herr K. gives Dora this same explanation when he makes advances on her, whereupon she slaps him. Dora's hysterical reaction, Freud argues, is the result of her feeling degraded to the status of a servant, since Herr K. had used the same words to seduce his governess. Freud ends his report by admitting his failure to successfully treat Dora's nervous symptoms – among which are 'loss of voice'. The reader is left with a sense of uneasiness over the dimensions and complexity of the perverse desires Freud has uncovered. Yet Freud appears no more concerned about Dora's decline than Dora's own father. The case of Dora, the incurable, nervous, and voiceless woman, becomes an allegory for the state of Viennese society at large.

The reflection on the fundamental rottenness of society inherent in family structures connects Freud's accounts of bourgeois sexual deviance with the work of Schnitzler. In his famous letter of 14 May 1922, Freud called Schnitzler his intellectual *Doppelgänger* [double] (Kupper and Rollman-Branch, 1959: p. 109). Indeed, Dora's case bears an uncanny resemblance to Schnitzler's novella *Fräulein Else* (1924) (Furst, 2003: p 19). While holidaying in Italy, Fräulein Else receives a letter from her mother urging her to rescue the family honour. Her father is about to be arrested for his inability to repay his debts. The only 'deal' to save the family's reputation is for Else to make herself available to a possible creditor, the Vicomte von Dorsday, who happens to be staying at the same hotel. After considering her options, Else concludes that her commitment to her father is the only way to salvage her family's position in society. She finds she is 'a depraved creature' and therefore is 'not made for a bourgeois existence anyway'. To make her parents proud, she wants to 'become a hussy, such a one the world has not seen yet'. She agrees to von Dorsday's demands, which involve Else posing nude for the Vicomte in his hotel room. Aware of the implied consequences of such an intimate encounter in private, and in a fit of hysteria, Else stands naked not in von Dorsday's room but in the hotel's music salon in front of the other guests. After her wilful exposure 'done only for Papa', yet 'with thrills running over [her] skin', she commits suicide. Written as an interior monologue, the novella captures the pressures of Else's psyche torn between private needs and public obligations. However, the key scene where Else exposes herself in public captures Schnitzler's notion of a diseased social system, one that cannot be limited to the deviance of an isolated individual (exemplified, for example, in Wilde's 1895 libel case) but rather to that of a whole society. The analogy between sexual and economic exchanges, which determine the bourgeois value system, brings home

Schnitzler's overt critique of his own highly educated, art-loving, well-off class, much like Klimt's *Faculty Paintings*, which also confronted the members of polite Viennese society with their own repressed, deviant desires.

Schnitzler's psychograph of a sexually overwrought society going in circles (suggesting the idea of the Ringstrasse) in *Der Reigen* [*Hands Around*] (written in 1897 and published for a group of friends in 1900) revealed, as Freud wrote to Schnitzler in 1922, '*everything* that I have had to unearth by laborious work on other persons' (Kupper and Rollman-Branch, 1959: p. 110). The play attacks the moral double standards and corrupt power structures plaguing Viennese society. Set in 1890s Vienna, the play uses important sites of the gleaming new bourgeois metropolis as a backdrop to the scenes covering up a syphilis epidemic. The play thereby emphasizes how the excitement of urban modernity conditions and aids the moral decay of the bourgeoisie. The play depicts a cycle of ten scenes, each showing couples before, during, or after sexual intercourse. Similar to Henrik Ibsen in his dramas devoted to social critique, Schnitzler paints a disarmingly honest *Sittengemälde* [portrait of mores] of fin-de-siècle Vienna: the whole of society is infected by sexual transgressiveness across class and professional boundaries, from the aristocrat to the proletarian. In an atmosphere of rising anti-Semitism, not surprisingly, Schnitzler received severe criticism and was condemned as a 'Jewish pornographer' (Schneider, 1995: pp. 188–93). Like the 'Klimt Affair', the controversy resulted in a court case known as the 'Reigen-Prozess'. *Der Reigen* was strictly censored and was not publicly performed until 23 December 1920 – not in Vienna but Berlin, where the notion of decadence and the decay of moral values had spread even more widely, penetrating all layers of society. Berlin in the 1920s and early 1930s would therefore continue to revel in what the German theatre critic Georg Hensel described as Schnitzler's 'Totentanz des Eros' [death dance of Eros] (1975: p. 776) – the very energy of excess that came to define the exuberance of the Weimar Republic.

iv

The fourteen-year period of the republic as an experiment in democratic governance between Germany's defeat in World War I and the rise of fascist totalitarianism in 1933 was a prelude to the destruction of a unified Germany by the Third Reich. While retrospectively appearing as a political disaster, the cultural richness of the Weimar Republic marks the interwar period as one of extreme cultural productivity. The era's many controversial cultural innovations in the wake of urban modernization led to a heterogeneous participation in a radically new society. Weimar Berlin worked as a 'frantic kaleidoscopic shuffling of the fragments of a nascent modernity': what seemed to some contemporaries as progressive technological and human advance appeared to others as the epitome of decadence. In order to reflect the sense of things falling apart in artistic practice, as Anton Kaes, Martin Jay, and Edward Dimendberg suggest, 'the multi-perspectivism of montage was often praised during the period itself as a technique that challenges synthesis and closure' (Kaes, et al., 1994: p. xvii). The idea of a fractured modernity feeds into definitions of decadence that are characterized by disintegration (Bourget), paradoxical pairings (Mahoney, 2015: pp. 18–19), and the anarchy of the parts in relation to the whole (Nietzsche). Modernity thus appeared to many Berliners as the harbinger of imminent social and cultural collapse, leading them to respond by anxiously indulging in the frantic spectacle Mel Gordon has called 'voluptuous panic' (2006).

By the end of the so-called roaring twenties, Berlin had superseded Vienna as the capital of Continental decadence. In his memoir *The World of Yesterday* (1941), Zweig documents his own experiences of the diametrically opposed vicissitudes of the two cities that were already emerging in 1902:

> Since 1870, when Berlin had changed from the rather small, sober, and by no means rich capital of the Kingdom of Prussia into the seat of the German Emperor, the homely town on the Spree had taken a mighty upswing. [. . .] Vienna above all, with its century of tradition, its concentrated power, and its innate talent, was still predominant over Berlin. But of recent years, with the rapid economic rise in Berlin, a new page had turned. [. . .] Vienna, bound to the ancient and worshipping its own past, was cautious and non-committal with respect to young men and daring experiments. But in Berlin, which wished to form itself more rapidly and more personally, novelty was sought after. (1943: p. 93)

Zweig, like no other chronicler of his generation, notes the different dynamics of Vienna and Berlin. In contrast to Vienna's luxurious decadence, decadence in Berlin was an excessive, hedonistic 'dance on the edge of a volcano' (Gay, 1968: p. xiv). The exuberance of *Lebenslust* [the lust for life] in Berlin contrasted with the restrained elegance of Vienna but was also a response to the vanishing contours of middle-class culture. Theories of cultural decline, such as Oswald Spengler's *Decline of the West* (written between 1918 and 1923), voiced anxious scepticism about the stability of civilization as a whole, which, according to Spengler, was particularly manifest in urban centres. Together with a number of other texts on urban degeneration (e.g., James Cantlie's lecture, 'Degeneration amongst Londoners' (1885)), Spengler identified the metropolis as a hotbed of human decline. In this climate, reflecting a sense of the imminent disintegration of culture, government, and economy, Berlin's entertainment industry prospered.

As with Haussmann's redesign of Paris during the Second Empire, Berlin saw rapid urban improvements, ranging from the construction of new sewer systems and transportation links to and from the provinces to the establishment of libraries, museums, cabarets, and theatres. The population of Germany expanded considerably, from 47.6 million in 1865 to over 70 million by 1914 (Marchand, 2015: p. 136). The rapid growth of Berlin brought with it an accelerated development of capitalist commerce and media, especially the new medium of film. The social and technological transformations progressed faster, more radically, and on a larger scale than in Vienna. The Alexanderplatz, the centre of urban reconstruction and nightlife in 1920s Berlin, became comparable to the Ringstrasse, a building site emblematic of the social and cultural changes brought about by rapid modernization.

The dramatic changes in economic and political certainties were also manifested in the visual arts, theatre, cabaret culture, and literature. Several factors led contemporaneous commentators to form an image of Berlin as a demonic Moloch: Germany had just lost a war and the resultant damage was not only visible in the urban wastelands but also in the mutilated bodies of returning soldiers. The impact of war breeding poverty and high unemployment rates was followed by the hyperinflation of 1923. The German-Jewish critic Walter Benjamin (1892–1940) witnessed these frenzied years of Weimar culture, remembering 'Demonic Berlin' in his 1930 essay of the same title. He recalls reading E. T. A. Hoffmann's gothic stories set in Berlin and their influence on Alfred Döblin (1878–1957):

> Hoffmann could be called the father of the Berlin novel. The traces of the city were subsequently submerged in generalities [. . .] until in our own time it sprang to life once more – in such works as Döblin's Alexanderplatz. He makes one of his characters say to another, standing in for himself: 'You had a definite reason for setting the scene in Berlin, and calling streets and squares by their proper names. But in my opinion it is not a bad idea in general to describe the scene precisely. Apart from the fact that the whole story gains the illusion of historical truth and thus bolsters a limp imagination, it also gains uncommonly in vividness and freshness for anyone familiar with the setting.' (Benjamin, 1999: p. 325)

In contrast to Hoffmann's romantic demonization of Berlin, which infused the cityscape with a gloomy yet enticing atmosphere, Benjamin insists that the reality of Weimar Berlin, similar to that captured in Dix's paintings and in Döblin's novel, already sufficed to make it appear demonic. As with Freud's and Schnitzler's Vienna, Weimar Berlin became synonymous with German decadent culture.

V

Social decadence and decay defined the aesthetics of three of the leading painters of the Weimar period: Max Beckmann (1884–1950), Otto Dix (1891–1969), and George Grosz (1893–1959). Dix's traumatic experiences during his military service and Beckmann's and Grosz's mental instability (both suffered nervous breakdowns) haunt their aesthetic of grisly grotesqueness and gross deformity. Their *Neue Sachlichkeit* [new objectivity] was Berlin's answer to Klimt's luxuriating sensuality, as it was to Schiele's and Kokoschka's more graphic eroticism. Dix's triptych *Großstadt* [*Metropolis*] (1928) (fig. 17.1) is a particularly good example illustrating the anxieties associated with decadence in Weimar Berlin. It represents Berlin's growing pleasure industry, bringing with it the conflation of gender boundaries, the widespread consumption of narcotics, the popularization of jazz as 'barbaric' intoxication, and the unsettling presence of war invalids in a city of glamorous ruins. Human shapes are deranged and deformed to appear as monsters and genderless bodies. The excessive luxury of the metropolitan elite displayed in the right panel clashes with the dire reality of the gutter on the left. Taking Dix's grotesques to the extreme, Grosz's depictions of skeletons wearing gas-masks, ageing nudes, and pregnant women with hollowed cheeks continue to emphasize the lurid titillation of urban decay and the sense of feverish excitement in face of impending doom that distinguishes Weimar decadence.

Far from the dandified prose or romanticizing accounts of Left-Bank Paris in the 1870s, the literature and arts of decadent Berlin portray low-class outsiders; petty criminals; impoverished entertainers; forced and gay prostitution; and extreme brutality towards women. The social divide in the mix of *haute-volée* [high-flown] types and impoverished, war-ravaged mobs is captured in Döblin's *Berlin Alexanderplatz* (1929). In nine books, the novel captures the grim economic reality of the 'kleiner Mann' [little man] and the necessity of crime and sexual labour. Like Schnitzler and Freud, Döblin drew on his professional experience as a doctor and psychiatrist. However, his accounts were based on practising in deprived

Fig. 17.1 Otto Dix's triptych *Metropolis* (1927–1928) represents three different social realties of Weimar Berlin: soldiers mutilated in the Great War, the elegant nightclub scene, and the thriving sex industry [Artists Rights Society / Art Resource, New York].

working-class quarters. His style rejects the introspective fiction of Schnitzler's fin-de-siècle interior monologue. Instead, as Ritchie Robertson notes, *Berlin Alexanderplatz* directs an 'anti-humanist gaze on contemporary Berlin'. Robertson remarks that '[t]he narration moves in and out of Biberkopf's thoughts, the collective consciousness of his fellow Berliners, and an unidentifiable voice that directs the story from an omniscient perspective' (2018: p. 18).

The novel follows Franz Biberkopf's struggles in Berlin, personified as the 'Whore of Babylon'. As an allegorical femme fatale, the city tempts him and leads to his undoing. Biberkopf is released from prison, where he has spent four years for the manslaughter of his lover, Ida. Despite his intention to become a better man and build a normal existence, the novel shows how his inability to live according to middle-class morality leads to his decline. Biberkopf himself perceives his release from prison as a punishment. He found prison comfortable because it shielded him from the onslaught of modernity, so when he is finally free he says, 'The Penalty starts now'. Upon his release Biberkopf, the born degenerate (a notion implied by his name, suggesting his animalistic nature as a beaver-head), immediately commits the next crime by raping Ida's sister. Biberkopf's own masculinity, however, is also in question: he is driven by his own homoerotic attachment to a sinister criminal, called Reinhold, who recklessly exploits Biberkopf. On one of the gang's robberies, Reinhold grows suspicious of Biberkopf's criminal integrity and pushes him out of the getaway vehicle. Biberkopf is hit by another car, and while surviving the accident, loses one of his arms. Now visibly scarred by life, Biberkopf then finds that his current lover, the prostitute Mieze, has been murdered by Reinhold's gang. Like one of Dix's portraits of urban deformity, Biberkopf has to admit his social, physical, and moral defeat: under suspicion for committing the murder of Mieze he is admitted to a mental health asylum. What makes Döblin's novel an excellent example of the energy of Weimar culture is the relentlessness of the narrative. While it does not judge the depravity of Biberkopf and the other characters, its descriptive, psychological approach exposes the everyday instinctive brutality necessary to survive in the jungle of the metropolis.

In 1928, while working on his own novel, Döblin was full of praise in his review of James Joyce's *Ulysses*. Both texts share the experimental usage of montage and modernist narrative techniques. Döblin uses montage, which he referred to as 'Kinostil' [cinema style], a device employed to immerse his readers in an epic about the chaos and frenzy of Berlin. In 1930, Benjamin praised Döblin's 'Montagestil', which loosely assembled newspaper scraps, biblical quotations, and popular song texts into a vibrant collage of 1920s Berlin. In keeping with the aesthetics of decadence as a 'demolished wholeness' (Krobb, 2004: p. 551), Döblin's narrative resembles the notion of *Verkehr* in its several senses. The ambiguity of the German word *Verkehr* [traffic, financial transaction, and sexual intercourse] captures three defining features of Weimar decadence: first, a shift from Viennese 'bourgeoisification' to a mass movement; second, widespread social decadence brought about by a sense of augmenting consumerism; and, third, as a result of the hyperinflation, the growth of Berlin's sex industry and sex tourism.

There are plenty of accounts by foreign authors and German writers that portray Weimar Berlin as the capital of sexual excess. Klaus Mann, belated dandy and son of Thomas Mann, paints a frenetic picture, reminiscent of Schnitzler's *Der Reigen*, in his description of 1923 Berlin:

> Boys with girls, boys with boys, girls with girls, men with boys and girls, women with men or boys or girls or tamed little panthers – what's the difference? [. . .] Millions of helpless, impoverished, bewildered people capered and swung in a delirium of hunger and hysteria. Dance was a mania [. . .]. The stock market danced. [. . .] The poets were convulsed with rhythmic spasms. The cripples, the prostitutes, the beggars, the reformers, the retired monarchs and astute industrials – all of them swayed and skipped. [. . .] They danced despair [. . .]. Berlin did a great job in displaying misery and vices on a colossal scale. (1942: p. 86)

To this Zweig adds: 'Berlin was transformed into the Babylon of the world. Bars, amusement parks, red-light houses sprang up like mushrooms' (1943: p. 240). After the hyperinflation of 1923 prostitution was omnipresent. As the mark rapidly declined in value, Berlin's sex industry attracted foreign visitors who could readily afford to purchase pleasures of all kinds. Gordon lists seventeen different types of outdoor and indoor prostitution. From child prostitution, mother-and-daughter duos, to gay, cross-dressing services, Berlin provided an apocalyptic 'circus of perversities' (Mann, 1942: p. 87). Journalist Luigi Barzini, who travelled to sex-crazed Berlin in the 1920s to meet Grosz, describes one saturnalian scene in his memoir, *The Europeans*:

> I saw pimps offering anything to anybody [. . .]. The story went around that a male goose of which one cut the neck at the right ecstatic moment would give you the most delicious, economical, and time-saving frisson of all – as it allowed you to enjoy sodomy, bestiality, homosexuality, necrophilia and sadism at one stroke. Gastronomy, too, as one could eat the goose afterward. (1983: p. 75)

These accounts, combined with Döblin's graphic description of political decadence and sexual violence, document the role of sexuality as an important economic product in Weimar Berlin. Isherwood's novellas, collected as *The Berlin Stories* (1939) (parts of which are widely known in adapted form as *Cabaret*) give complementary accounts of the 1930s leading up to a critical re-interpretation of Weimar modernity as a form of degeneracy. The unruly image of the *neue Frau* [New Woman] was partly embodied by Döblin's Mieze and Isherwood's Sally Bowles, who emerged as a natural progression of Schnitzler's female characters, aspiring to live 'for the present and according to [their] own desires' (Kaes, et al., 1994: p. 196). Isherwood's famed protagonist in the eponymous chapter of *The Berlin Stories* became a pop-culture icon. Sally is the face of Weimar aesthetics that were shaped by drastic social change: 'her fingernails were painted emerald green, a colour unfortunately chosen, for it called attention to her hands, which were much stained by cigarette-smoking and as dirty as a little girl's. She was dark [...]. Her face was long and thin, powdered dead white' (Isherwood, 2012: pp. 24, 25).

Both Döblin and Isherwood present the reader with fictional representations of social decadence and historical decline against a backdrop of Berlin facing the imminent ascendency of Nazism. Increasingly, anti-Semitism was believed to be the remedy to cleanse German culture of its cultural decline. As a result, 'decadence' as a term underwent yet another re-evaluation: from the artistic decadence of Vienna (ornament as crime), to the social decadence of the unleashed masses, to the decadence of human values in fascist totalitarian systems. Whilst decadence in Vienna was strongly connected to bourgeois circles and their separation into two camps (Secession), artistic decadence in Berlin was equated with social decadence. The importance of new media and forms of mass entertainment, mainly cinema, supported the sense of decadence taking hold of Berlin in its social entirety.

vi

While Viennese decadence celebrated anti-naturalistic, irrational, and psychological tendencies in art, Weimar decadence favoured naturalistic and expressionist forms. Political decadence in both cases conditioned rich cultural innovation. The phenomenon of socio-historical decadence thus locates Vienna and Berlin as two important cultural centres of intellectual modernism that shaped the way we perceive the connection between art and politics today. Despite the differences in the two cities, a comparison of their societies draws out the development of decadence from a primarily aesthetic principle to a social phenomenon: Vienna's double status as the capital experiencing the crumbling of one of the largest empires of the nineteenth century while also being the cradle of modernist innovation in culture and the arts marked by excessive artifice and ornamentation. The socio-aesthetic decadence of Berlin conveys a sense of political decline through even more radical forms of artistic expressionism, translating an artistic experience of distortion and displacement in modernity into theories of racial degeneracy. In many ways, the intellectuals and artists of Weimar Berlin continued the debate on aesthetic and social entanglement, which had emerged as a central development in Vienna around 1900, yet with a much darker and pessimistic outlook. For advocates of the German Conservative Revolution modernity all too often equalled decadence. Zweig poignantly sums up the result of the Weimar excesses:

> [E]verywhere it was unmistakable that this over-excitation was unbearable for the people, this being stretched daily on the rack of inflation, and that the whole nation, tired of war, actually only longed for order, quiet, and a little security and bourgeois life. And, secretly it hated the republic, not because it suppressed this wild freedom, but on the contrary, because it held the reins too loosely. (1943: p. 239)

By hardening the perspective of political and religious conservatives into fascism, the Nazi regime ended the careers of some of the greatest artists of the twentieth century through the notorious book burnings in 1933 and the *Degenerate Art Exhibition* of 1937. Social and artistic excess stand at both extremes of the socio-aesthetic histories of Vienna and Berlin. Decadence, then, can be understood as a thoroughly progressive and political concept situated in the historical context of central Europe. However, the socio-aesthetic histories of both cities also exemplify how decadence led bourgeois culture from a pluralistic metropolitanism towards an identification with retrogressive nationalist tendencies.

References

Banham, Martin (1995). *The Cambridge Guide to Theatre*, Cambridge: Cambridge University Press.

Barzini, Luigi (1983). *The Europeans*, Harmondsworth: Penguin.

Beller, Steven (2001). *Rethinking Vienna 1900*, Oxford: Berghahn.

Benjamin, Walter (1999). Demonic Berlin. In vol. II, part 1, of *Walter Benjamin: Selected Writings: 1927–1930*, Michael W. Jennings, Howard Eiland, and Gary Smith, eds., London: Harvard University Press, pp. 322–7.

Döblin, Alfred (2018). *Berlin Alexanderplatz*, Michael Hofmann, trans., London: Penguin.
Freud, Sigmund (1997). *Dora: An Analysis of a Case of Hysteria*, New York: Touchstone.
Furst, Lilian R. (2003). Girls for Sale: Freud's Dora and Schnitzler's Else. *Modern Austrian Literature*, 36(3/4), 19–37.
Gay, Peter (1968). *Weimar Culture: The Outsider as Insider*, London: Secker and Warburg.
Gordon, Mel (2006). *Voluptuous Panic: The Erotic World of Weimar Berlin*, Venice, CA: Feral House.
Hensel, Georg (1975). *Spielplan: Der Schauspielführer von der Antike bis zur Gegenwart*, 2nd ed., Frankfurt/M., Berlin, and Vienna: Propyläen.
Isherwood, Christopher (2012). *The Berlin Stories*, New York: New Directions.
Kaes, Anton, Martin Jay, and Edward Dimendberg, eds. (1994). *The Weimar Republic Sourcebook*, Berkeley: University of California Press.
Krobb, Florian (2004). 'Die Kunst der Väter tödtet das Leben der Enkel': Decadence and Crisis in Fin-de-Siècle German and Austrian Discourse. *New Literary History*, 35(4), 547–62.
Kupper, Herbert and Hilda S. Rollman-Branch (1959). Freud and Schnitzler – (Doppelgänger). *Journal of the American Psychoanalytic Association*, 7(1), 109–26.
Mahoney, Kristin Mary (2015). *Literature and the Politics of Post-Victorian Decadence*, Cambridge: Cambridge University Press.
Mann, Klaus (1942). *The Turning Point*, London: Fischer.
Marchand, Suzanne (2015). Central Europe. In Michael Saler, ed., *The Fin-de-Siècle World*, Abingdon: Routledge, pp. 131–49.
Nèret, Gilles (2000). *Gustav Klimt 1862–1918*, Cologne: Taschen Verlag.
Rasch, Wolfdietrich (1986). *Die literarische Décadence um 1900*, Munich: C. H. Beck.
Robertson, Ritchie (2018). Pared fingernails. *Times Literary Supplement*, 6001, 6 April, 18.
Schneider, Gerd K. (1995). *Die Rezeption von Arthur Schnitzlers Reigen 1897–1994*, Riverside, CA: Ariadne Press.
Schnitzler, Arthur (1995). *La ronde / Hands around*, New York: Dover.
Schnitzler, Arthur (2012). *Fräulein Else*, F. H. Lyon, trans., London: Pushkin Press.
Schorske, Carl E. (1981). *Fin-de-Siècle Vienna: Politics and Culture*, New York: Vintage.
Weir, David (2018). *Decadence: A Very Short Introduction*, Oxford: Oxford University Press.
Zweig, Stefan (1943). *The World of Yesterday: An Autobiography*, London: Cassell and Company.

CHAPTER 18

Decadence and Cinema

David Weir

According to the Internet Movie Database (IMDb), Oscar Wilde authored more than 250 screenplays, a remarkable accomplishment for someone who died in 1900, only five years after the Lumière brothers' invention of the cinematograph. In reality, the number of Wilde's IMDb 'credits' is a register of just how amenable the work of a pre-eminent decadent author is to cinematic adaptation, the first of several possible rationales for considering cinema and the concept of decadence. But a film need not be based on a particular decadent text to evoke the concept: surely the films of Kenneth Anger, Lucino Visconti, Derek Jarman, David Lynch, and Peter Greenaway, for example, qualify as decadent cinema for some combination of visual sense and scenario – lurid, overabundant detail in the mise-en-scène coupled with narratives of decline, decay, and perversity. But these recent exemplars of cinematic decadence owe a debt to certain key foundational figures, who are the focus of this essay: Erich von Stroheim, Ernst Lubitsch, Billy Wilder, Federico Fellini, and Pier Paolo Passolini. The cinematic exploration of decadence on the part of these directors is now regarded as classic, which points to another reason for considering the concept of decadence in the cinematic context: namely, that film has periodically undergone periods of extreme conventionalization that create the conditions – and the need – for artistic renewal. Like the literature of certain periods, cinema is supposed to have risen to a certain level of classical expression, only to enter a subsequent period of artistic decline. But repeatedly, reports of the death of cinema have been premature: time and again, some filmic form of decadence has brought the medium back to life.

i

Even in the silent era (1895–1927) concerns emerged that the most recent addition to the seven arts had already entered a period of artistic decline. In

1927, the future filmmaker Luis Buñuel expressed anxiety about 'the advent of colour and synchronized sound', innovations that he believed posed a threat to the art of cinema because the use of such technology suggested a return to the notion of the camera as a simple recording device. Buñuel urged his fellow filmmakers to place 'themselves under the auspices of the muse of silence, wrapped in the pure tunic of chiaroscuro' (2000: pp. 127–8). Buñuel's concerns were realized, in a way, the year after he made them with the release of *The Wedding March*, a film by Erich von Stroheim that in fact incorporated the 'decadent' elements Buñuel identified: colour and synchronized sound. True, the new cinematic resource of Technicolor was used only for certain segments of the film, and only the orchestral score was synchronized, the 'muse of silence' continuing to prevail by means of traditional intertitles for the dialogue. But von Stroheim's 1928 masterpiece, however decadent by Buñuel's then-purist standards, is classic today.

The Wedding March is set in Vienna in the last days of the Austro-Hungarian Empire, as the opening title card declares: 'Vienna – Anno Domini – 1914 – '. Stock footage of the city further establishes the locale, culminating in a long iris shot of 'its oldest guardian, St. Stephen's'. Henceforth extremely elaborate and expensive sets provide the basis for shots of the façade and interior of the great cathedral, as well as other Viennese settings. In 1927, the director described his Hollywood re-creation of the city of his youth to the *New York Times* in rapturous terms: 'It is Vienna! Vienna, before the great war of 1914 – Vienna the melodious, the romantic, the dramatic – my Vienna!' (Old Pre-War Vienna, 1927: VII, p. 5). Von Stroheim's nostalgia notwithstanding, what winds up on the screen is more decadent than romantic – 'no longer the Vienna of Strauss and Léhar, [. . .] but a melancholy town seen through the eyes of Schnitzler and Freud' (Kozarski, 2001: p. 209). The mere act of representing a society that no longer exists establishes the fact of historical decline, and that fact is matched by von Stroheim's treatment of an aristocratic class in its last days. Von Stroheim himself plays Prince Nicholaus ('Nicki') Erhart Hans Karl Maria von Wildeliebe-Rauffenbergh, the last scion of an aristocratic family noble only in name. After Nicki rouses himself from a night of debauchery, and after the maid refuses his morning advances, he asks his father for cash, whereupon he advises: 'Blow out your brains! – or marry money!' The latter solution would benefit the parents as well, so they manoeuvre a loveless marriage between Nicki and Cecelia (Zasu Pitts), the disabled daughter of a nouveau-riche corn-plaster magnate. The arrangement is certified in the drunken aftermath of a bordello orgy when Nicki's father agrees to ennoble Cecelia's father in exchange for 1,000,000 kronen. The orgy scene is intercut with Prince Nicki's seduction of Mitzi (Fay Wray), the woman he really loves, a commoner who became smitten with him at the Corpus Christi Day festivities in front of St. Stephen's. In the end, Nicki marries the corn-plaster king's daughter for the money, and Mitzi agrees to marry her jealous suitor Schani (Matthew Betz) to keep him from murdering the prince.

The ornate sets and aristocratic costumes are so lush and detailed that the mise-en-scène by itself is sufficient to establish the film as an example of cinematic decadence. The saturation of detail in some scenes is quite astonishing, even when the effect is supposedly natural. For example, Nicki seduces Mitzi on an old two-seater carriage parked in an apple orchard where blossoms rain down on the couple as they embrace and kiss. These blossoms were hand-made and designed to float down on the lovers on cue. The number of blossoms required for the scene has been variously estimated as somewhere between 50,000 and 500,000 (Kozarski, 2001: p. 217). Von Stroheim means to draw a contrast between Nicki's romance of Mitzi and his father's 'romance' of the corn-plaster magnate in the orgy scene, remarkable not only for the elaborate set but also for the wildly hedonistic action. According to first-hand reports by his cinematographer Hal Mohr and others, von Stroheim got the effect he wanted by staging an actual orgy, complete with call-girls and oceans of bootleg gin (p. 221). Such reports give credence to Kenneth Anger's characteristically over-heated description of von Stroheim's '*Alt Wien* decadence':

> The fancy brothel of *The Wedding March* had featured whores of all races, each with her erotic specialty; the fairies in white wigs and white body make-up who played stringed instruments had been blindfolded to prevent recognition of the 'nobs' present. The chastity belts of the Negro 'slaves' were sealed with heart-shaped padlocks; one refinement due more to Stroheim's imagination than to Austria-Hungary's depravity was a pretty pair of accommodating Siamese twins! (1975: pp. 173, 177)

Von Stroheim went to such excesses of direction for the sake of realism, assuming, reasonably enough, that the best way to get his performers to appear intoxicated was to get them drunk.

This idea of realism also extended to von Stroheim's off-screen persona, since he wanted audiences to believe that he actually *was* the decadent Viennese aristocrat he played on screen. In this respect von Stroheim emerges as kind of a male Theda Bara, the woman whose depraved vamp persona made her the first true movie star. Born Theodosia Goodman to a middle-class Jewish family in Cincinnati but given a fantastic new biography by the publicity machine of the old Willat Studio (later Fox) in Fort Lee, New Jersey, she was supposed to have been born in the shadow of the pyramids, the only child of Theda de Lyse, a beautiful French actress, and Giuseppe Bara, an Italian sculptor (Golden, 1996: pp. 1, 10). The difference in the case of von Stroheim is that the man himself, not some publicity-savvy studio head, devised the myth and the persona that brought him fame as 'the man you love to hate'. To this day, biographers disagree about the details of von Stroheim's life before he emigrated from Europe to the United States in 1909, but it is clear that von Stroheim took full advantage of the classic immigrant opportunity to remake himself in America. He may have left the port-city of Bremen, Germany, as Erich Oswald Stroheim, but by the time he got to Ellis Island he had transformed himself into Erich Oswald Hans Carl Maria von Stroheim (Kozarski, 2001: p. 3), the string of Christian names being very similar to those assigned to the fictional Prince Nicki in *The Wedding March.*

Von Stroheim was mostly successful getting audiences to buy into his screen persona, beginning with Lieutenant Eric Von Steuben, an Austrian officer in *Blind Husbands* (1919) who dies in the Dolomites when he is abandoned by the doctor whose wife he has tried to seduce. But Von Stroheim's monocled, dapper aristocrat, at once correct and corrupt (fig. 18.1), was to come back to life in film after film and is perhaps most familiar today as Captain von Rauffenstein, the German pilot turned prison-camp commandant in Jean Renoir's *La grande illusion* (1937). Where the role in Renoir's film is a kind of homage to the character, the von Stroheim persona is put to ironic use in Billy Wilder's *Sunset Boulevard* (1950). There, von Stroheim brings his aristocratic old-world bearing to the role of Max von Mayerling, the officious butler – and former husband – of Gloria Swanson's Norma Desmond, the faded silent screen star who chooses the role of Salomé as the vehicle for her deluded return to stardom. An especially layered moment from Wilder's film comes when von Mayerling screens a film for his mistress starring Desmond in her prime. As yet unreleased in the United States in 1950, the film within the film is *Queen Kelly* (1929), starring Gloria Swanson and directed by Erich von Stroheim. Clearly, by inserting a segment from a silent film directed by an actor in his own film and starring another Wilder effectively incorporates the decadence of an earlier cinematic age into his own contemporary narrative of Hollywood depravity. Like von Stroheim, Wilder grew up in Vienna, and, unlike von Stroheim, experienced the decline and eventual demise of the Austro-Hungarian Empire first-hand. Perhaps those twilight years in imperial Vienna informed, to some degree, Wilder's sunset saga of the woman who would be Salomé.

Fig. 18.1 Erich von Stroheim's militarized dandy brings the decadent tradition into the modern age of early cinema [Getty Images / ullstein bild Dtl].

ii

Norma Desmond's unrealized *Salomé* is almost certainly based on Wilde's play, as were at least thirty other treatments that were actually filmed. A closer look at Wilde's 'screenwriting' credits reveals some seventy or so adaptations of his various society dramas and more than twenty versions of his only novel, *The Picture of Dorian Gray.* Noteworthy versions of *Salomé* include Alla Nazimova's once artful, now camp, 1922 effort featuring costumes and set design inspired by Aubrey Beardsley's illustrations for the play and *Salome's Last Dance*, Ken Russell's delightfully tasteless recreation of 1988, in which the play is staged in a brothel run by Alfred

Taylor (the man who procured rent boys for Wilde and was convicted alongside him in 1895). Of the several rather unfortunate adaptations of *The Picture of Dorian Gray*, two stand out as being especially unfortunate: the 1945 Hollywood production, remarkable for Hurd Hatfield's dissociated, wooden performance as Dorian, and *Il dio chiamato Dorian* [The god called Dorian] (1970), directed by Massimo Dallamano. The film is set in late-1960s swinging London and follows the plot of the novel fairly closely, despite one glaring, distracting error: true to the novel, the other characters age while Dorian does not, yet the mise-en-scène remains the same – it is always the late 1960s.

Among the numerous cinematic adaptations of Wilde's society dramas one of the first and finest is the 1925 silent version of *Lady Windermere's Fan* (1892) by the German-American director Ernst Lubitsch (1892–1947). There are several reasons for making the claim that Lubitsch is Wilde's true cinematic successor. First, before he adapted Wilde to the screen, Lubitsch had begun to transform the rapid-paced sex-farce that had made his reputation in Germany into the kind of subtle, cosmopolitan, comic romance for which the director is best known today. This process of artistic maturation began with *The Marriage Circle* (1924), the first film Lubitsch made after securing a four-year contract with Warner Brothers that gave him complete artistic control over all aspects of production – choice of story, actors, set design, and so on, as well as supervision of the editing process (something few directors of the time enjoyed) (Hake, 1992: p. 61). One critic describes *The Marriage Circle* as a '*commédie matrimoniale* [. . .] very much in the manner of Wilde', with an 'extremely precise and detailed' plot, like, again, 'an Oscar Wilde play' (Dixon, 2011, p. 135). The critical and popular success of *The Marriage Circle* and the three other Warner romances leading up to *Lady Windermere's Fan* help to explain the decision by the estate of Oscar Wilde to allow Lubitsch – and only Lubitsch – to adapt the play (Thompson, 2005: p. 30).

Lubitsch transfers the main plot of the novel to the film in fairly complete form, eliminating some minor characters and the sub-plots that accompany them. But because of the silent medium the director could not convey any of Wilde's brilliant dialogue – where the decadence of the drama really resides. Of course, Lubitsch could have transferred Wilde's wit to title cards, an option he rejected. 'Playing with words is fascinating to the writer and afterward to the reader', he said, 'but on the screen it is impossible. Would much charm remain to long excerpts of Wilde's play if the audience had to ponder laboriously over the scintillating sentences on the screen?' Usually, commentators say that the director found 'visual counterparts for Wilde's dialogue' (Eyman, 1993, p. 114), and while there may be some isolated instances of such equivalence, Lubitsch's visual re-imagining of Wilde's play hardly depends on its verbal origins for its complex evocation of the world of fin-de-siècle decadent aristocrats, with their moral hypocrisy, diffident hedonism, social voyeurism, and conspicuous displays of wealth and leisure – all updated for the 1920s.

The film opens with Lady Windermere puzzling over the seating plan for the upcoming ball in celebration of her birthday, as a title card announces: 'Lady Windermere faced the grave problem – of seating her dinner guests'. The line is witty in its own right, Wildean even, but there is another reason that particular title card is the first thing the viewer sees: it announces the difficulty of arranging people in space, a problem faced not only by the character but also by the director. Physical placement reveals social standing, not only at dinner parties but also on the screen – and the stage. Indeed, we know from his letters to George Alexander, the actor who first played Lord Windermere and who staged the play in 1892, just how important Wilde felt the relationship of physical space to the production of social meaning to be. For example, Wilde tells Alexander that 'Windermere, being in his own house, can pace up and down – does, in fact, do so; Mrs. Erlynne, of course, cannot do anything of the kind' (Holland and Davis, 2000: p. 513). In the film, Lubitsch uses a stationary camera and deep focus photography to emphasize relationships between and among characters, most effectively in an interpolated scene set at the Ascot race track. When Mrs. Erlynne shows up, the other characters gaze at her, some through binoculars, and each for a different reason. Lord Darlington leers at her because he thinks Lord Windermere is having an affair with her, but Windermere's indifferent glance refutes the notion. Three elderly, gossipy dowagers stare at Mrs. Erlynne's jewelled fingers and also observe that her hair is starting to grey. Lady Windermere's view of Mrs. Erlynne is blocked, a visual cognate of the way she is kept in the dark about the woman's true identity as her mother. When Mrs. Erlynne looks for her daughter, Lord Augustus thinks she is looking at him and responds accordingly, ultimately pursuing her when she leaves the track. Through framing, cuts, close-ups, and impeccable eyeline matches, Lubitsch controls the cinematic space and conveys a wealth of social information every bit as layered and subtle as what Wilde achieves by means of dialogue and stage direction.

The film theorist David Bordwell uses the racetrack scene of *Lady Windermere's Fan* to explain 'the principles of classical cinema': 'Screen direction and eyeline matching are very exact. The space is "volumetric" [. . .]: the camera is "inside" the characters' space. [. . .] The film is especially precise in its composition of the frame. [. . .] If the frame is unbalanced, sooner or later a character will enter to fill the vacancy' (1997: p. 179). More specifically, Bordwell says of the racetrack scene that Lubitsch's technique involves 'shifting optical subjectivity to intensify disparities among various characters' knowledge' (p. 178). That observation comes into play in the first thing Lady Windermere says – via title card – to Mrs. Erlynne when she is forced to greet her at the birthday gala: 'I have heard so much about you – from every side'. The line helps explain why Lubitsch eschewed Wilde's dialogue for his own, since it can easily be read as a comment on the 'shifting optical subjectivity' on display earlier in the film at the racetrack. But the remark is also relevant to events that are shortly to ensue, once Lady Windermere leaves the interior space of the ballroom and goes outside to mope on the terrace. Lord Windermere does not see his wife leave and begins to look for her, walking screen right. In the next shot, the door to the terrace opens screen left, implying that Lord Windermere is entering. A cut to Lady Windermere holds with her alone in the frame, until a man's hand reaches for hers at the bottom right edge of the screen. She withdraws her hand and turns, facing screen right and registering surprise. The next shot reveals that the man is not her husband but Lord Darlington. He continues to woo her, and they leave the terrace for the formal garden just beyond, with its symmetrical rows of hedges. A long shot shows the two characters talking and occasionally ducking below the top of the hedge, but no title card clarifies either words or actions. A shot of Mrs. Erlynne on the terrace reveals that what we have just seen is from her point of view, evidently out of earshot (which perhaps explains the lack of title cards). She turns facing screen right to greet someone as Lady Windermere did earlier, whereupon the point of view shifts to that of Lady Windermere, alone in the garden after Lord Darlington's exit. She sees Mrs. Erlynne offer her hand to an unseen man, obscured by a bush, who takes the hand and kisses it. This is the climactic moment when Lady Windermere resolves to offer herself to Lord Darlington because she believes that the unseen man is her husband. But a 180° reverse angle reveals that the man is Lord Augustus. Lady Windermere does not on this occasion get to see Mrs. Erlynne 'from every side', a bit of dramatic irony fully consistent with the workings of Wilde's play. *Lady Windermere's Fan*, in short, demonstrates just how fully Lubitsch employed the cultural medium of decadence Wilde provided to develop classic cinematic technique.

iii

Billy Wilder idolized Ernst Lubitsch: 'For many years I had [a] sign on my wall. HOW WOULD LUBITSCH DO IT? I would *always* look at it when I was writing a script or planning a picture' (quoted by Thompson, 2005: p. 11). So if Lubitsch is the director who most successfully brought decadence from the silent era into Hollywood's golden age, Wilder would seem to be his heir apparent. Together with his writing partner Charles Brackett, Wilder penned the screenplays for two Lubitsch films, *Bluebeard's Eighth Wife* (1938) and *Ninotchka* (1939). But Lubitsch is not the only point of connection between Wilder and the decadent tradition. His collaborator Brackett had been a member of New York's Algonquin Round Table, a group whose latter-day, Jazz Age decadence is easy to see in relation to the fin-de-siècle original. Both the connection to Lubitsch and the collaboration with Brackett help to justify the association of Wilder with decadence, but Wilder was likely receptive to Lubitsch's influence and amenable to Brackett's contributions because of his own experiences in Weimar Berlin. Unlike Lubitsch, who left Berlin prior to the hyperinflation of 1923 that helped to transform the metropolis into the sex capital of Europe, Wilder lived and worked in the city from 1926 to 1933, arriving when he was only twenty years old. Prior to beginning what Wilder called his 'love affair' with the city of Berlin (Chandler, 2002: p. 59), he had worked for two years as a newspaper reporter in Vienna. His most celebrated scoop for *Die Stunde* [The hour] came at the end of 1925 when he interviewed – or tried to interview – Richard Strauss, Alfred Adler, Arthur Schnitzler, and Sigmund Freud (all on the same day!) on the subject of the rise of Italian fascism. Wilder managed to get the opinion of all of the Viennese luminaries on paper with the exception of Freud, who showed the teenage reporter the door (Lally, 1996: p. 11).

In Berlin, Wilder worked for a succession of newspapers, mainly covering crime and sports. Not surprisingly, the young man took full advantage of the multiple temptations of the great metropolis at a time when the city was at the height of its reputation for perversity and excess. Wilder's own adventures in the sex trade seem to have been rather modest, however. Some sources say he worked for a while as a gigolo – and Wilder himself did use that term (Madsen, 1969: p. 23), but the reality is that he found employment as an *Eintänzer* or 'tea dancer' at the ballroom of the Eden Hotel. He was paid to dance, mostly with matronly ladies while their husbands looked on (Lally, 1996: pp. 16, 18). So while Wilder may never have been a true gigolo, he had more than a passing familiarity with the profession, and it is hard not to see that Weimar experience lying behind the story of the screenwriter-gigolo Joe Gillis in *Sunset Boulevard.* More generally, 'the nihilistic cultural ambience of Berlin and the Weimar Republic', as one critic observes, played a major role in numerous Hollywood productions once the exodus of German filmmaking talent, begun by Lubitsch in 1922, came to its inevitable conclusion in 1933 (Wallace, 2006: p. xi). By the time of that necessary exodus, Wilder had established himself as a prolific screenwriter in Berlin, his most celebrated credit being for *Menschen am Sonntag* [*People on Sunday*] (1930), one of the last and best of the German silents.

Once in Hollywood, Wilder put his Weimar background to use in various ways, often in sanitized, that is to say, Americanized, form. For example, in *Some Like It Hot* (1959) the musicians played by Tony Curtis and Jack Lemon who dress in women's clothes and join a woman's jazz band to escape the mob seem like American cousins of the far more outré cross-dressers that Wilder, as a regular at the Romanishes Café on the Kurfurstendam, would have encountered strolling along that notorious boulevard. In a sense, Wilder's *Some Like It Hot* might be regarded as a comic conventionalization of the more genuinely transgressive films of the Weimar Era. To be sure, the musicians played by Curtis and Lemmon do not dress in women's clothes as an expression of transgressive sexuality: they do so to disguise themselves from the mob of gangsters who perpetrated the St. Valentine's Day Massacre of 14 February 1929, an event they accidentally witnessed. But Lemmon's character Jerry really takes to his disguise as Daphne, so much so that he becomes engaged to the wealthy, older playboy Osgood Fielding III played by Joe E. Brown. Daphne tries to get out of the engagement by pointing out that she is not a natural blond ('Doesn't matter'), can't have children ('We can adopt some'), has a terrible past ('I forgive you'), and so on. Exasperated, Jerry whips off his blond wig, and exclaims, 'I'm a man!' But Osgood is unfazed: 'Nobody's perfect', he says. That hilarious ending makes Osgood's obsession with what would have been, at the time, a rather inappropriate object choice tonally different from, say, Emil Janning's tragic attachment to Marlene Dietrich's cabaret singer Lola Lola in Josef von Sternberg's *Der Blaue Engel* [*The Blue Angel*] (1930), but there is still a kind of Weimar-meets-Hollywood feel to Wilder's film. In other words, Wilder could call on his experience of the permissive and transgressive nature of Weimar society as a creative resource, even as the creative conditions of Hollywood transformed that experience into something sanitized and conventional.

The transformation of transgressive Weimar culture into something both accessible and acceptable to middle-class, mid-century American audiences started with Wilder's very first Hollywood film, *The Major and the Minor* (1942). The film stars Ginger Rogers playing a young woman disillusioned with her life in Manhattan who decides to return to her hometown in Iowa. She does not have enough cash for the adult train fare so she disguises herself as a twelve-year-old girl and buys a half-fare child's ticket. On the way she is caught smoking between cars by the already-suspicious conductors, but she gives them the slip and sneaks into the compartment of Major Philip Kirby (Ray Milland), whose poor eyesight makes her little-girl disguise easier to bring off. She winds up spending the night with him in the bottom bunk of the sleeper, and when they are both awakened in the middle of the night by a thunderstorm, the Major snuggles with the 'child' to comfort her. The sexual frisson between the two is unmistakable, and, given that the older man actually thinks he is with a child, the scene conveys more than a hint of paedophilia. Wilder later described *The Major and the Minor* as 'prematurely *Lolita*' (Crowe, 1999: p. 95), and while the fifteen-year-old Sue Lyon makes a more believable nymphet in the title role of the 1962 Stanley Kubrick film than Rogers does as a thirty-one-year-old improbably masquerading as twelve, there is still something sunnily perverse about Wilder's film, a kind of wholesome depravity.

Wilder makes his Weimar background more directly apparent, if only in one scene, in his so-called 'Hitchcock' film, *Witness for the Prosecution* (1957). In that film Marlene Dietrich herself reprises her Weimar star turn as a cabaret singer in von Sternberg's *The Blue Angel* by means of a flashback that has her performing in a Hamburg dive to a group of GIs. A poster outside the nightclub *Die Blaue Laterne* [The blue lantern] advertising Christine Helm (Dietrich) is almost identical to the image of Lola Lola posted outside the cabaret in the earlier film: the same standing, spread-legged pose. Wilder is clearly having some fun with his Weimar source because this time Dietrich performs with the famous legs sheathed in trousers, which leads the disappointed audience of sex-starved soldiers to riot in protest. Nothing else about this film evokes the cultural memory of Weimar (aside from the worldly Dietrich), but the scene is one more reminder of just how insistent that memory was for directors like Wilder. As Lutz Koepnick observes, German filmmakers who began their Hollywood careers in exile would often 'recall their Weimar past to [. . .] express feelings of despair and dislocation' (2009: p. 246). That description certainly covers Wilder's case in *Sunset Boulevard*, but *The*

Major and the Minor and *Some Like It Hot* argue that the social and artistic past of the Weimar director is subject to more than one kind of subsequent valorization.

iv

All of our directorial exemplars of cinematic decadence thus far – von Stroheim, Lubitsch, Wilder – made films that are now regarded as classics. For cinema no less than literature has had its classical eras, such as the French interwar period (the age of 'poetic realism'), and its decadent ones: the French 'tradition of quality' in the 1950s prior to the *nouvelle vague* [new wave], for example. As this French example shows, the critical judgement as to what type of cinema might be classic and what might be decadent often involves the position of the filmmaker relative to the industry. It seems strange that *quality* and *tradition* should be seen as markers of inferiority, but that was precisely the case for François Truffaut and other critics-cum-filmmakers associated with the journal *Cahiers du cinéma* for whom the French studio system had become excessively formulaic and predictable. In the history of cinema, the concept of decadence as artistic decline has been invoked again and again, often in the context of technological innovation. Under the direction of a master like Lubitsch, silent cinema achieved classic status, so much so that the introduction of sound was regarded as a form of aesthetic decay; likewise, with colour, 3-D technology, and other, more recent technological innovations, such as computer-generated imagery (CGI).

A further rationale for considering cinema in relation to decadence includes the representation of modes of behaviour, mostly sexual, that are so far outside the norms of acceptable or expected moral criteria, usually bourgeois, as to cause condemnation (e.g., David Lynch's *Blue Velvet* (1986)). Another rationale is the aesthetic judgement, common in literature and the visual arts, that the manner of representation itself is so far removed from the norms of acceptable or expected artistic criteria, usually classicistic, as to invite denunciation (e.g., Kenneth Anger's *Inauguration of the Pleasure Dome* (1954)). Both of these rationales would seem to obtain in the case of two once-notorious adaptations of the literature from the two most foundational historical periods of decadence – the Roman Empire and libertine France: Federico Fellini's *Fellini-Satyricon* (1969) and Pier Paolo Pasolini's *Salò o le 120 giornate di Sodoma* [*Salò or The 120 Days of Sodom*] (1975). But in each film the evident offences against bourgeois morality and the violation of classicistic aesthetics render the judgement of decadence problematic, even as that judgement is in some measure validated. For example, both films include same-sex marriage ceremonies, 'decadent' by the bourgeois standards current at the time of the films' release, but hardly so in the context of the very different historical periods each film represents. As with the Roman novel *Satyricon* by Petronius on which *Fellini-Satyricon* is based (Fellini's film is so called because another director had secured the rights to the title *Satyricon* (Paul, 2009: p. 202)), homosexual relations between men cannot be the object of moral opprobrium because such relations were an accepted part of the classical world the film represents. As for *Salò*, Pasolini's choice to set the film in '1944–45 during the Nazi-Fascist Occupation' (as a title card has it) rather than in Sade's eighteenth century re-contextualizes the libertines' marriage to their respective victims as an ideological exercise of raw power, a form of perversity more political than sexual. In both instances, bourgeois morality is rendered moot as a measure of decadence.

Something similar happens with the question of aesthetic judgement based on classical principles of unity, balance, symmetry, and the like. There is no denying that *Fellini-Satyricon* is fragmentary, often to the point of incomprehensibility – but so is the classical text on which the film is based (Wyke, 1997: p. 189). Hence Fellini goes beyond the traditional concept of adaptation by attempting to capture not only the content of the source text but also its fragmentary structure, thereby making a larger comment on the nature of our knowledge of classical antiquity. Visually, the film takes inspiration from the Roman fresco, another classical art form known to us today mostly as a collection of fragments. The wide-screen process known as CinemaScope, together with the colour scheme of the film – the dusty ochre-orange tones – effectively suggest the look and feel of ancient Roman frescos. The conclusion of the film transforms the faces of the principal actors into images on ruined, weathered frescos, thereby implying that they are, in fact, part of classical antiquity. *Fellini-Satyricon* certainly challenges such traditional cinematic representations of classical Rome as, say, *Gladiator* (2000), but it also challenges our assumptions about what constitutes the concept of the classical in the first place. A similar instability emerges in the case of Pasolini's film, since *Salò*, for all its displays of sadistic sexuality (it was banned in Great Britain for 'gross indecency', the same basis for Oscar Wilde's conviction in 1895 (Green and Karolides, 2005: p. 34)), is classical and reserved in its cinematic technique; cold, in fact – a necessary adjunct to the dissociated action of the four fascist libertines. Indeed, in the light of all the sensational, effects-driven commercial films that appeared around the same time as *Salò* – mainly Stephen Spielberg's *Jaws* (1975) and George Lucas's *Star Wars* (1977) – Pasolini's 'decadent' film appears even more classicistic, or, as Gary Indiana puts it, '*Salò* has the retrospective aura of "the last art movie"' (2000: p. 24).

That assessment reflects a sense that cinema itself entered a period of decadence with the special effects wizardry of Spielberg and Lukas, while Pasolini eschews such effects and adheres fairly closely to the principles of classical cinema. At the same time, the reputation *Salò* still has as an especially decadent film persists, mainly because of its powerful cinematic representation of perversity (the famous scene of forced coprophagia being particularly memorable). The dual inclusion of *Salò* and *Jaws*, both about as unlike one another as two films can be, under the rubric of decadence seems strange at first, except that we are really talking about two different shadings of the concept. The decadence of *Salò* involves Pasolini's treatment of the libertine tradition that goes back to the eighteenth century, while that of *Jaws* inheres in Spielberg's effects-driven exploitation of the medium itself for craven commercial purposes. Simply stated, *Salò* is a classic film in the sense that it is mostly an exercise in traditional filmmaking, however sensational and salacious its content, whereas *Jaws* breaks with cinematic tradition through a combination of technological innovation (the mechanical shark, for instance) and audience manipulation, despite its normative narrative. Pasolini is fully aware of the larger tradition of decadence that includes not only Sade's novel but also later decadent developments; after all, the mordant sadists of *Salò*, transposed from the fading days of the ancien régime to the twilight of Mussolini's fascist dictatorship, have civilized conversations about Nietzsche and Huysmans. Pasolini's film, in short, has acquired the status of a cinematic classic, whereas Spielberg's unabashed, all-American embrace of popular culture seems, by contrast, more a product of calculation than art and so hardly qualifies as a candidate for the ranks of classic cinema.

Or does it? Clearly, there is a line between classic cinema by respected directors known for their devotion to the art of film and films that are too commercial or formulaic to merit a place in that classic category. These other films may not be designated 'decadent' in every case, but there is indeed a line between them and the classics. But this line keeps moving, and it has ever since the emergence of cinema as an art form early in the twentieth century. Spielberg may have crossed to the wrong side of that line in 1975, yet *Jaws* has since come to seem a classic work of cinematic art in the light of subsequent films that employ CGI effects to such an extreme degree as to make Spielberg's more limited analogue effects appear almost quaint by comparison. CGI, however, is only the most recent technology to mark the 'death' of cinema as an art form, just as sound technology and colour photography threatened its demise in 1927 for Buñuel. If electronic manipulation is indeed the most recent end of cinema, aesthetically speaking, that particular form of techno-decadence is, paradoxically, of critical importance to the continuing history of cinema. For most of motion picture history the very medium of cinema – the film stock itself – was subject to degradation almost from the moment images were recorded on it. But now, fortunately, digital 'decadence' can stay that degradation and preserve the classic films of the past.

References

Anger, Kenneth (1975). *Hollywood Babylon*, New York: Dell.

Bordwell, David (1997). *Narration in the Fiction Film*, London: Routledge.

Buñuel, Luis (2000). *An Unspeakable Betrayal: Selected Writings*, Garrett White, trans., Berkeley: University of California Press.

Chandler, Charlotte (2002). *Nobody's Perfect: Billy Wilder, a Personal Biography*, New York: Simon and Schuster.

Crowe, Cameron (1999). *Conversations with Wilder*, New York: Knopf.

Dixon, Bryony (2011). *100 Silent Films*, New York: Palgrave Macmillan.

Eyman, Scott (1993). *Ernst Lubitsch: Laughter in Paradise*, New York: Simon and Schuster.

Golden, Eve (1996). *Vamp: The Rise and Fall of Theda Bara*, Lanham, MD: Vestal.

Green, Jonathon, and Nicolas J. Karolides (2005). *Encyclopedia of Censorship*, new edn, New York: Facts on File.

Hake, Sabine (1992). *Passions and Deceptions: The Early Films of Ernst Lubitsch*, Princeton, NJ: Princeton University Press.

Holland, Merlin, and Rupert Hart-Davis, eds. (2000). *The Complete Letters of Oscar Wilde*, New York: Henry Holt.

Indiana, Gary (2000). *Salò or The 120 Days of Sodom*, London: British Film Institute.

Koepnick, Lutz (2009). The Bearable Lightness of Being: *People on Sunday*. In Noah Isenberg, ed., *Weimar Cinema*, New York: Columbia University Press, pp. 237–53.

Kozarski, Richard (2001). *Von: The Life and Films of Erich von Stroheim*, New York: Limelight.

Lally, Kevin (1996). *Wilder Times: The Life of Billy Wilder*, New York: Henry Holt.

Madsen, Axel (1969). *Billy Wilder*, Bloomington and London: Indiana University Press.

Old Pre-War Vienna Reproduced in Film (1927). *New York Times*, VII, 5, Jan. 2.
Paul, Joanna (2009). *Fellini-Satyricon*: Petronius and Film. In Jonathan Prag and Ian Repath, eds., *Petronius: A Handbook*, Malden, MA: Wiley-Blackwell, pp. 198–217.
Thompson, Kristin (2005). *Herr Lubitsch Goes to Hollywood: German and American Film after World War I*, Amsterdam: Amsterdam University Press.
Wallace, David (2006). *Exiles in Hollywood*, Pompton Plains, NJ: Limelight.
Wyke, Maria (1997). *Projecting the Past: Ancient Rome, Cinema, and History*, New York and London: Routledge.

CHAPTER 19

Transnational Decadence

Stefano Evangelista

Arthur Symons's 'The Decadent Movement in Literature' (1893) introduced decadence to English readers but was less original in what it had to say on the form than on the *space* of literary decadence. Symons gave decadence all the usual attributes, evidently culled from French periodicals: he set it up in relation to Late Antiquity, spoke of its 'self-consciousness', 'curiosity', and 'over-subtilizing refinement upon refinement', describing it as a 'disease of form' – the '*maladie fin de siècle*' (2014a: pp. 169, 170). When it came to locating decadence in space, however, Symons was more astute than his sources. While the examples he treated in detail were all French, or rather French-speaking – the Goncourt brothers, Paul Verlaine, Stéphane Mallarmé, Maurice Maeterlinck, Joris-Karl Huysmans – he closed the essay with a series of lightly sketched portraits that broadened its geographical remit: the Dutch Louis Couperus, the Italian Luigi Capuana and Gabriele D'Annunzio, the Spanish Emilia Pardo Bazán, and the Norwegian Henrik Ibsen, as well as English writers Walter Pater and W. E. Henley. Symons conceded that the decadent sensibility was more concentrated and thus more visible in Paris, where 'Decadence is in the very air of the cafés' (p. 177), but he also wanted to show that, in fact, it manifested itself simultaneously in many different countries, where it should not be seen, narrowly, as an imitation of French models but rather as a transnational network of ideas and authors, which of course included Symons himself. Indeed, Symons was clear from the start that decadence should be seen as '[t]he latest movement in *European* literature' (p. 169; my emphasis), quietly but firmly rejecting the proposition that decadence might have any exclusively national affiliation.

Before exploring in more detail this idea of decadence as a transnational network, it will be useful to establish more precisely what is meant by transnationalism. Sociologist Steven Vertovec has defined transnationalism as denoting 'sustained cross-border relationships, patterns of exchange, affiliations and social formations spanning nation states', a condition in which 'certain kinds of relationships have been globally intensified and now take place paradoxically in a planet-spanning yet common – however virtual – arena of activity' (2009: pp. 2–3). This definition was formulated within the field of sociology and against the historical backdrop of early twenty-first century theories of globalization. Nonetheless, it can be profitably transposed to the late nineteenth century, when increased international mobility and technological advances in travel and communication (including the international circulation of the periodical press) aided the process of formation of what we could anachronistically call the globalization of literature. Within this general trend, authors linked to decadence elaborated specific responses to the challenges of moving and working in a space that simultaneously ranged *across* nations and reached *beyond* the nation as an ideologically constructed marker of identity. This transnational re-orientation affected the decadents' taste, modes of production, individual identities, and what Vertovec calls 'patterns of exchange', i.e., the transmission of texts, critical alliances, solidarities, and forms of competition. In short, like Symons, decadents were aware of inhabiting a transnational field, and they knew that this very awareness formed a key constitutive element of their notoriously slippery shared identity.

The act of questioning national identity and national feeling was an important part of the decadents' ethos of transgression. When Théophile Gautier wrote that he 'should most joyously renounce [his] rights as a Frenchman and as a citizen to see an authentic picture by Raphael, or a beautiful woman naked' (1981: p. 39); or when Oscar Wilde threatened to 'take our letters of nationalization' to France if *Salomé* were refused a stage licence in London (1979: vol. I, p. 188), these half-joking remarks contained serious provocations to nineteenth-century concepts of citizenship and patriotism. They put forward the idea that literature could be a means of dissolving instead of building national cohesion, undoing the actual and symbolic borders of the nation in order to forge new loyalties and new identities. The transnational impulse of decadence was thus intimately related to its modes of dissenting from the bourgeois habitus and sexual morality, issues that have traditionally occupied critics.

In recent years literary scholars have become increasingly sensitive to the transnational dimensions of decadent literature, but by and large they have preferred to focus on cosmopolitanism, capitalizing on the philosophical connotations of this concept. In particular, Matthew Potolsky has seen nineteenth-century decadence as re-enacting the Enlightenment model of the republic of letters, in which authors' widespread practices of borrowing and expanding on each other aided the creation of a 'cosmopolitan community' (2013: p. 5). Potolsky notes that the decadents 'produced a remarkable number of collective manifestos and literary journals, but their interest in community is most powerfully evident in the themes and subjects of decadent writing, which look decisively beyond the frame of any localized national coterie to new and radically international frameworks for sociocultural belonging' (p. 7). For Regenia Gagnier, decadent individualism paradoxically developed alongside social, aesthetic, and scientific models of globalization, creating a 'tension of independence versus interdependence [which] constituted the anxiety of liberalism after a century of its development' (2010: p. 3). Late nineteenth-century theories of cosmopolitanism embraced by authors affiliated with decadence (Gagnier cites Friedrich Nietzsche and William Morris, among others) were the positive outcomes of these tensions.

Indeed, the transnational perspective gave decadent writers and their readers a new way of looking at the world and, with that, new insights into the aesthetic, ethical, and social dimensions of literature. The prefix 'trans', meaning 'across', 'through', or 'beyond', that describes the cross-border condition of transnationalism evokes the same element of fluidity that plays such a crucial role in decadent epistemology. As a phase of transition from one state to another, decadence denotes a process rather than an act of completion: it is a mode of becoming that opens up ideas and texts to transformative possibilities not only by stretching them in time but also by pushing them beyond the national contexts of their original formulations. The transnational dimension of decadence inheres in the two semantically related concepts of translation and transmission, both of which illustrate the importance of transnational space to literary practice.

Translation

Decadent authors did not approach translation as a demeaning activity or a utilitarian literary task aimed at financial profit. Rather, many of them saw translation as an essential part of their identity as writers and cultivated it as an important exercise in creativity and experimentation. Characteristically, therefore, decadent translations usually carried a level of meta-textual signification: they were not simply treated as a way of conveying effectively the meaning of an original text in a different language but as an opportunity to reflect on what it means to transfer literary material across languages and how that affects our understanding of literature more broadly. For this reason, decadent authors/translators often devised strategies that complicated an easy relationship between source and target texts, originals, and versions. Pater, for instance, embedded an extended translation from Apuleius' *Metamorphoses* within his historical novel *Marius the Epicurean* (1885). He set up the translation by making clear reference to a number of recognizably decadent tropes: Apuleius' book appears in a 'handsome yellow wrapper' and is 'perfumed with oil of sandal-wood, and decorated with carved and gilt ivory bosses' (Pater, 1910: pp. 55, 56); its fascination for Marius and his friend Flavian is anachronistically described as 'what the French writers called the *macabre*', glossed as 'that luxury of disgust in gazing on corruption' that makes some scenes from Apuleius 'worthy of Théophile Gautier' (pp. 60, 61). As Pater has his fictional characters read the 'original' Latin novel in his nineteenth-century translation, he superimposes not only the different decadent temporalities of Roman antiquity and the present but the different linguistic layers (Latin and French) and sensibilities that are contained within the deceivingly monoglot surface of his 'English' novel.

If we take Charles Baudelaire's foundational example, we can see that nineteenth-century decadence was truly born in translation. Baudelaire's two volumes of collected translations of Poe's tales, *Histoires extraordinaires* and *Nouvelles histoires extraordinaires*, were issued in 1856 and 1857, respectively one year before and in the very year *The Flowers of Evil* was published. The encounter with Poe, intensified and prolonged through the act of translation, aided the genesis of Baudelaire's own poetry and decadent sensibility. In an essay on Poe that introduced *Histoires extraordinaires* and that became a seminal document in the nascent history of modern decadence, Baudelaire showed how translation provided a platform to probe questions of national identity and international literary relations. He wrote passionately about how Poe's 'insatiable love of the Beautiful' (Baudelaire, 1986: p. 92) ran contrary to American national sentiment and therefore made him a foreigner in his own country. Baudelaire blamed Poe's marginalization on the materialism of nineteenth-century America, which he called 'a vast prison in which [Poe] ran about with the fevered restlessness of a creature born to breathe the air of a sweeter-scented world' (p. 70). This negative characterization, which has earned Baudelaire a reputation for anti-Americanism, only superficially set up a simple dichotomy between a materialistic and puritanical New World and an Old World which valued spiritual and artistic endeavours. In actual fact, Baudelaire constructed Poe as an alter ego to himself – a *poète maudit* who was at odds with modern social norms and a victim to bourgeois hypocrisy. In this respect, Baudelaire showed that their battle against bourgeois morality and provincialism made all decadents foreigners in their own societies.

In the preface to his second translation, *Nouvelles histoires extraordinaires*, Baudelaire further complicated the relationship between America and France. He still presented Poe's American background as an obstacle to his artistic success: American materialism, utilitarianism, and belief in progress were something that the poet must shake off in order to come to aesthetic maturity. At the same time, however, it was precisely the need to react violently to these false ideals of modernity where they were most powerfully concentrated that made Poe's decadence compelling and exemplary. America therefore emerged, paradoxically, as a hospitable context for decadence – a concept, it is worth remembering, to which Baudelaire always attached artistically positive connotations. Poe's decadent works should be seen as 'scraps of ancient wisdom floating back to us from a country whence one would least have expected them' (Baudelaire, 1986: p. 97). That the New World could export decadence back to the Old World was a paradox that Baudelaire cherished, and that he was quick to turn against French critics who attacked decadence for contravening natural laws of progress:

> [W]hat the professional pundits have not considered is that in the midst of the movement of life some complication, some combination may occur which is absolutely undreamt of in their schoolboy wisdom. When this happens their inadequate vocabulary is found to be lacking, as in the case when a nation *begins* with decadence and starts off where the others leave off – a phenomenon which may well repeat itself with variations. (p. 94)

As the case of Poe showed, this compromised origin was the situation in the United States, a 'new literature' (p. 94) that emerged on the global stage already in a state of decadence, disrupting traditional literary historiography. Decadence thus also upset hierarchies between one nation and another, when it came to artistic achievements, as well as the very dichotomy between civilization and primitivism:

> [I]f you will compare modern man, civilized man, with primitive man, or rather a nation called civilized with a nation called primitive – in other words, with a nation lacking all the ingenious inventions which dispense the individual of heroism – who will not agree that the whole honour lies on the side of the savage? By his nature, by necessity even, he is encyclopedic, while civilized man finds himself confined within the infinitely narrow limits of his speciality. Civilized man has invented the doctrine of Progress to console himself for his surrender and decay;

> while primitive man, a feared and respected husband, a warrior obliged to personal valour, a poet in those melancholy moments when the declining sun bids him sing the past of his ancestors, comes closer to the fringes of the Ideal. (p. 99)

The transgressive potential of decadence became apparent to Baudelaire precisely through the transnational perspective his Poe translations opened up. Indeed, as Baudelaire's essays amply demonstrate, removing Poe's works from their national context in no way caused loss of value, but rather endowed them with new meanings and potentialities. Translation redeemed Poe's decadence by liberating his writings from the restrictive aesthetic and moral perspective of the nation that as a social and political structure was complicit in the ideals of progress, materialism, and bourgeois philistinism both Poe and Baudelaire decried. As he bitterly observed in conclusion:

> [T]he censure which bad critics mete out to good poets is the same in all countries. As I read that article [i.e., an essay on Poe in an American biographical dictionary] I seemed to myself to be reading a translation of one of those countless indictments drawn up by Parisian critics against those of our own poets who are most in love with perfection. (p. 110)

The case of Poe in America showed, in magnified form, prejudices that were also rife in France. The transnational alliance forged through translation thus opened up an extraterritorial space of artistic freedom – the 'sweeter-scented world' described in his first preface – where future decadent writers could now also claim citizenship.

In the 1880s, for Mallarmé the act of (re)translating Poe was therefore a rite of literary initiation. Mallarmé concentrated on different works, focusing on poetry where Baudelaire had focused on Poe's prose: his translations of 'The Raven' ('Le corbeau', 1875) and *Les poèmes d'Edgar Poe* (1888), both published with illustrations by Édouard Manet, reinscribed Poe's work within a new wave of decadent literature. Despite the difference in genre, Mallarmé's translations were palimpsestic texts that superimposed themselves onto Baudelaire's, building on their discourse of decadence and carrying it forward into the fin de siècle. Even more significant is the fact that the Poe of Baudelaire and Mallarmé then travelled back to the English-speaking world. So that when writers such as Wilde, Symons, and Vernon Lee waxed lyrical about Poe and drew on him in their works (e.g., Wilde's 'The Portrait of Mr. W.H.' and Lee's stories in *Hauntings*), it was no longer simply the American writer they were evoking but the one that had been made more precious by the French patina, the translated and de-territorialized Poe created by the French decadent poets.

In Britain, but also in Russian- and German-speaking Europe, the chain of translation went on. Symons and John Gray included within their collections of original English verse translations or imitations of Baudelaire and other French decadents, such as Arthur Rimbaud and Verlaine, encouraging an understanding of French poetry in relation to their own, deliberately blurring the boundary between the crafts of translation and poetic composition. In Germany, the young Stefan George brought out his translation of *The Flowers of Evil* in 1901, explaining that his motivation was not 'to introduce a foreign author, but the primal pure delight of creation' (1982–2013: p. 5, my translation): George effectively re-enacted Baudelaire's own journey into translation as an apprenticeship in poetic form. The same phenomenon was even more pronounced in Russia, where translating and imitating Baudelaire became almost an obsession for poets of the so-called Silver Age, including Konstantin Balmont, Valery Bryusov, and the symbolist Vyancheslav Ivanov (Wanner, 1996: pp. 73–100, 145–65). All these translations and versions of Baudelaire enabled poets from different linguistic and national backgrounds to forge a link to decadence and at the same time helped to *create* decadence as a transnational movement. Decadence has often been labelled a French phenomenon; however, these examples show that it would be more appropriate to speak of a translated or a translational phenomenon.

In the English-speaking context as in France, decadence created a new ambition and new horizons of expectation for translation as a literary form. Symons, for instance, called Baudelaire's translation of Poe 'better than a marvellous original' and put it on a par with his poems and prose writings (2014b: p. 165). These remarks occurred in a periodical essay (*Saturday Review*, 1907) that migrated into a new edition of *The Symbolist Movement in Literature* (1919) and eventually became the preface to Symons's own translation of Baudelaire's collected poetry and prose (1926). In a somewhat acerbic review, T. S. Eliot complained that Symons had 'enveloped Baudelaire in the Swinburnian violet-coloured London fog of the "nineties", turning him into "a contemporary of Dowson and Wilde"' (Eliot, 2015: pp. 74, 71). Eliot realized how important translation was in broadcasting a decadent sensibility and for that very reason branded Symons's work as outdated, keen as ever to distance himself from his decadent predecessors. In fact, Symons had long been using translation as a means to promote decadence in England, alongside his poetry and critical writings. His career as translator started in 1894 with Émile Zola's lurid naturalist novel *L'assommoir* [*The Dram Shop*] (1876), followed by Émile Verhaeren's play *Les aubes* [*The Dawn*] (1898) and the interpolated poems in D'Annunzio's *Il piacere* [*Pleasure*] (1889). At the turn of the century, when D'Annunzio was at the height of his international fame, Symons became his most prolific English translator, specializing in his dramas: he published versions of *La città morta* [*The Dead City*] (1900), *La gioconda* [*Gioconda*] (1901), and *Francesca da Rimini* (1903); he also composed unpublished translations of *La figlia di Iorio* [*The Daughter of Iorio*] (1903) and *La fiaccola sotto il moggio* [*The Light under the Bushel*] (1905). These were complemented by periodical translations of poetry by Mallarmé and Verlaine, including bilingual versions of Verlaine in Symons's own periodical *The Savoy*. In his introductions, Symons was always keen to show off his personal connections to foreign authors: he cited Verhaeren's letter of endorsement in the preface to *The Dawn* and even dedicated the translation of *The Dead City* to D'Annunzio himself, capitalizing on the function of translation as sealing individual and collective cross-border alliances.

In an 1864 letter to Théophine Thoré, Baudelaire explained his decision to translate Poe as an attempt to investigate an uncanny affinity: 'The first time that I opened one of his books I saw, with terror and rapture, not only subjects that I had dreamt but SENTENCES that I had thought and he had written twenty years earlier' (1906: p. 362; my translation). In the same way, Symons translated in order to uncover – almost recover – correspondences between foreign authors and his own work, weaving his vision and voice together with theirs. He gave away this process in his introduction to his late translation (1935) of Pierre Louÿs' Spanish novel *La femme et le pantin* [*The Woman and the Puppet*] (1898):

> Pierre Louys [*sic*] derived the title of his passionate and perverse *La femme et le pantin* (1898) from one of those caprices of Goya I saw in the same year in the Prado in Madrid. [. . .] I spent two months in Seville and I went every night to the music-halls. Spanish women have often all the subtlety of the flesh and that kind of spiritual subtlety which comes from exquisitely responsive senses. I recognized it in the mournful pallor and that long and immobile gaze which seems to touch one's flesh, like a slow caress; that cold ardour (which I find in Conchita [the femme fatale of Louÿs' novel]) which is the utmost refinement of fire. (Symons, 1935: pp. 13–14)

By blurring the line between Louÿs' fictional world and his own experience during his Spanish travels, Symons established a correspondence between their decadent sensibilities, expressed here in the characteristic fixation with the body of the female dancer. When he described Louÿs' style as 'refined to such a point of mysterious malice' and possessing 'the subtlety of *maquillage*, the symbolic corruption of [. . .] painted women' (p. 25), he might as well have been describing his own style. Translating Louÿs thus became a way into Symons's own poetics. Crossing boundaries between languages, Symons encountered the uncanny strangeness that lies at the heart of the process of domestication: by way of the other's drives and desires, translation opened up a path into one's own unconscious. Decadent translation became a means to psychological introspection.

Transmission

In Baudelaire's *The Flowers of Evil* the lyric 'Franciscae meae laudes' stood out for being the only poem in the collection not written in French. Baudelaire explained his choice of using Latin in a short note appended to the poem in the first edition:

> Does it not seem to the reader, as to me, that the language of the last Latin decadence – the supreme sigh of a sturdy being already transformed and prepared for spiritual life – is singularly apt to express passion as it is understood and felt by the modern poetic world? [. . .] In this wonderful language, solecism and barbarism seem to me to convey the negligence caused by a passion that forgets and mocks the rules. The words, taken in a new sense, reveal the charming awkwardness of the northern barbarian kneeling before Roman beauty. (1857: p. 125, my translation)

A love lyric addressed to a modern woman therefore doubled as a declaration of love for the Latin language, paradoxically better suited to express the emotional complications of modernity. The Latin Baudelaire admired was not the classical Latin of Catullus and Cicero, but the quite different idiom of 'the last Latin decadence' ('la dernière décadence latine'): a language of artificiality, freedom, and transformation that eschewed what Baudelaire saw as the fixity and academic pedantry of the classical ideal.

Stylistically, the principal characteristics of this decadent language were 'solecism' and 'barbarism' – two related concepts that Baudelaire employed very deliberately. Solecism, meaning the breach of syntactical rules, took its name from the ancient city of Soles in Asia Minor (now Turkey), whose inhabitants were notorious for mangling the Greek language as spoken by the Athenians. Barbarism described the practice of importing a foreign term or usage into language; it derived from the word 'barbarian' with which the Greeks denoted foreign peoples, i.e., peoples whose languages were different from theirs. Both could designate genuine mistakes or deliberate strategies to challenge and transgress the academic standards that regulate literary language. Both simultaneously create and erode the distance between native self and foreign other. Spatially, therefore, decadence takes literary language away from the centre (Athens and Rome, but also Paris), imagining it as a site of contamination: it is where north and south, west and east, barbarian and native meet; where beauty is emphatically not synonymous with purity, either as a linguistic or a moral standard.

After Baudelaire, panegyrics to late Latin antiquity became a fixture of decadent literature. In his preface to the 1868 edition of *The Flowers of Evil*, Gautier extolled the innovations of a 'language already veined with the green hues of decomposition and almost gamey in flavour of the Lower Roman Empire and the complex refinements of the Byzantine school' (1868: p. 17, my translation). He compared this rich idiom, unfavourably, to 'the fourteen hundred words of the dialect of Racine [which] are not enough for an author who has given himself the difficult task of rendering modern ideas and things in all their infinite complexity and multiplicity of colours' (p. 18, my translation). Not only classical Latin, but classical French was downgraded to the status of 'dialect' ('dialecte racinien'). Instead, Gautier promoted the ideal of a modern idiom that, like the Latin of Late Antiquity, would be capable of embodying the networked transnational modernity of the second half of the nineteenth century, where the metropolitan centres of the modern colonial empires – notably, of course, Paris – created the conditions for productive aesthetic encounters between different peoples, idioms, and traditions. In this sense the spatial imagination of decadence was inextricably bound to the imperial and colonial geographies of the period. But the decadent hostility towards purity and fascination with barbarism were also profoundly antithetical to the nationalist discourses that gathered momentum towards the fin de siècle (in the French context, these were exemplified by the foundation in 1891 of the nationalist *école romane*, which would in fact take Racine as one of its models). The decadents' well-known comparisons with the end of the Roman empire thus looked back to antiquity in order to conjure a post-national future, in which the emphasis on national character that had been such a driving force in romantic literatures all around Europe gives way to a search for the hybrid, refracted, corrupted, and openly derivative.

Decadence, in this sense, was primarily an economy of transmission rather than innovation. Wilde captured this principle in his critical dialogue, 'The Critic as Artist' (1891), where he put forward a vision of the history of art and literature as a continuous process of reworking and refining that erases any meaningful distinction between original and copy, writing and rewriting, creation and criticism. The critic was thus Wilde's best artist because he 'deals with materials that others have, as it were, purified for him, and to which imaginative form and colour have already been added' (2007: p. 154). With a characteristic relish for provocation, Wilde went all the way back to ancient Greece, commonly regarded as the origin of European culture, claiming that the Greeks were in fact 'a nation of art critics' (p. 142). They too were busy reworking pre-existing models. Repeating the anti-classical gestures of Baudelaire and Gautier, Wilde moved the epicentre of the classical tradition from Athens to Alexandria:

> The tendency of creation is to repeat itself. It is to the critical instinct that we owe each new school that springs up, each new mould that art finds ready to its hand. There is really not a single form that art now uses that does not come to us from the critical spirit of Alexandria, where these forms were either stereotyped, or invented, or made perfect. I say Alexandria, not merely because it was there that the Greek spirit became most self-conscious, and indeed ultimately expired in scepticism and theology, but because it was to that city, and not to Athens, that Rome turned for her models, and it was through the survival, such as it was, of the Latin language that culture lived at all. (p. 144)

Wilde chose Alexandria, once again a decentred location in the colonial and imperial geographies of Greece and Rome, because it did not have an original or native tradition but rather rose to prominence by creating the conditions for the circulation, appropriation, and mobility of uprooted cultural forms. Greece and Rome were preserved on foreign Egyptian soil, where they, according to a quintessentially decadent logic, both 'expired' and survived. Alexandria was, in short, the centre point of a revised, decadent model of literary history that does not operate according to a temporal logic of evolution through innovation but to a spatial one of transmission.

Transferring this model to the nineteenth century meant questioning the cultural value of originality placed on literature by readers and critics as perpetuating a chimerical notion of purity that had significant repercussions in the field of national identity politics: the romantic and post-romantic search for authenticity (which Wilde in 'The Critic as Artist' identified with William Wordsworth) brought writers to invest in the native or local and thus allegedly unadulterated – in linguistic as well as thematic terms – leading to a hardening of the border between different national traditions. The decadent emphasis on the networked text, by contrast, placed the highest value on literature when it was at its most connected and impure, imagined as part of a transnational continuum in which borders between languages and traditions were highly porous. Indeed, in 'The Critic as Artist' as in many of his writings, Wilde put this revisionary ideal into practice by borrowing liberally, and sometimes silently, from a large number of sources.

Wilde's most radical experiment with decadent textual transmission, however, came with *Salomé* (1893), the work in which his antipathy for the national partition of literature brought him to cross the linguistic border into French. *Salomé* did not try to hide its sources (Gautier, Huysmans, Gustave Flaubert, Maeterlinck, the paintings of Gustave Moreau) because it aimed to go beyond the concept of source or original altogether: it translated on the page the spatial logic of transnational decadence, where texts exist simultaneously in a condition of intensified proximity rather than in a relation of influence. Once again, the late antique setting in a cosmopolitan and religiously diverse periphery of the Roman Empire was far from accidental. To paraphrase Baudelaire, with *Salomé* Wilde became a barbarian kneeling before French beauty. Wilde's French – with its linguistic mistakes famously corrected by his Parisian symbolist friends – was the ultimate embodiment of modern decadent barbarism: it posited the literary as a transnational territory of mobility, contaminations, and loss of national character.

As Baudelaire had noted of America, decadence was not a prerogative of old nations. Italy, for instance, had only come into being as a unified state in the 1870s. Yet, fin-de-siècle Rome was home to a decadent literary subculture that identified as a neo-Byzantine movement, refashioning the traditional backward-looking attitude of the new Italian capital into a self-conscious form of avant-garde culture. So-called Byzantine Rome had its decadent magazine, *Cronaca Bizantina*, founded in 1881, which adopted as its motto a couplet by the extremely influential classicizing poet Giosuè Carducci, displaying it prominently on its cover: 'When Italy was ready it called for Rome, | but was given Byzantium instead' (my translation). Carducci ironically contrasted the vigorous and heroic ideal of ancient Rome with the belated, languorous, and chaotic model of Eastern Late Antiquity, which the decadents seized on as a more appealing mirror for Italy's literary modernity. In so doing, and in opposition to the prevailing nationalistic tendencies of the time, they also implicitly counteracted the expectation that modern Italian culture should be the embodiment of a national continuum that stretched from ancient Rome to the present; instead, they envisaged the literature of the newly united kingdom as a transitional space and a site of productive contaminations. The magazine occasionally featured high-profile foreign contributors with symbolist and decadent leanings, including Sarah Bernhardt, Vernon Lee, and Catulle Mendès; and its target readership was an urban bourgeoisie that saw the unification of Italy as an opportunity to become more European and international. *Cronaca Bizantina* sought to encapsulate the new cosmopolitanism of the fin de siècle by mixing literary content (there was a strong focus on foreign literatures) with reportage on fashionable high society, resulting in what has been negatively described as 'a sometimes detrimental mix of high literature and sensationalist journalism' that determined the magazine's short life span of five years (Green, 2016: p. 545).

D'Annunzio, who was first contributor and then editor of *Cronaca Bizantina*, captured the atmosphere of the Byzantine Rome of the fin de siècle in his decadent novel *Pleasure*, where he depicted the new Italian capital as cosmopolitan in outlook, taste, and social habits. There was even something deliberately oriental in D'Annunzio's vision of Rome, which appeared to the eyes of the protagonist as 'entirely golden like a city of the Far East, under an almost milky sky, as diaphanous as the heavens mirrored in the southern seas' (2013: p. 37). This brief description captures the palimpsestic technique of D'Annunzio's Byzantine style, which distanced the reader from reality by interpolating multiple layers of literary and artistic references. The milky and diaphanous aesthetics evoked by D'Annunzio were probably a reference to James McNeill Whistler's artistic practice of transforming modern European cityscapes by viewing them through the representational conventions of Japanese art. By taking on this new Japanese look, D'Annunzio's Rome became a bit more like London and Paris: a de-nationalized space where foreign traditions crossed and melted into new forms. The novel itself changed shape and apparently increased in aesthetic value in the course of its international circulation, D'Annunzio refashioning its structure for the French translation by Georges Hérelle and then declaring to his English translator, Symons, that he was 'sorry' that Symons 'had read it in Italian rather than in French' (Symons, 1898: p. v).

D'Annunzio borrowed liberally not only from visual artists but from other writers, in *Pleasure* and throughout his works. The result was a literary mosaic that again recalled the aesthetics of Byzantine art and its practices of creative eclecticism, or Wilde's Alexandrian ideal in 'The Critic as Artist'. Needless to say, what decadent writers construed as transgressive acts of literary innovation could be interpreted by others as a breach to the literary rules of good practice. Both Wilde and D'Annunzio were openly accused of plagiarism. And at the same time – it is the very simultaneity of the accusations that is significant – they were both attacked for adopting foreign perspectives and writing, as it were, from outside the nation: Wilde as an Anglophone author who defected to France or as an Irish subject who climbed up the social ladder of literary London; D'Annunzio also as a foreigner trying to write in French and even, referring to his provincial origins in the rural Abruzzi, as 'the child of a semi-barbarous race' (Praz, 1954: p. 386) who stepped into the civilized culture of Florence and Rome as a foreign territory. In his seminal study of European decadent literature, Mario Praz built his whole picture of D'Annunzio around this idea of barbarism: D'Annunzio was 'like a barbarian who, exalted all at once to the throne of Byzantium, covers himself with all the jewels he can lay hands on' (p. 386). In this reading the bejewelled, archaic, and extenuatingly precious literary Italian characteristic of D'Annunzio's novels was a device by means of which the decadent writer turned his own mother tongue into a foreign language.

Despite his sharp judgements, Praz admired decadent authors and internalized their ways of thinking and looking at the world in his own writings, which projected the decadent sensibility into the second half of the twentieth century. Anti-decadent critics, however, could mobilize this line of argument in favour of open or covert nationalist ideology. Nowhere is this more blatant than in Max Nordau's *Entartung* [*Degeneration*] (1892–1893), where attacks on the allegedly pathological character of literary decadence went hand in hand with repeated accusations of plagiarism (directed at Richard Wagner, Nietzsche, Maeterlinck, and Herman Bahr, among others), and even plagiarism of plagiarism. Nordau reread the transnational cross-fertilization enabled by literary of decadence in perverse terms, as a network of contagion. In a sense, the real *bête noire* in *Degeneration* was the accelerated internationalization of literary culture: as literary content passed from nation to nation, leading to a global or at least pan-European economy of transmission, decadent writers allegedly lost touch with their domestic readers and were no longer subjected to the restraining influence of national character. Although Nordau never said so explicitly, the antidote to decadence was a hardening of the borders that protected inherently healthy nations against weakening foreign influences. Fears of miscegenation and of the transnational circulation of literature merged in this phobic vision.

It is important to remember that not all phenomena associated with literary decadence were transnational in orientation; and indeed that the liberal ethos that has been the focus of this essay would be put to a severe test when the work of some of the cosmopolitan authors analysed here, notably D'Annunzio and George, was subsumed into the chauvinist nationalist agenda of right-wing totalitarian ideologies. Yet, it is undisputable that, at the turn of the twentieth century, decadent writers were at the vanguard in finding new models for understanding and practising literature beyond the framework of the nation. Their experiments with literary translation and transmission aided the internationalization of literature at the fin de siècle and offered deliberate or indirect counterarguments to ideologies of nationalism. Today, recognizing the transnational orientation of decadence should encourage us to adopt transnational and comparative approaches aimed not only at recovering specific links that are difficult to see when working within a sealed national tradition, but also at providing a broader theoretical understanding of the radical logic of entanglement that defines the aesthetic and political mission of literary decadence.

References

Baudelaire, Charles (1857). *Les fleurs du mal*, Paris: Poulet-Malassis et de Broise.

Baudelaire, Charles (1906). *Lettres, 1841–1866*, Paris: Société du Mercure de France.

Baudelaire, Charles (1986). *The Painter of Modern Life and Other Essays*, Jonathan Mayne, trans., New York: Da Capo.

D'Annunzio, Gabriele (2013). *Pleasure*, Lara Gochin Raffaelli, trans., New York: Penguin.

Eliot, T. S. (2015). Baudelaire in our Time. In Ronald Schuchard, et al., eds., *The Complete Prose of T. S.* Eliot. *Vol. III: Literature, Politics, Belief, 1927–1929*, Baltimore, MD: Johns Hopkins University Press, pp. 71–82.

Gagnier, Regenia (2010). *Individualism, Decadence, Globalization: On the Relationship of Part to Whole, 1859–1920*, Basingstoke: Palgrave Macmillan.

Gautier, Théophile (1868). Charles Baudelaire. In Charles Baudelaire, *Les fleurs du mal*, Paris: Michel Lévy, pp. 1–75.

Gautier, Théophile (1981). Preface. In *Mademoiselle de Maupin*, Joanna Richardson, trans., London: Penguin, pp. 19–53.

George, Stefan (1982–2013). *Sämtliche Werke. Vol. XIII: Baudelaire, Die Blumen des Bösen, Umdichtungen*, Stuttgart: Klett-Cotta.

Green, Vivien (2016). Byzantium and Emporium: *Fine secolo* Magazines in Rome and Milan. In Peter Brooker, Sascha Bru, and Andrew Thacker, eds., *The Oxford Critical and Cultural History of Modernist Magazines. III: Europe 1880–1940*, Oxford and New York: Oxford University Press, pp. 536–59.

Pater, Walter (1910). *Marius the Epicurean: His Sensations and Ideas.* Vols. II and III of *The Complete Library Edition of the Works of Walter Pater*, 10 vols., London: Macmillan.

Potolsky, Matthew (2013). *The Decadent Republic of Letters: Taste, Politics, and Cosmopolitan Community from Baudelaire to Beardsley*, Philadelphia: University of Pennsylvania Press.

Praz, Mario (1954). *The Romantic Agony*, Angus Davidson, trans., Oxford and New York: Oxford University Press.

Symons, Arthur (1898). Introduction. In Gabriele D' Annunzio, *The Child of Pleasure*, Georgina Harding and Arthur Symons, trans., London: Heinemann, pp. v–xii.

Symons, Arthur (2014a). The Decadent Movement in Literature. In *The Symbolist Movement in Literature*, Matthew Creasy, ed., Manchester: Carcanet, pp. 169–83.

Symons, Arthur (2014b). Charles Baudelaire. In *The Symbolist Movement in Literature*, Matthew Creasy, ed., Manchester: Carcanet, pp. 165–7.

Symons, Arthur (1935). Introduction. In Pierre Louÿs, *The Woman and the Puppet*, Arthur Symons, trans., London: Butterworth, pp. 13–31.

Vertovec, Steven (2009). *Transnationalism*, London and New York: Routledge.

Wanner, Adrian (1996). *Baudelaire in Russia*, Gainesville: University Press of Florida.

Wilde, Oscar (1979). The Censure of *Salomé*. In *Oscar Wilde: Interviews and Recollections*, E. H. Mikhail, ed., 2 vols., London and Basingstoke: Macmillan, pp. 186–9.

Wilde, Oscar (2007). The Critic as Artist. In Josephine M. Guy, ed., *The Complete Works of Oscar Wilde. Volume 4: Criticism*, Oxford and New York: Oxford University Press, pp. 123–206.

CHAPTER 20

Decadence and Modernism

Gerald Gillespie

The period from the second half of the nineteenth century through the first half of the twentieth is remarkable for the number of artistic and literary movements in Europe and the New World. Sometimes announced by manifestos, sometimes named in serial acts of retrospection, these movements overlapped, yet were understood as both the successive and cumulative chapters of a major shift in Western culture loosely called modernism. The term 'modern' first gained currency in the 1400s but came to carry today's range of meanings only in the last two centuries. Other designations for significant trends in cultural history had meanwhile established themselves, most notably, the Renaissance as successor to the Middle Ages and the Enlightenment as successor to the Renaissance. Thus, the general idea of the 'modern' remained available as a kind of container term for the dynamic plethora of trends that followed from the end of the eighteenth century onward, including all the varieties of romanticism. In the profusion of creative impulses leading up to and following 1900, certain cultural themes often labelled 'modernist' are sometimes more prominent, whereas at other times they may continue as peripheral elements in some other cultural constellation. When 'modernism' began to take hold as a label for newer forms of consciousness and artistic expression, the term served as a catch-all for a tangle of initiatives crossing the threshold into the twentieth century.

The story of the term 'decadence' is somewhat analogous to that of 'modernism'. The concept of providential supersession in history was thoroughly woven into the Western cultural fabric through the influence of the Bible, with the Old and New Testaments leading to a host of derivative texts. The elaboration of a secular revision of biblical history was advanced in the Enlightenment. Edward Gibbon's *The History of the Decline and Fall of the Roman Empire* (1776–1789) is among the preeminent treatments correlating the rise of Christianity with historical decline, whereas the high romantic theorist Novalis' *Die Christenheit oder*

Europa [*Christianity or Europe*] (1801) seeks to restore balance by understanding the central role of the Christian belief system in European history in a series of major crises over the centuries, culminating in the disorders of the revolutionary era. G. W. F. Hegel's influential treatise *Phänomenologie des Geistes* [*Phenomenology of Spirit*] (1807) replaced the idea of providential guidance with the concept of history as a dialectical process. After Karl Marx famously claimed in the 1840s to have thoroughly secularized this concept as 'dialectical materialism' and posited a final solution to social problems through communism, the nihilist anarch Max Stirner, the founder of atheistic existentialism, ridiculed both communist millenarianism and modern humanism in *Der Einzige und sein Eigentum* [*The Ego and its Own*] (1844) as mere superstition. Slowly percolating under the Hegelian shadow in Europe was the key work of another philosophic atheist, Arthur Schopenhauer's *Die Welt als Wille und Vorstellung* [*The World as Will and Representation*] (1818), which would enjoy enormous resonance in the later nineteenth century and beyond.

Concern about cultural decline and desire for cultural rejuvenation were deeply ingrained habits well before the nineteenth century. After the tumultuous events stemming from the French Revolution and the Napoleonic period, it is hardly surprising that many writers would construe aspects of their own times as 'decadent'. Hence, alongside 'modern', 'decadence' emerges as a second useful container term for the profound sense of breakup and change during the late nineteenth and early twentieth centuries. But decadence also became a primary designation that artists and critics specifically applied to a predominant strain in art and thought from about 1880 to 1910. This strain was not monothematic but rather constituted a spectrum of attitudes during a period of dynamic change.

i

The very richness of the age challenges us not to simplify the cultural picture because the development of various arts, fashion waves, and social and class roles is not at all neatly coordinated, either within particular nations or across Europe as a whole. Architecture, sculpture, painting, and music were not neatly aligned with one another, let alone with literary production. Moreover, the breakthrough of romantic modes occurred somewhat earlier in Germany and England than in France, while neoclassical sympathies remained relatively stronger in the Netherlands, Italy, Spain, Scandinavia, and Russia. As Virgil Nemoianu has elaborated (1984 and 2006), the process of stocktaking and consolidation of cultural benefits across Europe were enormously important after the Napoleonic period. The sheer pace of transformation in the nineteenth century can also be seen as attaining an oppressive force, leaving old romantic hopes in the dust, as in Gustave Flaubert's novel *L'éducation sentimentale* [*Sentimental Education*] (1867). In starker contrast, Feodor Dostoevski's widely influential last novel *Bratia Karamasovi* [*Brothers Karamozov*] (1880) rejected the Western European heritage as corrupted in the revolutionary period and favoured a distinctly Christian pathway for Russia. In effect, the nineteenth century engaged in a vigorous debate about the future direction of the modern age. With the disturbing new doctrine of evolution already in mind, in the tragedy *Cain* (1819) Lord Byron had already posited the human struggle as a heroic response to the curse of existence, whereas in *The Martyrdom of Man* (1872) the Victorian philosopher and anthropologist Winwood Reade accepted not only the heroic role thrust upon modern humanity, but also the imperative of struggling for progress. As we learn from Max Stirner's disciple John Henry Mackay in the novel *Die Anarchisten* [*The Anarchists*] (1891), waiting alongside the purer moral anarchs in the shadows of Victoria's Jubilee in London is a cluster of various European and New World terrorists and revolutionaries who want to bring the whole system down. Among the markers which underscore the intensifying cultural atmosphere in the final decade of the nineteenth century are the collapse into dementia of Friedrich Nietzsche in 1889, whether from syphilis or a brain tumour, and the imprisonment of Oscar Wilde for gross indecency in 1895. Both men died in 1900.

The unsettling example of Nietzsche's end only enhanced contemporary interest in his rugged philosophic discourse about modern culture on the threshold of high modernism. If his avowed purpose was to 'correct' the aesthetic atheist Schopenhauer, in effect his broader message emphasized that a spiritual transformation was imperative, since European civilization was in the late and final throes of an epochal disintegrative crisis. This was spelled out initially in the polemical treatise *Die Geburt der Tragödie aus dem Geist der Musik* [*The Birth of Tragedy out of the Spirit of Music*] (1872). Nietzsche's shift into a psychological analysis of culture over the ages was significant. In his view, cultural achievement fluctuated according to the relationship between two inherent twinned capacities of the human mind, the Dionysian ('feeling') and the Apollonian ('shaping'). The Greek golden age had enjoyed creative equilibrium briefly, and the European Renaissance had exhibited such promise. In the longer run, however, through its imbalanced fostering of weakness, the Christian era was devolving into decadence. Nietzsche's radical move, as in the treatises *Jenseits von*

Gut und Böse [*Beyond Good and Evil*] (1886) and *Zur Genealogie der Moral* [*On the Genealogy of Morality*] (1887), was to posit the natural prerogative of the creative and strong human being to achieve both material and emotional fulfilment, and to rise above the counterforces of societal control, especially the influence of religion. In such works as the philosophical novel *Also sprach Zarathustra* [*Thus Spake Zarathustra*] (1891) and the posthumously published treatise *Der Wille zur Macht* [*The Will to Power*] (1901, 1906), he promoted the concept of the superior being or cultural champion, the *Übermensch* [superman]. Unfortunately, the Nazi movement appropriated Nietzsche's celebration of the superman for its own purposes. One of Nietzsche's most ingenious moves as a philosopher was to picture himself, as of the *Genealogy* onward, as knowingly a 'nihilist' on a higher plane who rejoiced in the creative challenge, whereas the decay of Christianity was producing a life-denying, unacknowledged nihilism. By embracing a defiant existential nihilism, he conjured for modernism a heroic alternative of creativity.

ii

Arrival at the fin de siècle is not something simple to define. The persistence of romantic themes and motifs into the later nineteenth century does not mean that neoromantic trends simply replicated the past. There was a perceptible, though gradual, shift during the nineteenth century away from the broad-based romanticism of the 1790s–1830s, which included empathetic exploration of earlier cultural history and diverse folkways in addition to more elevated Renaissance and Enlightenment emphases. The drift was increasingly towards interest in elite figures and attitudes within societies. Examples include the French novelist Stendhal, the mid-century English author Charles Dickens who imbues lower-class figures with sentimental value, and the Swiss writer of historical fictions Conrad Ferdinand Meyer who elevates the sentimental stature of protagonists of widely diverse past moments in European culture. In retrospect, readers today may find it curious how key elements of gothic story forms (e.g., a curse, a demonic double, baleful superstition) initially blossomed during the transition from Enlightenment to romantic writing and, in addition to being parodied, then reappeared in pseudo-scientific dress in naturalist fictions (e.g., malign genetic inheritance, addiction, degeneracy), and survived in authors of high modernism. That writers would find it useful to borrow from motivic and thematic repertories for purposes not obviously tied to the generic stream in which such elements were earlier operating is nothing new in the annals of literature. What further complicates the picture of such a richly inventive age is that, when we choose 'decadent' as a label, we are electing a polyvalent term. It both has a general purpose not tied to a specific phase of history and it names a narrower cultural time frame and therewith associated dominant trends acknowledged by key authors. Depending on which artist or thinker we approach, 'decadent' during the fin-de-siècle transition into the twentieth century can range in tone from negative to positive, over a spectrum of positions in differing mixtures.

One of the works that pre-eminently presents the clustering of traits critics will label 'decadent' is Joris-Karl Huysmans's novel *À rebours* [*Against Nature*] (1884). Its neurasthenic noble protagonist Des Esseintes not only exhibits in naturalistic terms the societal and bodily heritage of cultural lateness and decline, but a hypertrophy of aesthetic ripeness and an acute consciousness of thinkers, artists, and poets, old and new, who excite his sensibilities. He sketches the primary pantheon of decadent lore. In his hermetic inner world he indulges in imaginary voyaging and finds art more interesting than nature as the chief exemplar of the beautiful and of cosmic values. He rejects all the supposed classic golden ages in favour of what has emerged out of the wreckage from the Dark Ages onward and for its own sake as just pure art. From the synaesthesia of his experimental new 'music' of sensations there evolves an impressionistic, associational probing of the contents of the mind that foreshadows the Proustian experience, in *À la recherche du temps perdu* [*In Search of Lost Time*] (1913–1927), of the tasting of the madeleine whereby a myriad of synaesthetic connections is unlocked.

Des Esseintes' admiration for symbolist works by the dream-like Gustave Moreau and Odilon Redon is one of numerous instances of the building of a new aesthetic and its canon. Not content to just read Charles Baudelaire, poet of *Les fleurs du mal* [*The Flowers of Evil*] (1857), Des Esseintes attempts to plumb the vices personally, before a spiritual longing begins to invade and he realizes that he yearns for something genuine in the European heritage that is virtually suffocated by contemporary life. He rediscovers precious aspects of the Middle Ages and also the counterculture of evil, although philosophically he prefers Schopenhauer as primary guide. The horror of organic nature and threats like syphilis increasingly unnerve him. Marcel Proust will later borrow from Des Esseintes the flower suggestive of evil, the 'cattleya' orchid, the motif associated with the vamp Odette in *In Search of Lost Time*. All the horrors peak in Des Esseintes' nightmare of the bestial lurid whore, a trope which will reappear, for example, as late as in Jean-Paul Sartre's existentialist novel *La nausée* [*Nausea*] (1938). Borrowing from Flaubert, Huysmans's protagonist develops a sense of woman as 'chimera' and 'sphinx' even as his indulgence in the flesh devolves from the actual world into artifices and the imagination. His last major foray is his touristic discovery of 'actual' Dickensian London in a Parisian tavern frequented by English people. His decision ultimately to withdraw from the world in spiritual isolation exhibits the frequent religious turn among decadents of the fin de siècle. The novel concludes with a deepening appreciation of figures ranging from the Marquis de Sade and the arch-romantic E. T. A. Hoffmann to a contemporary line-up headed by Baudelaire, and Des Esseintes ponders a new kind of symbolist novel modelled on the work of Stéphane Mallarmé. This suggestion of a new species of narration based on correlated jewel-like virtual prose poems will recur in Rainer Maria Rilke's novel *Die Auszeichnungen des Malte Laurids Brigge* [*The Notebooks of Malte Laurids Brigge*] (1910). In these examples, we observe decadence metamorphose into modernism.

If Des Esseintes, angry at the degradation of his own times, finally exiles himself from history, Auguste Villiers de l'Isle-Adam's aristocratic couple in the drama *Axël* (1890) trump the refusal of banal, vulgar existence in a far more hyperbolic exit. Both protagonists are of ancient noble lineage. Axël abjures access to special powers and fabulous wealth, while Sara with the courage of a Wagnerian heroine refuses subservience to religious vows; together they realize they are so wonderful that there is nothing further worth their bother on earth. Even though theirs is a disdain that is defiantly secular, they commit suicide in a virtually hieratic as well as aesthetic gesture. Countervailing the sheer flamboyance which decadence reached in *Axël* was a simultaneous peaking of hardened naturalist, positivistic attitudes, which burst onto the international scene in 1892–1893 with the publication of Max Nordau's treatise *Entartung* [*Degeneration*], soon translated into English, French, Italian, and Russian. Nordau epitomizes a harsh triumphalist positivism which is now bolstered by the breakthrough of psychology and psychiatry as clinical sciences in Western Europe. Nordau stigmatizes a host of well-received British, French, and German authors – many today canonical – as mentally impaired or deficient and rejects a large post-romantic repertory of themes and motifs as symptoms of societal illness and a threat to public health. Nordau finds especially offensive what he detects as strains of mysticism in general, and notably in groups like the Pre-Raphaelites and symbolists whose work and human character he deems degenerate. He is appalled by innovative and experimental uses of language on the part of leading poets such as Mallarmé. Unrestrained and intemperate in his critical commentary, Nordau labels wide swaths of prominent writers by name as literally imbeciles or at best sick, however sophisticated. In short, Nordau serves as a hypertropic example of opposition to the deep cultural current of decadence that was feeding into modernism around 1900.

The most incisive depictions of new waves in the arts and literature often occur in retrospection. For example, by reading Flaubert's *Sentimental Education* and then the first two volumes of Proust's *In Search of Lost Time, Du côté de chez Swann* [*Swann's Way*] (1913) and *À l'ombre des jeunes filles en fleur* [*In the Shadow of Young Girls in Bloom*] (1919), we get to survey styles, trends, and cultural themes from the end of the Napoleonic period through the Revolution of 1848 and then to experience the second half of the nineteenth century densely packed with movements and manifestos. The oncoming central decades for decadence in the 1880s and 1890s are signalled by works such as Leopold von Sacher-Masoch's sensational *Venus im Pelz* [*Venus in Furs*] (1870), with its theme of the dominatrix. She will recur variously but unmistakably for many decades to come as, for example, Proust's Odette in *In Search of Lost Time*, Thomas Mann's Clavdia in *Der Zauberberg* [*The Magic Mountain*] (1924) and James Joyce's Molly in *Ulysses* (1922). It was not long before the broader neologism 'sadomasochist' linked Sacher-Masoch's name with that of the notorious Marquis de Sade. One of the prominent trends in the heyday of literary decadence was the use of biblical lore to depict the powerful realm of the flesh and senses, as in, for example, the exploitation of the Herodias and Salomé figures by such writers as Mallarmé, Flaubert, Wilde, A. C. Swinburne, and Guillaume Apollinaire. A major countertrend in literature, balancing accounts in favour of religion, was to contrast corruption in imperial Rome and the early promise of Christianity, as in the Polish author Henryk Sienkiewicz's international bestseller, the historical novel *Quo Vadis* (1895). As recalibrated for the decadent sensibility in Victorian Britain, the genre attained a high level in Walter Pater's *Marius the Epicurean* (1885), set in the Antonine empire of the second century CE, a time of fulfilment but uncertainty experienced as analogous to the modern fin de siècle.

Culminating in the core decades of decadence and into modernism, a fascination for the decaying city of Venice constitutes one of the most remarkable examples of widespread cultural focus on a complex symbolic entity. Venice became an important stop on educational voyages both for Enlightenment types, the romantics, and writers of the transition into the twentieth century; the number of foreign residents including many patrons of the arts increased markedly throughout the nineteenth century. Richard Wagner's prominent death in Venice in 1883 was a key marker underlying the title of Mann's novella of 1912. When the venerable Campanile of San Marco collapsed in 1902, devotion to decaying Venice was so strong that the iconic tower was rebuilt in an identical style within a decade. Rilke's modernist credo *The Notebooks of Malte Laurids Brigge* ends emotionally in Venice where Malte hears a Wordsworthian-like woman's voice singing in his native Danish. There were important secondary centres, such as Munich and Florence, and indeed the pre-eminence that Rome enjoyed as a world capital for artists well into the second half of the nineteenth century shifted extensively to Paris in the prelude to World War I. But Venice was somehow different in its very physical make-up, so that it could readily be perceived as a composite symbol of art and the Western will to form. Mann's novella *Der Tod in Venedig* [*Death in Venice*] (1912) stresses the city's physical vulnerability, being situated in marshes at a transactional border between the West and the East, symbolically on the edge where the Apollonian principle asserts itself heroically in the face of the Dionysian. Along with the leader of the British Arts and Crafts movement William Morris, Proust counted himself among key admirers of John Ruskin's influential treatise, *The Stones of Venice* (1851–1853). Ruskin analysed the many centuries of the city's rise and fall by reading the practice of the arts, above all, its architecture, as revelatory of its spiritual vitality. He divided the city's history into three grand episodes, the Byzantine, the Gothic, and the Renaissance, and was especially condemnatory of the Baroque tendency towards the grotesque, on top of Renaissance aridity that he thought had accompanied Venice's decline. Being prized by its foreign devotees, Venice served as an exemplar of a larger cultural life cycle that had finally lost genuine energy yet exhibited exalted achievements from its creative past. It was the perfect collective artefact to entrance Europeans obsessed once again with the spectacle of the passing of greatness. The Italian futurist Filippo Tomasso Marinetti heaped vituperation on efforts to restore Venice instead of modernizing it, but his contemporary Gabriele D'Annunzio counterbalanced that with decadent homage to the beautifully decaying city and supported Italian and international efforts to preserve it. In effect, the sophisticated Euro-American public had recreated Venice as a world inheritance (Pemble, 1996).

iii

The founding of key journals is an unmistakable indicator of the emergence of the concept of decadence as a complex of stylistic and thematic initiatives in the most highly developed large Western capitals, felt by many leading writers and artists as appropriate to the age. Paris led the way with *Le Décadent* (1886–1889) and London followed with *The Yellow Book* (1894–1897), whose more cautious title intimated autumnal ripeness, golden harvest, and decay. In between, the cultural idea quite naturally leaped the Atlantic to be explained to sophisticated Americans in Arthur Symons's article, 'The Decadent Movement in Literature', in *Harper's New Monthly Magazine* (November 1893). Further developments in the visual arts rapidly unfolded from the turn of the century onward, and some newer initiatives, such as Dadaism and expressionism, had important analogies in literature. While the cluster of impulses constituting modernism would continue well into the twentieth century, the eruption of World War I imparted a distinct sense of a catastrophic caesura in Europe. One province of prose literature which had already developed the capacity to represent the complicated repertories of deeply rooted cultures and their interactions within such a mammoth configuration as European civilization was the humoristic-encyclopaedic tradition in the novel, in the tradition of François Rabelais (1494–1553), Miguel Cervantes Saavedra (1547–1616), and Laurence Sterne (1713–1768). In this tradition, several of the greatest novelists of the first half of the twentieth century manifest encyclopaedic scope in rendering a composite picture of trends during the climax of modernism. Because their fame rests extensively on their attention to how aspects of European culture appeared during the heyday of decadence, the works of Proust (1871–1922), Mann (1875–1955), and Joyce (1882–1941) have a special relevance.

In *Swann's Way* and *In the Shadow of Young Girls in Bloom*, Proust charts the advent of modernism by painstakingly following his internal narrator Marcel's introduction as a youth both to new currents such as impressionism in painting and music and to the longer story of literature and the arts in France. The rich mixture of disturbing new cultural forces in Proust's novel does not yet include Nietzsche, but it does probe the power of music and Wagnerism. Marcel's gradual discovery of aspects of the ageing of complex cultural entities like a Gothic cathedral prepares us for the experience of a yet more involved construct like the city of Venice, that favourite cultural-historical reference of modernism. As Marcel matures, he deepens his appreciation of the cultural history of France and Europe and its contemporary legacy. He also encounters the sordid underworld of Parisian glamour in such institutions as homosexual bordellos and lesbian salons. Proust expands upon the thematics of contemporary decadence in later volumes, but programmatic decadence makes an early appearance most notably in the imposing personage of the baron Charlus, in whom a long aristocratic heritage defiantly asserts itself simultaneously in his homosexual deviance and his firm aesthetic views. *Le temps retrouvé* [*Time Refound*] (1927), the closing volume, includes the epochal experience of World War I and the strangeness of the passing of an era and of those who once defined it but who now are dying. Many years earlier, as a younger man, the narrator had noticed how the aged Princesse de Parisis, a famous hostess of the romantic era who had known many of the then leading lights in literature and the arts, was now rambling around the modern capital virtually unnoticed, like a relic of precious memories. Barely enduring World War I, a now ancient Charlus is outraged by the slaughter of handsome men and feels his kinship with Germanic nobles. (The French movie director Jean Renoir would reintroduce this latter motif as late as 1937 in the film *La grande illusion.*) Proust's narrator, now himself grown old as the war draws near, witnesses the bizarre saga of the eruption of death-dealing and the strangeness of Paris under air attack, surreal dream-like episodes which have their analogue in the new medium of cinema. The movie houses are like caverns in which classes merge in some mysterious primordial fusion (Gillespie, 2010: pp. 132–4). Proust does not suppress the complexity of the living culture of manifold impulses as he chronicles the emergence of modernism throughout *In Search of Lost Time*. Generations change, but the logic of new combinations and possibilities manifests itself in yet another iteration of evolving patterns.

Mann's first major triumph was his attempt in the novel *Buddenbrooks: Verfall einer Familie* [*Buddenbrooks: Decline of a Family*] (1901) to chronicle the downhill course from health, balance, and success taken by representatives of northern bourgeois society over the course of the nineteenth century. He lends a particularly Nietzschean twist to the grimly naturalistic story of how Wagnerian sickness invades Germany, when the appropriately named Gerda (as in Wagner's *Der fliegende Holländer* [*The Flying Dutchman*]) arrives with violin as the emissary of Dionysus, and soon music undermines the earlier stalwart but excessively Apollonian culture. The presumptive heir of firm and family, Thomas Buddenbrook, is too rigid, and he expires ominously when his tooth is pulled after his memories revive of having read Schopenhauer in his youth. The decay of the house of Buddenbrook climaxes in a feverish, ecstatic death by music, as his frail boy Hanno, the sole remaining male heir, rhapsodizes on the piano. Mann's novella *Death in Venice* starts from the Northern Cemetery in Munich when the Apollonian historian of heroic Western resolve, Gustav Aschenbach, feels attracted to Venice, the city set in a swamp and threatened by plague from the East. There eventually he will try like Faust to be rejuvenated and experiences a flamboyantly orgiastic Dionysian dream, but dies on the beach, watching the beloved ephebe Tadzio disappear into the water as if into the Freudian id. The novella opens explicitly under threatening skies, for Mann was concerned about the tense world picture on what soon proved to be the eve before the outbreak of the Great War.

In the war's aftermath, Mann wrote his admonitory novel *The Magic Mountain* which follows the young middleclass Hamburg engineer Hans Castorp through seven years of threat by sickness in a cosmopolitan Swiss sanatorium up to the war's outbreak. A cosmopolitan mixture of sick people have gathered there, mostly to die despite treatment, including Hans's alter ego, his beloved cousin Joachim, a decent Prussian officer who exemplifies the endangered Apollonian culture. Hans starts quite actively to explore fields of learning in the sciences and humanities; he becomes increasingly aware of cultural values and ultimately reintegrates music as part of his most precious human heritage. *The Magic Mountain* ends with Hans returning to the struggles in the lowlands as World War I erupts, but still resisting the lure of death against which he turned resolutely in the novel's famous 'Snow' chapter. The novel is structured as the deeper re-education of Hans. We readers are privileged not only to witness debates about life and culture over the ages by antagonistic spirits like the revolutionary bourgeois Settembrini and the Jesuit of Jewish origin Naphta, in whom are bundled strands of history over the millennia, but also to eavesdrop on Hans's own evolving reactions and emotional and intellectual growth as a humane person. The sanatorium intensely concentrates modern sickness in both real and figurative terms, and through Hans's sojourn it becomes the epicentre of the ideological and even evolutionary contestation which causes the world explosion of 1914. In facing the reality of suffering and sickness, physical, mental, and societal, Mann turns the mighty arsenal of past art and thought in the favour of life by positive reflection and action. Mann published *The Magic Mountain* during a period when as a public figure he was actively proposing in lectures and opinion pieces that defeated Germany should re-align itself with the major Western democracies as the way to a sane future. Through its suggestive encyclopaedism as a gateway to the myriad of subjects, experiences, and attitudes that elevate life over sickness, his novel – an admonitory post-mortem on the catastrophic Great War – has long outlasted the endangered public at whom it was first aimed.

Starting from his early years, Joyce was concerned over 'decadence' very specifically as the blighted cultural condition of his homeland Ireland. That did not prevent him from striving, at times exhibitionistically, for mastery of newer styles; for example, some passages in *A Portrait of the Artist as a Young Man* (1916), conveying the protagonist Stephen Dedalus' adolescent religious ecstasies and terrors, and his fantasies of being hallowed in the priesthood after spiritual struggles, attain a lushness reminiscent of the poetic prose of the older Italian literary decadent and political fascist D'Annunzio, while the book's general tone recalls the intensity of the heightened prose of Pater. Eventually Stephen Dedalus' travails give way in Chapter five of *Portrait* to a musical awakening from a 'dream poem' about creation '[i]n the virgin womb of the imagination' (Joyce, 1964: p. 217) as the Irish student begins to realize his calling as a writer and soon ventures forth in exile. In *Ulysses*, we re-encounter the maturing Stephen who is back in Dublin where he meets the Jewish businessman Leopold Bloom and Leopold's wife Molly. Stephen will depart again into life through their garden gate under a propitious Dantesque starlit sky, a symbolic passage of (re-)birth. But he like the Blooms ceases to appear further in Joyce's new magnum opus developed over a score of years, *Finnegans Wake* (1938). Joyce initially views the problem of decadence as not just culturally but also socially and politically oriented to Ireland's subordinate status under imperial Britain and in the grip of Catholicism, both experienced as stultifying in the *Portrait* and *Ulysses*. But thematically decadence becomes dispersed to the point of disappearance in the *Wake*. That is, Joyce projects the story of human achievement and decline onto a neo-mythological plane and recasts Ireland as a focal point where cosmic principles play out in a grander scheme. Although the *Wake* carries an enormous repertory of allusions to contemporary and more proximate historical matters, it is designed to suggest an enormous evolutionary process by which humanity became what we now perceive in history. The *Wake* seeks to capture this process within the governing framework of stages in the completion of a great cycle as conceived by the eighteenth-century anthropological philosopher Giambattista Vico in the *Scienzia nuova* [*New Science*] (1725). Hence, however many their variants and instantiations, the *Wake*'s key characters are now a symbolic basic family, the father and mother, a pair of antagonistic yet complementary sons, and a set of daughters – a panoply which we are invited to correlate to foundational Near-Eastern myths and scriptures, including biblical lore. Furthermore, Joyce deliberately pushes the narrative centre of gravity of basic paradigms back towards the primordial beginnings of Ireland, well before the arrival of St. Patrick and Christianity. Thereby the story of an older dynamic Ireland suffuses and liberates the present; modernity is effectively re-construed as a period of breakup and creative re-beginning. Joyce borrows from some eighty languages to gin up his own transmogrified English with multilayered puns and allusions in order to underscore that *Finnegans Wake* is a universal tale of becoming and rebirth and not just a paean to Ireland.

It is tempting to examine the essentially 'postmodern' *Wake* further, but in a stricter historical perspective *Ulysses* contains Joyce's major retrospection on the creative period or heritage labelled decadence as a prominent part of modernism. It starts from Stephen's worried thoughts about his own role, continues through Bloom's deconstructive thoughts about his world, expands into an enormous phantasmagoric symposium in the 'Circe' chapter set in the brothel district known as Nighttown, and indirectly arrives at an answer to life in Molly's famous interior monologue that closes with her affirmation, the word 'Yes'. Although *Ulysses* is extraordinarily complex underneath its simple structure of events of a single day and night in Dublin, Joyce's overt layering of a wealth of referentiality makes his novel more readily accessible as a modernist palimpsest. Joyce in *Ulysses* brilliantly melds Homeric narrative, Shakespearian plot, and Dantesque design and correlates this combined heritage meaningfully with the roles of his contemporary Irish protagonists (Weir, 2015). To that master framework we can add Joyce's unacknowledged rivalry with the non-Christian Goethe's *Faust*. Goethe's colossal palimpsestial example was simply too close for comfort for the ambitious Dubliner. It was bad enough that in *Wilhelm Meisters Lehrjahre* [*Wilhelm Meister's Apprenticeship*] (1795–1796) Goethe had already portrayed the title hero as suffering a deep psychological crisis in trying to stage Shakespeare and to play the role of Hamlet. Through its unique structure of contextualizing prologues in the tradition of the baroque world theatre and its stylistically independent parts I and II, Goethe's *Faust* had already achieved the incredible feat of combining a sweepingly wide range of genres and arts. As of 1832, Goethe's modern *Faust* employed rapid shifts of focalization and a combinatory art of quotation, while it investigated forces in cultural evolution over many millennia, ending in the final mystical vision of a transcendent principle, the 'Eternal Feminine', that echoed Dante's summation in the *Divine Comedy*. The enormous 'Circe' chapter, which in some respects resembles an independent synecdochic work inside *Ulysses*, can serve to illustrate Joyce's exponential recycling of Goethe's multi-referential phantasmagorias in parts I and II of *Faust* where poetic 'magic' (nominally directed by Goethe's theatre master Mephisto) plays a major role in marshalling themes and motifs and in engaging in ironic reflection on the nature of the enormous work in progress. Joyce demonstrates his own mastery in 'Circe' by updating *Faust* with contemporary materials from psychology, philosophy, and politics, and readily references such notables of modernism as Wagner, Nietzsche, Freud, and others, as well as recent discourse in Irish and European culture, and he blends all his own themes into the mix (Gillespie, 2002).

There are innumerable ways to regard the position which the great modern novelists take in retrospect towards the peaking of a thematics of decadence before World War I. Joyce expatiates on decadent traits with such encyclopaedic abandon in the 'Circe' chapter of *Ulysses* that they finally evince something absurd and mysterious in human nature, whereas in *In Search of Lost Time* Proust more tightly aligns decadent traits with the burden of personal character and societal malaise. Mann, in underscoring both medical and metaphysical aspects of decadence, links with Joyce and Proust at many points. And all three authors transcend mere scientific determinism by contextualizing the anxieties of their own times in the larger history of Europe and the human race. These prominent modernists reflect awareness of two basic polarities that emerged in the more narrowly defined decadent movement as it faced the fin de siècle. On one side of the spectrum was concern over disintegrative forces in the modern world and realization of the need to take spiritual and aesthetic shelter. On the other side of the spectrum was a sense of the imperative to harvest the gains which the opportunity of such a moment presented. In some cases, grappling with the felt reality of the collapse of a great civilization or its descent into mediocrity and banality elicited a heroic response. Linking all these insights was the sense of decadence as a kind of liberation (albeit perhaps also a species of martyrdom) at an axial moment in human affairs. A neoromantic renewal of appreciation of the Western religious and philosophical heritages flourished during the core years of decadence, but this reaction occurred alongside rampant deconstruction of cultural modes and widespread breakdown of confidence in the reality of personal rather than assigned identity. The rise of modern anthropology enabled a questioning of group identity as a stable universal, while simultaneously it furnished materials on earlier European and non-European mores for popular consumption via older and newer media, notably the cinema. The quickening pace of art manifestos at the turn of the century and the intensified proliferation of styles and modes of art, as World War I drew nigh, looked in retrospect like a parallel cultural explosion.

References

Gillespie, Gerald (2002). Harrowing Hell with Proust, Joyce, and Mann. In Jean Bessière and Sylvie André, eds., *Multiculturalisme et identité en littérature et en art*, Paris: L'Harmattan, pp. 305–17.

Gillespie, Gerald (2010). *Proust, Mann, Joyce in the Modernist Context*, 2nd rev. edn, Washington, DC: The Catholic University of America Press.

Huysmans, Joris-Karl (2003). *Against Nature*, Robert Baldick, trans., London: Penguin.

Joyce, James (1964). *A Portrait of the Artist as a Young Man*, New York: Viking Press.

Joyce, James (1986). *Ulysses*, Hans Walter Gabler, ed., New York: Vintage.

Joyce, James (2000). *Finnegans Wake*, Seamus Deane, ed., London: Penguin Classics.

Mann, Thomas (1988). *Buddenbrooks*, H. T. Lowe-Porter, trans., London: Vintage.

Mann, Thomas (1994). *Death in Venice*, Clayton Koelb, ed. and trans., New York: Norton.

Mann, Thomas (1999). *The Magic Mountain*, H. T. Lowe-Porter, trans., London: Vintage.

Nemoianu, Virgil (1984). *The Taming of Romanticism: European Literature and the Age of Biedermeier*, Cambridge, MA: Harvard University Press.

Nemoianu, Virgil (2006). *The Triumph of Imperfection: The Silver Age of Sociocultural Moderation in Europe, 1815–1848*, Columbia, SC: University of South Carolina Press.

Nordau, Max (1895). *Degeneration*, New York: Appleton.

Pater, Walter (1985). *Marius the Epicurean*, Michael Levey, ed., London: Penguin.

Pemble, John (1996). *Venice Rediscovered*, Oxford and New York: Oxford University Press.

Proust, Marcel (1992). *In Search of Lost Time*, C. K. Scott Moncrieff and Terrence Kilmartin, trans., London: Vintage.

Rilke, Rainer Maria (2016). *The Notebooks of Malte Laurids Brigge*, Robert Vilain, trans., Oxford: Oxford University Press.

Symons, Arthur (1893). The Decadent Movement in Literature. *Harper's New Monthly Magazine*, 87, 858–67.

Villiers de l'Isle-Adam, Auguste (1890). *Axël*, Paris: Maison Quantin.

Weir, David (2015). *'Ulysses' Explained: How Homer, Dante, and Shakespeare Inform Joyce's Modernist Vision*, New York: Palgrave Macmillan.

CHAPTER 21

Modern Prophetic Poetry and the Decadence of Empires: From Kipling to Auden

Chris Baldick

Literary history has in recent years been less inclined to treat the decadent literary tradition as a 'period' cul-de-sac and more inclined to rehabilitate it as a current contributory to the emergence of modernism. Decadence may now be redeemed in those terms as the essential preliminary raid against nineteenth-century bourgeois culture that cleared the way for that new dispensation. In this chapter, however, we set aside the academic construction of modernism, especially in its triumphalist presumptions (modernism as the destined apotheosis of all prior tendencies) and in its sectarian consequences (modernism as the sole authentic practice, all others being retrogressive). We shall instead be looking at the work of two non-modernist poets, Rudyard Kipling and W. H. Auden, after a preliminary glance at T. S. Eliot, recalling here that Eliot recognized – and published – Auden as the coming young poet, and that in the introduction to his *A Choice of Kipling's Verse* (1941) he significantly rebuked his contemporaries' habit of belittling Kipling's work.

We are concerned here not with a supposed literary revolution but with a continuity in the adoption of poetic subject-matter of a particular kind. Our object of study is a select body of early twentieth-century poems that concern themselves openly or allusively with the fates of empires and civilizations, especially with their fragility, decline, and disintegration – and so of course with their decadence. In these works, the decadent tradition persists under new twentieth-century conditions, not by echoing Baudelairean moods or manners but by rediscovering and reworking the underlying historical myth of *the* Decadence, which is the decline and fall of the Roman Empire, considered explicitly or implicitly as the model for the fates of all later empires.

There had been strong historical temptations for French writers in the wake of the double debacle of the Franco-Prussian War of 1870 and the Paris Commune of 1871 to imagine themselves as members of a doomed civilization under barbarian encroachment, as for instance in Paul

Verlaine's 1884 sonnet 'Langueur'; but in the half-century considered here, 1897–1947, world events pressed collapsing empires to the attention of writers on an unprecedented scale. This historical period opens with the Spanish Empire's loss of its last non-African territories in 1898–1899, continues in China with the overthrow of the last imperial dynasty, the Qing (1912), and then witnesses a conflagration of several Western empires in war and revolution: the Russian, Austro-Hungarian, Ottoman, and German, all in 1917–1919; it closes after the defeat of the Japanese Empire and with the major decolonization (India, 1947) that began the break-up of the British Empire. It should not surprise us that a few poets in such an epoch should have come forward with boldly 'prophetic' visions of a world order that they suggest, by reading the symptoms and auguries of the times, is undergoing general collapse.

Yeats and Eliot

Our academic canons recognize two early twentieth-century poems, both accredited as 'modernist' classics, as especially significant responses to the collapse of empires in the 1917–1919 phase of the period: W. B. Yeats's widely quoted 'The Second Coming' (1920) and T. S. Eliot's multiply allusive masterpiece *The Waste Land* (1922). The imaginative and poetic power of both poems rests in part upon their implicit yet audacious timeliness, their ability to rise to the tumultuous historic occasion. 'The Second Coming', though, names no particular contemporary event or historical process, the poem's apocalyptic resonance exploiting instead a sibylline vagueness as to what in its time is falling apart: nothing so specific as an empire or a social order, only the unidentified 'Things' of its famous third line. It can be guessed from the circumlocutory description of the Sphinx and the direct prediction of a coming birth at Bethlehem that we are approaching an epoch, in the stricter sense, at which the 2000-year Christian era will give way to its bestial opposite, as the poem's near-blasphemous title also implies. Yeats's poem does not invoke the fate of Rome, except by scriptural indirection in recalling and darkly inverting the epoch of the Nativity under the reign of Augustus. Yeats's conception of Antiquity in his other writings clearly favours Athens and Byzantium over Rome itself, for him merely a military power of no spiritual or artistic significance, although Rome's decline is alluded to in some late poems such as 'Meru' (1934) and again in 'Long-legged Fly' (1939), which begins: 'That civilization may not sink | Its great battle lost'.

The Waste Land is for many reasons an incomparable kind of work, but it still belongs centrally to the modern tradition of 'prophetic' verse, although without laying claim, as Yeats does, to visionary insight, nor even providing a single authoritative voice in which prophecies could be uttered. Rather, Eliot distributes oracular utterance among various named and unnamed voices – principally those of Tiresias, the blind Theban seer in the poem's third part and the unconvincing modern fortune-teller Madame Sosostris in its first, thereby casting the authority of oracles under ironic qualification. That process in fact begins with the poem's epigraph, quoted in almost-decadent style from the Latin and Greek of Petronius' *Satyricon*, in which the Cumaean Sybil herself expresses her wish for death. She, like all the poem's seers and witnesses, especially Tiresias, is accursed by the prolongation of her life, just as the persons, cities, and civilizations they witness seem to be blighted, surviving only in a half-life beyond their allotted span. Prophetic utterance appears not as privileged knowledge but as burden and affliction; accordingly, the blind Tiresias does not foresee the ills of the modern urban world: he foresuffers them.

We cannot here consider *The Waste Land* as a whole, except to remark that most critical interpretations of the poem agree that it addresses and defines the contemporary metropolis of 1920–1922 as doomed to repeat the accursed condition of ancient cities such as the Thebes of the Oedipus myth or the Carthage of Augustine's *Confessions.* London becomes the latest term in a succession of once-mighty cities whose power has crumbled: 'Falling towers | Jerusalem Athens Alexandria | Vienna London' (lines 373–5). Collapsing structures recur later and with more sinister proximity in the line derived from the children's song: 'London Bridge is falling down falling down falling down' (line 426). These features, taken with the poem's multiple motifs of drought, neurosis, and sterility, invite readers to take *The Waste Land* as a poetic augury of the decadence afflicting a city approaching its own fall. It might surprise us that Eliot's list of cities at lines 374–5 omits, perhaps on account of its very obviousness, the central case of Rome itself, although it could be remarked that Troy and Nineveh are likewise absent. Aside from its Petronian epigraph and some references to Ovid and Virgil in Eliot's notes, the poem's only overt Roman allusion is one late reference to 'a broken Coriolanus' (line 416) that remains unexplained. Eliot's thematic purposes require the typological forerunner of modern London to be not Rome but the Carthage of Augustine's unholy loves. The fate of the Roman Empire, including both its military exposure and its deepening Christianization, is then, as with

Yeats, to be recalled obliquely, here through Augustine's contemporaneity with Rome's collapse: the Christian bishop of Hippo had lived long enough to hear the appalling news of Alaric's sacking of Rome in the year 410 CE, and by the time of his death in 430 Vandal forces were laying siege to Hippo, going on to seize Carthage itself a few years later. Images of barbarian migrations encroaching upon the centres of civilization indeed arise just before the 'Falling towers' passage: 'Who are those hooded hordes swarming | Over endless plains . . .' (lines 368–9), at which point Eliot's notes refer us, via an essay by Hermann Hesse, to the chaotic state of Eastern Europe and thus to the Russian Revolution as the latest barbarian menace.

Kipling

Poetry in English in the period 1897–1947 is unusually rich in occasional poems that address moments of notable historical crisis. The examples still most celebrated now include Yeats's 'Easter, 1916' (1917) and Auden's 'September 1, 1939' (1939). Priority in that tradition, however, belongs to Rudyard Kipling, who had already made himself the master of occasional verse, and certainly its most widely read exponent, notably in his monitory poem about Queen-Empress Victoria's Diamond Jubilee celebrations, 'Recessional' (in *The Times*, 17 July 1897), and again in his verse response to Germany's invasion of Belgium in August 1914, 'For All We Have and Are' (again in *The Times*, 2 September 1914). In both cases, Kipling had addressed his large public in tones of solemn prophecy, specifically as the self-appointed prophet of the British Empire. It was indeed on the basis of his imperialism, and not despite it, that Kipling was able to exploit and powerfully reimagine the historical mythology of decadence.

Kipling had grown up amid family connections to English proto-decadent currents of Pre-Raphaelitism and Aestheticism, his Uncle Ned being the Pre-Raphaelite painter Edward Burne-Jones. Such links did not make Kipling a closet aesthete behind a philistine mask, but he still granted high respect to artistic work more refined than his own, notably the prose of Henry James and especially the poetry of A. C. Swinburne, whose metrical ingenuity indelibly marks his own verse. He also understood early that literature and art were respectable middle-class vocations, as in the case of his own father, an uncontroversial art teacher and museum curator. Accordingly, Kipling did not associate art with subversion, nor with decadence, which may be why we find him in 1895 attempting unsuccessfully to avert the dismissal of Aubrey Beardsley, a protégé of his Uncle Ned, from *The Yellow Book* by appealing directly to its publisher, John Lane (Lycett, 1999: p. 272). Kipling's devotion to the cause of empire being serious, he did not confuse inconsequential naughtiness on the part of marginal artists with genuine threats to the imperial order, such as those from Afghan or Boer riflemen.

Kipling did, however, believe that the British Empire, like the Roman, was susceptible to becoming rotten from within. The source of such rot, though, lay not among artistic minorities but in the dominant culture of the landed and educated classes, as codified by the great Public Schools and universities. For Kipling, it may surprise us to learn, the true decadents of his time were not the aesthetes but the athletic 'hearties'. Somewhat heretically in the context of imperial ideology, and in direct contradiction to Henry Newbolt's oft-quoted poem 'Vitaï Lampada' (1897), Kipling saw the playing fields of Eton not as a safeguard against imperial decadence but precisely as the problem. The most striking formulation of that view is another of his 'prophetic' poems, 'The Islanders' (also placed in *The Times,* 4 January 1902), this being the piece in which Kipling's much-quoted phrase 'the flannelled fools at the wicket or the muddied oafs at the goals' appears.

Prompted by recent British failures and inadequacies exposed in the Boer War, and specifically at the request of the National Service League, a new pressure-group calling for compulsory military service, 'The Islanders' sets out to urge upon the insular and sport-obsessed British the need for all young men to go through proper military training, as was already required in France and Germany. The poem tries hard to maintain the tone of an Isaiah or Jeremiah lashing his people mercilessly for backsliding into idolatry, in rather ill-fitting anapaestic hexameters of clearly Swinburnian derivation, right down to such rhyme-pairs as 'gods/rods' and 'whips/lips'. The 80-line poem proper (disregarding here the framing italicized lines added in 1919) begins:

> Fenced by your careful Fathers, ringed by your leaden seas,
> Long did ye wake in quiet and long lie down in ease;
> Till ye said of Strife, 'What is it?'; of the Sword, 'It is far from our ken';
> Till ye made a sport of your shrunken hosts and a toy of your armèd men.
> Ye stopped your ears to the warning – ye would neither look nor heed –
> Ye set your leisure before their toil and your lusts above their need.
> Because of your witless learning and your beasts of warren and chase,
> Ye grudged your sons to their service and your fields for their camping-place.
>
> (Kipling, 1993: p. 95)

Kipling had rebuked the British previously for their neglect and disparagement of their uniformed young men, as in the more popular ballad-monologue 'Tommy' (1890, originally titled 'The Queen's Uniform'), but had not until now expanded that complaint into such a sweepingly intemperate condemnation of institutionalized national decadence. In later lines, Kipling asks the sport-lovers of Britain whether they seriously expect to repel the next attempted invasion of their land with croquet-mallets or with dead pheasants; and his tirade culminates in a characterization of the British ruling class as 'Arid, aloof, incurious, unthinking, unthanking, gelt' (p. 97), that final term 'gelt' meaning castrated or emasculated. Not surprisingly, *The Times*, to which aggrieved cricket-loving readers wrote in complaint, distanced itself editorially from such excesses.

The terms in which Kipling characterizes British decadence in 'The Islanders' are explicitly scriptural in denouncing not only Indolence and Sloth (thus capitalized) but idolatry, the modern sport-cult being the latest Baal or false god. However, his historical conception of decadence as a creeping process of softening and emasculation is implicitly and almost inevitably a traditionally Roman one, drawing silently upon mythologies of decline formulated by poets (Horace, Juvenal) and historians (Livy, Tacitus, Suetonius) of the Augustan and post-Augustan ages. Suetonius had invited his readers to see connections between military defeats at the remote borders of the empire and the distractions of trivial entertainment or of vice preoccupying Rome and its imperial court. Kipling attempts likewise to trace the cause of humiliations overseas back to a culture of irresponsibility at home. The prevailing decadence of the imperial homeland is in turn diagnosed in his poem as the consequence of prolonged and leisured peace, and so of complacent failure to maintain military vigilance. In this respect, Kipling concurs again with Roman writers, notably Juvenal, who had blamed the moral corruptions of Rome upon peace and its attendant comforts and luxuries. The ideological genealogy of 'The Islanders' suggested here seems to be echoed in the poem's doctrinal core: its recommendation of temporary conscription for all young men is also recognizably 'classical', recalling, as every schoolboy of the time would know, the military obligations of warrior-citizens in the ancient city-states of Sparta, Athens, and of course Rome in its heroic Republican age.

'The Islanders' belongs to a phase of transition in Kipling's prophetic verse from Hebraic to Roman models and allusions. The earlier and certainly more dignified poem 'Recessional' presents itself as a hymn to the all-judging Lord God of Hosts, humbly recanting the boastfully complacent spirit, as Kipling saw it, in which the British had celebrated the success of their empire in the 1897 Jubilee. That poem's style is carefully stripped of Kipling's aitch-dropping colloquialisms and of his metrical Swinburnisms too, in its archaic diction and stately, unhurried rhythm. Its language is marked by phrases adapted, rather than directly quoted, from several biblical sources including Deuteronomy, Job, and Psalm 51. One of those sources is Paul's Epistle to the Romans, but there is nothing else 'Roman' about Kipling's hymn, which concerns itself not with decadence but rather with the ultimate prospect of the British Empire's obliteration, likened to the destruction of Assyrian and Phoenician powers long before the rise of Rome:

> Far-called, our navies melt away;
> On dune and headland sinks the fire:
> Lo, all our pomp of yesterday
> Is one with Nineveh and Tyre!
> Judge of the Nations, spare us yet,
> Lest we forget – lest we forget! (p. 82)

Five years later, though, Kipling's imagination, and along with it his prophetic verse, began to take a more consciously Romanized turn.

Once Kipling had settled in a rural mansion in Sussex from late 1902, he began to take an interest in archaeological traces of Roman Britain, then more widely in its history. He set to work diligently on Roman history, reading or re-reading Edward Gibbon's *History of the Decline and Fall of the Roman Empire* (1776–1789) and other sources. An early product of these interests is the short poem 'The King's Task' in Kipling's *Traffics and Discoveries* (1904), which summarizes the emergence of Saxon law and administration, but begins 'After the sack of the City, when Rome was sunk to a name' (1987: p. 143).

A more substantial result was a sequence of historical short stories, ostensibly for children, concerning a fictional British-born Roman centurion, Parnesius, who guards the border of the empire against Picts and Saxons on Hadrian's Wall in the late fourth-century: 'A Centurion of the Thirtieth', 'On the Great Wall', and 'The Winged Hats', all collected in *Puck of Pook's Hill* (1906). This set of tales comes accompanied, as was Kipling's habit when collecting his stories, by appropriate verses such as 'A British-Roman Song (AD 406)', 'A Pict Song', and the first stanza of the poem later extended as 'Rimini' (1912), the latter being a marching-song of homesick legionaries far from Rome. In a similar vein is the slightly later 'The Roman Centurion's Song' (1911), in which the speaker, a Parnesius-like figure although of earlier date (300 CE), has been ordered 'back' to

Rome, but decides that his true homeland is Britain. These works all have a double reference, legible under widely-assumed equivalences between the ancient *pax Romana* and the modern *pax Britannica*: ostensibly they describe events and persons of late Roman times while substantially they ventriloquize the attitudes of those who now serve at the outposts of Britain's Empire.

It was in this increasingly Romanized phase of his work that Kipling came to compose his most momentous exercise in prophetic verse, 'For All We Have and Are', at the outbreak of the 1914–1918 war. As in the earlier 'Recessional', Kipling's solemn style here is one of dignified simplicity, again seemingly scriptural in phrase, although the 'Commandments' invoked at lines 10 and 30 are again adapted (from Psalm 10) rather than directly quoted. A significant difference from 'Recessional', however, lies in the allusion by which 'For All We Have and Are' frames its crucial distinction between law-abiding and lawless peoples. That same distinction in 'Recessional' had been understood in biblical terms (from Romans 2:14) as that between God-fearing Jews within the Law and Gentiles outside it; but here it is recast in terms of Gibbon's account of the fifth-century Fall of Rome, now as a distinction between Roman citizens and invading barbarians. The immediate occasion of Germany's invasion of Belgium, its pillaging of Louvain and its campaign of deliberate *Schrecklichkeit* [frightfulness] towards Belgian civilians now shifts the focus of Kipling's fears for his empire from inner slackness to direct external threat.

The poem's fourth and most striking line, 'The Hun is at the gate!', condenses a complex historical allusion that of course casts the modern Germans as barbarian enemies of civilization itself, and so as outlaws on the international stage. (Kipling's next poem on this subject was indeed to be titled 'The Outlaws' (1914).) This allusion involves some historical inaccuracy, in that the original Huns had not been Germanic – as their rivals the Goths and Vandals had been – but probably of Central Asian origin; nor had they ever directly attacked the 'gate' of Rome but by their own migrations had pushed the Goths southward into Italy and the Vandals into Spain and North Africa. Nonetheless, Kipling's German-Hun parallel had seemingly been invited by a speech of Kaiser Wilhelm II's own, in which he had in 1900 asked his forces to show less mercy in suppressing the Chinese Boxer Rebellion than Attila the Hun had shown to his enemies. Kipling himself had thrown that simile back at Germany in an earlier, lesser-known poem, 'The Rowers' (1902), which refers to the German of that time as 'the shameless Hun' (2013: p. 1060). It was 'For All We Have and Are', however, widely reprinted because Kipling had renounced any royalties for it, that not only powerfully endorsed the British case that this would be a war for the survival of civilization itself but also fixed in the public mind the identification of Germans as barbarian destroyers. To Kipling's satisfaction, the 'Hun' usage came to be widely adopted by grateful newspaper sub-editors, propagandists, and speechmakers as a favoured ethnic insult; and it later came to be revived occasionally by both Winston Churchill and by Franklin D. Roosevelt during World War II.

Auden

The great inheritor and reinventor of the prophetic tradition in verse among the generations born within the twentieth century was W. H. Auden. This younger poet was neither a late decadent nor an heir to Baudelairean or symbolist traditions, nor indeed any kind of Francophile. Aside from his respect for a very few French literary heroes (Charles Baudelaire indeed among them, with Gustave Flaubert, Paul Valéry, and André Gide), he was largely indifferent to French culture. His decision to spend his post-university year 1928–1929 in Berlin rather than make the usual literary pilgrimage to Paris was a deliberate spurning of Francophilia, and one that helped redirect the interests – including interests in contemporary decadence – of his circle and his generation towards the German-speaking world, and so towards an alternative pantheon (Goethe, Marx, Freud, Rilke, Kafka). Having sampled the boy-bars of Berlin, he urged Christopher Isherwood to join him, the eventual result being the latter's 'Sally Bowles' (1937) and the other Berlin stories in which Isherwood presents the doomed condition of Weimar Germany under threat from political barbarism. (It was also Auden who had secured Isherwood a commission to translate Baudelaire's *Journaux intimes*, for which Eliot's 1930 essay on Baudelaire was written as the introduction.)

From the time of Auden's emergence as the young poetic prodigy of 1930, it was clear that he was a new kind of enigmatically oracular or 'prophetic' poet, his early work being distinguished by its repeatedly ominous suggestions of looming catastrophe and by its tendency to read auguries of the contemporary world as symptoms of some terminal malaise. In the words of the 1933 poem 'Doom is dark and deeper than any sea-dingle', the early verse suggests that 'gradual ruin spreading like a stain' is the essential condition of his times (Auden, 2009: p. 20). Earlier poems such as 'Consider this and in our time' (1930) and the fourth part of 'It was Easter as I walked in the public gardens' (1930) give us glimpses of apparently decadent upper-class figures who, in the latter poem, must die in order for new life to emerge, and in the former seem about to be overwhelmed by some epidemic infection or generalized neurosis. In 'Consider', an elite of financiers and academics is given notice that the 'game is up' and that it is too late to escape imminent destruction (p. 17). Doom, decay, and decadence are everywhere in this early verse, but it is notable that Auden does not at this stage invoke the historical mythology of decadence in its Fall-of-Rome versions. That was to come later; for now, the scene of decadence is strikingly contemporary to the Depression period, as in the imagery of industrial collapse and dilapidation that opens the 1930 poem 'Get there if you can . . .' (later titled 'Danse Macabre').

The early Auden achieves his powerful modernizing of poetically imagined decadence by ignoring Gibbon in favour of Freud, and especially his theory of the *Todestrieb* [death-drive]. Auden's new poetic mythology of decadence thus becomes clinical rather than historical, his mode of augury producing diagnosis from a reading of symptoms. In this mythology, the prevailing disease of the times usually involves the generalized 'wish for death' that is mentioned in 'May with its light behaving' (1935; later heavily revised as 'May'). An especially important example of this thematic preoccupation is Auden's 'Out on the lawn I lie in bed' (1934; later reduced from 16 to 12 stanzas as 'A Summer Night'), which may indeed be the defining 1930s poem of English decadence, here not diagnosed from outside but voiced from within an apparently besieged and doomed social class. (The text referred to here is the full 16-stanza poem, now to be found in the *Selected Poems* but not in the *Collected.*) Its twelfth stanza considers the cultural tradition in which 'we', a private circle of middle-class English friends, have been educated, finding that it now 'has little strength remaining' and in more Freudian terms that it 'has no wish to live' (Auden, 2009: p. 32). In the more openly prophetic stanzas that follow, the speaker envisages this walled enclave of privileged contentment being overwhelmed by a catastrophic 'flood' that seems to represent a coming social revolution launched by the unemployed hunger-marchers of the early 1930s. The hungry beyond the walls of bourgeois leisure are not disparaged as barbarian intruders but are still significantly assumed to be the inevitable victors over this enfeebled civilization. The poem's attitude and mood are, in a word, defeatist; and herein lies its own clearest link to the literary tradition of decadence. William Empson's parodic verses, 'Just a Smack at Auden' (1937), capture such terminal passivity well in their refrains: 'Treason of the clerks, boys, curtains that descend, | Lights becoming darks, boys, waiting for the end' (2000: p. 82).

Before moving on from the 'English' Auden of 1930–1938 to the much-transformed 'American' Auden of the post-1938 phase, we need to notice here his little-known and indeed long unpublished BBC radio drama-documentary *Hadrian's Wall* (1937), because it marks a significantly new Roman Empire motif in Auden's subsequent work. Auden's turn to Roman materials is initially informed by Kipling's own prior example, although it is not, as we shall see, a comparable 'Romanization' but something like its opposite. A reconstructed text of this radio script can now be consulted in Edward Mendelson's Princeton edition of the Auden-Isherwood *Plays* (1988), but Auden himself salvaged only one verse fragment of it in his lifetime, this being the song 'Roman Wall Blues' that he published in the 'Lighter Poems' section of *Another Time* (1940). 'Roman Wall Blues' is indeed a light and minor piece, the comic-pathetic complaint in seven rhyming couplets of a forlorn border-guard at Hadrian's Wall who misses his girl back home in (Belgic) Tungria. His woes may be read as symptoms of an imperial order in disintegration: he seems not to have been paid yet, he does not understand why he is stationed here, and he is annoyed by one of his comrades being a Christian who absurdly 'worships a fish' (Auden, 2007: p. 85). This last misunderstanding of the early-Christian ICHTHUS acronym lightly but tellingly evokes the historical irony of an empire that could not foresee its impending supersession by Christendom. The song is at the same time an obvious pastiche of Kipling's verses uttered by long-suffering legionaries, especially his 'British-Roman Song' and 'Rimini'. For the prose sections of *Hadrian's Wall*, Auden drew on a range of sources from the *Agricola* of Tacitus to R. G. Collingwood's *Roman Britain* (1932), but for the verse he clearly went back to Kipling for his models. This was an encounter between two poets who were both in different ways obsessed with frontiers, despite an evident political gulf between them. *Hadrian's Wall* concludes with a reflection quite foreign to Kipling's assumptions: that imperialism can be just as barbaric in its violence as the supposed barbarians.

Between *Hadrian's Wall* and his next significant encounter with Kipling the poet of empire, Auden rediscovered in the years 1939–1941 his Christian faith, in the Anglican (in the USA, Episcopalian) tradition in which he had been brought up. A dawning sense in the late 1930s that liberal-secularist optimism had failed became clarified for him by a sustained encounter with modern Protestant theology, especially with Charles Williams's *The Descent of the Dove* (1939) and Charles Norris Cochrane's *Christianity and Classical Culture* (1940). These works encouraged him to regard the Incarnation as an irruption of divine Love into human history, and specifically into the soullessly fatalistic world order of the Roman Empire, Roman power or *Romanitas* being in its idolatrous Caesar-worship directly antithetical to Christ's message. Auden's reconversion led him not only into a damning reassessment of the Roman Empire, but to a new conviction that modern political power-worship, of which Hitlerism was only one extreme instance, was a malign pagan cult, a neo-Caesarism. This he names in almost apocalyptic terms, for example in a pseudonymous contribution to the liberal-Catholic weekly *Commonweal* in late 1942 which condemns church-going anti-semites as unwitting devotees of 'the age-old imperial *Romanitas*, Leviathan, the Beast' (Auden, 2002: p. 172).

Auden returned to the consideration of Kipling in a belated review of Eliot's *A Choice of Kipling's Verse*, entitled 'The Poet of the Encirclement' (1943), by now confirmed in his own Christian form of anti-imperialism. Auden concurs with Eliot that Kipling's verse has its own merits, but he devotes his essay to defining the extraordinary difference between Kipling and 'virtually every other European writer since the fall of the Roman empire' (p. 199), this being that he is obsessed by external threats to civilization, to the exclusion of any reflection upon civilization's nature or its internal failings. The hero of a Kipling poem, Auden points out, will be some version of a sentry-figure, always on guard against the Pict or Hun, too defensively vigilant to think about what it is that he defends. The diametrically opposed focus of Auden's own work at this time was precisely upon the radical deficiencies of any civilization that promised salvation through political-administrative efficiency, whether this be the original Caesarism of Augustus or the neo-Caesarism of the 1940s. By this point, Auden had completed the most overtly Christian of his longer works, 'For the Time Being: A Christmas Oratorio' (1944), a verse sequence – with prose sections – on the Nativity, and thus on the fundamental challenge of the Incarnation to the soulless order of Caesarism, ancient or modern.

In 'For the Time Being', Auden presses home the contemporary relevance of that challenge, both by ironic mockery of Caesarist attitudes and by deliberate anachronism. The sequence's third part, 'The Summons', includes a 'Fugal Chorus' in which each stanza begins with the acclamation 'Great is Caesar', this chorus representing with obvious irony the gratitude of imperial subjects in their false worship of political power. It is striking, though, that Caesar's acclaimed achievements in economics, technology, and medicine are those of the twentieth century rather than the first. Here and throughout 'For the Time Being' an unashamed anachronistic principle prevails, so that Joseph and the three shepherds all speak like blue-collar Americans of the 1940s, and Herod speaks as a liberal rationalist intellectual of the same period. For Auden, this resort to anachronism was theologically justified in that the Incarnation is both an historical event and a perpetually recurring challenge for each subsequent generation. Accordingly, he re-activates consciously the anachronistic principle of late-medieval Christian art, emulating the Mystery Plays that re-enact biblical events in modern dress and modern idiom. This parallelism has its importance for the ways in which Auden was to imagine decadence as a phenomenon both ancient and contemporary.

Auden in the new age of the post-1945 *pax Americana* wrote a number of poems on Roman imperial subjects, including 'Under Sirius' (1949), 'Music Ho' (1951), 'The Epigoni' (1956), 'Secondary Epic' (1959), and the late poem suggested by Gibbon's account of Attila the Hun, 'An Encounter' (1971). The most intriguing and artistically satisfying of these is his 28-line poem in *abba*-rhymed quatrains, 'The Fall of Rome' (1947), which is unmistakably a poetic study of decadence of a highly original kind. Its founding conceit, rather bewilderingly to many readers on first acquaintance, is a flagrant anachronism which places us simultaneously in imperial Rome and in present-day 1940s America: the temple prostitutes (from an unreliable chapter of James George Frazer's *The Golden Bough*) and Cato, a statesman of Rome's Republican period, would seem to belong to Antiquity, along with Caesar (thus any of the Emperors from Augustus onward), but the poem obliges them to share their world with clearly modern figures. In place of the Praetorian Guard we find the 'Marines' upon whom modern American military power relies, while the scribe of Roman bureaucracy is replaced by a modern clerk and his paperwork. The purpose of these conflations of one era with another is of course to suggest that historical processes of decadence repeat themselves under all empires.

However, Auden's poem selects and highlights some aspects of imperial decay rather than others. Its title promises some version of Gibbon's narrative of decline, but the principal culprits in that narrative – the Christians and the barbarians – are in Auden's version strangely, or rather strategically, absent. These omissions may be explained on grounds of historical plausibility, there being no equivalent threats to America in 1947; but in the wake of Auden's 1943 essay on Kipling, they also indicate a conscious refusal to present civilization as externally menaced or encircled. The anachronized empire of the poem does indeed have an outside, glimpsed in the framing stanzas, but that exterior is (excepting the 'outlaws', a term that Kipling might employ) largely natural and therefore innocent: the erosive wind and rain of the opening stanza, the birds of stanza 6. Most significantly, the barbarian migrations of fourth- and fifth-century Roman history are replaced in the final stanza by the harmless migrations of reindeer. If there are any guilty parties to this story, the central stanzas find them entirely within the imperial culture's human failings.

'The Fall of Rome' revives, although with surer technical control, the ominous mood and sinister symptomatology of Auden's early soothsaying work; and here again the seemingly trivial signs of the times are to be read as auguries of disintegration: 'Fantastic grow the evening gowns' at the fifth line, an index of the over-refinement of taste with which decadence in any age is associated. Meanwhile, public obligations have given way to 'Private rites' and private fantasies, all the way up to the apex of imperial power, so undermining any true loyalty the individual – as soldier, taxpayer, or functionary – may feel towards the State:

> Caesar's double-bed is warm
> As an unimportant clerk
> Writes *I DO NOT LIKE MY WORK*
> On a pink official form. (Auden, 2009: p. 188)

The disaffected clerk here is 'unimportant' both to the erotically distracted ancient Emperor and to the impersonal technocracy of modern Caesarism, because neither of these powers, as Auden believed, can recognize the individual, and so each will collapse by failing to enlist the individual's freely chosen devotion. The implicitly Christian doctrine of anti-Caesarism, prosaically summarized here and in Auden's various essays of the period, may be found eccentric or otherwise unpersuasive; but in the poem it is the creative exercise of anachronism that brings home Auden's more compelling implications: that decadence is perennial, that the Fall of Rome is always taking place now.

References

Auden, W. H. (2002). *Prose, Volume II: 1939–1948*, Edward Mendelson, ed., Princeton, NJ: Princeton University Press.

Auden, W. H. (2007). *Another Time*, London: Faber and Faber.

Auden, W. H. (2009). *Selected Poems*, Edward Mendelson, ed., London: Faber and Faber.

Eliot, T. S. (1941). *A Choice of Kipling's Verse*, London: Faber & Faber.

Eliot, T. S. (2002). *The Waste Land and Other Poems*, London: Faber & Faber.

Empson, William (2000). *The Complete Poems*, John Haffenden, ed., London: Penguin.

Kipling, Rudyard (1987). *Traffics and Discoveries*, Hermione Lee, ed., Harmondsworth: Penguin.
Kipling, Rudyard (1993). *Selected Poems*, Peter Keating, ed., London: Penguin.
Kipling, Rudyard (2013). *The Cambridge Edition of the Poems of Rudyard Kipling, Volume II: Collected Poems II*, Thomas Pinney, ed., Cambridge: Cambridge University Press.
Lycett, Andrew (1999). *Rudyard Kipling*, London: Weidenfeld & Nicolson.

CHAPTER 22

The Gender of Decadence: Paris-Lesbos from the Fin de Siècle to the Interwar Era

Deborah Longworth

From 1900 to 1940 the citizens of Paris experienced a series of shocks rivalled only by the revolutionary era that began in 1789. The Third Republic, born in 1870 out of the collapse of the Second Empire in the aftermath of the Franco-Prussian War, was riven by the Dreyfus Affair at the fin de siècle and destroyed in 1940 with the Nazi occupation of Paris. Through it all Paris persisted, the interwar period in particular offering a remarkable flowering of culture, from the popular art of *chanteuses* like Lucienne Boyer and Edith Piaf, to the cinematic art of poetic realists like Jean Renoir and Marcel Carné, to the enigmatic art of surrealists like André Breton in poetry and René Magritte in painting. Parallel with these developments are the lesser-known but equally remarkable activities of the 'women of the left bank' who gave expression to same-sex concerns in both their poetry and their lives and so form the socio-cultural tradition known as 'Paris-Lesbos'. The tradition is one legacy of fin-de-siècle decadence, evident in the work of several Euro-American women writers living in Paris during the first half of the twentieth century. That work involves a complex intersection of decadence, 'sapphism' and 'sapphic fiction' from the Belle Époque to the interwar years. It includes the feminist and lesbian reappropriation of Sapphic decadence at the turn of the century and a later revival of the decadent mystique of the femmes damnées in the 1920s and 1930s.

The principal practitioners of this Sapphic form of decadence are Renée Vivien (pseudonym of Pauline Tarn), translator of Sappho and decadent poet (who died of pneumonia, exacerbated by anorexia and alcoholism, in 1909) and Natalie Barney, the multi-millionaire heiress and unashamedly self-proclaimed lesbian whose literary connections and love affairs among the social elite of the Belle Époque placed her at the centre of the legend of 'Paris-Lesbos' for half a century.[1] Vivien and Barney's intense relationship

[1] Natalie Barney inherited more than four million dollars on the death of her father in 1902, the equivalent of about a billion dollars today. See Jay (1988: p. 2).

in 1900 and 1901 inspired much of their work, while the aura they so clearly exuded to those around them has been conveyed in numerous literary portraits and romans à clef. Vivien, for example, is depicted by both Colette and Romaine Brooks as something of a high priestess of decadence, drinking eau de toilette in the bathroom and wearing serpents round her wrists, her darkened apartment fragrant with incense and decorated with glowing statues of Buddha. Barney, meanwhile, after the publication of her first collection of poems, *Quelques portraits-sonnets de femmes* [Some portraits and sonnets of women] (1900), became not only Vivien's muse but also inspired much of the fascination with the lesbian during the late Belle Époque. Liane de Pougy, the most celebrated courtesan of the era, published her roman à clef of her passionate affair with Barney in *Idylle saphique* [Sapphic idyll] (1901), and Vivien's collection of love poems, *Études et préludes* [Studies and preludes], appeared in the same year. As a result of her father's suppression of *Some Portraits*, Barney's poems to Vivien appeared as *Cinq petits dialogues grecs* [Five little Greek dialogues], also in 1901, under the pseudonym 'Tryphé', a term in classical Greek that implies a combination of luxuriousness, hedonism, and effeminacy. Colette included a cameo of her in *Claudine s'en va* [Claudine goes her way] (1903), before Vivien portrayed her again as Vally in *Une femme m'apparut* [*A Woman Appeared to Me*] (1903) and as Lorely in a revised version in 1905. Remy de Gourmont wrote his *Lettres à l'Amazone* [*Letters to the Amazon*] for her, and Ronald Firbank drew upon her in *Inclinations* (1916) for the character of Geraldine O'Brookomoore, the lesbian authoress who takes a young girl to Greece and is then left distraught when she abandons her. A decade later she appeared as Valérie Seymour in Radclyffe Hall's *The Well of Loneliness* (1928) and, in the same year, as Dame Evangeline Musset in Djuna Barnes' *Ladies' Almanack*.

i

Barney openly and confidently asserted her homosexuality throughout her life, declaring in *Souvenirs indiscrets* [Indiscrete memories] (1960), 'I am a lesbian. One need not hide it, nor boast of it, though being other than normal is a perilous advantage' (quoted in Souhami, 2004: p. 60). Extraordinary wealth, combined with a robust atheism and the outsider status of the expatriate, however, meant that she generally welcomed the advantages with little anxiety about the perilous, regarding scandal as enabling her freedom from societal constraint. Her poems, plays for performance in her private garden, and collections of epigrams and memoirs declare a vibrant sexuality, self-assured independence, and a veneration of female same-sex love. '[I]t's love that I love above everything else', she would write in an unpublished memoir, 'love is the difficult god whom I adore through each of my lovers, a god whom I cannot attain except through them' (quoted in Rodriguez, 2002: p. 78). The fêtes and performances that she held in the garden of her villa at Neuilly in the early 1900s and her weekly Friday salon from 1909 at her house at 20 rue Jacob on the Paris Left Bank recreated in modern Paris a social and artistic but also gender-fluid community of women (although not to the exclusion of Barney's equally large following of prominent male writers, both establishment and avant-garde), a space in which women's same-sex desire was welcomed, normalized, and legitimated. Vivien was more circumspect about directly revealing her lesbianism outside of her writing. Her translations of Sappho into French, which would earn her the posthumous epithet of 'Sappho 1900', indicate an equally self-conscious identification with the poetess from Lesbos through an eroticism of words and rhythm and a professional ambition to assume her role as the voice of same-sex love between women (Billy, 1951: p. 227).

The lesbian was a prominent feature of Parisian culture by the 1890s, as both a literary trope and also a reality within the relatively tolerant circles of elite salons. As Nicole Albert (2016) has exhaustively detailed, over the course of the second half of the nineteenth century a broad spectrum of sociological and sexological studies, literary and artistic works, erotic and pornographic texts, and the popular press had developed a voyeuristic fascination with the concept of female same-sex desire. By the end of the nineteenth century, Albert argues, the French imagination had constructed the lesbian 'as a threat and a fantasy, as a figure that could symbolize Decadence with a capital D' (2016: p. xii). With her instinctively 'unnatural' desires and ambiguous gender, the lesbian was a source of particular fascination as well as vicarious identification. The figure was particularly well-suited to the decadent aesthetic, which refuses the romantic equation of nature with what is good and beautiful and rejects mimesis as the standard for art, finding beauty in perversion and celebrating artifice and ornament.

The decadent tradition provides one explanation for the nineteenth-century fascination with the figure of the lesbian, and classical studies provides another. Interest in the Greek poet Sappho gained impetus from a new translation by Theodor Bergk in 1854 and, later, from the discovery of additional verse fragments in the 1890s. A prolific writer of love poetry, Sappho was said to have committed suicide by jumping from the cliffs of the Greek island of Lefkas when she was rejected by the boatman Phaon. Sappho's sexual identification had been unclear in classical Roman accounts, but assuming her heterosexuality from the story of Phaon, modern translators and critics largely interpreted her verses as being addressed to a man. When Henry Wharton restored the feminine pronoun in his 1885 edition of her fragments, *Sappho: Memoir, Text, Selected Renderings, and a Literal Translation*, he reframed the implication of intimacy with other women as that between teacher and female pupil. In her authoritative study of the representation of Sappho in France from the sixteenth century up until World War II, Joan DeJean demonstrates that the translation and representation of Sappho across the centuries has continuously and accumulatively reflected the fantasies and fears of both writer and epoch.

The lesbian Sappho may have become an inspiration for women writers such as Vivien and Barney in the early years of the twentieth century, but her voice had already been appropriated and her image had already been shaped by over half a century of male and largely decadent or proto-decadent authorship that not only framed but also *created* Sappho in many ways as a lesbian poetess for the modern author who tended to be, as DeJean notes, 'vehemently antisapphic' (1989: p. 265). The most influential example of this antisapphism was Charles Baudelaire in *Les fleurs du mal* [*The Flowers of Evil*] (1857), and the suppression of two lesbian poems as a result of the author's prosecution for indecency, 'Lesbos' and 'Femmes damnées: Delphine et Hippolyte'.

In 'Lesbos' Baudelaire portrays Sappho as instinctively lesbian rather than heterosexual or bisexual, describing her coupling with Phaon as an act of 'blasphemy' against 'the rite and the established cult' of Lesbos. With Sappho departed, leaving Lesbos ever after in torment, 'drunk every night with the tempest's howls', it is the male poet who assumes the role of giving voice to the pleasures and pain of lesbian desire. 'Lesbos chose me among all other poets', he claims, 'To sing the secret of her virgins in their bloom', 'the dark mystery | Of unbridled laughter mingled with tears of gloom' (Baudelaire, 1954: p. 134). Baudelaire proclaimed Sappho's sapphism in *The Flowers of Evil*, but in positioning her as the lost priestess for whom Lesbos continues to mourn, a Lesbos conflated with the landscape and spleen of modern Paris, he also made her a mythic heroine of decadence, her 'wan pallor, more beautiful than Venus!' and her 'black eyes ringed | With dark circles' (p. 135).

'Femmes damnées: Delphine et Hippolyte' follows a similar structure to 'Lesbos', opening with a depiction of sensuous love between women before dissolving into unsatisfied desire, pain, and damnation. Baudelaire again situates the lesbian woman in classical Greece in the figures of the young Hippolyta, newly initiated into the 'potent caresses' of another woman and now beset by 'heavy terrors' and 'black battalions of scattered phantoms', and the experienced Delphine, hungry with desire and consuming in her love (p. 137). In the dialogue between the two women, Hippolyta feels spiritual fear and regret as Delphine honours the physical pleasures of their act. Baudelaire initially seems to appreciate the 'strong beauty' of Delphine and the 'frail beauty' of Hippolyta (p. 136), but he attacks both women virulently in the final stanzas, in which the poet's voice, again taking over from and suppressing the female voices, curses the lesbian women into hell:

> Go down, go down, lamentable victims,
> [. . .]
> Mad shades, run to the goal of your desires;
> You will never be able to sate your passion
> And your punishment will be born of your pleasures. (p. 138)

While Baudelaire dressed his lesbian heroines of modernity as figures of antiquity and classical mythology, Pierre Louÿs in *Les chansons de Bilitis* [*Songs of Bilitis*] (1894) eschewed both modernity and mythology for a bogus antiquity of his own invention. The book is a pseudo-translation of sensual prose poems by the lesbian courtesan Bilitis, a contemporary of Sappho, complete with a scholarly account of her life and an appendix recounting the discovery of her tomb. Initial readers were unaware that the volume was in fact an elaborate hoax that was entirely the work of Louÿs, or that Bilitis and her tomb had never existed. Presented as the intimacies of female sexuality expressed by a female voice, Bilitis' poems were instead the imaginative fantasies of a late nineteenth-century male decadent author intended for a voyeuristic male readership. Nonetheless, Barney admired the poems and applied to Louÿs for advice on her early work. Louÿs had dedicated *Songs of Bilitis* 'aux jeunes filles de la société future' [to the young girls of the society of the future] (Louÿs, 2010: p. 9), and Barney later recalled that after visiting him with Vivien he sent them two deluxe volumes of the book, with the dedications: 'For Renée Vivien, this line of Keats: "Forever wilt thou love, and she be fair!" For N.C.B. young woman of the future, her admirer, Pierre Louÿs' (Barney, 1992b: p. 27).

In her memoirs, *Aventures de l'esprit* [*Adventures of the Mind*] (1929) Barney implicitly contrasted Louÿs' representation of Bilitis' lesbianism with Baudelaire's representation of Hippolyta and Delphine's. Louÿs, she wrote, 'who was no mystic when it came to love, surely preferred "Latin games and Greek pleasures" to the exaggerated preoccupations of "damned women" who, with their sense of sin, perhaps unconsciously sought to heighten and increase their passions through imaginary perils' (1992a: p. 33). She was also, in retrospect, identifying her own pagan belief in the love of multiple women with Louÿs' imagined Lesbos and Vivien's portrayal of love, pain, and sin with the mysticism, fear, and perverse passion articulated by Baudelaire. Here we see a divergence in the meaning that lesbianism held for the two women, with Barney rejecting the moral implications of lesbianism as outdated but embracing the socially progressive designation of the lesbian as 'a woman of the future'.

Vivien and Barney's ideal of love between women, however, also owes something to the aesthetic ideals of a broader but interconnected friendship group of extraordinarily wealthy young American women, once childhood friends, who had been living in or passing through Paris since the 1890s, among them not only Barney and Vivien, but also Violet ('Violette') Shillito, Mabel Dodge Luhan, and Eva Palmer. All possessed a passionate desire for knowledge and experience and found in the French capital a freedom from the social and educational restrictions of both America and England. Luhan's autobiographical writings capture the female affection among these women and the sensual intensity of their encounters. Both Shillito and Palmer read Greek, and Barney wrote of her love affair with Palmer in the summer of 1893 that she 'inspired me and taught me about love', and that 'poetry, Plato's *Banquet*, and nudism, all had a part in our Arcadian life' (quoted in Chalon, 1979: p. 12). Her 'Arcadian' experience with Palmer reveals Barney to be not so different from her libertarian compatriots in the home country who were likewise intent on establishing alternative communities devoted to more radical lifestyles removed from the American mainstream (see Berry, 1992). Indeed, Barney's Paris salon appears in this light like a more aesthetic version of a long-standing tradition of social experimentation in the United States.

Palmer remained close to Barney in the early 1900s in Paris but would marry the Greek lyric poet and playwright Angelos Sikelianos, brother-in-law of Isadora Duncan, in 1908, moving with him to Athens where they initiated the two-day Delphic Festival in 1927. If Barney was drawn to Palmer's paganism, however, Renée Vivien had a long-standing platonic entanglement with Violet Shillito. Recording her relationship with Shillito in 1896 in *Intimate Memories*, Luhan recalled, 'It was a more delicious life I felt in me than I had ever felt before. I thought it was a superior kind of living, too' (1999: p. 38). Luhan attributes to her something of a Paterian philosophy of life and experience, focused on the attempt to achieve 'la grande vie intérieure' [the life of the soul], the pursuit of a subjective aesthetic life achieved in moments of intense sensory experience (pp. 33, 36). Her retrospective account also situates Shillito within an essentially decadent aesthetic – her description of her as 'an unaging goddess fresh and unfaded, yet of the most ancient days' (p. 38), at once the culmination of her civilization and on the cusp of falling back into dissolution, echoes Walter Pater's description of the Mona Lisa as a modern goddess, 'older than the rocks among which she sits', a 'beauty [. . .] into which the soul with all its maladies has passed' and 'the embodiment of the old fancy, the symbol of the modern idea' (2010: pp. 70–1). Shillito seems to have embodied something of a spiritual Sappho for Luhan and for Vivien, who had known her in Paris as a child before her mother moved the family to London on her father's death in 1886, and who had re-established their friendship on her immediate return to Paris after inheriting his fortune twelve years later. Vivien was devastated by Violet's sudden death from typhoid in 1901 and ridden with guilt that in the whirl of her obsession with the ever-fascinating Barney she had turned her back on a deeper and more faithful relationship. Vivien's Sapphic vision, both the glimpse of an idyllic love that satisfied the soul as well as the senses, but also its corruption and loss, owes much to both the beliefs and manner of Shillito's life and to the shock of her untimely death.

Increasingly depressed by Barney's polygamy and her continued affection for Eva Palmer and Liane De Pougy, Vivien broke from her and entered a five-year relationship with the Baroness Hélène van Zuylen. The brief reconciliation with Barney on Lesbos in 1904 reinvigorated both her faith in a positive love between women and her role as a modern-day Sapphic poet:

> Now my soul has taken flight once more,
> Sweet mistress of my songs, let us go to Mytilene.
> . . .
> The tears of return will find our eyes:
> At last we will see the lands of lifeless love
> . . .
> Grow distant. (quoted in Barney, 1992b: p. 43)

'[W]e continued to dream on the murmuring shores of the Aegean Sea', Barney wrote of this Arcadian period on what seemed an 'enchanted island'. Both writers evidently regarded the trip as symbolizing the return of Sappho to Lesbos, an implicit challenge to Baudelaire's depiction of the torment left in the wake of her departure that is extended in Barney's decision to write a play that would 'destroy the myth of Phaon' and depict Sappho's suicide as the result of betrayal by 'the best-loved of her friends' (1992b: p. 46). The only record of their visit to Lesbos is Barney's biographical sketch, however, where we learn that it was Barney who made the suggestion that they create a poetry school on Lesbos, 'where young women vibrating with poetry, youth and love would come to us like the poetesses of old, traveling from all parts of the world to be with Sappho' (p. 45), in part because she knows it will delight Vivien. Vivien seems to have been enthusiastic, but when the Baroness demanded her return she complied, and although Barney was still hopeful of a reunion and arranged a villa for Vivien conjoining her own at Neuilly, once back in Paris Vivien's doubts and torment over their relationship returned. Elyse Blankley argues that Vivien's 'feminism and lesbianism guided her toward a vision of complete female isolation on Lesbos' (1984: p. 51). As her description of 'the lands of lifeless love' already suggested, Paris-Lesbos was very different from the utopian fantasy she could imagine of its Greek counterpart. The difference, again, points to the conflicting paradigms of lesbian love the two women embody, with Vivien connected much more closely to the decadent European tradition than Barney, who, despite her expatriate condition, relates more readily to a communitarian utopian tradition with roots in American radicalism.

ii

Vivien and Barney have become legendary figures in the history of lesbian women's writing, celebrated for a feminist reappropriation or reshaping of the late nineteenth-century decadent model of lesbian mystique. For Mary Ann Caws they are the 'leading proponents of the "lesbian-chic" movement in Paris in the 1890s' (2004: p. 107) while Shari Benstock (1986) makes Barney's salon the hub of the expatriate and international artist community in Paris in the interwar years. Most interpretations of Vivien's work distinguish between what critics identify as her 'decadent' poems, redolent with images of despair and populated by heroines derived from the work of later Pre-Raphaelites (Lilith, Viviane, Vashti), and her 'Sapphic' work, in which she seems able to free herself from the influence of the decadent, masculine gaze and to exalt lesbian love (see Benstock, 1986: p. 286). Diana Holmes understands Vivien's translations of Sappho as an attempt to define a female genealogy of poetry that avoided an otherwise inevitably patrilineal history of influence (1996: p. 95). Similarly, Susan Gubar argues that the rarity of Sappho's original texts offered Vivien an opportunity to develop her own lesbian voice in echo of, or as if in tête-à-tête with, her classical predecessor: 'the modern woman poet could write "for" or "as" Sappho and thereby invent a classical inheritance of her own' (1984: 46–7). Scott Bravman argues that 'Sappho, Lesbos and Greek paganism formed a central component of Vivien's and Barney's creative, erotic and emotional life together' (1997: p. 56), but while certainly true of Barney, Vivien's Sapphism was framed by a decadent rather than pagan temperament.

Lillian Faderman notes that Vivien's poetry 'most often associates lesbian love with vice, artificiality, perfume, and death', and a repertoire of decadent imagery pervades even the early *Studies and Preludes* (1981: p. 364). The woman depicted in 'Amazon', surely Barney, 'loves only lovers who offer her their mad | Wild agony and their fierce, proud fall', while in 'Troubling Resemblance' the speaker thinks of her lover as a serpent, her 'long lithe shape' reminding her 'Of slow, insinuating golden scales' (Vivien, 2015: p. 15). 'I have felt | A venom in the depths of your caress', Vivien writes,

> I hate you, but your beauty's suppleness
> Takes me, enthrals me, and draws me in its wake,
> And my heart, in terror at your cruelty,
> Scorns and adores you, my Goddess and my Snake! (2015: p. 15)

These poems articulate what would become Vivien's characteristic fusion of passion and cruelty, adoration and hatred, and the conviction that love and suffering cannot be separated. Barney's image, her dress, her mass of silver-blonde hair, and blue-grey eyes appear throughout the volume, typically associated with a cruel femme fatale. In 'Grey Eyes' Vivien writes:

> I interrogate your pupils' stagnant pools,
> They have the void of winter, dusk, and graves:
> I see eternal Limbos drifting there,
> The terrible dull endlessness of ocean waves. (2015: p. 13)

Barney recalls in her biographical sketch that by 1903 Vivien was becoming a recognized decadent poet and cites in particular Charles Maurras' description of her work as an example of 'feminine Romanticism' in his *L'avenir de l'intelligence* [*The Future of the Intelligentsia*] (1905) (1992b: p. 20). Maurras recognized Vivien's Baudelairisms, arguing that these were not just a collection of decadent tropes for the purpose of shocking a bourgeois audience, but instead deeply felt. '[W]here Baudelaire gives the impression of an eloquent hoax, this young woman touches us by her sincerity', he observes, 'And she is a virtuoso. The mere plaything of literary craftsmen becomes, in her hands, an instrument of joy and pain, springboard for deeply felt elegies or heart-rending tragedies' (quoted in Barney 1992b: p. 21). Perhaps most significantly, he regarded instead her 'Sapphisms' as the hoax, or rather the dressing up, of an essentially erotic sensibility that Mario Praz would later describe in terms of the Romantic agony: 'If we take a look inside the *peplum* [tunic], drop the *chlamyde* [cloak], a modern woman appears, fully clothed, complete with ideas about Life, ideas about the World imparted to her by the old romantics', he wrote, 'She is at her best when she leaves Lesbos and Sappho behind and translates herself' (quoted in Barney 1992b: p. 21). Louÿs had presented the young woman of the future as a sensuous pagan, personified in Barney; Maurras here saw her as the sensual mystic, and Vivien as characterizing her poetic voice.

Colette's description of her first visit to Vivien's apartment similarly emphasizes her tragic mysticism, although she is more critical of Vivien's decadent self-fashioning: 'Among the unstable marvels, Renée wandered, not so much clad as veiled in black or purple, almost invisible in the scented darkness of the immense rooms barricaded with leaded windows, the air heavy with curtains and incense' (1971: p. 71). She adds that 'nothing could dispel the uneasiness engendered by the strangeness of the place, bound to astonish a guest, the semi-darkness, the exotic foods on plates of jade, vermeil, or Chinese porcelain, foods that had come from countries too far away' (p. 73). Colette is nevertheless out of sympathy with the decadent sensibility. 'I am hostile to those who let their life burn out', she writes, noting of Vivien's poetry that it 'inhabits a region of elevated melancholy, in which the *amies*, the female couple, daydream and weep as often as they embrace' (pp. 83, 79). 'Our friendship was in no way literary', she pointedly remarks, reminding the reader of the difference between Vivien's tormented lovers and her own portrayal of lesbian alliances in her Claudine novels, adding that 'Baudelairism in the years 1900–1909 was for us rather late' (pp. 71, 79).

Barney was similarly unconvinced by Vivien's more clichéd decadent postures, particularly in her prose. 'She wrote two versions of our real-life novel [. . .] *A Woman Appeared to Me*', she recalled, 'in which she seemed to me to have given in to the worst excesses of "art nouveau"' (1992b: p. 24). Vally and Lorely, the two versions of Barney, share an '"undulating" body and eyes like "iced water under hair of moonlight"' (p. 24), which continue the images of the serpent and the grey eyes like 'endless waves' from her poems, while the Vivien alter ego of San Giovanni states: 'I saw everything filtered through the smoke of incense and aromatic herbs. My strange happiness filled my soul with mystic wonder' (1992b: p. 26). Barney was impatient of the decadent trappings and disliked Vivien's creation of these 'forced "femmes fatales" who resembled me' (p. 24). 'Renée believes I suffered from 19th century "spleen" in sudden fits only', she observed, 'whereas she made it the leitmotif of her life and art' (p. 24). In later works, however (such as *La Vénus des aveugles* [The Venus of the blind] (1903) and *Aux heures des mains jointes* [Hand in hand] (1906)), she observes 'how much stronger her poems had become. There were no more "perfumed pallors" and other insipidities trailing along. They were no longer languorous but heavy with images from her life, reflecting the cruelty of her existence against which she had at first rebelled' (pp. 48–9).

Barney ultimately puts Vivien's tragedy down to her inherent Christianity. 'The cross seems to have covered the entire world with its large shadow', she writes: 'Happy are those who have escaped the heredity of this creed! Renée Vivien, even into her first love, felt its inevitable obsession creeping, undefined, unrecognizable, but already present' (1992a: p. 186). Ellis Hanson observes that 'all the great works of decadent literature are conversion narratives' (1997: p. 10), and for Barney, the deathbed conversion was consistent with what she regarded as Vivien's inherently religious faith: 'Renée Vivien sought love and suffering, as the Christian woman who is unaware of herself; she had everything of a future believer, beginning with renunciation' (1992a: p. 186). While Barney presents Vivien as inherently Christian, she also praises the courage of her desire and her continuing rebellion against the faith: 'we can only admire this poet of decline, in whose works love of beauty, that intentional paganism, contrasts constantly with that unconscious sadism of enemies scornful of the flesh' (p. 187). Vivien wanted to be pagan, Barney notes, but it was not surprising that close to death she turned to Catholicism, 'the religion that was the most capable of satisfying her being that was always eager for ceremonies and images' (p. 188). Paganism takes strength in modern society (a strength she implies she has) and 'the Christian shadow reclaims its own when they are weakened by disillusion, remorse, and sickness' (p. 187). Colette had commented similarly on Vivien's conversion, noting that '[h]er paganism was so little rooted in her' (1971: p. 82).

iii

Richard Dellamora describes Barney as creating around herself from the 1910s a 'highly developed Sapphic culture – complete with rituals, a sacramental life, mythography, sacred texts, heroes and martyrs' (2011: p. xii). This culture centred on the salon she created at 20 rue Jacob, a house she rented in 1909, intending it for herself and Vivien, who never saw it before her death. In the communal garden was a small Doric temple, inscribed 'Temple d'Amitié' [Temple of Friendship], symbolizing both their pagan and spiritual worship of female love that would become the beacon of Barney's Sapphic community during the 1910s and the interwar years. In 1927 she launched the *Académie des Femmes* to honour contemporary women writers. The honour usually took the form of an introduction and reading by the writer at Barney's Friday salon, as recorded in *Adventures of the Mind*, with the women presented including Vivien (posthumous), Aurel (Antoinette Gabrielle Mortier de Faucamberge), Gertrude Stein, and Djuna Barnes.

While critics have celebrated Barney's salon as a hub of expatriate women's modernism (Benstock, 1986) and a lesbian cultural intervention (Winning, 2003), the women writers who were involved with it seem more equivocal. The portraits of Barney in introductions to the Friday salons, collected in *Adventures of the Mind* and in romans à clefs and memoirs from the interwar years, regularly associate her with the decadent imagery of the lesbian femme fatale. The writer Aurel, for example, records again a coolness and cruelty to her eyes – 'notice that their poetic blueness has some gleams of steel blades' – and depicts her as aloof from life, a cruel and Satanic dandy, a 'Fairy of destruction, [. . .] with a taste of pleasure that proves you right over nature' (1992a: pp. 135, 137). This is surely an extraordinary image of the purported leader of a feminist and lesbian community, and one that suggests a lack of genuine faithfulness beneath the magnetism of her personality: '[D]on't let the charm of her smile conceal from you the sarcastic corner of her mouth', Aurel writes, 'mistrust her dreadful left eyebrow when it raises during the seconds when irony passes' (1992a: p. 138). It also draws upon the decadent figures of the dandy and the vampire, rather than Sappho, to represent Barney's cool allure. If women writers, including Vivien and Barney, in the early twentieth century used Sappho as a means of valorizing the lesbian lyric, during the interwar years the literary depiction of the Sapphic lesbian (and lesbian Sappho) loses momentum, to be replaced by a return to the image of the lesbian as a figure of decadent vice and perversion, living in shame and torment. The change likely has something to do with the socio-political ferment of the post-World War I period in France, which included the re-emergence of anti-semitism and the rise of fascism, purist ideologies hostile to both racial difference and gender non-conformism.

Jennifer R. Waelti-Walters, in her survey of the lesbian in novels in France during the nineteenth and twentieth centuries, states: 'Half a dozen women produced lesbian novels in the permissive years of the Belle Époque. If women wrote any between 1910 and 1929 I have not been able to find them' (Waelti-Walters, 2000: p. 4). When the lesbian reappeared, most famously in Radclyffe Hall's *The Well of Loneliness* (1928), she was no longer a reclaimed Sappho, singing the pagan pleasures of languid female caresses, but instead the *femme damnée* asserting the naturalness of her 'inversion' while simultaneously tortured with shame and self-loathing. Hall's novel contains a lengthy, although again ambivalent portrait of Barney as Valérie Seymour, whom the protagonist Stephen Gordon, still concealing her sexuality, is directed to meet when she travels to Paris. Barney's constant avowal of the normality of her sexuality, her refusal to turn to the concept of sexual 'inversion', and the fact that she chose feminine dress rather than the mannish dandy fashion in clothing, haircut, and mannerism adopted by other prominent lesbians of the period (fig. 22.1), asserted a confidence in her lesbianism that Hall recognizes. 'Valérie, placid and self-assured', she writes, 'created an atmosphere of courage, everyone felt very normal and brave when they gathered together at Valérie Seymour's' (Hall, 2015: p. 571). Seymour offers a like-minded community and social safety: 'the freedom of her salon, the protection of her friendship'. Depicting Seymour as 'a kind of lighthouse in a storm-swept ocean', gathering to her 'the shipwrecked, the drowning', the 'men and women who must carry God's mark on their foreheads' (p. 571), she becomes here the human embodiment of the Statue of Liberty, 'MOTHER OF EXILES', a neoclassical American icon of freedom, returning to her natural home of Paris and welcoming to her the 'wretched refuse' of modern life.[2] Hall's representation affirms yet again that while Barney could take herself out of America, she could not take America out of herself.

The elite distinction of Seymour's salon, however, is a world that Stephen increasingly feels to be a space protected by wealth and lineage, the remnant of a past era of Belle Époque permissibility, out of touch with modern-day Paris-Lesbos. The salon is rather dusty and the large divan empty except for a lute, but no new poet can sing Sappho's songs of love because the strings are broken. When Seymour accompanies Stephen to the bars of the Paris underworld

[2] Emma Lazarus' sonnet 'The New Colossus' was written in 1883 to raise money for the pedestal of the Statue of Liberty. It was cast on a bronze plaque and mounted inside the pedestal in 1903 (see Schor, 2006).

Fig. 22.1 The photographer Brassaï captures Lulu de Montparnasse, owner of the nightclub Le Monocle, in the garb of the 'collar-and-tie' lesbian [©RMN-Grand Palais / Art Resource, New York].

she appears significantly and determinedly out of place. Setting herself apart from the homosexual company, she discusses instead her villa at St. Tropez: 'Stephen could hear her charming voice, so cultured, so cool – itself cool as a fountain; and she marvelled at this woman's perfect poise, the genius she possessed for complete detachment' (p. 629). There is an implicit criticism here not only of the kind of distance and cruelty Aurel described in her portrait of Barney, but also of the individualism of her uncompromising paganism. Her inability to contemplate the shame and struggle of others makes her insensitive: 'As for those who were ashamed to declare themselves, [. . .] she utterly despised such of them as had brains; they were traitors to themselves and their fellows, she insisted' (p. 662). Churchgoing is seen as a weakness, Seymour believing 'they must be a religion unto themselves if they felt that they really needed religion':

> But then of course she herself was a pagan, acknowledging only the god of beauty; and since the whole world was so ugly these days, she was only too thankful to let it ignore her. Perhaps that was lazy – she was rather lazy. She had never achieved all she might have with her writing. (p. 663)

Hall undoubtedly regarded Barney as a rival to her own assumption of the voice of the modern Baudelairean lesbian, 'the dark mystery | Of unbridled laughter mingled with tears of gloom'. In contrast with Seymour's laziness, she states that 'Stephen was one of the kind that did things – under different conditions of environment and birth she might very well have become a reformer'. Seymour, Hall implies, for all her calm acceptance of her own lesbianism, her welcoming of others into her circle of friendship, her refusal of any sense of moral sin, and her incredulity that others could not so easily acknowledge their non-normative sexuality, was not a reformer. Her salon was a rarefied retreat from the contemporary world rather than an attempt to transform it, a space of Sapphic conversion but one that could not understand, or support, the need of the 'invert' within the modern world for spiritual and social acceptance: 'For since all that to many of them had seemed fine, a fine selfless and at times even noble emotion, had been covered with shame, called unholy and vile, so gradually they themselves had sunk down to the level upon which the world placed their emotions' (2015: p. 631). More recent assessments of interwar lesbian communities understandably challenge the severity of Hall's, as when Benstock observes that '[i]t is Sappho who is invoked by "Lesbos", not a wrathful Old Testament God' (p. 57). But in Hall's *The Well of Loneliness*, Sappho seems to have been supplanted by that wrathful God, as Barney and Vivien's ideal of a Sapphic community becomes only an isolated and eccentric retreat from society.

References

Albert, Nicole G. (2016). *Lesbian Decadence: Representations in Art and Literature of Fin-de-Siècle France*, Nancy Erber and William Peniston, trans., New York: Harrington Park Press.

Barney, Natalie Clifford (1992a). *Adventures of the Mind: Memoirs of Natalie Clifford Barney*, John Spalding Gatton, trans., New York: New York University Press.

Barney, Natalie Clifford (1992b). *A Perilous Advantage: The Best of Natalie Clifford Barney*, Anna Livia, ed. and trans., Norwich, VT: New Victoria Publishers.

Baudelaire, Charles (1954). *The Flowers of Evil*, William Aggeler, trans., Digireads.

Benstock, Shari (1986). *Women of the Left Bank: Paris, 1900–1940*, Austin: University of Texas Press.

Berry, Brian J. L. (1992). *America's Utopian Experiments: Communal Havens from Long-wave Crises*, Hanover, NH: University Press of New England.

Billy, André (1951). *L'époque 1900: 1885–1905*, Paris: Jules Tallandier.

Blankley, Elyse (1894). Returning to Mytilene: Renée Vivien and the City of Women. In Susan Merrill Squier, ed., *Women Writers and the City: Essays in Feminist Literary Criticism*, Knoxville: University of Tennessee Press, pp. 45–67.

Bravman, Scott (1997). *Queer Fictions of the Past: History, Culture, and Difference*, Cambridge: Cambridge University Press.

Caws, Mary Ann (2004). *The Yale Anthology of Twentieth-Century French Poetry*, New Haven, CT: Yale University Press.

Chalon, Jean (1979). *Portrait of a Seductress: The World of Natalie Clifford Barney*, New York: Crown Publishers.

Colette (1971). *The Pure and the Impure*. Herma Briffault, trans., London: Penguin.

DeJean, Joan (1989). *Fictions of Sappho, 1546–1937*, Chicago: University of Chicago Press.

Dellamora, Richard (2011). *Radclyffe Hall: A Life in the Writing*, Philadelphia: University of Pennsylvania Press.

Faderman, Lillian (1981). *Surpassing the Love of Men: Romantic Friendship and Love Between Women from the Renaissance to the Present*, New York: William Morrow.

Gubar, Susan (1984). Sapphistries. *Signs*, 10(1), 43–62.

Hall, Radclyffe (2015). *The Well of Loneliness*, London: Vintage.

Hanson, Ellis (1997). *Decadence and Catholicism*, Cambridge, MA: Harvard University Press.

Holmes, Diana (1996). *French Women's Writing 1848–1994*, London: Athlone Press.

Jay, Karla (1988). *The Amazon and the Page: Natalie Clifford Barney and Renée Vivien*, Bloomington: Indiana University Press.

Louÿs, Pierre (2010). *The Songs of Bilitis*. Alvah C. Bessie, trans., New York: Dover.

Luhan, Mabel Dodge (1999). *Intimate Memories: The Autobiography of Mabel Dodge Luhan*, Albuquerque: University of New Mexico Press.

Pater, Walter (2010). *Studies in the History of the Renaissance*, Matthew Beaumont, ed., Oxford: Oxford University Press.

Rodriguez, Suzanne (2002). *Wild Heart, A Life: Natalie Clifford Barney and the Decadence of Literary Paris*, New York: Harper Collins.

Schor, Esther (2006). *Emma Lazarus*, New York: Schocken.

Souhami, Diane (2004). *Wild Girls: Paris, Sappho and Art: The Lives and Loves of Natalie Barney and Romaine Brooks*, London: Weidenfeld and Nicolson.

Vivien, Renée (2015). *A Crown of Violets*, Samantha Pious, trans., Sequim, WA: Headmistress Press.

Waelti-Walters, Jennifer R. (2000). *Damned Women: Lesbians in French Novels, 1796–1996*, Montreal: McGill-Queen's University Press.

Winning, Joanne (2013). 'Ezra through the open door': The Parties of Natalie Barney, Adrienne Monnier and Sylvia Beach as Lesbian Modernist Cultural Production. In Kate McLoughlin, ed., *The Modernist Party*, Edinburgh: Edinburgh University Press, pp. 127–46.

CHAPTER 23

Decadence and Popular Culture

Alice Condé

As a literary and artistic movement associated with marginalized figures, decadence celebrates opulence, artifice, and queerness, aspects that are crystallized in the figure of the decadent dandy. In 1864 Charles Baudelaire describes dandyism as a 'cult of the self' (1995: p. 27), an epithet that befits the present age in which individuals upload posed and filtered 'selfies' to social media platforms daily. He also refers to the expression of personal originality as a form of rebellion that 'appears above all in periods of transition' (p. 28). Our current age is one of global unease and uncertainty, with Brexit and the 2016 American presidential election heralding the return of the kind of conservative ideology that characterizes other periods of decadence in recent centuries. Conversely, in mainstream popular culture the fashion for androgyny, sexual fluidity, and edgy S&M aesthetics in pop music demonstrates that it is once again fashionable to be an outsider. Rebellious transgression is *en vogue* and in *Vogue*.

Oscar Wilde remains the 'High Priest of the Decadents' (*National Observer*, 1895: p. 547) in the popular imagination. So enduring is his popularity that in 2011 a glass wall was erected around his tomb in Père Lachaise Cemetery to protect it from damage caused by the lipstick kisses of his adoring fans. Wilde is the archetypal decadent dandy, a figurehead of the cult of personality and a proponent of 'art for art's sake'. He represents a nodal point between queerness and celebrity – one of the original personalities who was famous for being famous, whose caricatures in *Punch* were equivalent to articles in today's gossip magazines. As Roy Morris has observed, Wilde was a pioneer of modern celebrity, a blueprint for how the stars of today are 'created, cultivated, and commodified' (2013: p. 2). The way this marginal figure was assimilated into the popular culture of his time and ours is striking, for he remains a queer icon as well as being celebrated for his literary wit. As Kristin Mahoney has pointed out, Wilde's scandalously effeminate dandyism (as it was regarded in conservative late nineteenth-century Britain) is an example of one of the ways in which decadence highlights the performativity of gender; thus 'Wilde and Decadence can be understood as foundational to modern queer theory, as post-Victorian specters haunting late-twentieth-century discourses concerning gender and sexuality' (2015: p. 199). Wilde represents the serious implications of playfully camp, antinormative self-presentation at moments of perceived cultural degeneration. David Weir recognizes camp as a key aspect of the afterlife of decadence due to its association with excess and the cultivation of a taste for the distasteful (2018: p. 8). Decadence is characterized by excess with an edge, and it manifests in instances where bad or queer taste is celebrated. It is not objectively distasteful, but definitely plays on cultural anxieties.

Once the preserve only of an elite subset of the literary and artistic milieu of the nineteenth century, the decadent aesthetic has been adopted on a mass scale in popular culture of the twenty-first century. As in the case of Wilde, it is a phenomenon both in terms of subculture becoming merely culture, and in terms of the aesthetics of decadent taste. Decadence is evident in contemporary culture in the popular obsession with the practice of self-fashioning through dandyism, drag, or costume as a means of self-acceptance and of negotiating or overcoming social boundaries, often in a playfully transgressive manner. Glam rock is a modern form of dandyism and camp self-expression, while the aesthetics of opulence and excess take on a different significance when considered in terms of the association with social inequality in relation to New York's drag ball culture, a direct precursor to popular reality TV programme *RuPaul's Drag Race* (2009–present), in which drag queens compete in dazzling costumes and makeup to become 'America's next drag superstar'. Decadence in today's celebrity culture is exemplified by Lady Gaga's pop performance art, but this mainstream decadence is also accompanied by a counterculture pushing back against the mainstream using the same decadent paradoxes of beauty and decay, artifice and reality.

Decadence: From the 1900s to Now

Every decadent moment of Western cultural anxiety is accompanied by a subculture of almost nihilistic hedonism encompassing sexual licence, self-obsession, and fascination with degeneration. Legends of debauchery at the end of the Roman Empire inspired French and English decadents at the fin de siècle who were fascinated with decay and degeneration (see Chapters 1 and 3). The pleasure-seeking excess of the Roaring Twenties was a reaction to the economic prosperity and modernity after The Great War but tinged with trauma and unease about the emptiness of it all, as expressed by the Bright Young Things in Evelyn Waugh's *Vile Bodies* (1930). The novel satirizes the vacuity of modern hedonism in a world where human bodies are insignificant machines in the war that has devastated the world in which they live.

Decadence is never entirely about emptiness, however. Intellectualism flourished in Weimar Berlin during the interwar period, where scholars of sexual pathology and psychology represented a continuation of the curiosity and self-consciousness we find in both decadent characters and decadent authors. Joris-Karl Huysmans's Des Esseintes in *À rebours* [*Against Nature*] (1884) is a peculiar decadent specimen, exhibiting restless interest in matters of the brain, body, and sexual appetite. Wilde's trial and imprisonment for 'acts of gross indecency' in 1895 cast a shadow over the early twentieth century, and his plight was one of the motivating factors behind Magnus Hirschfeld's research and activism in Berlin (Bauer, 2017: pp. 52–6). Hirschfeld's *Institut für Sexualwissenschaft* [*Institute of Sexual Research*] dedicated to the study of gender and sexuality opened in 1919, featuring a sexological library, a clinical institution, and a residence for marginalized gay and transgender people.

The intellectual culture seeped into the exotic underground nightlife of Berlin fictionalized by Christopher Isherwood in *Goodbye to Berlin* (1939) and described in his autobiography *Christopher and His Kind* (1976), where a cast of queer outsiders explore sexual and intellectual liberation against the backdrop of Hitler's rise to power. Isherwood's stories inspired the 1966 Broadway musical *Cabaret* by John Kander and Fred Ebb and the 1972 film adaptation directed by Bob Fosse in which the decadence of the patrons of the Kit Kat Klub is paralleled by the cultural decadence outside as fascism takes hold of Germany. *Cabaret* represents the popular tendency to romanticize the interwar period in Berlin. Several recent episodes from the second season of Amazon's gender-identity drama *Transparent* (2015) depict the *Institut* as a safe haven populated by beautiful, liberated people engaged in aestheticized acts of decadent debauchery, although this activity also makes the abhorrent destruction caused by the Nazi regime appear more poignant when it occurs.

Decadence is typically associated with urban spaces: Paris and London in the nineteenth century, Berlin in the interwar period, and in the decades following World War II it reaches across the Atlantic for the second or third time, complementing its earlier manifestations in the 1890s and 1920s, in writing by Edgar Saltus, James Huneker, and Vance Thompson, and the social decadence of the Gilded Age and the Roaring

Twenties. In the 1960s and 1970s a queer, outsider art rock scene began to take shape in New York City, formed of the various creative figures who congregated around the Hotel Chelsea and The Factory, the studio of pop artist Andy Warhol.[1] These two locales represented the depth and superficiality of post-war American decadence. The Factory became a haven for figures on the margins of society: a cast of drag queens, transgender people, socialites with amphetamine habits, models, and adult film stars – all documented in Lou Reed's 'Walk on the Wild Side' (1972). Yet Warhol's creative output – particularly the mass-produced silkscreens blurring the lines between artworks and consumer goods – redirects art from the elite to the masses through industrial-level reproduction, indicating the emptiness and superficiality of fame. This practice contrasts with the more cerebral output of the Chelsea crowd such as poet and musician Patti Smith, who draws inspiration from Arthur Rimbaud, Paul Verlaine, and Baudelaire (she occasionally exclaims 'oh, Baudelaire!' in her improvised 'Babelogues'); and photographer Robert Mapplethorpe's documentation of the underground scene known as BDSM (the erotic culture of bondage, discipline, and sadomasochism).

In 1970s Britain, glam rock emerges as a reaction to the rise of right-wing Conservative politics. David Bowie cultivated androgynous, sexually fluid personas such as Aladdin Sane and Ziggy Stardust, in flamboyant costumes and makeup. This kind of camp decadent gender-play was regarded as a threat by moralizing traditionalists but is relatively clean when compared to the 'taste for the distasteful' (Weir, 2017: p. 221) as exemplified in popular (sub)culture by the collaboration between Baltimore filmmaker John Waters and Divine, the drag persona of Harris Glenn Milstead. Divine's infamous coprophagia scene in *Pink Flamingos* (1972), which carried the tagline 'an exercise in poor taste', established his position as a figurehead of extreme queer outsider art.

The hedonism of the underground queer scene suffered a devastating blow in the 1980s with the arrival of the AIDS crisis, documented in the memoir *Desire* (2017) by social theorist and Wilde scholar Jonathan Dollimore. Yet, as with the interwar period, decadence, excess, and camp are celebrated as a remedy for social anxiety. Jennie Livingston's 1990 film *Paris Is Burning* documents the ball scene of African American queer culture in 1980s New York, where individuals in dire financial straits manage to create exquisite costumes from the limited resources available

[1] Warhol briefly managed The Velvet Underground, whose 'Venus in Furs' (1967) is directly inspired by Sacher-Masoch's novella.

to them. As Zadie Smith succinctly puts it, camp is 'doing more than is necessary with less than you need' (2018: p. 181). Camp self-expression is not merely for the rich, but for anyone with refined enough taste to transform themselves, if only superficially, into an embodiment of luxurious extravagance.[2] Decadent excess was embraced sincerely in the 1990s by the Club Kids, spearheaded by James St. James and Michael Alig, New York's latter-day answer to Waugh's Bright Young Things. This group of personalities on the party scene was notorious for their outrageous costumes and pursuit of pleasure through drugs and sex. In his memoir *Disco Bloodbath* (1999), later adapted to film as *Party Monster* (2003), St. James recalls posing with a friend at a party 'saying deeply superficial things to each other, and looking very soigné doing so' (1999: p. 52). Drag queen RuPaul was part of the Club Kids coterie, and in recent years has been instrumental in bringing drag to the mainstream in the form of *RuPaul's Drag Race*.

The popularity of *Drag Race* reflects the obsession with appearance in our current age and directly feeds into the craze for Instagram and YouTube tutorials for drag makeup techniques such as 'contouring' – using makeup to create the illusion of a different face shape. There is a decadent irony in the everyday practice of using styles of makeup that draw attention to their own fakeness, and particularly their use by women who are emulating the exaggerated makeup techniques traditionally used in male impersonations of women. We have come full-circle: contouring recalls Des Esseintes' preference in *Against Nature* for real flowers that look fake. Artifice is celebrated whether through illusion created by powders and paints, through cosmetic procedures such as lip fillers and Botox, or in plastic surgery which ironically draws attention to the fact of ageing by trying to disguise it. Decadent works of the nineteenth century deal with moods and mentalities; they are solipsistic and psychological studies exposing and exploring neuroses and sexual proclivities. Decadence also involves an obsession with the body – what it feels, what it wears, how it looks. In the twenty-first century, popular contemporary manifestations of decadence are similarly focused around the body, but the symbolically closed space of the decadent sensorium, library, or cloister – the decadent spaces identified by Jessica Gossling (2018) – opens out into the virtual space of the social media and YouTube era in which imagery is rapidly consumed. Visual signifiers are privileged, and identity politics are expressed through the aesthetics of the body and performance.

[2] 'Camp taste is by its nature possible only in affluent societies' (Sontag, 2009: p. 289).

The association of decadence with queerness and marginalization has paradoxically propelled its ascendance into the mainstream, as exemplified by the *Drag Race* phenomenon, with contestants now acquiring an avid fan base and wide social media followings. In today's popular culture decadence manifests as a disproportionate interest in excess, hyper-focus on self-fashioning, and taste for the queer or distasteful. But it also loses some of its 'edge' in the process. Over a decade after *Pink Flamingos*, Divine finally achieved commercial success playing Edna Turnblad in the PG-rated *Hairspray* (1988) shortly before his death. Divine's long-held desire for stardom may not fit with the decadent mythology of deliberately cultivated outsider status, but actually it represents a decadent paradox: the desire to be accepted and admired is achieved by playing up one's 'difference' in order to become mainstream.

This mainstreaming of outsider culture is evident when we consider two record-breaking popular exhibitions at London's Victoria and Albert Museum in recent years centred on non-normative individuals: *David Bowie Is* (March–August 2013, 312,000 visitors) and *Alexander McQueen: Savage Beauty* (March–August 2015, 493,043 visitors).[3] Bowie fans flocked to see the costumes, props, and ephemera from the singer's archives, reflecting a fascination with his sexually fluid, androgynous self-fashioning and influence beyond the music. Bowie's mass appeal is evident, but his celebrity persona was far from superficial; his lyrics are rich with intertextual allusion and references from philosophy, spiritualism, and the occult.

The Bowie exhibition was the most visited in the museum's history until *Savage Beauty* arrived to showcase the work of avant-garde fashion designer Alexander McQueen. McQueen is a prime example of contemporary decadence. His dark and cerebral designs were displayed in provocative, artistic catwalk shows. One of the most memorable, *Voss* (Spring/Summer 2001), ended with a climactic tableau featuring the voluptuous naked body of fetish writer Michelle Olley surrounded by moths, head masked and attached to a breathing tube: an homage to Joel-Peter Witkin's photograph *Sanitarium* (1983). Like most decadents, McQueen was inspired by urban space – his native East London – and his designs combine the Gothic, romantic, and Victorian, often with a kinky sadomasochistic edge. 'I find beauty in the grotesque', he told *Harper's Bazaar*, a statement of pure

[3] The original version of *Savage Beauty* debuted at the Metropolitan Museum of Art, New York, in 2011.

decadent sentiment (Frankel, 2007).[4] There is something thrilling and threatening about his style, yet he became a huge mainstream success, mourned globally after his death in 2010.

Camp Glamour

As Mahoney has observed, there is a spectral presence of decadence in modern queer theory because critical studies of gender and sexuality often refer to the nineteenth-century decadent movement through the example of Wilde.[5] Thus 'The tone of Decadence has inflected the tone of queer theory and queer studies and underwrites the models of reading and appreciation that are central to those traditions of thinking' (Mahoney, 2015: p. 200). The playful, camp aspect of decadence, Mahoney claims, accounts for its enduring legacy in the twenty-first century (p. 199). In her influential 'Notes on "Camp"' (1964), Susan Sontag regards camp as a form of 'modern dandyism' (2009: p. 275). Modern camp is about appreciating vulgarity and is more vivacious and vital in comparison with the disdain and ennui adopted by the dandy of the nineteenth century, who occupies a position at the 'cleaner' end of the spectrum of camp. Wilde, Ronald Firbank, and Aubrey Beardsley are decadent examples cited by Sontag in her definition of camp as a 'sensibility' or 'taste' that – like decadence – is difficult to discuss because it is paradoxically both alluring and offensive, as well as unnatural. As Sontag describes it, 'the essence of Camp is its love of the unnatural: of artifice and exaggeration' (p. 275).

The correspondence between decadent behaviour and the performative queering or blurring of gender boundaries has antecedents in the nineteenth-century decadent movement. It is significant that the first text to promote the decadent credo of 'art for art's sake', Théophile Gautier's *Mademoiselle de Maupin* (1835), concerns a cross-dressing heroine who seduces the Chevalier d'Albert and his lover Rosette in male guise as the 'smooth and sinuous' dandy Théodore (Gautier, 2005: p. 130). Dandyism has been a mode of queer self-expression since its origins with George Bryan 'Beau' Brummell (1778–1840) and Jules-Amédée Barbey d'Aurevilly's treatise *Du dandysme et de Georges Brummell* (1845, English translation 1897).[6] In *Entartung* [*Degeneration*] (1892–1893), published in English translation in 1895 two months before Wilde's imprisonment for

[4] For further details of McQueen's decadent artistic imagination see Brown (2015).

[5] The most significant flourishing of queer theory in the 1990s included studies of Wilde by Cohen (1993), Dollimore (1991), Showalter (1990), and Sinfield (1994).

[6] For a full account of the history of the dandy, see Moers (1960).

acts of gross indecency, the German doctor Max Nordau proposes that Wilde's dandyism or his 'predilection for strange costume' is a 'pathological aberration of a racial instinct' (1895: p. 318). That is, because of his inflated sense of ego, Wilde dresses deliberately to shock and outrage, risking the degeneration of the 'race' by going against the common practice of dressing to attract a mate of the opposite sex in order to reproduce.

Dandyism offers an escape from such stifling conformism and can be connected with what Dollimore terms Wilde's aesthetics of transgression: 'One of the many reasons why people were terrified by Wilde was because of a perceived connection between his aesthetic transgression and his sexual transgression' (1991: p. 67). Wilde's cultivation of a distinctive personal style is reflective of his rebellious individualism. His outward appearance led to fear of his personality, his supposed sexual 'inversion', and even shaped the reading of his books which, as Dollimore notes, are much less explicitly immoral than they were perceived to be. In fact, as Ellen Moers points out, Wilde's florid dandyism changed as commercial success began to overtake his notoriety:

> In the 'nineties, when the success of his plays brought him a wide and deserved fame in place of a trivial notoriety, Wilde's dress became coldly and formally correct. He was content to express individuality [. . .] with a single detail: a green boutonnière, a bright red waistcoat or a turquoise and diamond stud. (1960: p. 299)

The wearing of beautiful clothes with playful hints at non-normativity is one element of Wilde's rebellion that connects with queerness, self-fashioning, and the decadent championing of artificiality over nature.

Wilde's awareness of fashion reveals the direct link between the artful wearing of clothes and the cult of celebrity. Think of the flamboyant, excessively opulent Liberace as an embodiment of the American dream: a working-class boy who transformed himself into the world's highest paid entertainer. Dandyism is a pose of elegance as well as the high camp that Sontag confines to the realms of the affluent. As Rhonda K. Garelick observes, 'It was inevitable that dandyism should merge with the culture industry, an apparatus designed to disseminate the charismatic personality. Equally inevitable was the shift of dandyism's culture of spectacle from Europe to America, corporate headquarters of the mass media' (1998: p. 154).

The appeal of rebellion-as-spectacle is clear in popular culture when the masses are thrilled or outraged by queer or transgressive self-expression, such as the refined elegance of 1970s glam rock stars who were directly influenced by the nineteenth-century decadent movement. Todd Haynes makes this explicit in his film *Velvet Goldmine* (1998), a drama about fictional rock icons Brian Slade and Curt Wild, modelled respectively after Bowie and a Lou Reed/Iggy Pop hybrid. *Velvet Goldmine* imagines Wilde as the extraterrestrial father of the glam rock movement, and his work is quoted numerous times in the film's dialogue. Indeed, the bibliography of Simon Reynolds's recent study *Shock and Awe: Glam Rock and its Legacy* (2016) contains a surprising number of references to works by and about decadents, including Wilde, Baudelaire, and others, such as decadent occultist Aleister Crowley. Reynolds calls Wilde 'the first philosopher of glam' (p. 91), pointing out the importance of self-consciousness as the 'crucial distinction' between glam and pop showbiz in general (p. 3). Reynolds identifies several aspects of glam that make it decadent: 'Amplifying the androgynous and homoerotic currents already present in fifties and sixties pop, flirting with new frissons of deviance and decadence, the glam performers used luridly over-the-top costumes and staged outrage to stun audiences into awestruck submission' (p. 4).

Decadence and Drag

Glam rockers like Bowie could drop visual and verbal hints about their sex lives and non-normative sexualities, but in spite of these teasing declarations of queerness the stars themselves remained relatively protected by their celebrity status. Like most of nineteenth-century decadence, glam rock is male, if not masculine, and limited to those in positions of privilege in terms of wealth, race, and gender. Drag is camp and confrontational for Bowie, hence Reynolds calls the Pre-Raphaelitesque cover of *The Man Who Sold the World* (1970), featuring Bowie in a dress, a 'drag-level provocation' (p. 110).

Bowie may have flirted with cross-dressing but remained in the realm of androgyny, an effeminate man, whereas drag queens embody decadent artifice more fully. Drag performance, as Judith Butler notes, highlights the performativity of gender roles: 'In imitating gender, drag implicitly reveals the imitative structure of gender itself – as well as its contingency' (1999: p. 175). Broadly speaking, 'drag' refers to the performative aspect of wearing the clothes of the opposite sex and has traditionally been the preserve of gay men impersonating women. It can, however, also relate to the performance of one's own gender through exaggerated signifiers, as in, for example, the excessive makeup and glamorous clothing worn by female drag queens.[7] Culturally assigned signifiers can be played with using a drag persona, challenging presumptions that gender is clearly defined. Through *Drag Race* we are most commonly exposed in pop culture to the 'feathers and sequins' kind of drag that crosses over into camp but is taken seriously as an art form, with hours spent making costumes, applying makeup, and designing wigs so contestants can compete in the guise of drag personas. This, again, is a male-dominated world of drag, with clearly defined boundaries between the self and the persona.[8]

Drag Race has roots in 1980s New York and the drag ball scene, which is particularly decadent because of the interplay between artifice and reality, as well as the socio-cultural context of New York City during the AIDS era. Livingston's *Paris Is Burning* documents drag performance in ball culture of the late 1980s in which marginalized and impoverished gay and transgender individuals from African American and Latin American communities experience another kind of decadence born out of discrimination and disillusionment. Members of competing teams who walk at the balls form 'Houses' with names that deliberately evoke or directly reference luxury fashion houses – the House of Xtravaganza or the House of Chanel, for example – but also act as families with 'mothers' and 'children'. The practice of voguing, a stylized form of dance resembling models' poses, reflects the concern with fashion and appearance that is also a celebration of beauty in the face of cultural anxiety. Beneath the surface of the costumery, these individuals faced very real threats of racism, homophobia, and transphobia.

The balls were a safe space for gay and trans people to be themselves, but achieved, paradoxically, through artificial means. As Butler explains, 'in *Paris Is Burning*, becoming real, becoming a real woman, although not everyone's desire [. . .] constitutes the site of the phantasmatic promise of a rescue from poverty, homophobia, and racist delegitimation' (2011: p. 89). Fantasies of opulent glamour are realized, if only fleetingly, and

[7] Recently, cisgender drag queens (women who identify with the gender they were assigned at birth) have become known as 'faux queens', a term preferable to 'bio[logical] queens' that can be seen as marginalizing transgender queens. They are also sometimes referred to as 'hyper queens', which refers to the hyper-femininity of their drag performance that calls beauty standards into question by pushing them to extremes.

[8] *Drag Race* is exclusively focused on female impersonation. In a recent *Guardian* interview RuPaul stated that he had no intention of allowing women to compete on the show. He was criticized for his comments which were felt to be particularly offensive to a number of transgender women who have appeared on *Drag Race*, the most recent of whom, season nine's Peppermint, was the first to openly apply and compete as a trans woman (others have revealed their identity during or after their appearances on the show). RuPaul's comments were also felt to be exclusionary of drag kings and the growing number of 'faux queens'. See RuPaul interview in Aitkenhead (2018).

offer a feeling of legitimacy and belonging that extends beyond the walls of the ballroom. As one of Livingston's interviewees puts it, 'A ball to us is as close to reality as we're going to get to all of that fame and fortune and stardom and spotlights' (1991). At the balls, individuals compete in various categories of 'realness', including passing convincingly for women or heterosexual businessmen. The idealized self often becomes rich and extravagant by contestants wearing clothes that have been made or 'mopped' (stolen). As drag queen Dorian Corey puts it:

> Black people have a hard time getting anywhere and those that do are usually straight. . . .
>
> In a ballroom you can be anything you want. You're not really an executive but you're looking like an executive and therefore you're showing the straight world that I can be an executive. If I had the opportunity I could be one because I can look like one. And that is like a fulfillment. (Livingston, 1991)

Ball commentator Junior LaBeija's legendary cry of 'O-P-U-L-E-N-C-E. You own everything!' (Livingston, 1991) reflects the desire for decadent glamour and luxury that can only be approximated through artifice. At the moment of walking in the ball they do own everything, but in reality, as Pepper LaBeija says, 'some of them don't even have two of nothing' (Livingston, 1991).

The aspiration to be 'real' is enacted through performative wearing of costumes and cosmetics; the fake should be indistinguishable from reality and the aim is to be 'unreadable'. 'Reading' in drag parlance relates to critiquing or insulting another person, often playfully, using quips reminiscent of Wilde's epigrams. Of the performance at drag balls, Butler states:

> when what appears and how it is 'read' diverge, the artifice of the performance can be read as artifice; the ideal splits off from its appropriation. But the impossibility of reading means that the artifice works, the approximation of realness appears to be achieved, the body performing and the ideal performed appear indistinguishable. (2011: p. 88)[9]

However indistinguishable the performer and the ideal may be, performance at the balls remains a reflexive artificial practice which both reveals and conceals itself. The very act of walking in a ball at night rather than in public during the day is a reminder of the unreality of 'realness'.

[9] Butler goes on to interrogate the problematics of this dynamic outside the safe space of the ball, noting the different fates of Willi Ninja, a gay man who can pass as straight and achieves fame and success, and Venus Xtravaganza, a pre-operative transgender sex worker who is murdered by a client, unable to fully 'pass' in a prejudiced world.

Exaggerated signifiers of wealth and femininity have significant connotations of stardom, power, and freedom for those who are socially marginalized. These signifiers are problematic, leading bell hooks to critique such aspirational 'reality' by pointing out that it reinforces the hegemony of white patriarchy. What viewers see, hooks explains, is 'not black men longing to impersonate or even become like "real" black women but their obsession with an idealized fetishized version of femininity that is white' (2015: pp. 147–8).[10] While seemingly subversive, the concept of 'realness' reinforces the norms it simultaneously disrupts. As Corey tells us in voiceover in *Paris Is Burning*, 'it's really a case of going back into the closet' (1991). However 'real' they may appear, the individuals documented in the film embrace a false identity in order to achieve self-acceptance. hooks notes that Corey 'urges all of us to break through denial, through the longing for an illusory star identity, so that we can confront and accept ourselves as we really are – only then can fantasy, ritual, be a site of seduction, passion, and play where the self is truly recognized [and] loved' (p. 156). Sadly, the aesthetics appeal to popular consciousness more than the recognition of selfhood; voguing was appropriated by Madonna in her video for 'Vogue' (1990), while very few of the stars of *Paris Is Burning* achieved wealth or stardom.

With the advent of *Drag Race*, RuPaul's championing of the underground scene and marginalized figures has led to recognition. Not only the makeup but the rituals and catchphrases of the ball scene, such as 'reading' or 'throwing shade', have entered contemporary culture. *Drag Race*, produced by US company World of Wonder, has been growing in popularity since its first season in 2009. It now airs internationally in Australia, Canada, the UK, the Netherlands, and Israel. Although it runs on channels aimed at an LGBTQ+ audience, it also appears on Netflix and has become a global phenomenon (Daems, 2014).[11] Drag performance is both superficial and symbolic of the social boundaries it is transgressing but is

[10] hooks is also critical of Livingston, as a white filmmaker, turning the ritual of the ball into a 'spectacle for the entertainment of those presumed to be on the outside of this experience looking in' (p. 152). My intention is not to analyse the film itself, but to consider the concept of 'realness' in relation to decadence and self-fashioning, and to show how the opulent artifice celebrated in *Drag Race* owes a debt to this earlier moment of decadence. Other explorations of this topic might pay attention to decadence and orientalism and the way white viewers of the film may position the participants as 'other' if they regard the balls merely as spectacle.

[11] *Drag Race* is the highest-rated programme on Logo TV in the US and has won multiple awards. In 2017 it was nominated for eight Emmys and won three, including the award for Outstanding Host for a Reality or Reality-Competition Program for RuPaul and was the winner of the 2017 MTV Movie & TV Award for Best Reality Competition.

increasingly becoming a consumer commodity in popular entertainment, as 'subversive' performances are assimilated into the mainstream. American rapper Brooke Candy's 2014 music video for 'Opulence' repeats LaBeija's 'I own everything' refrain and features drag queens in a luxurious orgy of decadent excess.

Lady Gaga: Glam Drag Monster

Lady Gaga is a female descendant of glam rock celebrated for the visual eccentricity of her costumes and performances. Known as 'Mother Monster' by her fans, she engages directly with what she calls the 'Fame Monster' (also the title of her 2009 album) and regards herself as a modern Warhol who both espouses the emptiness of celebrity and offers a safe haven for the marginalized. Blending strategies of the glam personas of Bowie and the self-reinvention of New York drag queens of the late-twentieth century, she liberates herself and others. The Haus of Gaga, the creative team responsible for her appearance and style, echoes the houses of the ball scene – we have been taken from couture to its imitation and back again. Gaga's music videos are often intellectually as well as visually stimulating, and she could be called a 'pop performance artist'.[12] Her 2013 *ARTPOP* album (a reverse of 'Pop Art') aimed to 'bring art culture into pop in a reverse Warholian expedition' (quoted in Thorpe, 2013).

In 2011 Lady Gaga appeared in male drag as 'Jo Calderone' at the MTV Video Music Awards. In 2017 she posed as a contestant during a cameo appearance on *Drag Race*. Gaga as a woman disguised as a man imitating a woman (complete with a 'male' alter-ego 'Ronnie' narrating to camera) brings the gender performance full-circle, exposing the contingency of gender and offering a modern-day example of Des Esseintes' delight in the irony of reality masquerading as artifice. Her emotionally charged reception by the queens of *Drag Race* also exemplifies the esteem she is held in as a champion of queer outsiders. Renowned for her outrageous and shifting aesthetic identities, paradoxically Gaga allows her fans to be themselves because she is *not* herself.

In true decadent fashion, an intellectual culture has built up around the seemingly superficial Gaga (see, e.g., Deflem, 2017). J. Jack Halberstam's

[12] For example, Reynolds claims that while musically 2009's pop-hit 'Alejandro' is 'perfunctory nothingness', the video is 'a visual tone-poem translation of the famous last sentences of Sontag's "Fascinating Fascism"' (2016: p. 628).

concept of 'Gaga feminism' refers to the socio-political movement as enacted in contemporary capitalist culture by Gaga as one of the 'poppiest' of pop culture celebrities. Considering her as a woman in terms of artifice as Halberstam does is interesting from a decadent perspective because Gaga is both superficial and natural, and reflexively self-conscious:

> Gaga feminism, or the feminism (pheminism?) of the phony, the unreal, and the speculative, is simultaneously a monstrous outgrowth of the unstable concept of 'woman' in feminist theory, a celebration of the joining of femininity to artifice, and a refusal of the mushy sentimentalism that has been siphoned into the category of womanhood. [. . .] she represents both an erotics of the surface and an erotics of flaws and flows, and she is situated very self-consciously at the heart of new forms of consumer capitalism. (2012: pp. xii–xiii)

Camille Paglia has expressed criticism of Gaga's emptiness, branding her 'a gangly marionette or plasticised android [. . .] calculated and artificial, so clinical and strangely antiseptic', and disparaged her 'manic miming of persona after persona' (2010). But is not this sterile artifice in fact a form of contemporary decadence? Gaga's 'illusory star identity', to borrow hooks's term, can be regarded as a somewhat troubling or uncanny mask, hiding the true person behind a spectacle of decadent artifice. Yet, as with decadence as a critical concept, artifice both reveals and conceals the nature underneath, via a morbid fascination with the self and the body. There is an interplay between substance and emptiness, and with Gaga we end up in a Wildean paradox of going beneath the surface or merely reading the symbol – each with its own peril. She is both artistically stimulating and empty; a personality with no personality, deliberately entrenched in the cult of celebrity.

Decadent Subculture

Gaga's video for 'Alejandro' (2009) features fascist military fetishism and iconography verging on the blasphemous. In a world where this is considered mainstream popular entertainment, some artists feel the need to go to even greater extremes in order to assert their queer identity. OutTV and World of Wonder's YouTube reality TV show *The Boulet Brothers' Dragula: The Search for the World's First Drag Supermonster* (2016–present) represents a subculture of drag that is thriving both because of and in direct opposition to the popularity of *Drag Race*. When compared with Holbrook Jackson's four chief characteristics of decadence – perversity, artificiality, egoism, and curiosity (1914: p. 76) – the opening lines of

Dragula's theme music could be applied to decadence as a critical concept. 'Drag. Filth. Glamour. Horror' are particularly appealing to those with a penchant for decadence as delight in what others would ordinarily find distasteful. The contestants on *Dragula* use aestheticized signifiers of degeneration, decay, and sacrilege to signify queerness within queerness. This outré tendency is clear in the contrast between the relatively sanitized John Waters-inspired challenge on the seventh season of *Drag Race* (2015) and *Dragula* contestant Vander Von Odd's vomit-eating homage to Divine in the finale of the show's first season. The *Dragula* finale, fashioned after the New York balls, required contestants to create three looks showcasing the aesthetics of filth, glamour, and horror. Another particularly decadent moment was provided by Melissa Befierce, whose 'filth' costume consisted of a blood-soaked nun's habit, naked from the waist down, with a rosary dangling from her anus. Darkness and deliberate shock tactics are used in order to show unity, self-acceptance, and championing of marginalized figures in a direct response to the rise of right-wing politics in the US.

A similar strategy was used by Bowie who experimented with darker aesthetics towards the end of his life. In the aftermath of his death in 2016 bereft fans turned to the *Blackstar* video directed by Johan Renck in attempts to decode hidden messages, including nods to Aleister Crowley's rituals, in its visual and musical symbolism. Bowie was less camp and glam in later years than in his earlier incarnations, but he remained an androgynous dandy to the end. He represents a trend for bringing references to the occult into the world of popular entertainment as a celebration of darkness in increasingly dark times. As Bowie suggests, occult imagery provides particularly fertile material for queer self-expression because of the double meaning of 'occult': secret and supernatural. This ambiguity is pushed to extremes in the drag performances of the *Dragula* contestants who use occult aesthetics to preserve the transgressive element of drag as an art form that is increasingly being assimilated into mainstream culture. In their performances, the magical and monstrous are made glamorous, filthy, and decadent.

Decadence in popular culture in the United Kingdom and the United States can be conceived of along two broadly intersecting lines. The aesthetics of excess and opulence, whether tasteful or distasteful; and queerness, primarily through the glam rocker as a modern effeminate dandy and the drag queen as an embodiment of artifice. In twenty-first-century popular culture, playful and tantalizing hints (with varying levels of sincerity) at glamorously 'transgressive' sexuality promote the message of acceptance in an appealing way that 'sells' to the more enlightened members of the social media generation. Indeed, this kind of self-expression increasingly takes place on social media, YouTube, and other video-sharing websites. The short, consumable format of the music video might have appealed to Wilde and other nineteenth-century decadent celebrities as an opportunity for self-promotion. *Drag Race* superstars have joined the masses of pop stars releasing music videos in which – as in the case of Lady Gaga – the music itself is secondary to the image. The 'cult of the selfie' may seem superficial, but, as the ball scene precursors to *Drag Race* demonstrate, the process of self-fashioning through drag, dandyism, or costume is in fact a process of self-acceptance and of negotiating or overcoming social boundaries. After all, as RuPaul says, 'if you can't love yourself, how in the hell you gonna love somebody else?'

Conclusion[13]

This analysis of popular culture reveals a rather dramatic shift in the political meaning of the concept of decadence. In the middle of the nineteenth century, the first intimations of a culture that found artifice more authentic than nature, taste more meaningful than morality, and decline more reliable than progress grew out of a real disdain for social and political modernity. Baudelaire's abhorrence of the bourgeois masses and their empowerment through the dual engine of liberalism – capitalist economics and democratic politics – led him to identify with the aristocracy, the one social class that was truly in a state of decadence during the poet's lifetime. And Baudelaire was not alone among the decadents in his preference for regressive politics. Even Wilde, a figure much admired by progressives today as a martyr to the cause of queer inclusion and gender equality, opined in 1879 that 'landed aristocracy and moneyed interests' are 'institutions in which the vulgar see only barriers to Liberty but which are indeed the only possible defenses' against tyranny (1989: p. 1130). Possibly, Wilde's politics were as closeted as his sexuality, but even when he 'came out' as an aesthetic anarchist in 1891 with 'The Soul of Man under Socialism' his ideological formulations still assume an aristocratic air, as when he avers that 'Art should never try to be popular. The public should try to make itself artistic' (p. 1090). At the same time, there is no denying Wilde's satirical critique of the British aristocracy in his society comedies, but we are still left with the sense that Wilde and other decadents of the nineteenth

[13] I would like to express my gratitude to Alcide Bava for his assistance with this conclusion.

century are hardly progressive and, sometimes, quite reactionary. Not so today: if Divine, David Bowie, RuPaul, Lady Gaga, and other outré figures of celebrity culture are regarded as latter-day decadents, they must also be understood as figures on the far-left edge of a socially progressive spectrum of liberal ideology.

The paradoxical concept of politically progressive decadence urges consideration anew of the perennial question of how art relates to society. Perhaps no one has thought more deeply about that question than Raymond Williams, who, despite his Marxist sympathies, rejected those 'descriptions of Western European literature of [the twentieth] century as "decadent" because its social system is judged "decadent"'. He decried such descriptions because they relied on 'a procedure which lumps together the bad art which reflects and exploits elements of disintegration, and the substantial art which, by the very seriousness of its procedure, shows the disintegration in process, and what it is like, in detail, to live through it' (1983: p. 281). That formulation for 'substantial art' reflective of social disintegration might be applied, retrospectively, to the poetry of Baudelaire – except that only a political reactionary like Baudelaire would regard an era of liberal social modernity as an age of disintegration. Indeed, the range of relations between the art of decadence and the society that gives rise to it appears to be quite varied. Paul Bourget and Friedrich Nietzsche both conceived of decadence as an aesthetic register of social disintegration, a manoeuvre that repeats the traditional formulation that imperial decline leads to bad art – defined as something mannered, precious, unoriginal, and excessively technical. In the case of the traditional formulation, the argument that the decadent art of fourth-century Rome was the cultural expression of a society less vigorous and sophisticated than the Golden Age of the Emperor Augustus is hard to refute. But the art that Bourget and Nietzsche described as decadent we would today describe as substantial, to use Williams's term, with the difference, again, that it was expressive of a decadent society only from an ideologically conservative perspective. By contrast, recent forms of popular art that draw on nineteenth-century traditions of dandyism, extreme artifice, and gender fluidity seem decadent by virtue of a different sort of relationship to society. If the queer art of camp culture is decadent, it is so partly as an affirmation of social developments that conservative ideology finds objectionable. Affirmatory decadence, no less than progressive decadence, is hard to contemplate in the nineteenth-century socio-political context. But surely the drag culture of the 1980s is nothing if not affirmative, all the more so because it occurred in the ideologically conservative context of Reaganism in the United States and Thatcherism in the United Kingdom.

The traditional association of decadence with marginalized figures has also acquired a different political resonance than it had in the nineteenth century. For the nineteenth-century decadent, social marginalization was in some measure a matter of choice: if bourgeois conformism was the norm, then of course the decadent preference was for a life outside that norm. That choice may still obtain to some degree today, in the case of self-conscious individuals who are aware of their own outsider positioning and seek to effect change by being a more exaggerated or excessive version of themselves. But it is also true that the power dynamic between mainstream society and marginal individuals is entirely on the side of the mainstream, so there can be no confusion about who is marginalizing whom. And while it is simply not possible to marginalize the mainstream, it is possible to mainstream the marginal, mainly for commercial purposes, whereupon the mainstreaming of the marginal acquires new socio-political meaning – when what was previously thought to be 'decadent' or 'degenerate' becomes normalized. Yet despite such normalization, decadence has a way of reasserting itself at critical moments of cultural change, when fears are played upon and difference is celebrated rather than downplayed, through artifice, paradox, and parody. One such moment was evident when the Tate Britain hosted an exhibition from April to October 2017 on *Queer British Art: 1861–1967*, including works by queer decadents such as Michael Field and Simeon Solomon, as well as the door of Wilde's Reading Gaol prison cell. Beside the museum label identifying the door, a visitor's handwritten response declared, 'Locking us up to keep us all in the closet. But we found the keys'.

Over 120 years after Wilde's imprisonment it may seem, thanks largely to the struggles of queer activists and campaigners, that the closet door has been unlocked for many worldwide (equal marriage was legalized in the United Kingdom in July 2013 and in all US states in June 2015). Yet it could be opened further still. The prospect of expanded social inclusiveness for gender-non-conforming individuals may seem slight in an era when far-right ideology is on the rise, not only in the United States but also in Great Britain and Europe. Indeed, the present age, marked by narrow ethno-nationalism and regressive social policies in many Western countries, might be considered an age of historical decline, if we take the post-World War II international order, with its rules-based system of trade agreements, security arrangements, international law, immigration protocols, and so on, as the standard. Hence the present socio-political context gives an especially enlightened charge to the concept of decadence, with its transnational aspirations, its embrace of eccentric individualism, and its wildly liberated attitude towards all forms of human sexuality. In short, Western culture seems to be in decline, so the paradoxical use of 'decadence' as both pejorative and celebratory – depending on the context – seems particularly apt. More importantly, we may have arrived at a moment when decadence in the affirmatory, progressive sense it has recently assumed seems less like a symptom of decline than resistance to it. The just society that progressives desire is hardly on the horizon, but the ever-paradoxical concept of decadence can be invoked as a way of recognizing its arrival, because the just society will finally exist only when the need to designate another human being as 'decadent' does not.

References

Aitkenhead, Decca (2018). Drag is a big f-you to male-dominated culture. *The Guardian*, 3 March, www.theguardian.com/tv-and-radio/2018/mar/03/rupaul-drag-race-big-f-you-to-male-dominated-culture.

Baudelaire, Charles (1995). *The Painter of Modern Life and Other Essays*, Jonathan Mayne, trans., London: Phaidon.

Bauer, Heike (2017). Dead Wilde. In *The Hirschfeld Archives: Violence, Death, and Modern Queer Culture*, Philadelphia: Temple University Press, pp. 52–6.

Brown, Susanna (2015). Nightmares and Dreams. In Claire Wilcox, ed., *Alexander McQueen*, London: V&A Publishing, pp. 285–302.

Busby, Mattha (2018). Far-right protesters including man in Trump mask attack socialist bookshop while chanting about Muslims. *Independent*, 5 July, www.independent.co.uk/news/uk/home-news/bookmarks-bookshop-attack-socialist-london-muslims-paedophilia-trump-a8478306.html.

Butler, Judith (1999). *Gender Trouble: Feminism and the Subversion of Identity*, New York: Routledge.

Butler, Judith (2011). *Bodies That Matter: On the Discursive Limits of 'Sex'*, Abingdon: Routledge.

Cohen, Ed (1993). *Talk on the Wilde Side: Toward a Genealogy of Discourse on Male Sexualities*, London: Routledge.

Constable, Liz, Matthew Potolsky, and Dennis Denisoff, eds. (1999). *Perennial Decay: On the Aesthetics and Politics of Decadence*, Pennsylvania: University of Pennsylvania Press.

Daems, Jim, ed. (2014). *The Makeup of RuPaul's Drag Race: Essays on the Queen of Reality Shows*, Jefferson, NC: McFarland.

Deflem, Mathieu (2017). *Lady Gaga and the Sociology of Fame: The Rise of a Pop Star in the Age of Celebrity*, New York: Palgrave Macmillan.

Dollimore, Jonathan (1991). *Sexual Dissidence: Augustine to Wilde, Freud to Foucault*, Oxford: Clarendon Press.

Dollimore, Jonathan (2017). *Desire: A Memoir*, London: Bloomsbury.

Frankel, Susannah (2007). The Real McQueen. *Harper's Bazaar*, 1 April, www.harpersbazaar.com/fashion/designers/a68/alexander-mcqueen-0407.

Garelick, Rhonda K. (1998). *Rising Star: Dandyism, Gender, and Performance in the Fin de Siècle*, Princeton, NJ: Princeton University Press.

Gautier, Théophile (2005). *Mademoiselle de Maupin, Helen Constantine*, trans., London: Penguin, 2005.

Gossling, Jessica (2018). 'Decadent Threshold Poetics: A Comparative Study of Threshold Space in Charles Baudelaire, Joris-Karl Huysmans, Ernest Dowson, and Arthur Symons', unpublished PhD thesis, Goldsmiths, University of London.

Halberstam, J. Jack (2012). *Gaga Feminism: Sex, Gender, and the End of Normal*, Boston: Beacon Press.

hooks, bell (2015). *Black Looks: Race and Representation*, New York: Routledge.

Isherwood, Christopher (1978). *Christopher and His Kind*, London: Magnum.

Isherwood, Christopher (1998). *Goodbye to Berlin*, London: Vintage.

Jackson, Holbrook (1914). *The Eighteen Nineties: A Review of Art and Ideas at the Close of the Nineteenth Century*, New York: Mitchell Kennerley.

Jacobs, Ben, Sabrina Siddiqui, and Scott Bixby (2016). 'You can do anything': Trump brags on tape about using fame to get women. *The Guardian*, 8 October, www.theguardian.com/us-news/2016/oct/07/donald-trump-leaked-recording-women

Livingston, Jennie, dir. (1991). *Paris Is Burning*, Miramax Films.

Mahoney, Kristin (2015). *Literature and the Politics of Post-Victorian Decadence*, New York: Cambridge University Press.

Moers, Ellen (1960). *The Dandy*, London: Secker & Warburg.

Morris, Roy, Jr. (2013). *Declaring His Genius: Oscar Wilde in North America*, Cambridge, MA: Belknap Press.

Nordau, Max (1895). *Degeneration*, London: William Heinemann.

Paglia, Camille (2010). Lady Gaga and the death of sex. *The Times*, 12 September, www.thetimes.co.uk/article/lady-gaga-and-the-death-of-sex-lnzbcd70zj3

Reynolds, Simon (2016). *Shock and Awe: Glam Rock and its Legacy from the Seventies to the Twenty-First Century*, New York: Dey St.

Showalter, Elaine (1990). *Sexual Anarchy: Gender and Culture at the Fin de Siècle*, New York: Penguin.

Sinfield, Alan (1994). *The Wilde Century: Effeminacy, Oscar Wilde, and the Queer Moment*, New York: Columbia University Press.

Skelly, Julia (2014). 'The Paradox of Excess: Oscar Wilde, Caricature, and Consumption'. In *The Uses of Excess in Visual and Material Culture, 1600–2010*, Julia Skelly, ed., Farnham: Ashgate, pp. 137–60.

Smith, Zadie (2018). *Feel Free: Essays*, London: Hamish Hamilton.

Sontag, Susan (2009). 'Notes on "Camp"'. In *Against Interpretation and Other Essays*, London: Penguin, pp. 275–92.

St. James, James (1999). *Disco Bloodbath: A Fabulous but True Story of Murder in Clubland*, New York: Simon & Schuster.
Thorpe, Vanessa (2013). Pop star or avant-garde artist? Lady Gaga wants to be the next Warhol. *The Observer*, 18 August, www.theguardian.com/music/2013/aug/18/ lady-gaga-artpop-album-avant-garde
Unsigned (1895). Notes. *National Observer*, 6 April.
Waugh, Evelyn (2000). *Vile Bodies*, London: Penguin.
Weir, David (2017). 'Afterword: Decadent Taste'. In *Decadence and the Senses*, Jane Desmarais and Alice Condé, eds., Cambridge: Legenda, pp. 219–28.
Weir, David (2018). *Decadence: A Very Short Introduction*, Oxford: Oxford University Press.
Wilde, Oscar (1989). *The Complete Works of Oscar Wilde*, New York: Harper & Row.
Wilde, Oscar (2005). *The Picture of Dorian Gray*. Vol. III of *The Complete Works of Oscar Wilde*, Joseph Bristow, ed., Oxford: Oxford University Press.
Williams, Raymond (1983). *Culture and Society: 1780–1950*, New York: Columbia University Press.

Select Bibliography

Anthologies of Decadent Writing

Beckson, Karl (1982). *Aesthetes and Decadents of the 1890s: An Anthology of British Prose and Poetry*, Chicago: Academy.

Blyth, Caroline, ed. (2009). *Decadent Verse: An Anthology of Late-Victorian Poetry, 1872–1900*, London: Anthem.

Boyiopoulos, Kostas, Yoonjoung Choi, and Matthew Brinton Tildesley, eds. (2015). *The Decadent Short Story: An Annotated Anthology*, Edinburgh: Edinburgh University Press.

Desmarais, Jane, and Chris Baldick, eds. (2012). *Decadence: An Annotated Anthology*, Manchester: Manchester University Press.

Hustvedt, Asti, ed. (1999). *The Decadent Reader: Fiction, Fantasy, and Perversion from Fin-de-Siècle France*, New York: Zone Books.

Rodensky, Lisa, ed. (2004). *Decadent Poetry from Wilde to Naidu*, London: Penguin.

Secker, Martin, ed. (1948). *The Eighteen Nineties: A Period Anthology in Prose and Verse*, London: Richards Press.

Showalter, Elaine, ed. (1993). *Daughters of Decadence: Women Writers of the Fin de Siècle*, New Brunswick, NJ: Rutgers University Press.

Stableford, Brian, ed. (1990). *The Dedalus Book of Decadence: Moral Ruins*, Sawtry, Cambs.: Dedalus.

Stableford, Brian, ed. (1992). *The Dedalus Book of Femmes Fatales*, Sawtry, Cambs.: Dedalus.

Stableford, Brian, ed. (1992). *The Second Dedalus Book of Decadence: The Black Feast* Sawtry, Cambs.: Dedalus.

Stanford, Derek, ed. (1971). *Writings of the 'Nineties: From Wilde to Beerbohm*, London: Dent.

Thornton, R. K. R., and Marion Thain, eds. (1997). *Poetry of the 1890s*, London: Penguin.

General and Critical Studies of Decadence

Albert, Nicole G. (2016). *Lesbian Decadence: Representations of Art and Literature in Fin-de-Siècle France*, Nancy Erber and William Peniston, trans., New York: Harrington Park Press.

Beckson, Karl (1992). *London in the 1890s: A Cultural History*, New York: Norton.

Berg, Maxine (2005). *Luxury and Pleasure in Eighteenth-Century Britain*, Oxford: Oxford University Press.

Bernheimer, Charles (2002). *Decadent Subjects: The Idea of Decadence in Art, Literature, Philosophy, and Culture of the Fin de Siècle in Europe*, Baltimore, MD: Johns Hopkins University Press.

Birkett, Jennifer (1986). *The Sins of the Fathers 1870–1914*, London: Quartet Books.

Boyiopoulos, Kostas (2015). *The Decadent Image: The Poetry of Wilde, Symons and Dowson*, Edinburgh: Edinburgh University Press.

Bristow, Joseph (1995). 'Sterile Ecstasies': The Perversity of the Decadent Movement. *Essays and Studies*, 48, 65–88

Calinescu, Matei (1987). *Five Faces of Modernity: Modernism, Avant-Garde, Decadence, Kitsch, Postmodernism*, Durham, NC: Duke University Press.

Carter, A. E. (1958). *The Idea of Decadence in French Literature (1830–1900)*, Toronto: University of Toronto Press.

Cevasco, G. (2000). *The Breviary of the Decadence: J.-K. Huysmans's À Rebours and English Literature*, New York: AMS Press.

Charlesworth, Barbara (1955). *Dark Passages: The Decadent Consciousness in Victorian Literature*, Madison: University of Wisconsin Press.

Constable, Liz, Dennis Denisoff, and Matthew Potolsky, eds. (1999). *Perennial Decay: On the Aesthetics and Politics of Decadence*, Philadelphia: University of Pennsylvania Press.

Daly, Nicholas (1999). *Modernism, Romance and the Fin de Siècle: Popular Fiction and British Culture, 1880–1914*, Cambridge: Cambridge University Press.

Davis, Whitney (2005). Decadence and the Organic Metaphor. *Representations*, 89, 131–45.

Denisoff, Dennis (2007). Decadence and Aestheticism. In Gail Marshall, ed., *The Cambridge Companion to the Fin de Siècle*, Cambridge: Cambridge University Press, pp. 31–52.

Desmarais, Jane (2017). *Monsters under Glass: A Cultural History of Hothouse Flowers, 1850 to the Present*, London: Reaktion.

Desmarais, Jane, and Alice Condé, eds. (2017). *Decadence and the Senses*, Oxford: Legenda.

Dowling, Linda (1977). *Aestheticism and Decadence: A Selective Annotated Bibliography*, New York: Garland.

Dowling, Linda (1986). *Language and Decadence in the Victorian Fin de Siècle*, Princeton, NJ: Princeton University Press.

Ellis, Tracey, ed. (1997). *Decadence and Danger: Writing, History and the Fin de Siècle*, Bath: Sulis Press.

Ellmann, Richard, ed. (1966). *Edwardians and Late Victorians*, New York: Columbia University Press.

Fletcher, Ian, ed. (1966). *Decadence and the 1890s*, London: Edward Arnold.

Fox, Paul, ed. (2014). *Decadences: Morality and Aesthetics in British Literature*, Stuttgart: Ibidem Press.

Gagnier, Regenia (2010). *Individualism, Decadence and Globalization: On the Relationship of* Part *to* Whole *1859–1920*, Basingstoke: Palgrave.

Gerber, Helmut E. (1960). The Nineties: Beginning, End, or Transition? In Richard Ellmann, ed., *Edwardians and Late Victorians*, New York: Columbia.

Gilman, Richard (1975). *Decadence: The Strange Life of an Epithet*, New York: Farrar, Straus and Giroux.

Gye, Joeng Meen (2002). Journey into Modern Literature: Realism, Naturalism, Pre-Raphaelitism, Aestheticism, and Decadence. *British and American Fiction to 1900*, 9(1), 165–80.

Hall, Jason David, and Alex Murray, eds. (2013). *Decadent Poetics: Literature and Form at the British Fin de Siècle*. New York: Palgrave Macmillan.

Hannoosh, Michele (1989). *Parody and Decadence, Laforgue's 'Moralités légendaires'*, Columbus: Ohio State University Press.

Hanson, Ellis (1997). *Decadence and Catholicism*, Cambridge, MA: Harvard University Press.

Härmänmaa, Marja, and Christopher Nissen, eds. (2014). *Decadence, Degeneration, and the End: Studies in the European Fin de Siècle*, New York: Palgrave Macmillan.

Harris, Wendell V. (1962). Identifying the Decadent Fiction of the 1890s. *English Literature in Transition*, 5(5), 1–13.

Harris, Wendell V. (1962). Innocent Decadence: The Poetry of the *Savoy*. *PMLA*, 77(5), 629–36.

Harris, Wendell V. (1968). John Lane's Keynotes Series and the Fiction of the 1890s. *PMLA*, 83(5), 1407–13.

Hawthorne, Melanie C. (2001). *Rachilde and French Women's Authorship: From Decadence to Modernism*, Lincoln: University of Nebraska Press.

Hext, Kate, and Alex Murray, eds. (2019). *Decadence in the Age of Modernism*, Baltimore, MD: Johns Hopkins University Press.

Hurley, Kelly (1996). *The Gothic Body: Sexuality, Materialism, and Degeneration at the Fin de Siècle*, Cambridge: Cambridge University Press.

Jackson, Holbrook (1913). *The Eighteen Nineties*, London: Grant Richards.

Jouve, Séverine (1996). *Obsessions et perversions dans la littérature et les demeures à la fin du dix-neuvième siècle*, Paris: Hermann.

Landgraf, Diemo (2014). *Decadence in Literature and Intellectual Debate since 1945*, New York: Palgrave Macmillan.

Ledger, Sally, and Roger Luckhurst, eds. (2000). *The Fin de Siècle: A Reader in Cultural History c.1880–1900*, Oxford: Oxford University Press.

MacLeod, Kirsten (2006). *Fictions of British Decadence: High Art, Popular Writing and the Fin de Siècle*, Basingstoke: Palgrave.

McGuinness, Patrick (2015). *Poetry and Radical Politics in fin de siècle France: From Anarchism to Action française*, Oxford: Oxford University Press.

Marquèze-Pouey, Louis (1986). *Le Mouvement décadent en France*, Paris: Presses Universitaires de France.

Marshall, Gail, ed. (2007). *The Cambridge Companion to the Fin de Siècle*, Cambridge: Cambridge University Press.

Moers, Ellen (1960). *The Dandy: Brummell to Beerbohm*, London: Secker and Warburg.
Munro, John M. (1970). *The Decadent Poetry of the Eighteen-Nineties*, Beirut: American University of Beirut.
Murray, Alex (2016). *Landscapes of Decadence: Literature and Place at the Fin de Siècle*, Cambridge: Cambridge University Press.
Nalbantian, Suzanne (1983). *Seeds of Decadence in the Late Nineteenth-Century Novel*, London: Macmillan.
Navarette, Susan J. (1998). *The Shape of Fear: Horror and the Fin de Siècle Culture of Decadence*, Lexington, KY: University Press of Kentucky.
Palacio, Jean de (1994). *Figures et formes de la décadence*, Paris: Séguier.
Palacio, Jean de (2003). *Le silence du texte: poétique de la décadence*, Dudley, MA: Peeters.
Pierrot, Jean, (1981). *The Decadent Imagination, 1880–1900*, Derek Coltman, trans., Chicago: University of Chicago Press.
Potolsky, Matthew (2013). *The Decadent Republic of Letters: Taste, Politics, and Cosmopolitan Community from Baudelaire to Beardsley*, Philadelphia: University of Pennsylvania Press.
Praz, Mario (1970). *The Romantic Agony*, Angus Davidson, trans., 2nd edn, Oxford: Oxford University Press.
Prungnaud, Joëlle (1997). *Gothique et Décadence: Recherches sur la continuité d'un mythe et d'un genre au XIXe siècle en Grande-Bretagne et en France*, Paris: Honoré Champion.
Reed, John (1985). *Decadent Style*, Athens, OH: Ohio University Press.
Ridge, George R. (1961). *The Hero in French Decadent Literature*, Athens, GA: University of Georgia Press.
Schoolfield, George C. (2003). *A Baedeker of Decadence: Charting a Literary Fashion, 1884–1927*, New Haven, CT: Yale University Press.
Sherry, Vincent (2015). *Modernism and the Reinvention of Decadence*, Cambridge: Cambridge University Press.
Spackman, Barbara (1989). *Decadent Genealogies: The Rhetoric of Sickness from Baudelaire to D'Annunzio*, Ithaca, NY: Cornell University Press.
Stableford, Brian (1998). *Glorious Perversity: The Decline and Fall of Literary Decadence*, Rockville, MD: Wildside Press.
Stephan, Phillip (1974). *Paul Verlaine and the Decadence, 1882–1890*, Totawa, NJ: Rowman and Littlefield.
St. John, Michael, ed. (1999). *Romancing Decay: Ideas of Decadence in European Culture*, Brookfield, VT: Ashgate.
Sturgis, Matthew (1995). *Passionate Attitudes: The English Decadence of the 1890s*, London: Macmillan.
Swart, Konrad W. (1964). *The Sense of Decadence in Nineteenth-Century France*, The Hague: Martinus Nijhoff.
Temple, Ruth Z. (1953). *The Critic's Alchemy: A Study of the Introduction of French Symbolism into England*, New York: Twayne.

Temple, Ruth Z. (1974). Truth in Labelling: Pre-Raphaelitism, Aestheticism, Decadence, Fin de Siècle. *English Literature in Transition*, 17(4), 201–22.
Thornton, R. K. R. (1983). *The Decadent Dilemma*, London: Edward Arnold.
Vance, Norman (2004). Decadence from Belfast to Byzantium. *New Literary History*, 35(4), 563–72.
Weir, David (1995). *Decadence and the Making of Modernism*, Amherst: University of Massachusetts Press.
Weir, David (2008). *Decadent Culture in the United States: Art and Literature against the American Grain, 1890–1926*, Albany: State University of New York Press.
Weir, David (2018). *Decadence: A Very Short Introduction*, Oxford: Oxford University Press.
Williams, Roger L. (1980). *The Horror of Life*, Chicago: University of Chicago Press.

Index